Vincente Minnelli

Also by Emanuel Levy

All About Oscar:
The History and Politics of the Academy Awards

Cinema of Outsiders:
The Rise of American Independent Film

Citizen Sarris, American Film Critic (editor)

George Cukor: Master of Elegance;
Hollywood's Legendary Director and His Stars

John Wayne: Prophet of the American Way of Life

Small-Town America in Film:
The Decline and Fall of Community

The Habima–Israel's National Theater, 1917–1977:
A Study of Cultural Nationalism
(1980 National Jewish Book Award)

Vincente Minnelli

Hollywood's Dark Dreamer

EMANUEL LEVY

ST. MARTIN'S PRESS ☙ NEW YORK

VINCENTE MINNELLI. Copyright © 2009 by Emanuel Levy. All rights reserved. Printed in the United States of America. For information, address St. Martin's Press, 175 Fifth Avenue, New York, N.Y. 10010.

www.stmartins.com

Book design by Christopher M. Zucker

Library of Congress Cataloging-in-Publication Data

Levy, Emanuel.
  Vincente Minnelli: Hollywood's dark dreamer / Emanuel Levy.—1st ed.
      p. cm.
  Includes bibliographical references.
  ISBN-13: 978-0-312-32925-9
  ISBN-10: 0-312-32925-3
  1. Minnelli, Vincente.   2. Motion picture producers and directors—United States—Biography.   I. Title.

PN1998.3.M56L48 2009
791.4302'33092—dc22
[B]

                                                        2008028751

First Edition: April 2009

10   9   8   7   6   5   4   3   2   1

*This book is dedicated to
my aunt Retti and my cousin Lina
for all the movies and other experiences we shared together.*

Contents

Introduction and Acknowledgments · *ix*

Prelude · *1*

One Childhood · *3*

Two Chicago · *15*

Three Radio City Music Hall · *27*

Four New York, New York · *41*

Five Broadway · *55*

Six Hollywood: Early Years · *70*

Seven The First Peak: *Meet Me in St. Louis* · *96*

Eight A Fresh Look at Old Genres: *Ziegfeld Follies* and *The Clock* · *115*

Nine Falling in Love · *128*

Ten Husband and Father · *147*

Eleven The Great Debacle: *The Pirate* · *160*

Twelve Scandalous Melodrama: *Madame Bovary* · 172

Thirteen Problems with Judy · 182

Fourteen An American in Paris · 194

Fifteen Minnelli's Masterpieces: *The Bad and the Beautiful* and
The Band Wagon · 223

Sixteen Minnelli Loves Lucy · 241

Seventeen Up and Down: Contract Director · 257

Eighteen Personal Films: *Lust for Life* and *Tea and Sympathy* · 269

Nineteen The Height of His Career: *Gigi* · 295

Twenty Master of Melodramas: *Some Came Running* and
Home from the Hill · 316

Twenty-one The Party Is Over · 331

Twenty-two Being Idle · 354

Twenty-three Life Is a Cabaret · 365

Twenty-four The Swan Song · 379

Conclusion: Minnelli's Legacy · 395

Notes · 407

Index · 427

Introduction and Acknowledgments

THIS BOOK OWES ITS EXISTENCE to three incredible individuals, the acclaimed director Vincente Minnelli, his kind widow, Mrs. Lee Anderson Minnelli, and Stephen Harvey, the late critic and curator at the Museum of Modern Art's Department of Film, and to one incredible organization, the Margaret Herrick Library of the Academy of Motion Picture Arts and Sciences, which contains the invaluable Special Minnelli Collection.

To the best of my knowledge, there are, quite shockingly, only three books about Minnelli. The first is Harvey's *Directed by Minnelli,* which is arranged by genres, rather than chronologically, and deals with the making of the pictures. The second is *The Films of Vincente Minnelli,* by the bright scholar James Naremore, an excellent academic study of five of the director's films: *Cabin in the Sky, Meet Me in St. Louis, Father of the Bride, The Bad and the Beautiful,* and *Lust for Life.* And the third is *I Remember It Well,* Minnelli's own memoirs, cowritten with Hector Arce and published in 1972 (fourteen years before Minnelli's death). All of these books are now out of print.

By contrast, there have been at least a dozen books written about such directors as Howard Hawks, John Ford, and George Cukor, who was Minnelli's rival at M-G-M. If I draw extensive comparisons between

Cukor and Minnelli, it's because they were contemporaries and Metro's top directors, both arrived in Hollywood after working in the New York theater, and both imbued their work with what some scholars now call queer sensibility, a concept I am not fond of. However, while Cukor was openly gay, Minnelli could be defined as bisexual, as he was a complicated man who married four times and channeled his sexual and other anxieties into his work in both manifest and latent ways.

To this day, when I mention that *Vincente Minnelli: Hollywood's Dark Dreamer* is the first full-length biography of the director, movie lovers raise highbrows and say, "You must be kidding." I am not.

Why the neglect? I have no idea. Is Minnelli too flamboyant? Too complex? Too much of a stylist? A victim of working in the popular and "feminine" genres of the musical and the melodrama rather than in the more "macho" genres of war, action-adventure, and suspense thrillers? Perhaps the critic Andrew Sarris put his finger on the reason for this neglect when, after Minnelli's death, he observed that "a director whose big claim to fame is the musical genre is doubly handicapped for posterity, first because musicals are inescapably more collaborative affairs than are other genres, and second because most intellectuals do not take musicals seriously enough, and are thus seldom able to talk intelligently about them."

Minnelli was not modest, but he was shy, often insecure, and truly mysterious, which made him a tough, almost unreachable subject for interviewers and scholars. In *The Men Who Made the Movies*, my colleague and film critic Richard Schickel observes, "Next to Sir John Gielgud, Vincente Minnelli is the most difficult person I've ever interviewed. Like Sir John, he is unfailingly polite and totally impenetrable. Unlike Sir John, however, he gives the impression of really trying to help you, which makes the interviewer's frustration more bearable and leaves him with a warm regard for a man he must assume is making a brave effort to overcome his natural shyness and what may be genuine pain over self-exposure."

Minnelli didn't like to explain his work. Nor did he know how to talk about it analytically or intellectually. He was an intuitive artist par excellence.

In this book, I aim to explore several issues about Minnelli: first, that he was one of the earliest truly modernist artists at work on Broadway and then in Hollywood; second, that he was not the victim of the studio system in general and M-G-M in particular. My main goal is to demonstrate that Minnelli was much more than a stylist, that he was a genuine auteur in both the thematic and visual senses of this term. I am particularly intrigued by the ways in which Minnelli reflected his sexual anxieties in his films, and how he criticized the American conformist culture of the 1950s. Considering that he was apolitical (and seldom even voted), his movies are highly political in terms of sexual politics and gender roles.

To address and, I hope, to answer these queries, I place Minnelli against the socio-cultural-political contexts in which he lived and worked, from his early life in the Midwest—in particular, Chicago, where he was first exposed to the modernist movement in art—to New York in the 1930s, to Hollywood in the 1940s through the 1960s.

In other words, I seek to elevate the stature of Minnelli as a film artist of the first rank, alongside more recognized titans such as Alfred Hitchcock, John Ford, Douglas Sirk, and George Cukor. Apropos of Cukor, the differences between him and Minnelli could not have been sharper. Cukor was primarily an actor's director, who perceived cinema as an extension of theater and drama. Minnelli, in contrast, was a modernist artist who viewed film as a medium closer to painting and music than to theater. Like King Vidor, Rouben Mamoulian, and Orson Welles, Minnelli was an experimental filmmaker, an innovator who developed a uniquely and specifically cinematic language.

My interest in knowing more and possibly writing about Minnelli began in 1978, when I was a beneficiary of a Minnelli retrospective at Carnegie Hall Cinema and Bleecker Street Cinema in the dead of winter, between January 17 and March 9, which opened my eyes to his rich, intriguing oeuvre. What better way than to spend cold snowy nights with Minnelli's musicals and melodramas?

My encounter with Lee Anderson Minnelli began with a letter that she sent me in 1996, after reading my book *George Cukor: Master of Elegance,* inquiring whether I would be interested in writing about her late husband. I met with Mrs. Minnelli several times, and she shared with me invaluable information and materials (letters, drawings, photographs, and so on). However, it took some time to launch the project, as I was in the midst of writing *Cinema of Outsiders: The Rise of American Independent Film* and editing a tribute volume for the critic Andrew Sarris, *Citizen Sarris.*

The knowledgeable and resourceful Stephen Harvey wrote the first book about the filmmaker, *Directed by Minnelli,* one of the most handsomely produced volumes about a Hollywood director, and based on exhaustive research of his films—but it was not a study of his career or life. The book coincided with a retrospective of Minnelli's work at the Museum of Modern Art in 1989. I attended as many screenings as I could and benefited from conversations with him. In fact, the last conversations I had with Harvey before he passed away in 2002 were about my intent to write a biography of Minnelli, using his book extensively, and about his contribution to the Sarris festschrift, which he began writing but was too ill to finish.

The Margaret Herrick Center for Study is one of my favorite places to conduct research. I have done several books based on their collections, including *All About Oscar, George Cukor,* and now *Vincente Minnelli.* I would like to thank the director of the library Linda Meyer, as well as Sandra Archer, Fay Thompson, Barbara Hall, and all the other members of the loyal staff. Likewise, allow me to express appreciation to the staffs of the Lincoln Center Library for the Performing Arts, and the libraries of the American Film Institute, the Museum of Modern Art, UCLA, and USC.

Over the past two decades, I have offered several courses on the American musical at Arizona State University, Wellesley, Columbia, and UCLA, courtesy of the deans in those schools, and I'd like to thank particularly Joseph Comprone and Thomas Keil at ASU and Robert Rosen at UCLA. Benefiting from freedom in choosing the musicals, I admit to have favored Minnelli's musicals, the excellent ones, such as *Meet Me in St. Louis* and *The Band Wagon,* which had every reason to be included in a survey course, as well as the mediocre ones, such as *Brigadoon* or *Kismet,* which were semi-legit choices for such a course.

I dedicate the book to my aunt Retti and my cousin Lina, who along with my parents, particularly my mother, Matti, cultivated passion for cinema early on, during my childhood in the austerity that prevailed in

Israel. Who would have believed that I saw my first Minnelli musical, or the first Bergman film, on the grass of Kibbutz Ginegar (where my cousin resides), surrounded by members seated on blankets with a huge temporarily set white screen.

Television was introduced to the Israeli public rather late, and in a limited way. There was one channel, which broadcast only several hours per evening. Hence, movies were—and in many ways still are—the primary medium of entertainment.

My parents were both avid moviegoers. My father was a womanizer, who loved beautiful women (onscreen and off), so we saw many dramas, women's pictures, and musicals. But he also loved John Wayne and Gary Cooper westerns, Hitchcock thrillers, screwball comedies, and crime-gangster pictures, so my movie education was well rounded. After my parents' divorce, I was taken to the movies at least twice a week by my mother and my aunt, who was an officer and could always get inexpensive tickets, even at the very last moment.

Many friends and colleagues have read and commented on earlier drafts of this book and papers on Minnelli I've presented at various conferences. I would like to thank Edward Johnson, Marykate Harris, Baruch Grabov, Tom Brueggerman, Pamela J. Riley, Bill Shepard, Jack Richmond, and Andrea Weinstein for providing helpful comments.

While helping to organize centennial tributes for Minnelli, in 2003, I benefited from discussions with Lawrence Kardish at the Museum of Modern Art, Ian Birnie at the Film Department of the Los Angeles County Museum of Art, and Michel Ciment, the noted French critic of *Positif.* I have enjoyed many conversations about film and popular culture with several of my professors at Columbia University, including Sigmund Diamond, Meyer Schapiro, Arthur C. Danto, Alan Silver, Andrew Sarris, and others. Also, when I screened numerous Minnelli films at the City University of New York, Columbia, Wellesley, UCLA, and ASU, my students have contributed immeasurably to my evolution as a scholar and critic by challenging my ideas about the intricate links between film, culture, politics, ideology, and society. Their candid, often spontaneous remarks have made teaching film a stimulating, rewarding enterprise, with many unanticipated results.

I am grateful to the National Endowment for the Humanities for providing support and travel funds for my research.

I would like to single out the work of three research assistants, Tamara Blaich, Lauren Caputo, and the resourceful and indefatigable Beth A. Mooney, who helped in gathering information, conducting meticulous library work, and preparing and typing various appendices for the book.

Michael Homler, my editor at St. Martin's, joined this book project rather late, but with his considerable skills, he managed to bring it to fruition, while contributing substantially to its final shape.

Finally, this book could not have been written without the encouragement, trust, and support of two close friends, Nathan Waterman, and Rob Remley, my devoted companion. No writer could ever hope for more inspirational encouragement and blissful support than those provided by Rob. His painstaking criticism, high standards of thinking and writing, and meticulous editing have contributed immeasurably to the depth, clarity, and quality of my writing.

Though I am trained as an academic, for this biography I have tried for a more popular style that keeps scholarly jargon to a minimum. This book aims to reach educated people who love movies and want to know more about them. It is my hope that *Vincente Minnelli* will increase their understanding of the various facets of his talent and rich work, and of the history, aesthetics, and politics of American movies.

EMANUEL LEVY
Los Angeles, August 2008

Vincente Minnelli

Prelude

THE EVENING OF MARCH 20, 1952, when that year's Academy Awards were presented at the RKO Pantages Theatre in Hollywood, had special meaning for Vincente Minnelli as a director and man. He had been nominated for the Best Director award for *An American in Paris,* which had received the Best Picture nomination. All his life he had been waiting for this moment, and the timing could not have been better since he had just gone through some frustrating years in his career and a divorce from Judy Garland, in 1951, which turned out to be nastier and uglier than necessary.

While acclaimed by his colleagues in the industry and widely considered M-G-M's top director, Minnelli had never received an Oscar nomination before. With *An American in Paris,* he became the first filmmaker to be nominated for directing a musical since 1942, when Michael Curtiz earned a nod for *Yankee Doodle Dandy.* Many felt that Minnelli had deserved the honor in 1944 for *Meet Me in St. Louis,* his first masterpiece, but the country was at war then and that film, while a success, didn't get its due recognition from the Academy voters.

When *An American in Paris* opened the previous October, the critics had praised George Gershwin's score, Gene Kelly's innovative choreography, and Leslie Caron's youthful charm. Minnelli was disappointed that the film was regarded as just another M-G-M musical, albeit one with a classier score and a long, dazzling ballet sequence. The movie was a huge box-office hit, grossing more than $8 million in the United States alone. *An American in Paris* had received eight nominations, but few people in the industry expected it to win the Best Picture Oscar. The front-runners of that year's race were Elia Kazan's *A Streetcar Named Desire* and George Stevens's *A Place in the Sun,* both powerful dramas based on prestigious literary sources.

The Oscar evening was fraught with intense emotions and bittersweet feelings. The Academy's Board of Governors bestowed on Gene Kelly an Honorary Oscar for his "versatility and brilliant achievements in the art of choreography on film." Kelly, who was in Germany, asked Stanley Donen, his friend and codirector of the upcoming musical *Singin' in the Rain,* to accept the statuette on his behalf; Minnelli was offended that Kelly had not asked him.

The Best Picture award was presented by the veteran producer Jesse Lasky. Opening the envelope, Lasky exclaimed, "Oh, my! The winner is *An American in Paris.*" The audience greeted the announcement with polite applause, but not with roars of approval.

An American in Paris represented the biggest, most expensive, most challenging, but also the most troubled musical of Minnelli's career to date, and for the second time that night he wondered if this might be the peak of his career. The first time had come when George Stevens won the award for best director; Minnelli must have wondered then if his work as film director would ever get its deserved recognition. Tears were rolling down his face as he began to recall crucial episodes of his life. But sadly, there was no intimate companion in his life to share those memories—his precious daughter, Liza, was then just six years old.

One

Childhood

VINCENTE MINNELLI'S SHOWBIZ CAREER must have been preordained. He was literally born in the trunk, as Judy Garland, his future wife-actress, would famously sing in her 1954 movie, *A Star Is Born*.

Lester Anthony Minnelli entered the world on February 28, 1903, in Chicago, Illinois. He would change his name to Vincente, a Latinized version of his father's name, in the 1930s while working as an art director at Radio City Music Hall in New York.

Minnelli's father, Vincent Charles, and his uncle Frank founded the Minnelli Brothers Tent Theater, a company that toured the summer circuit of small towns in Ohio, Illinois, and Indiana, bringing culture to the provinces. During the winter the members of the troupe were forced to go their separate ways because engagements for the company were scarce.

Minnelli's father viewed his work as a job since his great passion was for music. His self-image was validated by the townspeople of Delaware, Ohio, who regarded him as a well-known music conductor and horn player. Among other accomplishments, Minnelli's father wrote Sousa-type marches, and several of his songs, such as "White Tops," were popular with the circus bands.

Mina Mary LaLouche LeBeau, Vincente's mother, was the company's multitalented leading lady, as she could act, sing, and dance quite well. Mina, who was known to her husband and those who loved her as May, worked until the last moment of her pregnancy, a tough challenge considering she was playing ingénues and had to conceal her growing belly. When the time to deliver arrived, Mina left the company and went to Chicago, where her mother and sister lived. Soon after giving birth she returned to the troupe with her infant son in tow.

Before Minnelli was born, his older twin brothers had died from some mysterious childhood disease. Another brother, Willie, curiously bearing the same name as the dying son in *East Lynne,* a play in which Minnelli would later perform, died when he was an infant. After these traumatic tragedies his parents decided not to have any more children. The Minnellis buried their grief deep inside, seldom talking about their losses in public. But the losses also meant paying much greater attention to their surviving son and having more exacting expectations for him.

Minnelli's mother was not so much domineering as overprotective; after all, he was her only surviving son. Born when his mother was in her thirties and his father even older, the young Minnelli was always told that he was a special kid. This label put tremendous pressures on him to excel and to prove that he deserved to be treated as special.

The whole Minnelli family performed in *East Lynne,* an old chestnut of a play based on Mrs. Henry Wood's 1861 novel. His mother played a dual part, Lady Isabel and Madame Vine, and at the age of three Vincente played Little Willie, her son. In the melodramatic plot the wife elopes with a scoundrel, but upon hearing that her son is fatally ill, she returns, disguised in gray wig and spectacles. Pretending to be a nursemaid, she is hired by her former husband and his new wife to take care of the dying boy.

Minnelli's mother tried to rehearse Vincente onstage, but already stubborn, he resisted. Realizing that the stage, with two chairs standing in for a bed, was not realistic enough as a setting, Mina decided to rehearse her son at the boardinghouse. She reminded Vincente time and again, "Just pretend that you're dying." Mina coached Vincente indefatigably until he learned his lines for his big emotional death scene.

Minnelli did the reunion scene beautifully. Years later he recalled having read his lines with "great panache." After Little Willie's death, the mother has a great hysterical scene in which she throws off the wig and says, "Willie, speak to me, tell me that you're not dead!" Mina's sobs were so heart-wrenching that Minnelli decided to "comfort" her. All of a sudden he got out of bed and said in a firm voice, "No, Mom, I'm not dead. I'm not dead. I'm just acting!"

Of course, the whole audience burst out laughing, and Minnelli's father, who was in the box office, rushed in to see what was wrong. Smiling broadly, Minnelli turned his head from side to side, while his mom managed to finish her speech. Then, as soon as the curtain came down, so did his father's wrath. Minnelli viewed this episode as the first of his long series of flawed performances at best and stage debacles at worst.

Minnelli was a lonely, awkward, painfully shy boy, more interested in painting than in sports or other games that appeal to most boys his age. Vincente, or Lester, as he was then known, spent much of his time alone, in his backyard "studio," a converted chicken coop. He would sit in a packing crate in the backyard and fantasize about being on an airplane or in an army tank. Minnelli's fertile imagination always gravitated toward the theater world with all its mysteries and intrigues.

Astrologists are inclined to predict that Pisceans are shy, imaginative, superstitious, emotional, and low-key. By his own account, Minnelli was certainly all of the above. As a child, he was cursed with a short attention span and found it hard to concentrate. For the rest of his life, Minnelli suffered from vagueness of memory for names, people, and places, a problem that caused him many public embarrassments.

Minnelli attributed his shyness to his strict upbringing, a combination of rigid Catholicism with a strict puritanical work ethos. As soon as his family's troupe reached a new destination, Mina took her son to an early mass. However, he wasn't blessed with his mother's piety and his experience as an altar boy was very brief.

One of Minnelli's most vivid childhood recollections was staring at his image in front of the mirror on the medicine cabinet and telling himself: "Here you are, nine years old, and what have you done? You're nothing, nothing but a failure." That persistent anxiety, the urgency to achieve higher and better, continued to haunt Minnelli for the duration of his life, even when he was at the peak of his career as M-G-M's highest-paid and most acclaimed director. No matter how much he accomplished, it was never enough.

Vincente's grandmother, May LeBeau, was not the typical stage mother, though she was aware of her daughter's talent and took Mina to auditions in Chicago, where the family had settled after emigrating from France. Minnelli's mother adopted the stage name of Mina Gennell, her surname deriving from a distant branch of her family. Minnelli believed that his mother could have become a Broadway star had she really been ambitious or liked the theater. But Mina was a reluctant star who lacked an emotional affinity for her calling. His mother's dislike of the stage rubbed off on Minnelli. Forced to perform, he felt like a boy who's unwillingly conscripted into the military.

Mina's sister, Amy, performed a trapeze act with the Ringling Brothers Circus, and Mina's brother was an equestrian. Minnelli didn't remember much about his uncle except that he, too, died young from a mysterious illness. Stories in the family circulated of how his uncle was humiliatingly reduced to being a circus clown. After his death, Aunt Amy left the circus and retired to Chicago with her sister. Never married, she looked after Grandmother LeBeau until the latter died.

Despite the rigid limitations, Minnelli never considered his upbringing to be horrible or boring; at times, it was even glamorous. Whenever they arrived in a new town, children bombarded him with questions about theater life on the road. To compensate for his loneliness, Minnelli would fabricate all kinds of tales that made road life sound much more fascinating than it really was.

Minnelli remembered the old Pullman trains, which took them from town to town. The company was composed of his father, mother, uncle, eight actors, and a manager, who all rode in the passengers' cars, while the crew were placed in the baggage cars with the tent. His father and uncle supervised the construction of the theater tent on a vacant lot, rented by an advance man, who also took care of the troupe's housing and other basic needs.

One of the early lessons Minnelli learned concerned the coexistence of two codes of behavior—in public and in private. If he misbehaved or broke something at home, he was just cautioned to be more careful in the future. But it was a different story if he caused a problem on the road or involved hotel property. His father would then cast a warning look at him, and physical punishment would follow.

Minnelli's mom was in a road show when she met his father, then working as the show's musical conductor. Vincent Charlie Minnelli was a handsome, good-natured Sicilian. At their very first meeting, the couple fought hard over the kind of music to be used in Mina's act. His father thought that Mina was standoffish. For her part, Mina found him to be not only stubborn but a downright snob. Which meant that they were made for each other and their marriage was inevitable; it was only a matter of time before it happened.

After his parents got married, Mina joined the Minnelli Brothers Tent Theater. Though she didn't like the theater, Mina didn't find it easy to quit, as she was on her way to becoming a big star—"a Dresden China doll," a Chicago critic called her. But, ultimately, for Mina, acting was just a way of making a living.

Minnelli's parents were utterly devoted to each other. They conveyed a sense of commitment, almost in defiance of the more prevalent image of showbiz couples, notorious for their eccentricities, tempers, and quirks. There was not much erotic passion between them, but they compensated for sex with tenderness and love. As a mature man who would divorce three times and would finally find happiness with his fourth wife, Lee Anderson, during the last decade of his life, Minnelli became even more appreciative of the durability of his parents' union than he was as a boy. And like his parents, he learned quickly how to separate sex from marriage, or sex from love, particularly during his first marriage, to Judy Garland.

Minnelli's father became a musician, just like his father, Professor Minnelli. His grandfather moved from the bustling city of Palermo in Sicily to the small town of Delaware, Ohio, to head the music department of Wesleyan University. After settling in Delaware, he became known as the town's most eccentric resident. Professor Minnelli walked to work while singing to himself oratorios from beginning to end and whacking at flowers with his rattan cane. Half a block later he would run back to whack any flowers he had missed along the way the first time. Living up to the stereotype of academics, Professor Minnelli was vague and easily distracted. Following in his footsteps, Minnelli would become as absentminded as his grandfather, but without the academic career to match the stereotype.

Each morning before going to school, Professor Minnelli worked in his garden. He typically wore a black Prince Albert coat, a heavily starched white shirt, and white trousers. Grandma would often force him to change his muddy clothes before leaving for school. One morning, Professor Minnelli set out to prune the branches off a tree, when the branch he was sitting on suddenly collapsed. He died from his injuries the following morning at the hospital. The details of the accident would become the stuff of family folklore, told and retold by Minnelli to his friends in different versions.

After her husband's death, Minnelli's grandmother married a farmer named Maine, but it was not a happy marriage. They had one daughter together, and when she was grown up, they divorced. Minnelli remembered the care with which his grandmother prepared for Christmas in Chicago, the beautiful crystal and china she displayed, the quantities of food she made.

One of his most treasured toys was the Dancing Sambo his grandmother gave him as a child, though at the time he was unaware of the toy's racist character. Later, in Hollywood, he would seldom display the Sambo in public, instead keeping it in a secret place, but he never got rid of it.

Minnelli also recalled the disapproving glances of Grandmother Maine whenever Aunt Stella, Uncle Frank's second wife, was in the same room. Stella was young and pretty, but from his grandmother's religious perspective, Stella was frivolous. Stella was a far cry from Aunt Edna, Frank's first wife. Uncle Frank had built Stella a special room in the house, and the young Minnelli loved visiting them. In the future, he would accommodate Judy Garland's request to have a private space of her own in their house, fondly recalling Frank and Stella.

As a young boy, Minnelli felt the sadness in his family, a logical result of the multiple deaths they had endured. Aunt Edna and her daughter Francine, with whom Minnelli shared a love for music and literature, had both died of consumption.

For one year Minnelli went to school in Wheeling, West Virginia, where his mom was appearing in stock. He hated the experience because it called for yet another relocation and readjustment. His mother would

get up early in the morning to go to mass, then return home to fix breakfast and take him to school. After four hours of rehearsals, Mina would
take Minnelli back to the boardinghouse for lunch, walk him to school,
and then head back to the theater for the matinée performance.

After school, Minnelli would go to the theater and watch his mother
perform from the wings. When he got tired, he would slip into her
wardrobe trunk for a catnap. At the end of the show Mina would take
him home, feed him, put him to bed, and return to the theater for the
evening performance. As a child, Minnelli liked to sing himself to sleep.
He would make up tunes while holding at bay the goblins beneath the
bed. It was a way to endure the intolerable loneliness that continued to
plague him for the rest of his life.

Because of endless touring, Minnelli understood why his mother was
desperate to establish roots somewhere—anywhere. In later years, Minnelli would experience the same yearning for home but would never
have it, in the real sense of the word. In their efforts to settle down, the
Minnellis bought a house in Delaware, Ohio. Situated across town from
where his grandmother and aunt lived, the Minnellis' house was at the
end of the trolley line, about one mile from the center. It was an ordinary
house, but to his mom, just having a permanent residence was a cause
for joy and celebration.

To avoid paying royalties, it was customary at the time to use pirated
editions of Broadway shows and tunes. Because the offerings of the touring companies weren't sufficient enough entertainment for the culturally
starved residents, the towns produced their own plays with local talent.
For years the Minnellis themselves toured the Plains states every summer, bringing "real culture" to people like the Smith family in Minnelli's
future musical film, *Meet Me in St. Louis*, set in 1904. Soon, though, silent movies killed the tent-show business. Money became scarce and the
Minnellis experienced rough times.

Delaware was a conventional town. The birthplace of Rutherford B.
Hayes, it was located a few miles north of Marion, where Warren G.
Harding ran a newspaper. Minnelli would recall the tree-shaded streets
of this university town set in a semirural area. The houses were furnished
with bilious green sofas, tiny rosebuds in the ceilings, wallpaper, and

pongee curtains, all of which Minnelli would later re-create in his movies.

Starting up housekeeping at a relatively late age, Mina didn't possess the Victorian attitude that other housewives had at the time. More modern, she decorated the house with golden oak furniture and chintz fabrics. Minnelli learned to appreciate these decorations by looking at them through his mother's eyes. He would stand in front of an art object and stare at it for hours from different perspectives, a skill he would later use as a director.

Significantly, Minnelli's formative years were shaped by a uniquely female sensibility since he was always surrounded by women. This background would account for his effeminate behavior and for what was considered to be distinctly female aesthetics.

Minnelli's father would come home and talk for hours about everything he did or saw during his professional travels. Already enormously curious, Minnelli insisted on hearing about each and every detail of life on the road. From a very young age Minnelli learned how to recycle his life experiences and apply them to new creative endeavors. His most basic mental images stemmed from his childhood days on the road. Minnelli perceived life as one endless free association, linked by strong imaginative flights and random experiences that often defy clear logic or rationality.

Minnelli was seven when his mother took him to a matinée show in the city. When the curtains parted, he saw a blond girl sitting on a crescent moon. The stage was black, with a single spotlight on the young girl, who sang "Shine On, Harvest Moon." The effect became even more dazzling as the moon started to move toward the audience. Years later Minnelli would use the same device, a crane covered in black velvet pushed around by men also dressed in black velvet, in his Broadway show *The Show Is On*.

Similarly, Minnelli would borrow the red tam-o'-shanter that his aunt Anna used to wear for the costume of the maid (played by Marjorie Main) in *Meet Me in St. Louis*. And he would turn Aunt Anna into the character of Aunt Elsie in his movie *The Long, Long Trailer*, starring Lucille Ball and Desi Arnaz. In that film Lucy says, "This is poor Elsie," by way of introduction of the silent woman. Desi Arnaz's eyebrows shoot up. "Well, she's very shy," Lucy explains. "She doesn't meet people, she doesn't shake hands," all references to Minnelli's real-life aunt.

Minnelli again revisited his childhood when he re-created the small-town carnival for his 1958 melodrama, *Some Came Running*. Booths were set up in front of the stores, which were just like those on Sandusky, the main street of Delaware, Ohio, along with a merry-go-round and Ferris wheel. Banners and bunting transformed the dreary business streets during these fall shows, which were attended by people from all the neighboring communities.

Minnelli's boundless flights of fantasy took him to the exotic locales in the books he was reading. He would transport himself to Kipling's *Barrack Room Ballads,* or envision himself in the midst of an O. Henry story. Minnelli became such an expert on his father's books that after hearing just a few lines, he could guess from which book the text was drawn. With his imagination fully absorbing the tall tales, Minnelli determined to be far nobler than a character like Sydney Carton in *A Tale of Two Cities.*

Minnelli didn't make it as an actor in the tent theater, but by immersing himself in those books, his imagination became more limitless and filled with derring-do. In time, Minnelli didn't need books to stimulate him. Stretched on the floor with a pad, he began creating his own fanciful images, placing himself in all kinds of idiosyncratic locales.

Minnelli could quote from *Snappy Stories, Life,* and the other magazines Uncle Frank had lent him. More sophisticated than his dad, Uncle Frank became a mentor, exposing Minnelli to a wider world. Minnelli was already envisioning life on a grander scale, with an insatiable hunger for sophistication that would continue into his teens and twenties.

Though they couldn't afford drawing lessons, Minnelli's parents encouraged him to pursue his artistic interests. After school his father allowed him to use the chicken coop in the backyard as a studio. It was there that Minnelli spent his loneliest—and happiest—hours. By that time, as painful as it was, Minnelli had already learned to value his solitude and take full advantage of the amazing bursts of creativity that it enabled. Occasionally Minnelli would ride his bike with friends or go skating and swimming in an abandoned quarry. He would also fight with neighbors for the privilege of swinging the trolley car around when it reached the end of the line. But his heart was really not in those male activities.

Along with his tours as music conductor, Minnelli's father had local engagements. Making a living was more difficult after his father became afflicted with rheumatism. Minnelli's mother scraped by in near-poverty to raise the family in a normal, satisfying way.

Though encouraging his son's artistic inclinations, Minnelli's father refused to allow him to study music because there was no money in it; somebody in the family had to be pragmatic. When Minnelli showed him his paintings, his father would look at them and say, "It's good, but it isn't up to your usual standards"—as if he had established any standards. Minnelli would then go back to his chicken coop and try to do better. In later years Minnelli realized that his father was teaching him a useful lesson: Never be fully satisfied with your work, always strive to do better.

Minnelli's parents didn't hang his drawings on their walls, nor were his "artworks" shown in school. But he didn't worry. While Minnelli was still in grade school, a sign painter offered him a job making show cards to be displayed in store windows. Minnelli's apprenticeship was cut short due to the drinking habits of his boss, forcing him to fill in for his absent employer to deliver an order on time. Gradually he inherited all of his supervisor's customers, who much preferred dealing with him than with his stern boss.

At one point he was hired to go to Columbus, eighteen miles away, to paint show cards and do artwork for various conventions. Minnelli gave his entire wages to his parents. Family money was so tight that he couldn't indulge himself in any luxury. The family's frugal existence taught Minnelli to get as much use out of his clothes and shoes as possible. Even after he became a successful director, waste of any kind was a cardinal sin in Minnelli's vocabulary.

One summer, a neighbor got Minnelli a job helping a farmer. He had to report at six o'clock in the morning to help with the daily chores. Not used to any physical work, Minnelli came home on the verge of collapse after the very first day.

"How much do you get paid?" Minnelli's father inquired.

"A dollar a week," Minnelli said.

His father strongly disapproved.

The next day the farmer brought a steer and asked Minnelli to hold it before hitting the steer with a sledgehammer right between the eyes.

After letting out a horrible sound, with blood trickling down its face, the steer collapsed. The farmer then asked Minnelli to hold a hose on the carcass, while he began butchering it. Minnelli could barely control his nausea. When he came home, he was sick and threw up all night.

The boy was too sensitive for this kind of grueling job. After a brief family consultation, his father decided that Minnelli was not going back to work. Inspired by his industrious mother who, to make ends meet, always kept busy, Minnelli began looking for another job right away.

At age thirteen, Minnelli accomplished his most ambitious assignment to date. He repainted the curtain of the local movie theater. The painted pillars had draperies with square boxes at each side, to be filled in with ads. A truck arrived at Minnelli's house and the enormous curtain was unloaded. Unfortunately, while he was painting the curtain, it began to rain and the colors started running, threatening to damage the fabric. To protect it from the rain, his father placed a canvas over the curtain, and Minnelli was forced to finish the job much more quickly than he had intended. Needless to say, the end result didn't please him.

Minnelli spent the first three years of high school at St. Mary's, where Sister Patricia became his mentor. A tall, slim woman, regal in bearing, Sister Patricia instilled in him enormous faith in himself and his personal hobbies. Because St. Mary's had no twelfth grade, he was sent for his last year to Willis High School in Columbus.

Minnelli tried acting again, playing Deadeye Dick in the school's production of *H.M.S. Pinafore*. This was followed by the lead role in *The Fortune Hunter* at the Delaware opera house, which was left vacant after the town was dropped from the vaudeville circuit.

Too shy to court girls, Minnelli worshiped them from afar, perceiving them as "goddesses to be placed on a pedestal." He was too timid to ask a girl for a date out on the town. During this period he had cultivated only one friendship with a girl, a classmate who introduced him to the work of F. Scott Fitzgerald and other writers.

Minnelli's shyness would become a major problem when he moved to Hollywood, an industry known for its toughness and aggressiveness. But his courtly, gentlemanly manner would prove a major asset in dealing with and courting women, who found it an old-fashioned yet vastly appealing quality. Some of the problems he would encounter in his marriage to Judy Garland, and in his role as father of Liza Minnelli, were based on what he himself knew was an "unrealistic" approach to women, treating them as deserving of soft and special treatment, even if it meant spoiling them.

With a population of six thousand, Delaware was too small to have an upper class, but Columbus boasted one with a lifestyle to match. Minnelli got his chance to experience it when, in his senior year, he attended high school in that city. At school, Minnelli came into contact with kids from the upper echelon and found socializing with them quite easy and natural. Minnelli shared his interests with them, particularly his love for classic literature and paintings and for the silent clowns Charlie Chaplin and Buster Keaton.

Lacking any specific career plans, Minnelli felt that college would serve as a useful stopgap, allowing him time to figure out what he wanted to be or do. But the family could not afford to send him to college anywhere, not even in Ohio. Hence, at the young age of sixteen, having just graduated from high school, Minnelli left rural and provincial Delaware, Ohio, for urban and urbane Chicago. To this Midwestern adolescent, Chicago epitomized the Big City, with all the culture and sophistication he desired to experience.

Two

Chicago

IN 1919 CHICAGO WAS A VIBRANT PLACE for a curious sixteen-year-old boy. It was a most exciting and vital time, during which Minnelli absorbed with gusto the city's raucous vitality. Chicago became a transitional point between the small town of Delaware and the big city of New York, to which Minnelli would relocate in 1930.

Minnelli moved into the modest house of Grandmother LeBeau and Aunt Amy on Polk Street. The house was in the midst of the so-called French Colony, an area that would soon gain notoriety as one of Chicago's more dubious neighborhoods. His grandmother would say, "What can you expect with all those Italians moving in?" But actually she liked all minority immigrants, be they black, Polish, or Italian. The only ethnic minority Minnelli didn't come much into contact with were Jews, a group he would encounter in Hollywood, where most of the executives were Jewish.

The house was close to a church, which made Minnelli's failings as a Catholic all the more upsetting to his family. Shortly after dawn, his grandmother and his aunt would go to an early mass. They would be the first to arrive, even before the priests themselves. Later, back home, the conversation over breakfast always revolved around the various doings of the nuns or priests. "Father Crepto didn't look well this morning,"

Grandmother would comment. "Do you really think so?" Aunt Amy would say.

Grandmother's sweet simplicity and generosity were a family legend. Minnelli's mother once said, "I think you would have something nice to say about the devil himself." To which his grandmother responded, "Well, I don't think he's as bad as they say."

To accommodate Minnelli, Aunt Amy gave up her room and shared Grandma's brass bed. This arrangement produced some unintentionally funny moments. Coming home late one night, Minnelli heard the creaking of bedsprings as the women were settling down for the night. "Move over, Amy," his grandmother said. "I'm over as far as I can get," Aunt Amy replied. After a brief pause, the bedsprings creaked again. Grandmother was checking whether Aunt Amy had moved. "Go on, Amy," she instructed. "There's room for another party here."

Minnelli knew that his presence disturbed the household's routines. Though given full freedom to come and go as he pleased, he still felt inhibited, and he determined to move into his own apartment as soon as he could afford it financially.

The most urgent order of the day was to find a paying job. A day after his arrival, Minnelli took his portfolio of watercolors and started on his job search. As he approached the intersection of Washington and State, he was taken by the elaborate window display of Marshall Field, where an artful arrangement of merchandise was placed in front of a Florentine garden. Marshall Field's windows were considered to be the finest in the country, emulated even in New York City. Later, New York would take the lead, and Salvador Dalí's windows at Bonwit Teller would become the apotheosis of classic design. But at that moment, Chicago was leading.

Minnelli asked to see Mr. Frazier, the store's chief designer and head of the display department. Frazier took one brief look at Minnelli's portfolio and hired him on the spot as one of his apprentices. The job at Marshall Field was not as creative as he had hoped, but it offered useful learning experience and some necessary cash.

Minnelli was not bothered by the notion that artistic creativity was deemed by some a "feminine" or "unmanly" activity. He adopted as his

role models Frazier's assistants, all of whom were married men with refined tastes. Confident about their skills, they taught him the meaning
of professionalism. They were all men who, as he described them, "could
happily function as the male animal and still give vent to their so-called
feminine traits." This combination of traits would define but also stig-
matize Minnelli as a person and as a filmmaker in Hollywood.

Store windows at Marshall Field were changed four times a year, and
for each season Frazier would design elaborate themes. At first, Minnelli
was assigned to the men's store, which was rather big. It was there that
he began noticing his physical attraction to men, as they were going in
and out of the fitting rooms, even if he dared not stare or follow them.
However, the work itself was not stimulating enough, as it more or less
boiled down to choosing the proper tie for the proper suit.

Working on the fashion windows was the store's most coveted assignment. Gradually, moving up in the ranks, Minnelli was first trans-
ferred to the less desirable windows on Wabash Avenue, which displayed
furniture and antiques. Changing those windows every season was a
grueling task, because it had to be done in a very brief time. As moving
the furniture around took an entire night, to hide their activities from
passersby, the designers would roll down the curtains over the windows
while working.

Minnelli pursued his ambition to become a painter by enrolling at the
Art Institute of Chicago. He took several classes, but working full time,
he couldn't keep the schedule up. Besides, the classes didn't inspire him,
and he didn't learn much.

Instead of classes, he began sketching for himself images from all the
shows he was seeing. He would attend a show and, later that night, do
two kinds of sketches for it. One reflected what he had seen on the stage;
the other was his own version, or what he would have done with it,
based on his taste and aesthetic sense.

Minnelli paid his grandmother a nominal fee for his room and board.
He also sent money home to supplement his parents' meager income.
Living extremely modestly, he was even able to save some money to
move into his first apartment.

Minnelli was making enough money to go to the theater or take an
occasional meal at Henrici's, the bakery-restaurant where Chicago's
famous people hung out. Shy and insecure, he would sit there for hours

at a time, not talking to anyone, merely observing the comings and goings.

Minnelli's work in Chicago provided good schooling for a future movie director. Assisting a society photographer taught him about light, composition, and perspective. Dressing windows at Marshall Field taught him how to arrange a scene in three dimensions. Both kinds of skills would prove useful to a Hollywood director who paid the utmost attention to mise-en-scène, specifically in positioning humans vis-à-vis objects and sets.

At this time, Minnelli became transfixed by the stage work of scenic designer Robert Edmond Jones, and through Jones he began to see the similarities between set design and window display. He started to think of ways to modernize the windows' conservative look, though deep down he realized that this was not his calling.

In Chicago, Minnelli made one last attempt at acting. A blind woman came into the store one day, accompanied by a young girl, to borrow props from Frazier. She had an affiliation with a group that put on plays in a small theater. They were doing an evening of Eugene O'Neill's one-acts, and she asked Minnelli to join the group.

Minnelli agreed, and read for a lesser part in one of O'Neill's foreboding, doom-laden pieces, that of a retired sea captain going mad along with his son. However, doubting his skills, and disliking the play's pregnant pauses, Minnelli once and for all rid himself of the acting bug. When he told his mother of the debacle, she sympathized with him, supporting him fully in his decision to pursue another career in the arts.

Minnelli had time to explore the area on the North Side around the Ambassador Hotel. He found a charming L-shaped flat in a house owned by Chicago society's grande dame, Mrs. Potter Palmer. Grandmother and Aunt Amy were at first upset by his decision to move out, even if they understood his desire to become more independent.

It was easy to move into the tiny apartment, since he had few possessions. Minnelli's only valuables at the time consisted of a record collection and some inexpensive reproductions he had bought in secondhand stores, a habit he cultivated in Chicago.

An acquaintance recommended that Minnelli contact Paul Stone, a professional photographer of celebrities. Upon examining Minnelli's work, Stone said, "If you can do that, you can learn to photograph." Minnelli went to work for Stone, photographing the notables of the day. Since he was very shy, he liked the idea of standing behind the camera, sort of hiding.

Paul Stone's studio was in the heart of Chicago's theater district. His business was equally divided among society and showbiz clients. Stone's soft, cultivated voice appealed to the gentry, while his high-strung nervousness appealed to the more frantic showbiz crowd. His style of photography emphasized shooting in sharp focus so that his pictures would reproduce well on the printed page.

Minnelli learned the different effects and moods that could be created through the use of varied lighting. Stone threw different fabrics over plain blue backdrops to create various looks, which were further varied by the dimming lights. His boss didn't believe in retouching, which he considered a last resort, done when all other methods failed.

Minnelli learned how to distinguish between photographers who were genuine artists and those who were just craftsmen, a skill he would find useful in Hollywood while working with various cinematographers. Despite being very shy, Minnelli tried to emulate Stone's mode of interaction with his clients. Minnelli trembled with nervousness when he photographed the legendary stage actress Ina Claire. The notoriously stubborn actress claimed to know which were her best angles, and Minnelli had to jolly her out of her wrong conception. This became his first experience in learning how to "handle" erratic and temperamental stars.

A few months after Minnelli began working, Stone had a nervous breakdown, and Minnelli was forced to do all the photos of actors, weddings, and business portraits by himself. Minnelli developed such efficiency that Stone let him continue taking most of the photos after he returned from the hospital.

All along restless and discontented, Minnelli felt that something basic was missing from his life, a clear and exciting direction for the future. Stumbling upon Elizabeth Robins Pennell and Joseph Pennell's biography of James McNeill Whistler, the expatriate American painter who had dazzled nineteenth-century London and Paris with his style and wit, he read the book from cover to cover twice, after which Whistler became an inspirational role model, an artist Minnelli could easily identify with.

Minnelli envied Whistler's childhood at the Russian court, his youth as a West Point cadet, his adult years as a starving artist in Paris, and, above all, his devotion to his wife. Whistler's multifaceted personality enthralled the young Minnelli. A pioneer in interior design, Whistler introduced blue-and-white decor and Japanese china to London. Whistler had an emotional affinity to the color yellow, wearing yellow gloves while brandishing a long cane.

In the future, Minnelli's work uniform, modified for California's warmer climate, would consist of gray slacks and yellow shirts. Yellow became one of Minnelli's two favorite colors (the other was red). This became evident in the sets and costumes he designed for the stage and for the screen. There's hardly a frame in a Minnelli movie that doesn't contain an item in yellow, be it a dress, a scarf, a pillow, a couch, or a flower.

As Whistler violated conventions of contemporary taste by painting the interiors of his house in arresting colors, so did Minnelli, who decorated one room of his California house in stark black and white; the walls were black, the furniture white. Whistler enjoyed a stylish life, and so did Minnelli, who hired a Filipino to take care of his household. Both Whistler and Minnelli wore smart clothes, lived in smart houses, and liked to be pampered by servants and maids.

There were limits, however, and Minnelli couldn't copy Whistler in every respect. If Minnelli could effortlessly relate to Whistler's famous habit of giving his paintings titles from musical works, he couldn't emulate his wit. A dandy and a snob, Whistler originated epigrams that Oscar Wilde would later pass off as his own. Indeed, the painter was as famous for his sharp tongue as he was for his art. Minnelli, in contrast, could scarcely be articulate, let alone witty.

Whistler was handsome; Minnelli was unattractive. With a receding chin, an aggressively long nose, and drooping eyes, Minnelli was so unappealing that some of his coworkers described him as a dinosaur or goldfish. What made Minnelli's physical defects all the more noticeable were facial tics—an occasional twitch in the right eye and a continuous pursing of the mouth. "To tell the truth, I couldn't really look at him," said Kathryn Grayson, a leading lady in Metro musicals who worked with Minnelli on *Ziegfeld Follies.* "He was totally unattractive."

It was in Chicago that Minnelli discarded completely his provincial past and reinvented himself as a Whistler type of man. By the time Minnelli reached New York, the transformation was complete in image and ideal, if not practice. He was no longer Lester, a timid boy from Ohio who liked to draw and who hid in the background. He now perceived himself as the newly born Vincente Minnelli, an aesthete and man of the world.

Whistler's was the first biography of an artist Minnelli read, and he was now eager to read more of that genre. Since neither family nor friends had such books in their libraries, he frequented Brentano's bookstore. In addition to books about art and artists, he began reading translations of Guy de Maupassant and Chateaubriand, the romantic novels of the Brontë sisters, the fiction of Somerset Maugham, the plays of G. B. Shaw—anything literary he could put his hands on.

A few years later, Minnelli told playwright William Saroyan, who was beginning to work at M-G-M, of his experience discovering the joy of literature. Saroyan found Minnelli's innocence amusing and used it in his screenplay, *The Human Comedy.* Minnelli was flattered to have provided the inspiration for Saroyan, though he was quick to point out that he was much better read and more sophisticated than Macauley, the protagonist of Saroyan's script (played in the film by Mickey Rooney).

Though college education was not yet the norm in the 1920s, Minnelli's lack of formal education was a major frustration for him, and he hoped to conceal it by engaging in meticulous research and voracious reading. More than anything else, Minnelli wanted to be perceived as a suave and sophisticated artist. He subscribed to the *New York World* during the paper's heyday, when the opinions of writer-critics such as Heywood Broun and Alexander Woollcott were de rigueur. Itching to move ahead, Minnelli felt he was the right age to be brash, even if it was presumptuous to present himself as a connoisseur of the theater and art worlds.

Like Whistler, Minnelli yearned to be an active participant in the art world rather than a passive spectator. As the scholar David Gerstner pointed out, Minnelli was inspired by the set designs of Gordon Craig and Robert Edmond Jones and by the costumes of James Reynolds and

Robert Locher. He was aware of the art and literary movements in Chicago, led by writers such as Carl Sandburg, Theodore Dreiser, and Sherwood Anderson, and he followed the new styles in jazz sparked by Bix Beiderbecke, Eddie Condon, Jimmy McPartland, and Benny Goodman. And though he didn't know many painters or writers, he was aware of the various cliques that made up Chicago's art scene. Minnelli first became aware of the impressionists, the fauves, and the surrealists through the Chicago Art Institute. The works of Henri Matisse, Marcel Duchamp, Max Ernst, and Salvador Dalí inspired Minnelli's rapidly expanding visual imagination.

Minnelli's absorption of the contemporary avant-garde served as an important element to his restlessly creative mind. His exposure to Cézanne, Van Gogh, Renoir, and Dufy was instrumental, particularly because he saw a creative convergence among forms of painting such as cubism, surrealism, and impressionism—a sensibility that he would later blend with his childhood visions of Midwestern Americana in films like *Meet Me in St. Louis* and *Some Came Running*. In the future, Minnelli would become famous for his ability to mix seemingly divergent genres and styles in his effort to bridge high culture and popular art.

Around this time Minnelli also immersed himself in reading about surrealism, a movement that was already present in the novels of Ronald Firbank and the British artist Aubrey Beardsley's art nouveau drawings, such as "The Peacock Skirt," which would influence Minnelli's own drawings for *Casanova's Memoirs,* one of his first projects when he moved to New York.

He admired the experimental films of Jean Cocteau and Luis Buñuel and the writings of Freud, whose radical psychological theories influenced the art world. Minnelli was particularly intrigued by Freud's writings on the interpretation of dreams, a fascination that would become manifest in Minnelli's two signature genres, melodramas and musicals, most of which contain reenactments of dreams, fantasies, and other surreal elements, in various forms, such as ballets.

Minnelli attended regularly the Chicago Theatre on North State Street, which was part of the Balaban and Katz chain. The troupe presented elaborate stage shows along with films, a format later copied by the new

Radio City Music Hall in New York City. Drawing on his decision to be more assertive, Minnelli decided to see Frank Cambria, the head of the Chicago Theatre.

Cambria looked at Minnelli's portfolio of photographs and watercolor paintings.

"What do you have in mind, young man?" Cambria asked.

"I think you should start your own costume department," Minnelli found himself saying, "and I think I should be put in charge."

Cambria's eyes narrowed, and Minnelli couldn't tell if the man was affronted or amused by his audacity.

"What do you know about costume design?" Cambria wanted to know.

"Well," Minnelli answered in a cool tone, "I grew up in the theater, and I'm familiar with the work of James Roberts, Robert Locher, and Lee Simonson."

"Do you sew?"

"No."

"Then how do you expect to accomplish this?"

"Anything I don't know now, I'll learn."

Cambria turned pensive. Then he rose. "Come with me." Cambria took Minnelli to A. J. Balaban, who repeated the same line of interrogation.

Minnelli was asked to leave the room while the men conferred. After what seemed like endless minutes, the door opened and Cambria said, "All right, young man, you're hired!" Minnelli's uncharacteristic self-assurance, in reality a façade, and his insistence that he could learn to design fast, had done the trick. That night he didn't need to ride the El to take him home; he was practically flying.

Balaban and Katz were used to renting their costumes, but now Minnelli's job was to give the shows a "special touch," a vague term that no one, least of all Minnelli, knew how to define. At first, under the delusion that his budgets were unrestricted, he allowed himself to be extravagant. Months later, Minnelli was surprised to learn that the new department was operating under a tight budget and that he was accountable for every penny he spent.

To save money, the costumes and sets were carefully disassembled for future use, and pieces of material were recycled over and over again until the fabric literally disintegrated. Though they still rented part of the wardrobe, Minnelli was asked to prepare several costumes for the specialty acts and the dancers.

By designing some elaborate productions, Minnelli became accomplished in the baubles, bangles, braids, and spangles of his craft. It was the hardest, most detailed work he had done to date. Creating costumes for the stage shows of Balaban and Katz, Chicago's biggest theater chain, introduced him to the dramatic uses of color, a knowledge he was to exploit effectively in his Hollywood movies.

Running a week at each house, the shows opened at the Chicago Theatre before moving on to the Tivoli and the Uptown. Balaban visited each of the theaters with Cambria and Minnelli every Monday, when the shows changed. They would catch the first show at the Chicago Theatre downtown, then go to a second show at the Tivoli. After a short dinner break, they would drive to the North Side and see the last show at the Uptown.

Slowly, Minnelli's social life was becoming more interesting. As a photographer, he had only rubbed elbows with celebrities; now he had the chance to meet and get to know them in person.

One of Chicago's most fascinating salons was presided over by Lillian Rosedale Goodman, a former concert singer. Still attractive at an older age, Lillian looked like a Russian opera star, with her black hair combed back and long and ornate earrings. Lillian took an immediate liking to Minnelli, who offered an attentive ear to her stories. Soon he was put on her A-list of invitees, which included artists and art lovers, most of whom were latently gay or married men living double lives. Lillian's salon became the first legitimate place for Minnelli to encounter and socialize with gay men.

His attendance at this salon began two patterns for Minnelli. First, he socialized with older women, often escorting them to public events, since he was hesitant to go out with male partners to see shows or have dinner. Second, because most of the gay men he met were married, he realized that he didn't have to choose one lifestyle at the expense of another. Still uncertain about his sexual orientation, Minnelli found it useful to have brief encounters that seldom involved commitment on any level, not even sexual. Having sex with either men or women was almost a side effect, never a goal, of these relationships.

Among others, Minnelli socialized with Leo Stahr, a jolly German who designed sets, and his wife, who invited him for dinners, as did the Cambrias. He also befriended an older man, Victor Young, who was hired as the company's music arranger and would become a distinguished, Oscar-winning Hollywood composer. Young fascinated Minnelli with his stories about the Polish and Russian theaters with which he had toured as a violin prodigy. As they were all working at night, there was plenty of time for stories and jokes to be told.

In many ways, Minnelli got to know his theater associates better than their wives knew them, because he saw them more often and in crisis situations. However, as intense as these relationships were, they would dissolve as soon as he moved on to new projects since each project involved a different set of people. The ephemeral nature of these relationships suited Minnelli's shyness, insecurity, and doubts about his sexual orientation. It also allowed him to sleep with some of the gay men he worked with, knowing that he would not see them again. All along, Minnelli continued to date women, mostly showgirls who passed through Chicago. His courtship philosophy could be summed up as follows: "As long as no one was hurt." The directness of it all, Minnelli felt, made it easier to overcome his shyness."

Soon Minnelli was drawn into an affair with a beautiful dancer who was much older than he. When they first met, she vaguely mentioned the existence of her husband-actor, a piece of information he immediately dismissed. The relationship was nearly sexless, as most of Minnelli's relationships at that time were, but he enjoyed her company. Besides, it was nice to be seen in public with a female escort who was a celebrity. All went well, until Minnelli heard that her husband was in town performing.

One day there was a knock on Minnelli's door. He opened it and there stood a distinguished-looking man of about forty.

"May I come in?" he asked in a friendly manner.

"You're quite young," the husband observed.

Minnelli stuttered something, expecting a Noël Coward kind of confrontation with barbs exchanged over drinks.

"Don't be nervous," the man said. "You have nothing to fear. I was just curious. I wanted to see who you were."

Minnelli breathed a little easier, and they sat down and talked for a while. Minnelli found the man to be worldly and charming, and with a mature understanding of relationships that was rare. Needless to say, that meeting ended the affair with the dancer.

When Balaban and Katz merged their venture with Paramount-Publix, the three-theater operation became part of a bigger national chain. Minnelli was occasionally sent to New York City to work on shows that would later go on tour. No doubt, he would have appreciated Chicago and its sociocultural scene more intensely and pleasurably had his mind not been set on living in New York.

New York was everything Minnelli expected it to be, and more. Working on the shows at the Paramount Theater on Broadway, where the units originated, provided his first taste of Manhattan. Once the rigors of mounting a new show were over, he had time to explore the magic of the city. It was at this time that he began to explore his homosexual inclinations. Late at night, he would take a walk on the dark streets of Greenwich Village, following, or being followed, by men who looked gay. He seldom took the initiative in beginning a conversation, and often would change his mind after a couple of blocks and turn back.

Minnelli usually stayed in a midtown hotel on the East Side so that he could walk to the theater district. He was particularly drawn to Times Square and the surreal colors of its neon lights. He now fully comprehended G. K. Chesterton's observation upon seeing the letters and trademarks that advertised everything from pork to pianos: "What a glorious garden of wonders this would be to anyone who was lucky enough to be unable to read."

It was only a matter of time before Minnelli's talents took him to Broadway. Moving to New York now became his major goal. Suddenly, life in Chicago seemed provincial and purposeless. Unbeknownst to him, Balaban and Katz wanted to move him to New York for their own reasons. In fact, Cambria gave Minnelli an ultimatum: If he wanted to stay with Balaban and Katz, he would have to move to New York. At this particular point, Minnelli couldn't have been given a better order. He totally obeyed.

Three

Radio City Music Hall

MINNELLI SPENT MOST OF HIS FREE TIME in New York going to the theater. The Broadway scene was rapidly changing. Musical reviews were replacing the drawing room comedies and operettas of the 1920s. Lavishly mounted, they served as entertaining distractions in the early years of the Depression.

The successful musical revues of the day included *The Band Wagon, Ziegfeld Follies of 1931, Earl Carroll's Vanities,* and *George White's Scandals.* Minnelli liked musical theater, but he had no idea that this would be his future direction. He certainly couldn't have anticipated then that he would make two of these shows, *The Band Wagon* and *Ziegfeld Follies,* into big-screen musicals for M-G-M.

Minnelli lived in a tiny Greenwich Village apartment, which he sublet from a dancer, Jacques Cartier, whom he had met through gay acquaintances. The predominant furniture in the room was a big bed, which served multiple functions, including as a place to have dinner for two. But the modest apartment fulfilled his needs. Its greatest advantage was its location. The apartment was across the street from the speakeasy Chumley's, a popular hangout for struggling artists like Minnelli.

One of the first people Minnelli met in New York was a charming lady named Eleanor Lambert. Married to Seymour Berkson, one of

Hearst's right-hand men, she was launching a new business, a public relations firm. One day, after looking at Minnelli's portfolio, Lambert said, "I'm going to represent you soon. You're going to do great things." Utterly insecure, Minnelli listened to her remarks with skeptical curiosity before dismissing them.

At Paramount, Minnelli's work blended smoothly with that of the other artists. At first, he designed costumes exclusively and was excluded from doing sets because he didn't belong to the set designers' union, the Society of Painters and Paper Hangers. But his work enabled him to meet some of the most admired craftsmen in the field, such as Robert Edmond Jones and James Reynolds.

Minnelli worked hard, designing costumes for all the productions that traveled the Paramount circuit. The Paramount-Publix units traveled fifty-two weeks a year. One such unit went out each week, and each had its directors and designers. Though Minnelli did one out of the three shows, it was a full-time job, amounting to the equivalent of doing a new Broadway show every week.

It was not easy to gain union membership; only a few set designers were accepted each year. Minnelli was introduced to Woodman Thompson, a prominent stage designer who instructed him on matters of technique and scale. With Thompson's sponsorship, he gained acceptance into the Society, the first professional organization he belonged to, and one to which he would remain a loyal member for the duration of his life.

Touring in these units was a young pianist named Oscar Levant. Minnelli didn't meet Levant until a couple of years later, when the musician became the wisecracking guest of the Gershwin social salon, where New York's cultural elite gathered. Levant was equipped with a huge supply of jokes about his neuroses, and God knows, he had plenty of them. Thus began a tentative acquaintance that would blossom into close friendship and collaboration, with Levant appearing in several Minnelli pictures, including *An American in Paris* and *The Cobweb,* in which Minnelli cast him as a neurotic mental patient.

E. Y. (Yip) Harburg, the lyricist who wrote such classics as "Over the Rainbow," was the first member of the Gershwin salon Minnelli met, at a party given by the theater critic Gilbert W. Gabriel. Minnelli was drawn to Harburg's good nature, and, in turn, Harburg saw in Minnelli a bright if socially awkward kid who needed help in acquiring polish and dash.

Along with designing costumes for a different show each week, Minnelli was doing other jobs. He illustrated a new edition of Casanova's memoirs, titled *The Story of My Life,* in the Aubrey Beardsley style. To supervise the work and also expedite the process, the publisher would turn up at Minnelli's tiny apartment and wait for him to finish the drawing. Invariably, the publisher would fall asleep on Minnelli's bed while the artist continued to work late into the night.

Minnelli was then hired by Earl Carroll to design a 300-foot-tall, all-girl curtain for his 1931 *Vanities,* similar to the ones Erté had done for the Folies Bergère. George White had been doing something similar for his show, *George White's Scandals*, and now it was Carroll's turn. Though Minnelli had never taken on such a massive job, he was eager to execute it. Minnelli had never been to France, and so he tried to imagine how an American might execute an Erté concept.

Using absinthe-colored chiffon seven times the width of the stage, Minnelli incorporated silver embroidery in the material. The reviewer Robert Benchley criticized the design for its "Negroid sense of color," but Minnelli dismissed the review, claiming that Benchley was unaware of the bold use of color in the European theater, inspired by Leon Bakst and executed by Nicholas Remisoff and Serge Soudeikine for the Ballets Russes. Benchley had adopted an inaccurate stereotype that implied mismatched colors, which Minnelli perceived as an insult to Negroes, as well as a slap at him as an artist.

Fortunately, Carroll liked the design and before long put Minnelli in sole charge of designing both sets and costumes for the 1932 *Vanities.* A young musician Minnelli admired, Harold Arlen, was writing some of the *Vanities* score. After winning an Oscar for "Over the Rainbow" in *The Wizard of Oz,* Arlen would contribute the song "Happiness Is Just a Thing Called Joe" for Minnelli's first movie, *Cabin in the Sky.*

While working on the show, Minnelli fell for one of the *Vanities* girls whose lovely legs showed through the curtain—that is, until he found out she was Carroll's girlfriend. A soft-spoken but no-nonsense man, Carroll always wore headphones over his ears during rehearsals, coolly putting the girls through their paces. When Carroll found out about Minnelli's infatuation, he denied him an invitation to his secret place, where the show's voyeuristic backers could have a peeping look into the dressing room of the showgirls.

Around that time, the diva-singer Grace Moore asked Minnelli to supervise the art direction for the operetta, *The Dubarry,* which was scheduled to open in November 1932. To revamp the work to Moore's specifications, the original librettists Rowland Leigh and Desmond Carter were brought from England, where the show had first been produced.

Minnelli found Moore to be an opinionated artist with too-strong ideas. Moore complimented Minnelli on a ballroom set, done in chinoiserie style, but she was not excited about his other ideas. Even so, the friction between them was reconciled, and after an out-of-town tryout in Boston, the operetta went to New York, where it enjoyed a modest run of eighty-seven performances.

Minnelli's relationship with Moore was never more than cordial. On opening night, he sent her a good-luck telegram. To his shock, Moore didn't even acknowledge it. A couple of days later, producer Morris Green reproached Minnelli. "She thinks you insulted her on purpose," he said.

"What?" Minnelli said.

"The telegram you sent was not very smart," Green said. It turned out that Minnelli had inadvertently addressed the telegram to Florence Moore, a very popular singer-comedienne of the day. In the end, Moore accepted Minnelli's already notorious lack of memory for names as an excuse and even laughed about it. Working with Moore offered the first valuable lesson Minnelli learned about prima donnas with big egos. It would become handy in Hollywood when dealing with Judy Garland, Katharine Hepburn, and Judy Holliday, among other stars.

Based on his track record, the Paramount executives broadened Minnelli's duties to include set design, and he was asked to arrange girls in glamorous costumes and costly tableaus, just as Ben Ali Haggin was doing for the *Ziegfeld Follies.*

Shortly after, the operations moved to Astoria, Long Island, where Paramount's East Coast studios were located. But Paramount decided that traveling units were not economically feasible and replaced them with big bands. As a result, in the winter of 1933, Minnelli found himself out of a job.

Lacking any real sense of money, Minnelli had spent every penny he earned buying books and art supplies. When he was down to his last dollar, he bought two pounds of beef, potatoes, and onions, and cooked up a huge stew which lasted for days. But Minnelli didn't starve for long. Out of the blue he got a call from an administrator at Radio City Music Hall, inquiring whether he would be interested in becoming its costume designer.

Radio City Music Hall had opened at Rockefeller Center in December 1932. With a capacity of 6,200 seats, it became the world's largest theater, presenting musical extravaganzas by Robert Edmond Jones, while a second space in the house showed movies. When neither concept proved successful, it was decided to close both houses temporarily.

After Jones's departure, S. L. Rothafel, nicknamed Roxy, was hired. The new plan for the Music Hall was to present movies, preceded by vaudeville acts. The egomaniacal Roxy was notorious for his rambunctious nature and fault-finding; nothing was good enough for him. As a result, Minnelli, his youngest and most defenseless employee, became an easy target for Roxy's caustic barbs.

Each week, Minnelli, art director Clark Robinson, and dance director Russell Markert worked together hard for the Thursday opening. No movie, not even the popular ones, was held over in those days. Every movie had just a one-week run, as did the stage presentation. Minnelli had been at the Music Hall for only a few weeks, when Clark Robinson suddenly resigned. In trying to find a quick replacement, Roxy asked Minnelli to take over Robinson's job, in addition to handling costume design.

The first week of December 1933 marked the end of a historic era: Prohibition was repealed. For Minnelli, however, the date was significant in another respect. The highlight of the ambitious show that week was the *Scheherazade* suite of Rimsky-Korsakov.

The *New York Times* reviewer marveled at "the Persian rugs, muezzins, elephants, janizaries, and veiled houris," and a proud Roxy had the newspaper in hand when he met Minnelli in the conference room over lunch. Looking at Minnelli, Roxy said, "You know, I've been picking on this fellow, but all that picking brought good results. He's an artist." From then on, Minnelli's relationship with Roxy was cordial. Though it was a painful way to whip Minnelli into shape, it had proved effective.

Roxy's abrasiveness pushed Minnelli to creative heights he didn't even know he was capable of.

Unfortunately, Roxy's extravaganza proved too much for the board and he was fired, supposedly for "artistic differences." W. G. Van Schmus, a public relations executive, was appointed as managing director. Highly methodical, Van Schmus created a different, more restrictive climate at the Music Hall. While Minnelli didn't mind the numerous sleepless nights and endless work, he did mind the budgetary cuts.

The workload followed the same routine. Minnelli worked steadily through Wednesday night, and the cast then came in at eight the next morning for a final rehearsal before the first show at noon. Minnelli would then wake up from his Thursday-night collapse in time for the Friday business-lunch meeting. As inspiration had to come regularly and reliably, Minnelli discovered within himself extraordinary energy and an abundance of ideas.

Though it was meager, Minnelli's social life came at the expense of sleep. But young and enthusiastic, he was able to get by with only four hours of sleep per night. Minnelli spent most of his free time with Lester Gaba, also a designer, whom he had met at a party.

The relationship involved sex, but Minnelli wasn't able to commit either to a man or to a woman. They dated regularly, but the peculiar relationship proved frustrating to Gaba, who was less cautious about being known as homosexual, at least to theatrical colleagues, and wanted a more permanent relationship.

Minnelli and Gaba were almost mirror images. Their physical resemblance was so close that Gaba might have been mistaken for Minnelli's twin. Like Minnelli, Gaba came from a small town (Hannibal, Missouri) and had worked for Marshall Field and Balaban and Katz in Chicago, where they had met. Gaba and Minnelli had been given the same first name, but it was around this time that Minnelli dropped "Lester" and became known as "Vincente."

Though Minnelli and Gaba maintained separate apartments, they spent most of their nights together. Their friends always paired their names—Vincente and Lester, Lester and Vincente—as if they were an established couple. Dorothy Parker, known for her wicked tongue, was particularly intrigued by the duo. "Here come Lester and Lester," she would say when they arrived together for a party, often dressed similarly and wearing makeup.

There was no malicious gossip, though, of the sort Minnelli would encounter a decade later in Hollywood. In New York's theatrical circles, as long as you had talent, it seemed to be okay to be effeminate, even to wear light makeup, as Minnelli and Gaba occasionally did.

When Minnelli was working at Radio City Music Hall, Gaba would sit in the front row every night, patiently waiting for him to finish his duties backstage. As was the norm with many gay men in that era, the two often escorted women to dinner and nightclubs before retiring to Minnelli's place late at night.

Around this time, Minnelli realized how much safer it was to get involved with women older than himself, or with women uninterested in steady relationships, sex, or marriage. There was not much sex with these usually older women, who served more as companions and escorts to premieres and social events. In this milieu it was okay to be gay so long as you didn't flaunt it in public.

Though he didn't really enjoy it, out of both courtesy and duty, Minnelli occasionally double-dated with Russell Markert. It was important to stay close to Markert, who had recently begun a dancing troupe under Roxy and would later supervise the group's transformation into the famous Rockettes.

Markert was seeing a gorgeous redheaded woman named Lucille Ball, but Minnelli and Lucille didn't become friends until much later, after they both moved to Hollywood. Initially, their meetings were mostly at parties, but even then Minnelli was struck by Lucille's vivaciousness. Minnelli saw Ball as a sophisticated Myrna Loy type (recalling her role in *The Thin Man,* in which she made a big splash in 1934) rather than the female Charlie Chaplin she would later become in her TV show. He certainly couldn't anticipate that he would be directing Ball in a zany comedy, *The Long, Long Trailer,* in 1954.

Occasionally, Minnelli went out with one of the Giersdorf singing sisters. Mostly, though, he socialized with his coworkers. He went out several times with leading lady Nell O'Day. Through O'Day, Minnelli met Marian Herwood, who was so efficient in administrative matters that he hired her as his permanent secretary. With her devotion and good skills,

Herwood literally changed Minnelli's work patterns at Radio City Music Hall, presenting him each day with a summary of the tasks to be accomplished. With her intervention, the job became more manageable and enjoyable too.

Though he liked living in Greenwich Village, Minnelli decided it was time to move uptown, closer to the Broadway scene. His new apartment, on East 52nd Street, wasn't quite so far from the Gershwins' house. Composer George, his lyricist brother, Ira, and Ira's wife, Leonore (known as Lee), lived together on 72nd Street, and Yip Harburg took Minnelli there regularly.

It was not easy to gain full acceptance into the Gershwins' salon. The two criteria for admission were talent and joy of life, vague as these concepts were. However, once you were in, you became a lifetime member, unless and until you violated a sacred norm. "Regulars" at the salon included such diverse artists as Harpo Marx, Dashiell Hammett, Lillian Hellman, Heywood Broun, John O'Hara, Dorothy Parker, and Moss Hart.

The wit of the group was Oscar Levant, who aimed his most ferocious lines at himself. Levant knew everyone, from newspaper publishers to waiters at chic restaurants and scary gangsters. Levant's company was highly sought out, and since he wasn't often active professionally, he had plenty of time to socialize. A sponger, Levant adjusted easily and smoothly to the company and needs of the moment. The joke in town was that Levant changed his girls as often as his underwear. Lacking Levant's social skills and ease with every kind of company, male or female, Minnelli looked upon him with envy, only later to realize that the pianist's behavior masked a deeply neurotic personality, in constant need of reassurance.

No one was immune to the nasty tongue of Dorothy Parker, whose wit was different from Levant's. Parker was a quieter but sharper observer than Levant. She would look at Minnelli with her enormously curious eyes and then, as soon as he left the room, would say something humorously wicked about him. Minnelli always made sure to exit in a discreet, nondemonstrative manner.

Then there was Moss Hart, who belonged to a different breed from Levant. Hart was totally unprepared for his first big success, _Lifetime,_ in 1930. Like Minnelli, Hart was a working-class, self-educated man, and had to learn from scratch how to behave properly in public, how to stir his teacup with a little spoon, how to light a lady's cigarette, where to place his friends' photos, the proper way to tie his shoelaces, and so on. Both Minnelli and Hart were determined from a young age to rise above their station at all costs—and they did.

If Levant was "the man who came to dinner," Moss Hart was the "golden boy," to borrow terms from the titles of two noted theatrical plays of the late thirties. Hart was often the guest of honor at a party, but he would forget to show up. Too ashamed to admit his error, Hart would decide to "cool it," until the following Friday, when he would ring his hosts' doorbell promptly at the appointed hour, only seven days late. The hosts might be in pajamas and wrappers, but after apologies for the misunderstanding, they would invite him into the kitchen for a hot meal, since Hart was always hungry.

Occasionally, George Gershwin also came down from his apartment. George was then writing his folk opera, *Porgy and Bess,* with his brother, Ira. George's muse accompanied him wherever he went. He would take over the piano as soon as he arrived at a party and then play all evening long. In irritation, other composers would throw darts at George, but he would remain oblivious to them and continue to play the piano.

A known womanizer, George had engagements with a different girl every night. Unlike Ira, George liked his freedom and didn't want to settle down into "boring" domesticity. George knew that he was gifted and had no false modesty about it. Because of his lack of social skills and awkward shyness, Minnelli felt doubly lucky just to be around people like the Gershwins. Minnelli saw George often, but he never got to know him well because he was always holding court and surrounded by people.

The exposure to these larger-than-life talents and personalities had an enormous influence on Minnelli. The Ira Gershwins took Minnelli under their wing, and in due process, they became his closest friends. Ira was the kind of person who became more attractive as you got to know him. Unlike George, Ira didn't seem to realize, or at least didn't show, what a great talent he possessed. No ego was involved. Ira just accepted that George was the family's genius and relegated himself to "just an ordinary songwriter."

As usual, it was easier for Minnelli to socialize and bond with older women and wives. He was more comfortable in the company of women than men because there was always something to talk about and there was no sense of rivalry. Ira's wife, Lee, was charming, vivacious, and kind, and she opened their house to visitors at all times of the day and night, with liquor and food in abundance.

In due time, Lee became more important to Minnelli as a friend and close confidante. He could talk to Lee about matters that he couldn't share with Ira. Lee made a special effort to introduce Minnelli to many people, and was always willing to help during rough times, both in New York and later in Hollywood, during his tumultuous marriage to Judy Garland.

At Radio City Music Hall, Minnelli was given freedom so long as his taste did not "offend" the more conservative patrons and didn't call for an inflated budget. The experience offered enormous challenges, such as designing sets that used elevators and interlocking turntables. Getting the lighting right was particularly tricky, as it sometimes involved juggling through a complicated technique with as many as one hundred cues. Minnelli learned how to examine effects from the perspective of technical resources and the capability of the tools at hand, skills that would prove useful when he became a film director.

One of his challenges was to design four to five scenes a week, but he could work only one week ahead of time. Minnelli could not afford to be sick, nor could he be uninspired, and he looked for inspiration from every possible direction. He tried to add touches of surrealism, a movement then in vogue, to several productions, experimenting with color and shadings under varied lighting conditions. One week, Minnelli designed Ferde Grofé's *Tabloid Suite,* using newspapers for the sets; the following week, he used the very same papers as backdrops.

Minnelli applied equally eclectic taste and resourceful energy to furnishing his own lodgings, his 52nd Street apartment, which was done in blue and white with a bright red bathroom. The apartment was so close to Radio City that he could walk to work. Minnelli could even take time to walk home for dinner on work nights. He liked the idea of taking a break in the midst of a long workday.

Again inspired by Whistler's lifestyle, in his new place, Minnelli decided to hire a valet. Through friends, he was introduced to a young Japanese named Hara.

"The furniture hasn't arrived yet," Minnelli said. "Can you start next Wednesday?"

The furniture still wasn't there when Hara showed up for his first day of work on Wednesday. Hara was full of doubts about the job.

"You sure you want Japanese butler?" he asked.

Minnelli reassured him, and Hara moved in.

Vocal and extremely opinionated, Hara could say the most outrageous things in public. After attending the opening night of each show, Hara would offer a most severe, totally unsolicited criticism. Hara was such a colorful character that Minnelli's friends invited themselves for dinner just in order to meet the flamboyant helper.

One evening, songwriter Kay Swift ("Can't We Be Friends?"), who was then dating George Gershwin, came for dinner. During the meal, a piece of steak got stuck in her throat and she was gasping for air. The guests were frantic, trying to get the meat out of Kay's windpipe. Unfazed, Hara walked over, pushed everybody aside, looked straight into her face, and said, "I think she die." This colorful episode circulated among Minnelli's friends for years, adding to Hara's rapidly growing reputation.

Hara took care of all of Minnelli's household needs, and for the first time, he found himself living a comfortable existence. As soon as he made enough money, Minnelli moved his parents to St. Petersburg, Florida, where the weather was good for his mother's angina and his father's rheumatism and liver trouble. His parents continued to live in the same house until their deaths, seldom visiting their son in New York or in Los Angeles. The relationship between Minnelli and his old folks gradually lost its natural warmth and was now mostly conducted from a distance, via letters and occasional telephone calls.

In 1934 Van Schmus decided that Minnelli, his prime employee, should try his hand at producing the weekly shows. The responsibility was alternated with conductor Leon Leonidoff, choreographer Florence Rogge, and Russell Markert.

Minnelli's first show, *Coast to Coast,* was scheduled to open on October 25, 1934. Yip Harburg volunteered to write a song for it, and collaborating with Jerry Sears, he supplied an answer song to "Eadie Was a Lady," naming it "Jimmy Was a Gent." Duke Ellington's "The Mooch" was also introduced in that show. A chromium turntable, which opened the show, revealed the Côte d'Azur set done in the style of Raoul Dufy. Other sets included the Ascot royal enclosure for the Gold Coast, black sculpture for the Ivory Coast, and a barroom act followed by a suggestive brass bed that was meant to represent the Barbary Coast.

To celebrate Minnelli's producing debut, a party followed the opening night in the upstairs penthouse, where receptions were held when out-of-town celebs visited New York. It was one of Minnelli's least favorite functions, even when he felt good about his work, because he had to schmooze, and that never came easy to him.

The Music Hall's publicity release on Minnelli's sets and costumes proudly proclaimed: "Vincente Minnelli demonstrates a flair for the unusual and picturesque, sticking to his modern style. Modernistic dances and blue torch songs are the mediums in which he revels."

One day, Yip, Lee Gershwin, and Minnelli were walking out of 21, the famous restaurant, when they bumped into the ticket broker, Harry Kaufman.

Lee introduced Minnelli to Kaufman.

"I know you," Kaufman said to Minnelli. "I know your work."

Minnelli realized that he was becoming a known quantity.

After Kaufman left, Lee said, "Harry's now working with Lee Shubert. They're trying to create class productions. Do you think you might be interested in directing a Broadway show?"

Minnelli could not believe his ears.

He continued to work at Radio City Music Hall into 1935, taking his turn at producing a weekly show, in addition to his other duties. Though he was still young and didn't require much sleep, he was beginning to wonder whether his energy was boundless.

Switching to a more legit style of theater meant starting at the bottom, and the bottom in those days was the Shubert organization. The snobbish Lee Shubert was aiming to establish his respectability. He had already produced two John Murray Anderson shows, *Ziegfeld Follies of 1934* and *Life Begins at 8:40*.

For the first time in his career, Minnelli worked with such A-list talents as Fanny Brice, Bert Lahr, Ray Bolger, and Ira Gershwin and worked more closely than before with Harold Arlen and Yip Harburg.

"I want to move on to quality shows," Lee Shubert told Minnelli. "I think you should be with us. How would you like to produce all the Shubert musicals?"

Minnelli made a point to be cautious, as the Shuberts were notorious for exploiting fresh talents like his. The legal issues were handed over to his lawyer, and indeed Minnelli's contract stipulated that he would have total control over his shows for as long as they ran, and that he could also hire the musicians and actors. Once the details were worked out, Minnelli accepted a lucrative offer to produce three Shubert shows. Marian Herwood, who had become an indispensable assistant, helped him tender his resignation from the Music Hall in a graceful way.

One afternoon in Times Square, Minnelli ran into Boris Aronson, who had recently designed the sets for *Three Men on a Horse.*

"That was a great saloon set," Minnelli said. "I liked those dingy shades of green and brown."

"Well," Aronson said, "the brown was for the cockroaches, and the green for the powder that exterminates them."

That kind of dry wit was characteristic of Aronson.

Soon after, Minnelli recommended Aronson as his replacement at Radio City Music Hall. Aronson took the job, but he was too slow and methodical a craftsman to endure the pressures, and didn't last very long.

Scouting around for a studio, Minnelli found a brownstone on 53rd Street, next to the Museum of Modern Art. The studio had an enormous room with a carved ceiling and wall panels, and two bay windows that faced the street. Across the hall, there was a three-room apartment that he was allowed to use as extra space to design the shows.

Minnelli's studio soon became a Sunday-afternoon hangout for the elite of the theater and music worlds. Ira and Lee Gershwin, George Balanchine, Yip Harburg, Oscar Levant, Richard Allen, Vernon Duke, Dorothy Parker, Paul Bowles, Pavel Tchelitchev, all stopped by. Among the regulars was also photographer Man Ray, whom Minnelli helped support financially when in need. Minnelli also befriended the photographer Alfred Stieglitz and his artist-wife Georgia O'Keeffe, who also became regular guests at his studio. While Minnelli was still at the

Music Hall, O'Keeffe had painted the mural in the ladies' lounge, much to the chagrin of Stieglitz.

Kay Swift named the glitterati salon the "Minnellium," which he loved. Minnelli was always at his happiest among his fellow artists. At that time, he was still dreaming about going to Paris to become a painter, and the "Minnellium" was perceived as a stepping-stone.

Four

New York, New York

IN JULY 1935, MINNELLI BEGAN REHEARSALS for a show scheduled to open in October, planning to perform all of the duties: to direct, design the costumes and sets, and supervise the lighting. After all the bad stories he had heard, Minnelli found the Shubert organization to be a pleasant place to work, perhaps because of the complete autonomy granted to him. There was no interference, and no expenses were spared in mounting the productions.

The show's original title, *Not in the Guidebook,* was later changed to *At Home Abroad,* a kind of a geographical revue that unfolded as a musical holiday trip through Europe, Africa, Japan, and the West Indies. Howard Dietz and Arthur Schwartz composed the score, and Dietz, Marc Connelly, Dion Titheradge, and Raymond Knight wrote the sketches.

Beatrice Lillie was signed to star in the show, along with Reginald Gardiner, who was brought over from London. Eleanor Powell, who had already begun a screen career, was cast for the tap-dancing routines, and ballet dancer Paul Haakon, who had worked at Radio City, was hired as her partner. Ethel Waters and Herb Williams rounded out the cast, adding variety to it.

Dietz didn't like two songs, Paul Haakon's "Death in the Afternoon" ballet and Powell's "Lady with a Tap." Minnelli, however, felt that the songs were necessary and insisted that they remain. The conflict became a bit nastier when Dietz's lawyer got involved with Minnelli's, and the two lawyers realized that the Shuberts had given both Dietz and Minnelli identical contracts, with each artist led to believe that he had the final say. Since the Shuberts didn't take sides, a big argument ensued. Dietz and Minnelli reached an impasse, just before heading to Boston for the tryout.

With no time to pack, Minnelli instructed Hara, "Please pack my suitcase. You do know how, right?"

"Of course," Hara said coldly, offended by the question.

The bags were left at the theater to be sent to the Boston hotel.

But in Boston, when Minnelli prepared to dress for dinner, he was shocked to realize that his suitcases had arrived totally empty.

"Pack" must have been the Japanese word for "clean," for that's what Hara did. Minnelli had to rush out of the hotel in time to buy a new wardrobe for the evening.

Before the opening night, Dietz approached Minnelli. "Look, it's you and me, and to hell with the Shuberts. Let's talk this out." The Powell and Haakon numbers remained intact, and Minnelli was pleased, because he respected Dietz and wanted them to remain friends.

One of the show's highlights, "Lady with a Tap," was a spoof of filmmaker Ernst Lubitsch, with Eleanor Powell playing a spy who sends secret messages by tapping the code with her feet. Another number, "Death in the Afternoon," used innovative lighting and sets to tell the story of a matador going from his dressing room to his death. Minnelli designed a long red corridor leading to the bullring. A tango interlude in the middle of the number introduced the bullfighter's sweetheart, who had a premonition of a fatal tragedy; nevertheless, the matador fights the bull to the bitter end.

One of Minnelli's favorite songs in that show was "Antonio," but, to his chagrin, Bea Lillie didn't want to do it. "I just can't sing a song with too many words," she said, tripping over the fast tempo of the opening bars. The set was an arena for bicycle riders with real bikes wheeling about upstage and represented by marionettes at the rear of the stage. Knowing that Bea wanted to be in "Get Yourself a Geisha," toward the end of the show, Minnelli struck a bargain with her. Bea could do that number only if she sang "Antonio."

The diva consented for a while, but she continued to have a terrible time with "Antonio," which Minnelli insisted on her doing with a credible Italian accent and the speed of a Rossini aria. The number was finally cut, after much haggling.

Bea Lillie was then a huge star. Onstage, she registered big; each gesture of hers was hilarious. All she had to do was raise a finger and the public would respond with laughter. But offstage, Bea was not very talkative; in fact, she was quite somber. For Minnelli, the main problem of directing Bea stemmed from her volatile unpredictability. She would do something brilliant in one performance, and then something totally different in the next one.

"What became of this number, or that gesture?" Minnelli would ask after one uneven show.

"I don't remember," Bea would say.

Bea was as intuitive as a child, and as spontaneous as an animal. However, once her shows reached New York, Bea demonstrated that she was "the greatest opening-night performer." In time, Minnelli learned that Bea's secret was to save all of her energy out of town for the Broadway critics and her fans.

As a result of Minnelli's guidance, the Boston reviews were ecstatic, singling out his use of colors and lighting without resorting to opulence. One critic wrote that Minnelli "filled the stage with rich glowing colors that give the whole work an extraordinary loveliness." In fact, the reviews were so good that *At Home Abroad* went straight to New York rather than to other cities.

The stage at the Winter Garden in New York was not as deep as that of the Boston theater. Minnelli had a hard time getting the lights right, and several cues were missed on opening night. It became a nightmare, and Minnelli was so exhausted that he saw only the negative aspects of the show, and he longed to go back to Boston where things had been easier.

Minnelli went to bed early, anticipating a bad, sleepless night. Several hours later, however, the phone rang.

"Where are you?" Dietz said. "We're waiting for you."

"Be there soon," Minnelli said.

He got out of bed and dressed quickly. By the time he arrived at the Lombardy Hotel, the reviews were out. Dietz read them loudly and proudly, beginning with *The New York Times*'s Brooks Atkinson: "At last the season has begun."

Even the performers who were not mentioned in the reviews were glad that the show was a hit. Minnelli always admired the theater's esprit de corps, the one selfless aspect of showbiz that he would miss the most after relocating to Hollywood. The reviews articulated what Minnelli's special gifts were, what he brought to the theater, and what he had accomplished—so far. At this juncture, he treated the notices as "gospel."

In his stage work, Minnelli developed an innovative concept, the integrated musical, in which singing and dancing advanced the story line with elegance, satire, and wit. He brought sophistication, urbanity, and a personal style to the old-style variety shows. Minnelli's productions highlighted his modernist designs, fostering at once a sense of unity and individualistic expression, and were based on a strategy that he described as "a feeling of variety within harmony."

Unlike Bertolt Brecht's radical separation of elements in musical theater, Minnelli's shows were strongly unified with his personal touch. For one thing, Minnelli did everything. He chose the themes, guided the performers, and even designed the sets and costumes. An innovative concept, "variety within unity" also blurred the old distinctions of highbrow versus lowbrow entertainment, which also would characterize the good Minnelli musicals at M-G-M.

In the next few months, Minnelli became, in his words, "the Great White Way's new white hope." He had done several shows before at Radio City, but most of them received only scant attention. But now, with such glowing reviews, his ambitions got higher, and he could ask for more money for his productions as well as his services.

Minnelli treasured a laudatory letter from a fan who praised profusely his theatrical innovations. It turned out that the fan was none other than the writer S. J. Perelman, Minnelli's longtime idol. When Perelman asked Minnelli to join him for drinks at the Lombardy Hotel, he was full of trepidation, but he was pleasantly surprised by the way Perelman put him immediately at ease. As a result, they went on to become fast friends.

A few weeks later, *The New Yorker* ran a profile of Minnelli, titled "Prodigy":

> It's time you know something about Vincente Minnelli, the youngster who directed *At Home Abroad,* and designed the settings and costumes. We're told that never before in the history of Broadway and musical shows has one man undertaken these three important jobs (at least nobody has tried it and got away with it). The impetuous Shuberts now have him under contract to do the same thing for five of their forthcoming shows. Up to a few years ago he habitually dressed in a way to remind you of Easter Sunday in Harlem, but lately he has tapered off to gray suits and light-green ties. He reads Saki and Huysmans more than he does any other writers, and has added Daumier and Roualt to his painting gods.

Fashion publicist Eleanor Lambert, who in the meantime had taken on Minnelli as a favorite client, was responsible for giving him a new celebrity status. Minnelli, however, felt that she and the press were trying to confer on him a fake "flamboyant personality" that he simply didn't possess. "I'm not used to this treatment," Minnelli complained to his friend, photographer George Platt Lynes. "You'd better learn," Lynes said. And he did, rather quickly.

Being a celebrity meant, among other things, having gossip about your life printed in the social columns, and, on a more pragmatic level, getting a desirable table at a chic restaurant. In one of his gossip columns, Walter Winchell reported that Minnelli and Marian Herwood were going to get married. After reading about it in the newspapers, Minnelli's mother called from Florida in a state of shock.

"You should have told me first," she said hurtfully.

"Mother," Minnelli protested, "there's no truth in that. Marian is my secretary and assistant. We go out a lot because we're always working. We're good friends. We're not going to get married. You'll be the first to know if I do."

In truth, Minnelli's mother wished he would get married. Like many other people, she was beginning to suspect that "something might be wrong" with her son, then in his mid-thirties, though she couldn't articulate yet what the problem was. The evidence suggests that Minnelli never felt comfortable enough to discuss his sexuality with his parents, and there was no need to; in Hollywood, he certainly had the strong alibi of multiple marriages, even if the first one, to Judy Garland, did not occur until he was forty-two.

At Home Abroad was still enjoying a successful run when Lee Shubert assigned Minnelli to direct the latest version of *The Ziegfeld Follies*. John Murray Anderson was meant to do another installment, but the Shuberts had difficulty getting title clearance, which forced them to rename their revue. The Shuberts' second *Follies* again used the veteran actress Billie Burke, Ziegfeld's widow, as a co-producer. Lee Shubert asked Minnelli to design the costumes and sets as one of the shows in his contract.

Anderson, a former dancer, and Minnelli were friends even before working together on the show. A founding father of the American revue, Anderson began staging shows after his wife and dancing partner had died. Many of the effects for which Minnelli would be credited were learned during his work with Anderson—the best free training he could get.

Anderson's shows were casually charming yet stylish. The artists who had worked with him had already established reputations in costume or fashion design: Howard Greer, Charles Le Maire, Adrian, James Reynolds. Anderson brought the modern-dance movement to Middle America, spotlighting Martha Graham, Doris Humphrey, and Jack Cole in the *Greenwich Village Follies*.

Anderson was generous to a fault, even selfless, and so there was no backbiting or jealousy; each artist and craftsman was allowed to cultivate his own talent at his own pace. Gradually, Anderson turned over the directing chores to Minnelli, though he never got credit for it from the management or the critics.

During his Radio City days, Minnelli went to Harlem with his colleagues. One day, they got hold of marijuana, which was then easy to obtain. As they sat in a bar puffing away, they got to laughing hysterically. The evening ended in the apartment of an eccentric old lady, who had a lot of money but thought that her money was really dirty. She would wash the twenty-dollar bills and then spread them out on newspapers to dry.

Minnelli woke up the next morning with no hangover but also no special desire to do drugs again. Anderson made up nicknames for everyone, and after Minnelli told him this story, he became known as Mister Reefer.

Ira Gershwin and Billy Rose wrote a number, "Modernistic Moe," for Fanny Brice to sing in the 1936 *Follies,* for which Minnelli asked her to wear a long dark wig, large false feet, and a jersey dress split up on both sides.

In one rehearsal, Ira Gershwin called out, "Fanny! Revolt!"

That's all she needed to hear.

"Okay, kid," she yelled back, then stomped from one end of the stage to the other, striking dramatic poses and screaming, "Rewolt! Rewolt! Oy, am I hungry!"

Also featured in the *Follies,* and for the first time on Broadway, was a surrealist ballet, choreographed by George Balanchine, the Russian immigrant who would go on to found the New York City Ballet. Minnelli achieved striking effects with that number thanks to his own ingenuity, aided by a score by Ira Gershwin and Vernon Duke. Three dancers dressed in green stood at the top of a ramp, while three figures clad in black were lying at a sharp angle from them, suggesting the dancers' shadows and repeating their movements. The number ended with the men who had cast the shadows "losing" the star, Harriet Hoctor, to the black silhouettes, while rising from the ground.

David Freeman, a good sketch writer, supplied some comic work, including the classic "Sweepstakes Ticket" sketch for Fanny Brice, which Minnelli would use in his 1946 movie, *Ziegfeld Follies,* again with Brice. In some sketches Brice was paired with the then rising star Bob Hope. In one, Hope was asked to pursue Eve Arden while singing "I Can't Get Started."

While *At Home Abroad* was done with a simple design (a map filled in with bright schoolbook colors), *Follies* was executed in the elegant and stylish spirit of fashion photography. The opening number was a teaser: The master of ceremonies sang a song that implied there were no girls in the show. Then an enormous tableau depicted girls in mirrors and on swings. Since many previous *Follies* had used period costumes of the Louis XVI era, Minnelli decided to update the look.

For "That Moment of Moments," he chose as inspiration the elaborate hairstyles, bustles, and long trains on gowns of the 1880s. The setting was an adaptable three-foot ramp, which was moved around in several configurations to serve as backdrop for the specialty numbers.

Also in the cast were Gertrude Niesen and Judy Canova. The Shuberts had also offered a contract to St. Louis–born Josephine Baker, who returned to the United States after causing a sensation in Paris at the Folies Bergère.

Baker arrived in New York with her husband, a dashing Italian count, two beautifully groomed dogs, and a large assortment of Louis Vuitton luggage. A day later she swept into Minnelli's studio in a stunning burgundy velvet suit trimmed in sable. Embodying a vision of French chic, she said in a melodramatic tone that stressed every syllable, "Mr. Minnelli! This is how they present me in Paris. The curtain goes up on a huge white lace chocolate box, with all the beautiful girls as bon bons. At the center of the box, there is a lovely chocolate drop—moi, Josephine!"

Minnelli listened patiently, then coughed politely. "Miss Baker," he said, "I have a slightly different conception of how to present you. George Balanchine will create a ballet especially for you, and we will design a beautiful gold dress for the spectacular 'Maharanee' number." Minnelli later draped Josephine in a shimmering sari that showed her sensual body to great advantage.

Baker's second number, "5 A.M.," was semi-autobiographical. To indicate her African roots, Minnelli designed a magnificent gown of glittering gold clinging mesh. The design was so unique and challenging that he had to find a factory that manufactured metal mesh bags to have it made to his specifications. The extremely heavy dress, weighing about one hundred pounds, was covered with a spectacular whirling burgundy ostrich-feather cape, but it clung to Baker's sexy body like a second skin.

For Baker's "Island in the West Indies," Ira Gershwin wrote some of his best lyrics, and Minnelli supplied a costume ornamented with white tusks.

As the show's starry cast included, among others, Fanny Brice, there were also the usual ego problems. Baker had only three numbers whereas Brice had seven. Baker felt that she had proved she could sing in *La Creole,* that she was a known quantity as far as touching the viewers' hearts. Feeling insecure and underestimated, she claimed that Minnelli wanted her to "start all over again," and do it in costumes that might cause her embarrassment and ridicule.

Vernon Duke and Ira Gershwin wrote two highly spiced tropical arias, "5 A.M." and "Maharanee," with ornamentation that, according to Duke, "would scare Lily Pons out of her wits." In addition to Baker's well-publicized flair for rotating her derrière, she also possessed a small but exquisite coloratura soprano. Duke recalled that "Josephine mastered the acrobatic intervals and larynx-defying trills like a trouper, although she was seldom audible, whereas Niesen was too audible."

It was not easy working with Baker, who was at once confident and insecure. She kept asking her companions and confidants how she should express herself—she found fault with everybody and everything. Minnelli later said that he didn't know how he survived the ordeal: "Everybody, not just Josephine, would come to complain and ask for changes, like 'I can't dance in that dress,' or 'The lighting is too harsh.'"

While some critics—all men—complained that Josephine posssessed a small, thin voice that couldn't fill the theater, they were unanimous in their praise of her gorgeous figure. Even so, Minnelli was upset with the notices because the reviewers paid more attention to Baker's body than to his work.

In his memoirs, Vernon Duke described Minnelli in the following way: "I don't think there has ever been a greater disciplinarian or more exacting perfectionist in the musical theater than Vincente Minnelli. Whereas other directors wasted valuable time wrangling with costume designers, arguing with overpaid stars, or kidding around with chorus girls, with Vincente, once rehearsals started, it was all work and no play. We felt like cogs in Minnelli's magical wheel and kept ourselves well-oiled." According to Duke, most revues were not finalized until dress rehearsal time, and the routines kept being changed nightly while out of town. But not with Minnelli: "Once the material was decided upon and whipped into shape, it was blocked out and put together like pieces in a solved jigsaw puzzle; very little of the running order was changed for the New York opening."

All the reviewers commented on the show when it opened at the Boston Opera House, on December 30, 1935. Elliot Norton's *Boston Post* review stated: "Young Vincente Minnelli, who doesn't appear on stage, is the real star of the new *Ziegfeld Follies*." Minnelli was thrilled by the reviews, but he felt that they unfairly treated the other talents that had helped him.

Freddie de Cordova, who years later became the producer of Johnny Carson's TV show, was then Minnelli's second assistant director, serving next to his first assistant, Eddie Dowling. Disregarding one of the sacred rules of their bosses, to avoid fooling around with the girls while they were in rehearsals, on New Year's Eve Eddie and Freddie bought booze and waited for the girls to show up in their hotel. They left the door of their room wide open, but no one showed up. Minnelli happened to walk by after midnight, and he couldn't hide his amusement at how naïve they were. He could have predicted that the two men would end up alone. All the girls were in bed asleep, preparing for the next day's performance.

After the show opened, the *Post*'s Elliot Norton did a follow-up story. "It will be hooted down in some quarters," he wrote, "and here and there, it will probably serve to curl a well-rounded lip into an unbecoming sneer or two. Nevertheless, it is the well-pondered opinion of this column that Minnelli, who designed the costumes and scenery for the current new *Ziegfeld Follies,* has a greater theatrical genius than the late Florenz Ziegfeld. This does not necessarily mean Mr. Minnelli has or will develop flair for self-aggrandizement such as Ziegfeld had. What it does mean is that Florenz Ziegfeld, with all his vast capacity, never had any such amazing ability to create and project the theatrical beauty as has this young Italian-American."

In the number "The Gazooka," Minnelli satirized the *Broadway Melody* style of movie musical, exploiting all of the genre's clichés. David Freeman's comedy scenes and the other sketches were a takeoff on the Dick Powell–Ruby Keeler Depression-era Warner musicals, such as *Forty-Second Street*. Fanny Brice played the chorus girl who fills in for the star on opening night, and Bob Hope was cast as her boyfriend. Upon meeting in an agent's office, they tell each other, "You're different," and fall into a passionate embrace.

These scenes, designed in black-and-white, were followed by a production number full of color that imitated the novelty of a Technicolor finale to black-and-white movies, which in the 1930s was popular in Hollywood movies. For irreverent fun, Minnelli decided that the color sequence should be as blurred as some early Technicolor movies were. In this way, the sets and dancers were covered in colored cellophane, which gave them a blurred edge.

Minnelli created a surrealist ballet done with such panache and sophistication that it revolutionized the conventions of musical theater. As a result of this and other novelties, the press labeled Minnelli "Broadway's wunderkind."

The new *Follies* opened at the Winter Garden on January 30, 1936, to smash reviews. Brooks Atkinson wrote in *The New York Times*: "Minnelli has burst into the Winter Garden with a whole portfolio of original splendors. He has managed this season to reanimate the art of scenic display and costumery. Although he is lavish enough to satisfy any producer's thirst for opulence, his taste is unerring and the *Follies* that comes off his drawing board is a civilized institution. Every number looks well when Minnelli dresses them." This and the other glowing reviews were read at the opening night party, hosted by Lorenz Hart.

For a much-needed change of pace, Minnelli went to the West Indies with Lee and Ira Gershwin for a three-week vacation. He was so tired during the cruise on the S.S. *Britannica* that he spent most of the time sleeping. The trip began in Barbados and Martinique, and from there they continued to Curaçao and Trinidad. Unfortunately they arrived in Trinidad at the start of Lent, a religious season that offered little by way of entertainment. With no airplanes available to take them back, they had to wait for another two weeks for the next boat.

One morning, when Lee went to the hairdresser, she had to wait for hours because a deposed dictator from a South American banana republic was staying at their hotel, and the hairdresser, fearing for her life, was instructed to give priority to his entourage.

There was one moviehouse, which changed its program twice a week. Since there was nothing else to do culturally, Minnelli and the Gershwins waited in line every night for the doors to open. They saw a Warner musical and a Jerome Kern operetta on four consecutive nights. Ira Gershwin quipped, "I didn't like the movie in the U.S., but it looks pretty good here."

Lee must have heard rumors about Minnelli's secretive sex life. While they were playing tennis one day, she suddenly turned to Minnelli and said, "Isn't it time you started thinking of getting married?"

"I've always wanted to get married, but I'm afraid of passing on the Minnelli curse," Minnelli said in reference to the divorce and infant-mortality rates in his family.

At which point, Ira and Lee giggled and left it at that.

During the trip, Lee urged Minnelli to tell over and over again the story of his grandfather's peculiar demise. People at parties found it uproarious that the old man sawed a limb from under him, which caused his own death. In time, Minnelli enjoyed not only the story, but the telling of it, each time with slight exaggeration.

Back in New York, the *Ziegfeld Follies* of 1936 was doing good business. After five months, the show closed for the summer, and then reopened for another five months. Minnelli wasn't involved in the revival, as he had to start right away on his new project. The new Shubert revue, *The Show Is On*, featured Minnelli's name above the title—in big letters. This elevated status meant that he could now afford to hire his close friends. Together, they formed a kind of fraternity, a clique of collaborators, fulfilling Minnelli's dream of being involved in intimate teamwork, albeit with him as the undisputed leader.

Minnelli tried to buy songs from all of his friends. Ted Fetter and Vernon Duke provided "Now" and "Casanova," Lorenz Hart and Richard Rodgers "Rhythm," Yip Harburg and Harold Arlen "Song of the Woodman," and Stanley Adams and Hoagy Carmichael "Little Old Lady." Replete with stage clichés, "By Strauss," as sung by Grace Barrie and Robert Shafter and danced by Mitzi Mayfair, was meant to be a spoof.

Minnelli and his coterie hung out at Harms Music Company, located across 53rd Street, near his own studio. When they didn't see each other, they spoke on the phone, exchanging gossip such as "This show is in trouble, it may not reach Broadway" or "I heard Fanny was a temperamental bitch last night."

Harold Arlen and Minnelli had remained close friends ever since their days with Earl Carroll. Minnelli became a chaperon when Arlen courted a showgirl named Annie, who later became his wife. Both Minnelli and Arlen worshiped the music of the Gershwins and Jerome Kern, which were vastly different. Kern's impudent humor was at odds with the plaintive melody of his songs, a peculiar combination of his rabbi father's wails with Harlem blues. Vastly accomplished, Kern had already written dozens of musicals, including *Show Boat* and its signature ballad, "Ol' Man River."

When Lee Shubert became ill during rehearsal, his brother Jake filled in for a few weeks. Jake Shubert called Minnelli to his office one day and said, "There's too much money being spent, cut it down! Get rid of some of the chorus. Use cheaper materials. Less money all around!" Unfazed, Minnelli said, "Mr. Shubert, you're going to die of apoplexy." For the first time, he talked back and stood up for himself. Back at rehearsals, Minnelli burst out laughing, shocked at his own uncharacteristic audacity.

Freddie de Cordova used to tell horrendous stories about Jake Shubert's cruel fierceness. One time, Jake yelled at de Cordova, "Get your hat and coat, go over and tell them I want seven hundred and fifty yards of material, tomorrow and no later!" Freddie ran out, but then he realized he didn't know where he was going or who was he to talk to, but he was afraid to come back. Years later, the arrogant Shuberts told Freddie, "We must have taught you right."

Moss Hart was working with David Freedman on the sketches, to be performed by Beatrice Lillie, Bert Lahr, and Reginald Gardiner. It was a satire of John Gielgud's version of *Hamlet,* with Gardiner sensing disaster in his performance that evening. Lillie had wonderful asides interrupting the prince. In the finale, Gardiner ends up in the audience with Lillie in a state of a quivering mess.

Another sketch was based on Edna Ferber and George S. Kaufman's smash play, *The Royal Family* (which George Cukor had already made into a popular Hollywood picture). Bea plays a Folies Bergère star accompanied by her manager, husband, and lover to the reading of a play, and Gardiner impersonates a seedy John Barrymore type. Minnelli tried to re-create a picture of the reading he had seen, and to light it as a tableau vivant.

One actor was stretched on a bearskin rug, the other lolling around him. Hart and Freedman inserted one instruction: "Actor enters through door at stage left, provided Minnelli hasn't placed red velvet sofa in front of it." It was a none-too-subtle criticism of Minnelli's penchant for décor, and he got the point. After the reading, there is silence, and the author asks, "What did you think of the play, madame?" "I did not understand a goddamned word!" she says.

Bert Lahr's number, "Song of the Woodman," was a rendition of a popular Nelson Eddy number. "What do we chop when we chop a tree," Bert recited, "a thousand things that we often see." He then enumerates all the things made of wood, with stagehands throwing chips in his face as he is chopping.

The show's funniest sketch was about a hundred-dollar tax rebate. Furious that he's been overcharged, Bert Lahr enters the office of the tax accountant.

"Sit down," the accountant says, "and we'll discuss it. By the way, who is Nina Lahr?"

"She's my grandmother," Bert says, "a darling lady. She's almost eighty."

"You have her here as a gag man at two hundred dollars a week," the auditor says.

The tax officer goes through the return, point by point, and Bert ends up paying the government $200,000.

When the show opened, its conductor Gordon Jenkins was a newcomer to Broadway. Minnelli had been critical of the brassy quality and crude musical arrangements in most theater orchestras. After listening to Jenkins's arrangements on the radio, Minnelli hired him to conduct and to do the arrangements. Jenkins had introduced guitars and vocals that had not been done before. Indeed, conservative musicians complained that Jenkins's arrangements were impossible to play.

Already a perfectionist who had never accepted no for an answer, Minnelli called for extra orchestra rehearsals, for which he paid with his own money. He also invited Bea Lillie to come over to a meeting with Lee Shubert and himself. The diva was delighted, as she was not used to such treatment from her bosses.

The show opened on Christmas Day, 1936, and ran for 237 performances. A reprise opened in September 1937 and played for two weeks before going on the road. Brooks Atkinson wrote in *The New York Times*: "*The Show Is On* skims gaily through an evening of radiant high jinks," and John Mason Brown of the *Evening Post* thought it was "a revue with great effectiveness and rare good taste." Taste seemed to be the key word in evaluating Minnelli's work.

Five

Broadway

IN 1937, MINNELLI HAD THREE SHOWS running on Broadway. He didn't want to go to Hollywood, but all his friends said he had to at least give it a try. Minnelli got into a kind of agents' war, and chose the agent that got him the best offer.

Paramount promised to pay him a large salary and also offered to bring out his staff. Minnelli wanted to embark on a Hollywood career in a way that would use his Broadway experience to his advantage.

After the premiere of *At Home Abroad*, the playwright Lillian Hellman, who was a close friend, took Minnelli to meet the Hollywood mogul Samuel Goldwyn, who was staying at the Waldorf Astoria. Having worked with Goldwyn before, Hellman had praised his unusual honesty and integrity in dealing with writers.

However, Minnelli's first impression of Goldwyn was that of an aggressive and presumptuous man. It might have been based on a misunderstanding, since Goldwyn assumed that Minnelli came to ask for a job and negotiate a contract with his company.

"You'll find that the quality of the Goldwyn pictures is much better than anyone else's," the producer said, implying that Minnelli was already under contract to him.

Minnelli, however, interrupted Goldwyn before he could continue.

"That's very nice, Mr. Goldwyn. But I plan to stay in New York. I like the theater too much to leave Broadway."

Goldwyn looked at Minnelli as if he were an idiot or imbecile, and the conversation rapidly deteriorated into uncomfortable silence.

Minnelli was therefore surprised when, a few months later, *Variety* reported that he was going to M-G-M as an associate producer of musicals. His first picture, according to *Variety,* was to be *The Goldwyn Follies*, with music by George and Ira Gershwin. It was strange, since no one had talked to Minnelli about it, and he had no plans of moving west.

All along, Minnelli's friends kept saying that he shouldn't fight what was preordained for him, to work for "the pictures industry," as they referred to Hollywood. They pointed out that, with the exception of Ernest Hemingway, virtually every noted American writer went to Hollywood, including William Faulkner, F. Scott Fitzgerald, Ogden Nash, Dorothy Parker, and S. J. Perelman.

Some writers returned to New York with a lot of money, and a lot of sarcasm, aimed at the "suntanned Philistines" they'd met on the West Coast. Most writers, however, chose to stay in California. This love-hate relationship, or as Minnelli put it, the "war" between refined aesthetics and the mighty buck, seemed to be going on at full rage.

Many of Minnelli's songwriter friends commuted back and forth between the coasts with no visible damage to their creativity. Harold Arlen, Yip Harburg, Irving Berlin, the Gershwins, Cole Porter, Jerome Kern, and Dorothy Fields had been writing songs for the movies for years, and they all had the cash flow and lifestyle to show for that labor.

Since Minnelli didn't know anything about the movie studios, he left the matter entirely up to his agents to get the best movie offer possible. After playing off one studio against the other, his agents settled on the highest offer. Paramount beat out the bids made by Goldwyn and M-G-M. According to the contract, as a producer-director, Minnelli would be getting $2,500 per week, and he could bring two members of his staff, secretary Marian Herwood and technical assistant Al Coppock.

Minnelli appreciated musical films, but he wasn't impressed with their quality. He liked Rouben Mamoulian's *Love Me Tonight* (1932), which interweaved cleverly the Rodgers and Hart songs into the story.

He particularly liked Mamoulian's treatment of one number, "The Son of a Gun Is Nothing but a Tailor," and the effective denouement. The songs bounced from one character to another, when each discovers that Maurice Chevalier is an impostor posing as a nobleman. Overall, though, Minnelli found most Hollywood musicals lacking a unified style. Bringing sophistication and panache to the musical genre would become Minnelli's self-declared mission in Hollywood.

The European films of Luis Buñuel, Sergei Eisenstein, Carl Theodor Dreyer, and Jean Cocteau, with their stylistic experimentation, were more to Minnelli's taste. These works grasped film's full potential as a distinctive medium in ways matched by few American pictures at the time. A French film that particularly appealed to Minnelli's aesthetics was Jacques Feyder's *Carnival in Flanders* (1935), which was shot in two languages simultaneously. Exhibiting poetic realism, the film impressed Minnelli with its production design, specifically Lazare Meerson's extraordinary sets.

When Minnelli arrived at the Pasadena train station, he received a hero's welcome from a delegation headed by the leading lady Dorothy Lamour, soon to be famous for Paramount's road movies with Bing Crosby and Bob Hope. After the photographers did their job, Lamour and Minnelli were whisked away in different cars. At the Beverly Wilshire Hotel, Minnelli went through yet another photo shoot, this time around with actress Virginia Bruce, filling in for Lamour.

As the studio's brass was eager to meet Minnelli and offer him any possible help, the following morning, he reported to William LeBaron, Paramount's head of production, for a formal orientation. Optimistic about Minnelli's future at the studio, LeBaron told the novice that Paramount planned to break out of their bland radio musicals, such as *The Big Broadcast* movies, and the Bing Crosby musicals, and move into more ambitious pictures, for which Minnelli would be responsible. Minnelli was then assigned a specific writer, Leo Birinski, and began working the following day without much fanfare.

On Minnelli's first day, an upsetting telegram from Eleanor Lambert awaited him at the front desk. Apparently, S. J. Perelman had written a "dangerous" profile of Minnelli for *Stage Magazine*. Lambert's message said: "Stop Perelman piece immediately. People believe such things. It will ruin you. Copy follows." But, Minnelli wondered, how bad could it be? There was no way to tell without seeing it for himself.

A few days later, Minnelli received a copy of the Perelman article, in which the writer reported on their meeting in the New York Public Library. The piece was full of anecdotes, including a funny reference to Minnelli's pot-smoking adventure. Highly amused, Minnelli sent a telegram back to Eleanor: "Piece stands as is. All my life I've been trying to achieve that reputation."

The first phase in Minnelli becoming a full-fledged Californian was renting a nice house on Camden Drive in Beverly Hills, which was easy. Lack of driving skills, however, proved to be a more daunting and urgent problem. Driving hadn't been necessary in New York but it was a must in Los Angeles. Minnelli was advised to buy a car and hire a chauffeur to take him to the studio and teach him how to drive along the way.

The first words the newly hired driver uttered, when Minnelli was behind the wheel and a car swerved in front of them, were: "Hey, look out, you son of a bitch!" This scared Minnelli to death, and he literally froze. On the following Saturday, the driver brought Minnelli home and parked the car in the garage. "Now, don't touch the car until I get here Monday morning," the chauffeur said before leaving. Ever curious, and unaware of his dubious skills, Minnelli settled into his car. The first time he drove, he got into an accident.

At Paramount, Minnelli began to develop a mystery titled *Times Square,* a film that was to incorporate scenes from current Broadway productions. The writer assigned to him, Leo Birinski, a cigar-smoking Russian who trailed ashes behind him, captured the film's spirit right away. The plot was based on a race against time, with the characters jumping from one theater to another to piece together the vital clues. Minnelli felt that creating an all-star movie, with Broadway performers acting out scenes from their hit shows, was a nice way of introducing stage players to a larger movie audience.

He discussed the project with Adolph Zukor, then head of Paramount, but Zukor didn't commit right away. Most of the discussions were held with LeBaron, whom Minnelli found too diplomatic and vague. "Keep up the good work," LeBaron would say. "It's wonderful having you with us." However, nothing concrete happened. Minnelli's assistants Marian and Al were sitting at the studio twiddling their thumbs. Was Minnelli's pace too fast for an industry like Hollywood? Paramount's senior executives had no intention of experimenting with an unknown quantity like Minnelli and his untested ideas.

In the 1930s, Paramount's roster of stars was just as impressive as M-G-M's. The studio also employed two of the biggest star-directors, Cecil B. DeMille, who headed his own unit, and the more subtle and admired Ernst Lubitsch. Minnelli was introduced to DeMille, who looked down on him and treated him as a novice. It was clear right away that no friendship or any contact would develop between them. Lubitsch was slightly friendlier, but Minnelli didn't get to know him either, since Lubitsch was formal and kept himself at a distance. Though vastly different directors, both DeMille and Lubitsch were self-aggrandizing snobs.

At Paramount, Minnelli met another émigré from New York, composer Kurt Weill, and the two talked about the possibility of working together in the future. Weill thought that Minnelli's fascination with surrealism and psychiatry would fit well with his own eccentric ideas. *Lady in the Dark,* which Weill wrote with Ira Gershwin in 1941, was made into a movie three years later. Under Mitchell Leisen's helm, it expressed Weill's philosophical concerns even though he wasn't directly involved in the production. Minnelli didn't understand why this Technicolor adaptation of Moss Hart's groundbreaking Broadway show omitted most of the Weill–Ira Gershwin songs, and he also thought that Ginger Rogers was miscast in the lead.

Idle, Minnelli was beginning to feel guilty for making too much money without doing any work. To demonstrate his presence, Minnelli would self-consciously walk through the lot on his way to the commissary, hoping that the studio's top producers and executives would see him from their windows.

Minnelli's happiest times in Los Angeles were spent with Ira and Lee Gershwin, who had taken a house with George Gershwin on Roxbury Drive in Beverly Hills. He enjoyed many pleasurable weekends around the pool with his ex–New York friends. Among the stars that he met and liked was the vivacious Paulette Goddard, who was dating George at the time.

Ira and Minnelli had long been close friends, sharing a love for word games and light verse with Yip Harburg. They also shared a similar cockeyed view of human foibles. But now, Minnelli was finally getting to know George better. Minnelli and George talked about working together, possibly directing a Spanish gypsy opera or a Jewish opera based on S. Anski's play *The Dybbuk*. Both he and George were impressed with the Yiddish-language movie based on the play that had been directed by Yevgeny Vakhtangov in Moscow for the Habima theater. George was also interested in turning to the classics and composing orchestral pieces.

George and Ira were working on a Fred Astaire–Ginger Rogers musical at RKO, whose title kept changing until they settled on *Shall We Dance?*, to be directed by Mark Sandrich. The Gershwins preferred to work quietly at home, and at their own pace. They would go to the studio only when a problem needed immediate solution.

Joining them at RKO one day, Minnelli was able to observe their modus operandi. When Minnelli remarked how impressed he was by the short time it took them to compose the "Walking the Dog" sequence, Ira snapped back, "What do you mean short time? It took a lifetime." Ira was right. The Gershwins' genius was so perfect that everything they did seemed easy and effortless.

As busy as he was, George always found time for his social life, which included tennis, golf, and Sundays around the pool. But for a number of reasons George was not happy in Hollywood. George had been idolized all his life; he was used to people making special trips from all over the world to meet with him. In California, however, he was put off by the casualness with which the Hollywood crowd treated him, favoring stars over any other talent group, be they writers or composers.

The attitude of most of Minnelli's friends toward the movie industry could be described as a conspiracy of silence. Most of them didn't really like Hollywood, though none dared to voice too loudly his or her frustrations. It was considered a cheap shot to accept the money and then grouse at the crassness of the Hollywood executives, the people who guaranteed that flow of cash in the first place. Quietly and discreetly,

Minnelli, too, instructed his agents to get him out of what he perceived as a "gold-plated straitjacket," if not an outright cage.

George and Ira started working on *The Goldwyn Follies,* which George Marshall was to direct. (That old *Variety* news item about Minnelli was wrong in reporting both director and studio.) Minnelli put *Times Square* on the back burner, realizing that it would never materialize. Instead, he turned his attention to *Artists & Models,* if only in an advisory capacity, with Raoul Walsh as director and George and Ira as composers.

Two of the songs were almost completed when Minnelli invited George to join him and two young women for a Saturday evening dinner, in June 1937.

George arrived in his usual high spirits.

"This is George Geshwin," Minnelli told the starlets.

The girls cast a blank stare; neither had ever heard of George. Pretending not to notice, George continued to play the piano for them.

The next week, when Minnelli reported for his regular Sunday at the Gershwins, George wasn't feeling well and stayed in bed. His presence was very much missed, but he didn't want to see anyone.

A couple of days later, Lee told Minnelli that George was suffering from strong headaches, but the doctor couldn't find anything wrong with him. A second physician was consulted, but he too couldn't diagnose the problem.

Minnelli went to the Gershwins for dinner a few nights later. This time, George joined them. Looking pale and frail, he was accompanied by a male nurse.

George and Minnelli were left alone in the living room for a few minutes, during which silence prevailed.

Then George suddenly said, "Don't let them get you, Vince, or complicate you."

Minnelli was stunned. This was an unusual thing for George to say since he was always so vital and cheerful.

When dinner was over, the nurse took George back to a dark room, to avoid causing pain to his eyes, which couldn't tolerate any light for too long. Frustrated, the doctors still couldn't diagnose the problem. Ira asked the studio to take him and George off the picture, temporarily, until the crisis was over, thinking the illness would last only a matter of days.

After many false diagnoses, the doctors determined that George had a brain tumor and needed an immediate operation. On the day it was scheduled, Minnelli waited with Ira and Lee downstairs in the hospital's lobby. A member of the Gershwins' inner circle would periodically come down with updated reports. At dawn, the doctor himself reported that the operation had been successful, and George was resting comfortably. Relieved, they all went home, and got some sleep for the first time in weeks.

However, on the morning of July 11, 1937, Minnelli received an alarming call from Lee. George was dead at the age of thirty-eight. Apparently, the operation had been done too late, and he never regained consciousness. While George had certainly accomplished much, he died with so many ambitions unfulfilled. Ira, who worshiped his younger brother, was inconsolable. There was no way he could return to work. Vernon Duke and Kurt Weill had to finish the assignment.

Back at work, the news that Harold Arlen would do the music for *Artists & Models* was a minor consolation for Minnelli. He and Arlen conceived one number, "Public Melody Number One," a spoof of gangster movies, such as Jimmy Cagney's powerful *Public Enemy,* that featured Louis Armstrong and Martha Raye. Arlen dedicated the sheet music to Minnelli. After brainstorming, he came up with the idea of a surrealist ballet that involved the stars, but his detailed concept was rejected. As shot, Minnelli found the production number messy and devoid of nuance.

George's death precipitated a major artistic crisis in Minnelli. All of a sudden, he asked himself, "What am I doing in Hollywood, when there are so many things I'd rather be doing in New York?" After endless negotiations, Minnelli bought himself out of his Paramount contract and returned to the East Coast.

Lee Shubert had just offered him a show in New York. Minnelli sighed with relief as he boarded the train east, realizing the absurdity of the fact that he'd spent most of his time in Hollywood trying to get out of a most lucrative contract.

Minnelli had been away in Hollywood for seven months. Upon his return, he found the Broadway scene utterly changed. There were new shows and dramas about people from all walks of life. There was working-class theater such as the Federal Theatre's *One Third of a Nation,* as well as Clifford Odets's *Golden Boy,* Orson Welles's *Julius Caesar,* and *I'd Rather Be Right,* a musical spoofing FDR and the New Deal by George Kaufman and Moss Hart.

Moss Hart had gone on a cruise with Cole Porter and Monty Woolley to write the musical *Jubilee.* "There won't be any place for us in the theater when we get back," Hart told his friends, in light of the rising popularity of political theater. He was wrong, and *Jubilee* proved to be a huge hit.

Though Minnelli had no fears about his place in the "new" theatrical milieu, he did realize that the New Deal and its aftermath had brought new artistic challenges. The most obvious casualty was the musical revue. A year earlier, Minnelli had enjoyed the greatest success of his career with *The Show Is On,* but now, with revues in decline, he thought that the "book show" format was on the rise. Paradoxically, it was the revue *Pins and Needles* that contradicted the prevailing theory and broke all records for a musical show, running 1,108 performances. Though amateurish, it brought social significance to a genre that had always been decidedly nonpolitical.

When the Shuberts asked Minnelli to stage *Hooray for What!,* he was given only three months to put the show together for its scheduled opening, on December 1, 1937. Harburg wrote the lyrics and Harold Arlen composed the score for a story that was very much of its time.

While Minnelli was in Hollywood, Harold Arlen had taken over his apartment, so he had no place to live. He decided to stay in the Lombardy Hotel for a couple of weeks, until he could find a permanent residence. Because Minnelli's old studio was now rented to the Theatre Guild as a rehearsal hall, he found a new space a block away, on East 54th Street.

In his absence, his valet, Hara, too, had defected to new, easier employers on the East Side and couldn't be lured back. Minnelli hired a woman housekeeper to come in daily, but the interaction with her was strictly limited to work, with nothing like the rapport and fun he'd had with Hara.

After being idle for so long, Minnelli was anxious to get back to work, direct shows, design sets—anything he could get. Raoul Pène Du Bois, who assisted Minnelli with the *Ziegfeld Follies,* designed the costumes, and Howard Lindsay and Russell Crouse supplied the book.

It was great fun working again with consummate professionals, and the team had no problem rewriting and repolishing the show until it pleased him completely.

Soon, the specter of Nazism was beginning to be felt in America, even in theater circles. But, like other apolitical artists, Minnelli was naïve, failing to realize its danger and consequences. Lillian Hellman, whose work began to reflect the new social concerns, engaged in heavy political discussions, one of which he attended. Minnelli was bored by the ideological nature of the talks, the clearly leftist orientation that Hellman was taking. Instead, he and his closest friends immersed themselves in work, pretending that the problems were out there, in Europe, and would not reach the domestic front.

Minnelli approached his first book show as a revue, the only difference being that one set of characters carried through from beginning to end. As usual, the action began with a title song. The second act ridiculed the Nazis, which was timely enough. This show opened long before Chaplin's political satire, *The Great Dictator,* which, together with other issues, later caused the comedian problems with the authorities, and eventually forced him into exile outside the United States.

Putting the show together was a frantic race against time. It became even more nerve-wracking when the company reached Boston for a tryout. The previous show took longer than expected to vacate the theater, and the week planned to raise the sets was cut back to only three days, which meant three sleepless nights.

A colleague, fearing the frantic pace would break Minnelli, suggested extra medication for help. He gave him two pills, one for sleep, the other for waking up. Minnelli went back to his hotel and obediently took the sleeping pill, then he woke up and obediently took the other pill. The pills worked their magic.

The next day, Minnelli flew through rehearsals, getting everything right in record time. He took it all in stride—before collapsing. His system simply couldn't take any drugs, medical or recreational. It's not that he was against them for health reasons, since he was always a heavy smoker. But in the future, he would be overly cautious about all kinds of pills. And this intensely traumatic experience would forever taint his attitude toward drugs and physicians, particularly after marrying Judy Garland, who was addicted to both.

Working with Ed Wynn on *Hooray for What!* turned out to be a delightful experience. The *Time* review, dated December 13, 1937, stated: "Sharing credit with Ed Wynn for the show's success is able Vincente Minnelli, trained in the hard school of movie stage-shows, who directed it and designed the scenery." Another favorable review appeared in the January 1938 issue of *The Stage*.

The success of *Pins and Needles* and *Four Saints in Three Acts* motivated Minnelli to stage a surrealist revue, now that his contractual obligation to the Shuberts had ended. Minnelli considered working again with Beatrice Lillie. He began by preparing a presentation for a surrealist fantasy called *The Light Fantastic*. Lee Shubert said he might be interested in producing it, if Bea played the lead. Trying to persuade her, Minnelli simply wrote, "It's a show that sets out to prove that the world today is completely screwy."

Minnelli offered Bea Lillie four musical numbers and four sketches. When Bea, then in England, took too long to reply, he moved on to his next idea.

Initiated by Vernon Duke, it was a musical version of *Serena Blandish,* S. N. Behrman's play, adapted from Enid Bagnold's *A Lady of Quality*. Unfortunately, the wheeling and dealing for *Serena Blandish* turned rockier than the negotiations for other productions. There were too many artists on the payroll, which made it impossibly expensive. Bagnold was to get her customary author's cut, as would Behrman, Sid Perelman, and Cole Porter. Minnelli tried his best to find a way to do the show, but it was economically unfeasible. After spending six frustrating months, Minnelli dropped *Serena Blandish* for good.

It was time to take a vacation, before the political situation worsened in Europe. A travel agent made all the arrangements for Minnelli to take his first—and highly anticipated—European trip. Though he sailed alone, Minnelli was armed with letters of introduction to people in the arts.

One important letter was addressed to writer Louis Bromfield, who was then staying in London. Gathering courage, the shy Minnelli called Bromfield at the Ritz Hotel.

"We are having a crowd at the Ritz," Bromfield said. "Would you please join us?"

Minnelli accepted the invitation gladly.

Upon arrival, looking into the dining room, Minnelli noticed a sea of unfamiliar faces. Overcome by attacks of shyness and anxiety, he made a hasty retreat. The next day, he called to apologize, but he never got another opportunity to meet Bromfield.

With free time on his hands, Minnelli forced himself to be more social. Bea Lillie took him under her wing and introduced him to her British friends. After London, Minnelli departed for Paris, where he spent all his time visiting museums and palaces. On his trip back home, he resolved to get to know the Continent better, particularly Paris, but his fantasy of becoming a painter was somehow diminished, now that he had witnessed works of the great French artists in museums, and many aspiring painters on the pavement along the River Seine.

When songwriter Dorothy Fields visited New York, Minnelli invited her to the Metropolitan Opera. They were standing at the opera bar between acts, when Minnelli noticed two familiar faces, but, as usual, he couldn't remember their names. As the couple approached them, Minnelli suddenly summoned up their names.

"Why, hello," Minnelli said, smiling. "So nice to see you, Mr. and Mrs. Schulte. I would like you to meet my companion." But now he blanked and couldn't recall his own companion's name.

"Dorothy Fields," the shocked songwriter said, barely recovered from the initial humiliation.

Many other embarrassing incidents would stem from Minnelli's vague memory for names and places, and his inarticulate forgetfulness, as some of his friends referred to the problem. For a filmmaker, it would prove to be a major deficiency, particularly on the set while trying to evoke names or ideas as part of his direction. Actors often joked about the paradox of having an extremely precise and demanding director who was also absentminded and easily distracted.

In times of crisis, Eleanor Lambert always proved to be helpful. Aware of his indecisiveness about the future, Lambert said one day: "There's this marvelous soothsayer on the West Side. You must see her. She's absolutely uncanny." Thereupon, without waiting for his approval, she set up an appointment with the psychic.

The lady, her pompadour in a hairnet, operated out of an apartment that was heavy with oak furniture and had a musty odor. A piano stood in the corner, and every soft surface in the main room was covered with chenille.

"You're in the entertainment business," she said. "And you're going out West to work in the movies."

"Oh, yeah?" Minnelli said.

"You're going to have a dog, and you'll be crazy about him. And you're going to marry a star. Your first project will be very successful. I see something all-black."

Minnelli assumed that she meant black-and-white pictures, as was the Hollywood norm then.

He had barely gotten home when the telephone rang. It was Lambert, of course, curious to know what had happened. "What did the psychic tell you?"

"You know," Minnelli mumbled vaguely. "All the usual things."

Though he disregarded the prophecies, deep down, there was a growing sense of anticipation for things to come. And years later, in Hollywood, while directing the musical *Cabin in the Sky* with an all-black cast, Minnelli remembered the conversation with the psychic.

He was debating the merits of reviving *The Light Fantastic,* when Max Gordon came up with an offer to direct *Very Warm for May.* Oscar Hammerstein was to write the book and lyrics, and Jerome Kern would compose the score for yet another musical about putting on a show in a barn theater.

Minnelli designed the sets, including a barn with dark woods and a hayloft that was meant to be a tribute to his childhood in Delaware. The barn was then remodeled, and the second set transformed it into a stage by stripping down the wood while maintaining the geometric lines.

Initially, Oscar Hammerstein didn't believe in the first act, which featured the song "All the Things You Are." Hiram Sherman, playing the pretentious producer, was to hold the entire show together. But for Minnelli, it was the second act that could not be saved, because its only merit was a "psychological" ballet, with Sherman serving as narrator while the dancers went through their paces. Sherman talked about every phobia that afflicted him—masochism, sadism, Oedipus complex. The dancers danced it straight and somber, while the action satirized it. "I took a hell of a beating," Sherman's character said about his emotional health, and the dancers brought out lighted neon rods and whacked away. Minnelli would repeat the same device in "The Girl Hunt" ballet in his 1953 musical, *The Band Wagon.*

Minnelli tried to rearrange the second act in different ways, but to no avail, nothing worked. Finally, the show opened at the Alvin Theatre on November 17, 1939. There was tension in the air as *Very Warm for May* was the first Kern-Hammerstein show in eight years. In his highly critical review, Brooks Atkinson noted that Minnelli "has not resolved the confusion of the story," and that "the direction throws away the point of the music." It was the first pan he had received and he was deeply hurt. Also, it was the first time that Minnelli resorted to extracting favorable phrases out of context and single words from disastrous reviews, twisting them into a kind of encouragement that his work was not all that bad. This was the only way Minnelli could react to his first big flop, a show that ran for only fifty-nine performances.

Around that same time, William Saroyan was having better luck with his first full-length play, *The Time of Your Life,* which had opened just a few weeks before *Very Warm for May.* That show put Saroyan on the forefront of the theatrical map. Minnelli welcomed Saroyan's friendliness. Spontaneous and good-humored by nature, Saroyan was the opposite of Minnelli. Saroyan went through life finding marvelous human stories in every encounter and wisdom in the most unexpected places. Minnelli treasured Saroyan's vitality and innocence, and he could never understand how Saroyan ended up so embittered later in life.

"That man is a genius," Saroyan would say to Minnelli about an anonymous driver after getting out of a taxicab. Later, in Hollywood, Saroyan would look at Minnelli's black poodle, Baba, go through his paces, and echo the same sentiment. "That dog is a genius, too!"

Minnelli and Saroyan decided to do a surrealist musical comedy based on a Rodgers and Hart score. Minnelli discussed his ideas for the show, and Saroyan put them to work. Saroyan wrote a sketch at one sitting, then handed it over to Minnelli. Minnelli had seen David Freedman work for hours on just one line, tightening the text so that it became as succinct as possible. But Saroyan was unable to do this. He would rather write another sketch than rework the original one. Eventually, the joint project fell apart, but Minnelli and Saroyan remained friends.

In the spring of 1940, Minnelli stood at a crossroads. Restless, he was itching to get on, feeling that life had much more to offer. He now remembered vividly the psychic's prophecy, which for him translated into "Young Man, Go West!"

Six

Hollywood: Early Years

ON A WARM SPRING DAY IN 1940, Yip Harburg brought producer Arthur Freed to Minnelli's office in New York. Freed began his career as a lyricist, writing with composer Nacio Herb Brown such pop classics as "You Were Meant for Me," "Temptation," and "Singin' in the Rain." Before long, M-G-M's Louis B. Mayer set Freed up with his own production unit within the studio to develop new musicals. It soon became known as the Freed Unit. A great appreciator of talent, Freed sought out the best for his company, giving creative people the freedom to experiment.

Along with Minnelli, other directors, such as Stanley Donen (who would become Minnelli's competitor) and Richard Brooks, began their careers at M-G-M. Minnelli always credited Freed as Hollywood's true innovator of the movie musical. Freed and Minnelli would establish a wonderful rapport that would last two decades and produce such memorable films as *Meet Me in St. Louis, An American in Paris,* and *Gigi.*

In the 1930s, M-G-M had few successes with innovative musicals: *The Broadway Melody* and *The Great Ziegfeld* had won the Best Picture Oscar in their respective years, but they were both stagy and conventional. As for the Jeanette MacDonald–Nelson Eddy films, they were saccharine operettas as far as Minnelli was concerned. The one major exception was *The Wizard of Oz* (1939), which Minnelli perceived as a fable-fantasy rather than a legit musical. Freed had bought the rights to *The Wizard of Oz* from Goldwyn, and insisted—against producer Mervyn LeRoy's objection—that Yip Harburg and Harold Arlen's song "Over the Rainbow" be kept in the film. As is well-known, this troubled production became a legendary story within the industry, elevating the stature of Freed, making him a desirable figure to work with.

Freed had just finished his first picture as a solo producer, *Babes in Arms*, starring Judy Garland and Mickey Rooney, and that film's commercial success gave him a lot of latitude with M-G-M's top brass.

"How would you like to work at Metro?" Freed asked Minnelli after the introduction.

"Well, I don't know, Mr. Freed," Minnelli said. "Things didn't go too well for me the last time I was in Hollywood."

"The job at Paramount?" Freed asked.

"Yes, as soon as I got there, I knew it wasn't going to work out. I spent the next seven months trying to get out of my contract."

"Unfortunately, that happens in Hollywood," Freed conceded.

"Why don't you try it my way for a year? You won't have a title, but you'll be learning the business. Other producers will call on you for services. You'll read scripts and make suggestions. You'll direct musical numbers, and you'll work in the cutting room. If you don't like it after that time, and if you see that you don't have a future in pictures, then you can go back to New York. But if you like the work and decide to stay, I have the feeling you'll make a damn fine director."

"Well, that sounds very good," Minnelli said hesitantly, "but I don't know if . . ."

Before Minnelli had a chance to complete the sentence, Freed interrupted, "What do you think your living expenses would be?"

"I could probably get by on three hundred dollars a week," the insecure Minnelli said quietly.

"You're on!" Freed said, shocked by Minnelli's ultramodest request.

Minnelli received a much smaller salary than he had received at Paramount, but he really didn't care, because he felt that he was in good hands this time.

Other producers, such as Joe (Joseph) Pasternak, had put together similar groups before, but Freed's was the first unit to be composed entirely of newcomers. Freed imported many talents from New York: Gene Kelly, vocal coach Kay Thompson, and choreographer Robert Alton, all of whom would work with Minnelli. Later, Freed brought from Broadway costume designer Irene Sharaff, lyricist Alan Jay Lerner, choreographer and future director Charles Walters, and set designer Oliver Smith, all joining composer-arranger Roger Edens and the others as the nucleus of the Freed Unit. It was just the kind of group Minnelli wished to belong to, one that would allow him individual expression as well as teamwork— the Hollywood equivalent of Broadway's esprit de corps.

With his enthusiasm for Hollywood once again rekindled, Minnelli set off immediately for Los Angeles on the Super Chief. Overly excited and anxious, he didn't sleep at all, his mind preoccupied with how to apply his theatrical experience to a medium that was totally new to him, in a city that he had not particularly liked the first time around.

The Goldwyn Follies of 1938 notwithstanding, Minnelli didn't see much novelty in the musical film since his last visit. This was probably a too-general and inaccurate assessment, but it helped the feelings of a novice, ambitious filmmaker. After the Paramount debacle, Minnelli no longer thought of himself as "the musical's great savior." However, endowed with chutzpah, he believed that he could contribute something new to the evolving genre, whose high points were still defined by the RKO black-and-white musicals with Fred Astaire and Ginger Rogers.

The first time Minnelli noticed a ballet in a film was in a Goldwyn picture. Though choreographed by New York City Ballet maestro George Balanchine, it was shot in a conventional manner, with the ballerina Vera Zorina entering and leaving the stage through a diving bell device in the middle of a marble pool.

There weren't many great musical talents in Hollywood, in front or behind the camera, that impressed Minnelli. The notable exception was Fred Astaire, whose dance numbers were the brightest spots in the RKO musicals, but the stories in these films were archaic and insipid. Nor was Minnelli impressed with Busby Berkeley's spectacular effects at Warner's, though he found Berkeley's recent work at M-G-M more pleasing. Berkeley's devices were ingenious, but they bore little relation to the stories they were meant to serve. Like most musicals of the thirties, Berkeley's films often were "backstage" stories, containing songs that were not integral to the plot; in fact, they stood apart from it, in sharp contrast.

Musical numbers would begin on a proscenium stage and then unrealistically open up, with hundreds of girls dancing on the wings of an airplane or forming the shape of flowers. Minnelli didn't object to the use of fantasy, but he felt that fantasy nevertheless should have physical limitations. Moreover, he was vehemently opposed to the montage school of cutting and splicing, the essence of Berkeley's film choreography. In fact, Minnelli would become known for his gloriously fluid and detailed mise-en-scène.

Minnelli found most big-screen adaptations of Broadway shows to be disappointing. He was particularly critical of the poor quality of the sets and costumes, and the general lack of imagination. Many of the original numbers that had helped make these shows successful were inexplicably dropped, while new songs, which didn't have the flavor of the original ones, were written to fill in the gaps.

Filmmakers didn't seem to care much about the musical's structure as a whole, so long as it contained big splashy production numbers that delivered exciting moments, if not authentic inventiveness. The pyrotechnics were visually impressive, but the overall strategy was ludicrous and often even banal. Minnelli saw his challenge as applying greater "unity" and "coherence" to the film medium.

The first logical area for Minnelli to experiment with was lighting, an aspect where films lagged behind the theater. With the exception of close-ups granted to the stars, lighting in most pictures was conventional and flat, either too bright or too harsh.

Minnelli was impressed by the French film *Carnival in Flanders,* which was shot by cinematographer Harry Stradling, who had recently come to America. Anxious to meet the respected lenser, Minnelli requested to see Stradling, and a lifelong dialogue began, including collaboration on *On a Clear Day You Can See Forever.*

Like other film artists in the 1940s, Minnelli regarded John Ford as the most accomplished American filmmaker, he who was blessed with a particularly strong eye for stylized, expressionistic lighting and astute visual composition, as evident in his Oscar-nominated films *Stagecoach, The Informer,* and particularly *The Grapes of Wrath*.

Minnelli didn't understand why other filmmakers didn't use lighting to establish mood and ambience more sensitively and accurately. Within a year, though, a genius named Orson Welles, then twenty-five, and working on *Citizen Kane,* would take the industry by storm. Welles would become Minnelli's idol, and someone to whom he paid tribute in several movies, most notably in *The Bad and the Beautiful*.

No studio brass met Minnelli upon his second arrival in Hollywood. Checking in at the M-G-M lot in Culver City the next day, he was assigned an office to share with Eddie Powell, a musical director from New York.

Driving his jalopy to work, he had to park off the lot; his low apprentice status didn't grant him any privileges. Minnelli had to walk through the lobby of the administration building to his office, which was in the writers' wing. In the first year, Minnelli's work was like an office job. He arrived promptly at nine in the morning and stayed until five or six in the afternoon.

On March 27, 1940, the first agreement between Minnelli and M-G-M promised him "limited" employment, at $300 per week plus expenses for several trips to New York. His first title, for lack of a more accurate name, was dance director, even though he knew little about choreography. Upon his request, just weeks later, Minnelli signed another agreement in which he was given "advisory capacity," but no final say, in staging production numbers. Clearly, the studio didn't know what to do with him, so the document was rather vague, mentioning counseling, collaboration, and codirection.

With all the excitement of starting a new chapter in Hollywood, there were tensions about Minnelli's hiring. Serious questions about his duties and responsibilities were raised by Cedric Gibbons, M-G-M's powerful art director, who oversaw every production directly or indirectly through his assistants.

In an April 2, 1940, memo to top executive Eddie Mannix, which carelessly misspelled Minnelli's first and last names, Gibbons wrote: "We have signed Vincent Manelli, a New York stage designer. This was done through Arthur Freed. In speaking to Arthur on Saturday he told me about this man and said he was engaged as a dance director. I said, 'Nothing else?' And he said, 'For ideas on dance numbers and musical settings, etc.' I am afraid, Eddie, that this will probably be another Harkrider-Hobe-Irwin-Oliver-Messel situation and if you remember you and I chatted at great length about this type of thing sometime ago—and I want to reiterate that I absolutely refuse to work under any conditions with any man designing settings unless he is brought through to me as a member of my department."

Gibbons elaborated: "The man may be the world's greatest genius. If he is, by all means give him my job. I find it tough enough as it is to work with the most sympathetic assistants I can secure. I do not feel that any of my men should take orders from anyone other than myself in the matter of set design, whether it be for musical numbers or the interiors of submarines. Do you think we need further experience in these expensive experiments? Not just the man's salary, but what he actually costs us. I, for one, had thought we had learned our lesson."

Minnelli was unaware of this memo, but he would experience creative differences and explicit tensions with Gibbons and M-G-M's art department. As the scholar David Gerstner pointed out, Minnelli's modernist sensibilities and creative vision were often at odds with the department, which he once, in a state of frustration, labeled "a medieval fiefdom, its overlord accustomed to doing things in a certain way."

In June 1940, the agreement was extended for another ten weeks, and Minnelli was asked to contribute to the Marx Brothers' comedy *The Big Store* and the Judy Garland–Mickey Rooney musical *Strike Up the Band*. Minnelli visited the sets of the Marx Brothers, but there's no evidence of what he did.

Minnelli was not particularly happy or fulfilled in the next two years, during which his employment continued to be extended. However, determined not to repeat his first frustrating Hollywood chapter, he tried to make the most of it. Though under direct sponsorship of Arthur Freed, his greatest supporter at M-G-M, he made a point to meet with the heads of the other units, such as Jack Cummings and Pandro Berman, for diplomatic if no other reasons. In fact, Berman would prove essential as producer of some of Minnelli's best and most popular films:

Madame Bovary, Father of the Bride and its sequel *Father's Little Dividend,* and *The Long, Long Trailer.*

In early 1941, Minnelli flew back to New York at M-G-M's expense for a "shopping" trip, to survey what was playing on Broadway with the goal of reassessing the fare's "movie potential." It was a fun job that he totally embraced. He would have gone to see the shows in any case, on his own coin. However, to be paid by M-G-M as a scout not only afforded a nice expense account, but also reaffirmed his prestige among his East Coast colleagues and friends, who were beginning to wonder, "What exactly is Vincente doing in Hollywood?"

Among other shows, Minnelli saw *Pal Joey, Lady in the Dark, Panama Hattie,* and *Cabin in the Sky,* all of which would be later made into musicals at M-G-M or other studios. He went backstage to meet some of these plays' performers, such as Ethel Waters, who would become the leading lady of his first solo directorial effort, *Cabin in the Sky,* in 1943.

Back in Hollywood, he read and commented on Freed's production of *Lady Be Good,* and advised Pandro Berman to change the beginning of the picture *Rio Rita.* In March 1941, Minnelli's contract with the studio was changed, explicitly stating that he was to render services as a director, producer, associate producer, and even screenwriter, a capacity in which he never felt comfortable. Unlike many directors, who were also producers, Minnelli never received a writing credit, and though he helped shape some of his scenarios, it was in terms of structure rather than content.

When *Strike Up the Band* began principal shooting in June 1941, Minnelli was asked to design a musical sequence for Judy Garland and Mickey Rooney, while Busby Berkeley did the rest. His sequence "Ghost Theater" has the couple perform a medley of songs made famous by George M. Cohan, Fay Templeton, and others. But Minnelli was unhappy with the end result because it bore Berkeley's signature, not his.

In 1942, Minnelli was finally given real authority (and credit) when he contributed to *Panama Hattie,* which he had seen in New York with Ethel Merman. Centering on a provincial singer who falls for a young, handsome man, the story was stale and the Broadway show ran for a full year largely due to its star power. The show was not top-drawer Cole Porter, who had written such uncharacteristically mediocre songs as "Let's Be Buddies" and "Make It Another Old Fashioned, Please."

From the beginning, it was clear to Freed—who didn't tell Minnelli—that Merman would not be invited to Hollywood to reprise her role. Minnelli had little say in casting Ann Sothern when the movie went into production in September 1941 under the helm of vet Norman Z. McLeod (who had done a much better job with *Topper* in 1937 and *Merrily We Live* the following year). Minnelli was familiar with but didn't like Sothern's work in the *Maisie* film series; he never worked with her in his own pictures.

After the first, disastrous preview, Freed decided to restructure the picture, requesting a new script and replacing McLeod with Roy Del Ruth, a more reliable craftsman, who had helmed *Broadway Melody of 1936* and *of 1938*. With his blessing, Freed cast Lena Horne, whom Minnelli had met in New York. The movie, a rather dull romance between Sothern and Dan Dailey, doesn't take advantage of its better talent, Red Skelton, Rags Ragland, and Ben Blue. The lowbrow musical is marred by silly dialogue and a song celebrating getting drunk, "Did I Get Stinkin' at the Savoy," with Skelton mugging.

Minnelli is credited with staging the musical numbers. The opening song, Roger Edens's "Hattie from Panama," displays the singers in impressive white tropical suits and dresses but suffers from fake black dialects and Sothern's poor singing. "Berry Me Not," the first song by the Berry Brothers, dressed in white and black, is performed with canes and shot in a dynamic way, the camera moving down to a close shot of the singers' legs before pulling back to a long shot of the jumping dancers.

For "Good Neighbors," which depicts sailors trying to pick up women on a patterned floor, Minnelli instructed the cinematographer to set up a crane shot from an elevated angle, showing the dancers in two triangles, with three men in the middle and three women outside. With as much attention to music as to geometry, this number points to Minnelli's more intricately structured song-and-dance numbers in the future. The rousing ending, "The Son of a Gun Who Picks on Uncle Sam," draws on the prevailing climate of American patriotism, but the staging is static and slow. The entire cast faces front in one long shot, with lyrics like "We've got a wood kimono for the Mikado/We've got a mausoleum for Mussoleen."

No doubt, the best things in *Panama Hattie* are Lena Horne's songs, and as Stephen Harvey has observed, Minnelli deserves credit for shaping the screen image of the first black star in the Hollywood sound era by cultivating her exotic and suave appeal. Nonetheless, in the 1940s, Horne, like other black actors, couldn't share the screen on equal terms with white performers, and was relegated to guest or minimal onscreen appearances, at times amounting to no more than five or six minutes per movie.

In this picture, adorned in black net with ball fringe, Horne uses a Caribbean accent to sing her lyrics, "a tricky, icky dance they call the Spring," performed by her and the Berry Brothers, while a drummer is on a movable platform traveling across the dance floor. Lovingly framed by Minnelli, Horne delivers the most memorable moment in the movie, "Just One of Those Things," borrowed from Cole Porter's Broadway score for *Jubilee*.

Restructuring *Panama Hattie* made some improvement, but not enough to impress the critics. *The New York Times* rather atypically mentioned the film's troubled history: "Metro revised it with scissors and pen but couldn't put the movie together." Even so, the public, seeking innocuous entertainment during the early years of World War II, made it a moderate hit. Moreover, *Panama Hattie* is important sociologically if not artistically because it features talented black performers such as Horne and the Berry Brothers in a more integrated way than was the norm.

In the early 1940s, M-G-M still had "more stars than there are in heaven," as its slogan proudly announced: Garbo, Norma Shearer, Joan Crawford, Clark Gable, Spencer Tracy, and Katharine Hepburn, to name a few. But times were changing rapidly. The enormous success of *Gone with the Wind,* which M-G-M distributed for producer David O. Selznick and which swept the 1939 Oscars, and the popular reception to *The Wizard of Oz,* marked a new era for the studio. M-G-M's brand of glossy women's pictures—the typical Shearer, Garbo, and Crawford vehicles—were on their way out domestically, and the loss of foreign markets during World War II made it worse. In 1942, Shearer and Garbo would retire, and Crawford would be fired after eighteen years of service and move to Warner.

The threat of war in Europe led to a cycle of propagandistic and nostalgic films, such as *Goodbye Mr. Chips* and *Mrs. Miniver.* The star of these films, the new studio queen, was Greer Garson. Minnelli never liked Garson—and never worked with her—during his lengthy M-G-M tenure. Garson was too ladylike, too solemn, too mannered and humorless for his taste. It was with his encouragement that Judy Garland would render a comic impersonation of Garson in a sketch titled "A Great Lady Has 'An Interview' " in Minnelli's 1946 musical, *Ziegfeld Follies*.

The climate at Metro seemed ripe for innovation. Given the opportunity to experiment, Minnelli and the other newcomers found the creative climate encouraging, and the top echelon's approach benevolent. He took Freed's advice, that he should get an intense course in filmmaking, with absolute seriousness. And he also embraced Freed's desire to make musicals about small-town America, in anticipation of the changing times, specifically the public's more conservative taste during the war years for well-made, old-fashioned, escapist fare.

Minnelli was impressed with Metro's personnel in each and every department. The teams were so passionate about their jobs that they worked overtime willingly. Though there was competition, each worker wanted to succeed individually, while also helping the others. In the 1960s, with the demise of the old studio system, this esprit de corps and unique camaraderie would be very much missed by contract directors like Minnelli and George Cukor, directors who were not the producers or writers of their features.

Whenever a musician was in trouble or needed help, his colleagues got together, usually at Eddie Powell's house. Since composers had to produce music very quickly—by demand or commission—the whole team would work hard, sometimes all night. The same solidarity applied to the other craftsmen, who demonstrated professionalism and dedication, qualities Minnelli had previously associated exclusively with the theater world.

Minnelli couldn't aspire to be in livelier or wittier company, encountering on a daily basis Dorothy Parker, Lillian Hellman, and S. J.

Perelman, with whom he lunched in the commissary or off the lot. He got used to these writers' carping about their exploitation, though he never heard them carp about their sizable paychecks. Tales about Hollywood's dehumanization of movie stars and writers "forced to sell out" both amused and bemused Minnelli, who perceived the former as "animated robots" and the latter as "willing whores." More alarming was the prevalent studio practice of assigning several writers to the same script, unbeknownst to one another.

Still a novice, Minnelli seldom complained. Besides, whining was not in his nature. Never one to look down at M-G-M, or the industry, he was proud to identify himself as a Hollywood director.

Physical constraints simply didn't exist in Minnelli's work vocabulary. No matter how difficult the task at hand, he tried to find a quick, inexpensive resolution to it. His pragmatic approach meant that each problem was thoroughly handled until a satisfying resolution was found.

Minnelli had an opportunity to demonstrate his pragmatic philosophy when Freed asked him to visit the set of Busby Berkeley's *Strike Up the Band*. The musical starred Judy Garland and Mickey Rooney, a new team that the studio was exploiting as an onscreen romantic couple, youthful counterparts to the older, more mature teaming of Greer Garson and Walter Pidgeon.

"Mickey, this is Mr. Vincente Minnelli," Freed said.

"Hi, ya," Rooney said.

Minnelli found Rooney to be boyish and cocky, just as he was in his pictures.

He was curious about Judy, but she was not present on the set that day.

Casual chitchat was not what Freed had in mind; he needed Minnelli's opinion on a specific problem.

"We need a big production number here," Freed said. "Mickey and Judy are in the house and he's telling her that he wants to be a famous band leader."

"Who else is in the house?" Minnelli asked.

"Nobody. They're alone," Freed said.

Minnelli looked around and noticed a bowl of fruit on a table.

"Why don't you take that bowl and have Mickey set the fruits as if they were musical instruments, apples for fiddles, oranges for brass, bananas for woodwinds. Then have Mickey conduct with his hands as if the pieces of fruit are his puppet characters of musicians."

"Good," Freed said. "Thank you." All Minnelli did was supply an idea, but his speedy resourcefulness impressed Freed.

The remainder of the job was executed by the technical departments. This was one of the great facilities of the studio system. The research department found a layout in *Life* magazine, and artist Henry Fox was instructed to use it as a model and create a tabletop of musicians out of fruit. It was so simple yet so ingenious that Berkeley, Judy, and Mickey all loved the idea.

Louis B. Mayer would later introduce Minnelli as "the genius who took a bowl of fruit and made a big production number out of it." As the new pragmatic genius, Minnelli was now given several problems to resolve, as fast as he could.

Minnelli's first meeting with Judy Garland followed a different path from that with Rooney. Arriving on the set one day, after Judy had finished a dance routine with Mickey, Freed said, "This is the new production assistant Vincente Minnelli, the New York director and stage designer."

"Glad to meet you, Mr. Minnelli," Judy said cheerfully and politely.

Minnelli was taken by Judy's simple, open, and friendly manner.

The meeting with Judy was brief and cordial. Though still a teenager, Judy was already a big movie star.

Judy later recalled that her first impression of Minnelli was of a tall man with enormous black eyes and a nervous stammer, but who possessed a courtly manner. For Minnelli, there was no indication that the eighteen-year-old girl he had just met would become his first wife and the most influential woman in his life. The same goes for Judy, who was married at the time to David Rose.

Mayer's idea to have talent auditions one night a week didn't sit well with his contract directors. The mogul must have sensed his directors' resentment, and this practice was quickly dropped. Minnelli didn't mind conducting auditions in the evening because he wasn't busy socially. At that point, the notorious Hollywood Sunday pool parties, where both gossip and useful information were exchanged, were mere theory for Minnelli, simply out of his league.

With plenty of time to spare, he experienced a worse time acclimating to Los Angeles than he had anticipated, and a much less pleasant time than the first time around. Having made only a few friends, he felt quite isolated. It was a relentless, unrelieved loneliness, with a touch of melancholy and depression, of a kind he hadn't experienced before. In New York, Minnelli could walk across town for work and meet dozens of people he knew on the street. The crowds, the traffic, the city lights of Times Square and the theater district gave Manhattan the kind of tempo and buzz that Los Angeles decidedly lacked.

The social landscape of L.A. was vastly different, and it affected Minnelli's routine evenings. He would leave the studio at dusk and go home. It took him a while to realize that most of the entertainment was done at home, instead of going out to nightclubs, like the Copacabana, Mocambo, or Ciro's. Even after moving into his own apartment, at the Regency on Doheny, and later to a house in the Hollywood hills, he was indifferent to Los Angeles. How could anyone get excited about a town made up of houses that were spread around and inhabited by lonely people like him? Nonetheless, Minnelli hadn't been idle in his spare time. He frequented projection rooms and movie theaters, trying to learn about every aspect of his new medium.

While the themes of movies might have become more mature, visually and technically speaking, they still relied heavily on theatrical and literary traditions and on the use of stationary, uninventive camerawork. He liked King Vidor, a director who understood the medium's unique properties, as manifest in his innovative silents *The Big Parade* and *The Crowd*. However, by and large, Minnelli thought that the fluidity and mobility of silent films had been lost with the advent of sound. He much preferred Vidor and other directors' silent films to the early sound pictures.

Max Ophuls and other French directors became Minnelli's role models. Unlike most American talkies, which were stagy and verbose, in Ophuls's films (*Liebelei, Une Histoire d'Amour,* and the later masterpieces *La Ronde* and *Le Plaisir*), the camera swirled with movement, waltzing about the décor and the actors inhabiting it. In Ophuls's pictures, the moving camera played an active role, heightening both dramatic and emotional effects.

Minnelli soon learned that no one could teach him how to move the camera inventively, or how to manipulate it in order to create variable emotional effects. Rhythm, he came to realize, was innate to the director, and plotting camera movement was a form of elaborate yet subtle choreography. For Minnelli, the trick was not to make the audience aware of the camera, but to let the camera's movement glide along with the performers. Minnelli was proud of what he described as "my inquisitive and restless" camera. He devised movements toward or away from the action that illuminated the shifting mood of the movie's various scenes.

Holding that motion was used too little in Hollywood, Minnelli planned to exploit it in his first picture, and he continued to improve on that aspect with each succeeding film. In Minnelli's opinion, directors were spending too much time on the master shot, which he found unimaginative and repetitious. Since most scripts were too wordy to begin with, Minnelli felt that dialogue and long monologues could be reduced and sometimes even eliminated by the use of a more expressive visual style and a more pronounced mise-en-scène.

Another frequently used device that slowed up the movie's action was the use of fade-out as a means of transition from one scene to the next. Minnelli opted to use dissolves of different lengths as a smoother way of progressing the action, or moving the characters from one locale to another.

While Minnelli's trial period at Metro progressed smoothly, he had no idea whether the top brass felt he was ready to direct. He was just a one-year apprentice, and they opted to go with more tested talents. Commercially proven directors, such as Sam Wood, Victor Fleming, Clarence Brown, and George Cukor—all Oscar-nominated or Oscar-winning filmmakers under contract at M-G-M at the time—had first choice of the best properties. Despite his Broadway reputation, Minnelli would have to prove his worth all over again.

One day, Freed summoned Minnelli into his office. "What do you think of *Cabin in the Sky?*" he asked.

"I think it is true and human, a wonderful story," Minnelli said, since he knew about the script.

Showing no emotion, Freed then said, "How would you like to direct it?"

Minnelli was stunned.

If *Cabin in the Sky* had not been a small, risky picture, Minnelli would have had to wait much longer for his break. The original Broadway show lost $25,000, and M-G-M was able to buy the property for $40,000.

Cabin in the Sky concerns Little Joe, a good-natured gambler who becomes the center of a dramatic conflict. On one side stands his devoted wife, Petunia, trying to keep him on the straight and narrow path, and on the other, is the beautiful and seductive nightclub singer Georgia Brown, who attempts to make him leave his wife for a career of gambling and high life.

Later on, when the wounded Little Joe lies on his deathbed, the struggle goes on, this time for his immortal soul. After some complications between good and evil, Little Joe is saved by his wife's unfaltering faith. Recovering from his wounds, he declares he has learned the errors of his ways.

Surprisingly, Minnelli was allowed to tackle his first assignment with more freedom than anticipated. Minnelli was not aware until years later how hard Freed had to fight for him. He also didn't realize the extent of Freed's battle to obtain a decent budget (the picture cost $662,141.82, to be precise) for a second-tier film, an all-black musical.

However, Minnelli *did* feel Freed's faith in his abilities when he was given free rein on his first directorial assignment. This decision met with great resistance in certain quarters, as there was a select clique of "seasoned" directors on the Metro lot. But, to his credit, Freed fought the battle and won.

As a safeguard, however, Freed appointed as associate producer Albert Lewis, a man with considerable experience, who was to assist and to advise Minnelli in technical and all other matters. Andrew Marton, another Metro director, was to guide Minnelli on his first venture as to the camera's possibilities and limitations.

Minnelli was eternally grateful for Freed's protection, which guaranteed his insularity. Not knowing anything about studio politics—the cruel in-fighting, the heartless backstabbing—was an advantage at that point. In later years, when the studio system would collapse, Minnelli wouldn't know how to fend for himself. Like other contract directors, he naïvely yet conveniently thought that the system would last forever. The dream factory was in full blossom in the 1940s, with the industry's best years, right after World War II, yet to come.

Freed had wished to make a film out of *Porgy and Bess* before *Cabin in the Sky,* but the property was not available. *Cabin in the Sky* therefore became the first all-black musical to be produced by a major studio since King Vidor's *Hallelujah!* in 1929.

When Metro announced that Arthur Freed would produce an all-Negro musical based on a Broadway show that had been an artistic but not a popular success, there was almost universal disapproval in Hollywood. The white executives were apprehensive as the militant black press was critical of the endeavor in general and its perceived patronizing tone in particular. Their misgivings derived from Warner's 1936 *The Green Pastures,* a film protested by the black community and the black press for reflecting a black mentality that was ludicrous, condescending, and false. It was therefore good diplomacy on Freed's part to give extensive interviews to several black papers before and during the production.

In his speeches and statements, Freed said: "All of America has learned a lot from the Negro in the theatre. With originality and talent, he has rendered a great service to the world of entertainment and the culture of the nation. The motion picture industry in its basic forms will never discriminate. More than ever before, we are aware of the Negro problem and are daily moving toward a better understanding. One that in the end will result in a dignified presentation of a peace-loving and loyal people."

Freed's pronouncements sounded like the launching of a message picture, which *Cabin in the Sky* was not. In fact, Minnelli intended the film as a musical fantasy depicting the humor and religious beliefs of blacks as a distinct ethnic group.

Minnelli himself had some reservations about the story, which reinforced the naïve, childlike stereotypes of blacks. In *Cabin in the Sky,* the characters are marked by an essential simplicity, embodying absolutes of good and evil, lacking shading or ambiguity. However, once he committed to the project, Minnelli decided to approach the material with passion and affection, giving no serious thought to any potentially negative reaction from black and other liberal-minded groups.

Cabin in the Sky was a courageous undertaking, reaching for a different dimension of filmmaking. Said Freed: "I will spare nothing and will put everything behind it. It will be a picture on par with any major film under the M-G-M banner."

It did help that a foreword, written by playwright Elmer Rice, opened the picture and placed the story in context.

Ethel Waters, who had appeared in Minnelli's Broadway musical *At Home Abroad*, became his good-luck charm when she agreed to repeat her stage role of Petunia. Minnelli wanted Dooley Wilson to re-create his Broadway role of Little Joe, but as Wilson's name was not as big as Eddie "Rochester" Anderson's, he was overruled. Had they waited a couple of years, after Dooley's great success in *Casablanca*, he would have easily gotten the part.

Along with Waters as Petunia and Anderson as Little Joe, the cast included Rex Ingram, also from the Broadway cast, who played the dual role of Lucifer Jr. and Lucius. Georgia Brown's character, instead of being the dancing part that Katherine Dunham had played onstage, became a singing role tailor-made for the up-and-coming starlet Lena Horne. The film also featured Louis Armstrong in a dramatic role and Duke Ellington and His Orchestra.

A most important element in the picture was the participation of the Hall Johnson Choir. Initially, Johnson, a highly educated man, had a measure of anxiety about the project, reflected in a detailed letter he wrote to Lewis:

> Thanks for giving me an opportunity to read the present script of *Cabin in the Sky*. You are to be commended for your desire to include nothing which might give offense to the Negro race, a consideration too often overlooked in this business of motion-picture making. I think my nose is particularly keen in that direction but, so far, I have been unable to detect anything in this script which could possibly offend anybody. *Cabin,* as it now stands, may be offered to the general public without reservations—needing neither explanations nor apologies. To this day, Negroes have never forgiven the slanderous misrepresentations of *The Green Pastures,* and when after five successful years on the stage it was finally made into a picture, they did not hesitate to express their true feelings about it.

Johnson went on to comment:

> The dialect in your script is a weird but priceless conglomeration of pre–Civil War constructions, mixed with up-to-the-

minute Harlem slang and heavily sprinkled with a type of verb, which Amos and Andy purloined from Miller and Lyle, the Negro comedians; all adding up to a lingo which has never been heard nor spoken on land or sea by any human being, and would most certainly be "more than Greek" to the ignorant Georgia Negroes in your play. The script will be immeasurably improved when this is translated into honest-to-goodness Negro dialect.

If your director is as sympathetic and intelligent as your script writer, you will turn out a picture which will delight everybody and offend no one without an inferiority complex, an affliction, by the way, which has almost completely died out among modern Negroes. We love nothing better than to laugh at ourselves on the stage, when it is ourselves we are laughing at.

Lena Horne arrived at M-G-M at about the same time as Minnelli. She had first met Minnelli in New York, at the famous Cotton Club, in Harlem. Back in New York, the two toyed with the notion of Lena playing the lead in *Serena Blandish,* a musical that never materialized. Bonding right away, Minnelli and Horne became known in Hollywood as the high-strung New Yorkers.

Lena had complained to Minnelli that because she was black, her numbers were not integrated into the scripts of her films. The reason for that was simple: If Southern distributors expressed any objection, the black performers' songs could be easily deleted from the film. Minnelli thought that this was a contemptible practice, but characteristically, he didn't raise his voice to protest.

Cabin in the Sky was the first picture in which Lena played a major part. Georgia was Lena's first real acting role, after making her film debut in *Panama Hattie,* a Red Skelton vehicle, in which she did a number with the Berry Brothers. One of Minnelli's first assignments was to stage Lena's musical numbers in *Panama Hattie* at minimum cost and maximum style. Minnelli costumed Lena in a lavish gown, positioning her carefully in front of changing sets in a way that didn't call too much attention to them. Lena's numbers were shot on a proscenium stage, and he had to learn quickly how to move the camera swiftly.

A few weeks after *Panama Hattie,* Minnelli ran into Lena at Freed's office and was greeted warmly by her.

"Wouldn't it be wonderful if we could finally do something together," Minnelli said. "Should I do *Cabin in the Sky?*"

"Yes, you must do it," Lena said.

In *Cabin in the Sky*, white characters not only are invisible, they're irrelevant to the story. As Stephen Harvey observed, the degradations that whites have imposed on blacks are not even mentioned. Poverty is seen simply as a fact of life, passively accepted by the blacks. In fact, it was the absence of black anger in *Cabin in the Sky* that made it palatable to white audiences. For a country that was at war and needed to feel unified, it was comforting and reassuring that blacks (and other ethnic minorities) were "content" with their lot. Nothing in the film suggested that blacks were kept in their place by the white majority.

Ethel Waters played the deeply pious Petunia, a woman praying for the soul of her weak gambler-husband. Minnelli wanted Petunia to look as appealing as possible, but this was a challenge as Waters was not physically attractive. In contrast, turning Lena Horne into a beautiful siren posed no problem at all. Minnelli gave her a great deal of confidence and she trusted him blindly.

No major problems with the press arose during production, though there were tensions and manifestations of anger from within the cast itself. Waters, who was older than Horne by two decades, became jealous and felt threatened by the younger singer, endlessly complaining to Minnelli. Waters later said: "I objected violently to the way religion was being treated in the screenplay. All through the picture there was so much snarling and scrapping that I didn't know how in the world *Cabin in the Sky* ever stayed up there."

Horne did everything possible to enjoy herself during the shoot, but as she later recalled, "The kids who were working in scenes with Ethel Waters told me she was violently prejudiced against me. Waters was not notably gentle toward women, and she was particularly tough on other singers, if they were younger and attractive."

"I was kind of a bulwark between them," Minnelli later recalled, "because I loved Lena and I loved Ethel, but Ethel didn't like Lena at all. It always seemed so ridiculous to me, because Ethel was such a great artist." In New York, it had mostly been Waters's show, but now it was divided between Waters and Horne. There was the new element of the "beautiful colored girl," which Waters simply could not tolerate.

On screen, the sensuality of the materialistic Georgia Brown, Petunia's nemesis, is viewed as a threat. Minnelli embellishes Georgia's portrait with brief alluring touches, as when she snatches a magnolia from a tree and fashions it into a seductive hat. Minnelli felt that the only way for Horne to compete with Waters's intensity was to play Georgia as a helpless, utterly sensual woman. Since Waters had the sympathetic part—the good woman protecting her marriage at all costs—Minnelli gave Horne's role more complexity and visual excess, not realizing at first Waters's jealousy.

Among the film's highlights is Ethel Waters's belting of the title song, "Cabin in the Sky," shot in one of the film's fakest sequences, a hillside and pond fabricated on the backlot. Making things worse—and borderline racist—was the decision to surround Waters with a chorus of mammies wearing bandannas and boys projecting the image of urchins. Indeed, despite Minnelli's seemingly tactful efforts, he didn't really solve the problem of black stereotypes. Waters, resigned to her situation, spends a lot of time on her knees, with her eyes uplifted to the Lord imploring help to vanquish the Devil's messengers.

As Stephen Harvey noted, in the movie, the competing forces of heaven and hell are presented as more urgent than the stress of everyday life. The title song suggests that Petunia's vision of heaven is a replica of her life on earth. The cabin will be on a cloud "as the angels go sailing by." Even so, Minnelli showed his gift for integrating a diverse group of characters into a more or less coherent narrative: the robust Ingram, Louis Armstrong (in a nonmusical bit) as the Devil's chief man dressed in a harlequin bathrobe, Kenneth Spencer as God's good emissary, and Anderson in a more humanized treatment than his scripted role suggested.

Though Freed had gotten an adequate budget for the musical, it was not large enough to bankroll Minnelli's endlessly vivid imagination. As a result, about half of the action takes place in Petunia's cabin, which made the film too stagy. And there are too many theatrical tableaux, such as Little Joe and Petunia's march to heaven. Hell is depicted as a white-deco office suite, while heaven is a painted staircase to infinity, surrounded by clouds of dry ice with black cherubs sitting on what seem like broken Greek columns.

The film was shot entirely in sepia, which was quite original. The fantasy sequence was a photographic feast for the eyes by the standards of the time. Minnelli showed his talent for imbuing objects with the symbolic and the fantastic. For example, oil lamps flare with the arrival of the emissaries, and when Georgia grabs a magnolia from a studio-made tree, she turns it into a sexually alluring hat.

Without Minnelli's stylized direction, the film would have been arch and simplistic. He deployed the camera's power to shape the distinctive mood of each scene without calling much attention to itself. Minnelli was beginning to show the kind of uniquely filmic technique that in the future would make him the most vibrant stylist of Hollywood's directors, in musicals as well as other genres.

Not everything went smoothly, though. Minnelli's first real contact with the art department resulted in a battle. Most novice directors accepted passively the department's rather dictatorial rule. For Minnelli, however, it was worse—a medieval division too accustomed to doing things its old-fashioned way. When the art department showed him sketches of the cabin, Minnelli's temper, which his bland exterior usually kept hidden, flared up. As far as he was concerned, the designers had missed his intent of showing that the characters were poor but not disheveled or miserable.

Indeed, the main obstacle Minnelli had to overcome was the resistance from the art department to his nontraditional ideas. It was Minnelli's intention at the outset to show the black race in the most beautiful terms possible; *Cabin in the Sky* was never conceived as a realistic picture.

In the Arlen-Harburg musical number "Ain't It the Truth," Lena Horne is shown in a bubble bath. The set was a prettied-up version of a slum, and Minnelli wanted a room in a house inhabited by poor people. He raised hell and the set was changed to his specifications. Horne looked beautiful, and the song was a charmer, but it had to come out of the picture due to pressures from Joseph Breen, head officer of the Production Code Administration. Freed said he had no choice. But, for his part, Minnelli was devastated; it was his first but not last major encounter with censorship.

Minnelli thought that Petunia would try to make her surroundings as pleasant as her limited funds would allow. At Minnelli's request, handsome but inexpensive wicker furniture was used to transform the cabin. Similarly, Minnelli wanted the street in the Southern ghetto to have a warm golden look, despite its being reworked from a studio version of a New York street. Eventually, Minnelli adjusted to the department's style as it did to his, resulting in a workable compromise.

The musical sequences are filmed succinctly. Waters is bathed in a saintly key light from above for her song "Happiness Is Just a Thing Called Joe." A radiant Horne in a froth of white plumes sings "Honey in the Honeycomb." In the first number, the Sunday meeting "Little Black Sheep," Minnelli's camera zigzags backward through the church, pausing to focus on the soloists and gossipy residents.

A number of songs intended for the movie were excised, but M-G-M was notorious for not wasting material, as was Arlen. "Ain't It the Truth" was later used by Harold Arlen in the 1957 Broadway musical *Jamaica*. The "Cabin in the Sky" number, as photographed, was used in a Pete Smith specialty, a Metro short. Another number called "I Got a Song," was cut from the picture and later used in *Bloomer Girl*.

Cabin in the Sky displays themes and images that would preoccupy Minnelli for the rest of his career. Mirrors would become emotion-fraught objects, more often than not exposing the characters' worst fears about themselves. In *Cabin in the Sky,* the mirror reveals the characters' true nature, such as Little Joe's moral ambivalence, Georgia's self-satisfaction, Petunia's deep faith, and so on.

Though there's pain, and the plot is motivated by greed, adultery, and homicide, *Cabin in the Sky* uses fantasy as sublimation for more realistic human conflicts. Most of the action is set within a dream, using a narrative structure similar to that of *The Wizard of Oz*. In all of Minnelli's work, dreams and fantasies have the ability to turn painful nightmares into beautiful experiences.

When the picture opened, most of the reviews were good. *The New York Times* called the musical a "bountiful entertainment," and predicted a "long tenancy of the Metro picturization of the Negro fantasy at Loew's Criterion," based on its being "sparkling and completely satisfying as was the original stage production." The *Daily Variety* critic thought that *Cabin in the Sky* was "a fantastic piece of American folklore, a morality fable stated in elemental, earthy terms, replete with pathos and comedy."

The *Hollywood Reporter* held that M-G-M "has a natural, first, because it is jammed with entertainment; secondly, because, being all colored, it presents an unusual picture, a show that will get box-office talk." As for Minnelli, "he has done a really inspired job in the direction of the picture, without which it would not be the good entertainment it is. It is his first picture effort and the job stands out."

Even more gratifying was the response of Oscar Hammerstein, who loved the picture, as he reported to Arthur Freed on June 7, 1943: "I saw *Cabin in the Sky* a couple of nights ago and thought it a very beautiful picture. The audience seemed to love it. Please congratulate Vincente for me on his first directorial assignment. I thought he did a fine job. The whole thing was intelligently produced, and for the first time, I realized the double-barreled courage that it needed, because it was not only a Negro picture but a fantasy as well, and both these elements have been on the taboo list for some time."

After their meeting in Freed's office, Minnelli got close to Lena Horne and an enjoyable, undemanding relationship evolved, with no pressure of any kind. She later recalled: "We did not go out. Vincente had a beautifully run house with a wonderful library and fine paintings on the wall and we spent most of our time together there. Occasionally, he would come over to my place, and I would cook dinner for him. He was living like a displaced New Yorker, just as I was, and we shared a dislike at that time for Hollywood life."

During the shoot, Minnelli didn't see much of Horne, using his nights to prepare for the next day's work. One night, the couple broke their rule against socializing during work and went to a party given by the singer Ella Logan. It was there that Lena met her future husband, Lennie Hayton. Hayton was noodling around at the piano while the comic Rags Ragland told bad-taste jokes about Negroes. Horne got so mad that night that she insisted they leave the place immediately. On their way back home, she took all her anger out on Minnelli.

On their dinner dates, Minnelli did some patronizing of his own.

Rather cowardly, he would call restaurants beforehand, to find out whether black customers would be turned away. If he noted any doubt or hesitation in the response, he would call Lena and pretend that the chosen restaurant was not a good choice, after all. For her part, Lena never suspected Minnelli's motivation for the last-moment changes.

One night, Minnelli, Horne, and jazz musician Hazel Scott, who would appear in his next film, went to the famous Alabama nightclub to hear Winonie Harris sing. They spent the night having a ball, smoking and drinking. Lena had to drag herself to work the next day. No matter how much they partied, she and Hazel always managed to do their scenes adequately.

One evening, while celebrating at the Francis Edwards, a bar across the street from Metro where studio people used to hang out, Lennie Hayton turned up again. Minnelli asked him to join them for drinks. When Hayton left, Minnelli told Lena she was fated to marry him, having met him twice by accident in the same week, with Minnelli in attendance.

After *Cabin in the Sky,* Minnelli was assigned a trivial comic romp, *I Dood It,* starring Red Skelton and Eleanor Powell. Shooting began in November 1942, just three weeks after completing *Cabin in the Sky.* The film's story is both simple and slender. Skelton plays a clumsy tailor's assistant who, adoring a Broadway star (Powell), attends every performance of her Civil War melodrama. To annoy her lover (John Hodiak), who is taken with another woman, the star then impulsively marries Skelton, her fan.

Minnelli was replacing a second-tier director, Roy Del Ruth. At first, he was flattered that the producers had turned to him for help, only to realize that he had no choice. Minnelli knew that it wasn't politically smart for a novice to balk at his second job at a studio like M-G-M.

The studio was stuck with bad footage shot by Del Ruth, including two musical numbers: an Eleanor Powell production number on a battleship and an exercise in twirling ropes. Metro's executives pretended that it was up to Minnelli to decide whether to use the existing materials. To save money, Minnelli was "encouraged" to keep some of the old footage. Metro then asked Sig Herzig and Fred Saidy to rewrite the slipshod script, a remake of Buster Keaton's last silent film, *Spite Marriage* (1929).

In updating the narrative, the writers made the Skelton character expose Hodiak as a spy, since saboteur plots were popular during the war years.

Among its few rewards, *I Dood It* gave Minnelli a good look at the comedian's real psyche. Skelton had to deliver one-liners but he was unsure how funny they were and which style to use to deliver them. On this picture, Minnelli was of no help. "I'm not funny," Skelton complained to his wife and manager, Edna, as they looked at the rushes. "You're crazy," Edna said. "You have never been funnier." Red continued to agonize, knowing deep down that his instincts were right. So did Minnelli.

I Dood It featured only pale traces of the Keaton picture. There's a long slapstick routine in which Skelton carries his comatose bride to bed on their wedding night after Powell has mistakenly taken the drink she'd concocted to knock him out. The film's slender humor was based on the collision between Powell's self-centered callousness and Skelton's clumsy masochism; his suicide attempt fails because the gas has been turned off.

Though he had previously worked with Powell on *At Home Abroad,* Minnelli never liked her dancing much, which was too athletic for his taste. Moreover, Powell proved an uninspiring foil for Skelton, and her tap dancing was neither exciting nor elegant. Some of her solos were "borrowed" from previous movies, like a hula dance from *Honolulu.* But others, like the cowgirl song "So Long, Sarah Jane," were shot specifically for this movie.

Even visually *I Dood It* is below mediocre. Minnelli's spark shows only once, in the Penthouse-in-the-Sky routine. Framed as a producer's audition for Powell's new show, and easily excisable to placate Southern exhibitors uncomfortable about black performers, it's shaped as a battle between two divas, Hazel Scott and Lena Horne.

Horne and Scott's rendition of "Jericho" is staged by Minnelli too self-consciously. Scott launches into "Taking a Chance on Love," as a mock concerto turned boogie-woogie, while Minnelli's camera circles 180-degree arcs around her baby grand. Then, against a starry cyclorama, a white-gowned Horne sweeps in, saying, "I'm terribly sorry, I just couldn't find a taxi," a line that prompted mirth in several public screenings. A café society version of the fall of Jericho follows, as a genteel

Horne and her chorus belt out the Kay Thompson arrangement. This was the one vibrant note in an otherwise dull movie. In another mildly entertaining sequence, Skelton dons a beard to play a Yankee scoundrel in a Civil War drama opposite his wife.

After *I Dood It* was released, Minnelli received a letter from an outraged fan who hated the scene in which Skelton, confused about his predicament, is sitting on a park bench next to Butterfly McQueen (as Powell's maid) and her black dog (played by Minnelli's own pet poodle, Baba). In a mildly amusing bit, a bewildered Skelton talks first to Butterfly, then to the dog. "How dare you make fun of black people by equating them with dogs?" the angry fan wrote. Minnelli was shocked by the misinterpretation; it was the last kind of reaction he had anticipated from such a trivial scene.

The New York Times's Bosley Crowther faulted the movie's story for "sagging about halfway along," claiming that "too much responsibility has been piled upon Red Skelton in what is basically a one-man comedy," and that the film contained few flashes of Powell's dancing skills or Skelton's comedy antics. From the outset, the movie was doomed by an unappetizing title, and the influential *Times* critic felt that, "for grammar like that, maybe Skelton's got what he deserves."

Minnelli did his best to please the movie's producer, Jack Cummings, but in the end, he, too, was disappointed with the results. Coming as it did after an auspicious debut, he would always refer to it as "my sophomore jinx." After the triumph of his next picture, *Meet Me in St. Louis,* Minnelli would never again work on such silly and banal material.

Seven

The First Peak: *Meet Me in St. Louis*

MINNELLI WAS NOT AWARE THAT by assigning him to direct *Meet Me in St. Louis,* Arthur Freed was catapulting him into the major leagues. The film was based on a series of articles that Sally Benson had written for *The New Yorker,* which were later published as a book. Freed wanted to create a nostalgic mood piece out of Benson's childhood memoirs.

Freed's selection of a director was puzzling, since Minnelli had little experience for such a large-scale musical. Freed had originally wanted George Cukor to direct, but Cukor had been mobilized into the war effort. Minnelli had volunteered for the Army, too, but was rejected because of his age and other ailments.

It didn't take much to persuade Minnelli, who found the book's evocation of a bygone era affectingly warm, despite its sentimental nature. What appealed to him about the text was one mischievous sequence, set during Halloween, which had a dark, even malicious tone for a musical. The children, longing for horror, envision the burning of feet and slashing of throats. Far from Hollywood's traditionally innocent approach to Halloween, this was the type of fantasy cultivated by children raised on the Grimm Brothers' fairy tales.

As an artist, Minnelli saw great possibilities for endowing the story with extra color and emotion. After a second reading of the script, he rushed to Freed and told him he'd be glad to direct the picture.

Because there was no conventional plot to Benson's articles, Minnelli suggested that a stronger narrative might be achieved through sharper characterization. In deference to his director, Freed hired writers Fred Finklehoffe and Irving Brecher and instructed them to center the tale on Esther Smith, which would be Judy Garland's role.

Minnelli worked on the script with Finklehoffe and Brecher, and whenever they ran out of ideas or inspiration, he asked them to go back to Benson's stories, which vividly conveyed the flavor of her childhood. The writers constructed a story out of a slim but charming episode, revolving around the imminent transfer of paterfamilias Alonzo Smith (played by Leon Ames) to New York, and the effects of this seemingly traumatic move on each member of the three-generational family.

At age twenty-one, and recently separated from her first husband, David Rose, Judy Garland intended to move into playing more adult roles. From her viewpoint, it was a mistake to play again a seventeen-year-old girl. Having just starred in *Presenting Lily Mars,* she felt it was the first step in her desired transition toward onscreen female maturity. Judy kept talking about the end of *Lily Mars,* when she whirls about in black tulle as the star of a big production number, a sequence that Minnelli particularly hated.

She had always been subjected to conflicting advice from the studio executives, who pretended to know what was best for her. However, this time, Judy was pleased that most of her "well-wishers" concurred with her notion that *Meet Me in St. Louis* would be a career setback to the child roles such as Dorothy Gale of *The Wizard of Oz.*

Minnelli's first contact with Judy, whom he hardly knew, was not encouraging. Informed about the studio's commitment to do the picture, Judy decided "to go in and talk to this Mr. Minnelli." Judy walked into Minnelli's office with the script in her hands. It was difficult for her to confront her director bluntly, so she just said, "It isn't very good, is it?"

"I think it's fine," Minnelli contradicted. "I see a lot of great things in it. In fact, it's magical."

Minnelli wasn't aware of Judy's feelings when he first discussed the role with her, but she couldn't see the magic in the script he was talking about.

A courtly man, especially when female guests visited his office, Minnelli would leap from behind his desk, get a chair for his guests, and offer them coffee or candies. As soon as they were in his presence, and taken by his natural charm and generosity, the guests learned how to disregard his nervous, fidgety quality and the stammer that got worse when he was either anxious or excited.

Judy tried to get her point across, but Minnelli was just as stubborn as she was. Realizing that *Meet Me in St. Louis* represented his chance to break into the front ranks, Minnelli did his best to change her mind. Minnelli's response was so assured that Judy was surprised. Minnelli couldn't understand why she had protested against the project in the first place. No one had told him that Judy had already gone to Louis B. Mayer, and that there had been several conference calls behind his back.

All along, Freed knew that if staged by one of the studio's stock directors, *Meet Me in St. Louis* would be a routine film. Skilled at making everybody around him happy, Freed protected his directors by keeping them in the dark about studio politics. This was Freed's modus operandi. He endeared himself to the artists in his Unit by leaving them to their own devices and, more important, defending them against bureaucratic interference from the top.

Mayer called Freed into his office and told him, "For once, I have to agree with Judy. I've read the script and there's no plot." Freed stood firm. His track record was so solid that Mayer was forced to consent. Freed felt that after a long string of successes, the studio owed him a "failure," if that's how *Meet Me in St. Louis* was perceived.

Having gotten nowhere with Minnelli's soft-spoken yet stubborn approach, Judy remained bewildered. Before a final decision was made, Mayer consulted his script reader, Lillie Messenger, known for her remarkable abilities and candid talk to the mogul. If Messenger liked a script, she would retell it in an eloquent fashion that stressed its strong potential and concealed its weaknesses.

Minnelli was lucky that Mayer gave the script to Messenger. "O.K.," the mogul said, "tell me what you think." Messenger enthused: "The script is a fine kind of Americana, and it was about the family. Don't forget that the country is at war." That's all Mayer needed to hear. He decided to go ahead right away. It was determined that the script would expand Judy's part to a more central role. Minnelli finally got his desirable, if reluctant, leading lady.

As for the music, Ralph Blane and Hugh Martin, who had written other Freed musicals, created three of the most melodic songs for Judy: "The Boy Next Door," "The Trolley Song," and "Have Yourself a Merry Little Christmas." All three songs would become classics in Judy's future solo concerts and other appearances.

Freed prevailed against strong opposition, for *Meet Me in St. Louis* was a risky endeavor. However, both Freed and Minnelli knew that they were gambling their reputations on a seemingly problematic movie. If the picture scored a hit, no one would question their judgment; if it failed, both would be blamed. For both, the stakes were high.

With screenplay and songs in acceptable but not final shape, Minnelli began to labor over the film's visual look. In New York, he was used to supervising every detail, from the first sketch to the last lighting cue. But at Metro he again found himself at odds with the art department, which had its own way of doing things.

On *Meet Me in St. Louis,* however, he worked with Lemuel Ayres, who had arrived from New York as one of Broadway's leading set decorators. For costumes, he hired Irene Sharaff, another Broadway vet who was now in Hollywood.

Finklehoffe's departure in the midst of the shoot, to become a Broadway producer, was a snag, and Minnelli had to rely on Irving Brecher to continue tightening up the script.

The main interior set, the Smiths' home at 5135 Kensington Avenue, was an elaborate and challenging proposition. Apart from the question of accurate period detail, Minnelli didn't want to be confined by conventional sets. Instead of building separate sets, one for each room, with breakaway walls to facilitate camera movements, he decided to shoot on a continuous set that would be constructed like the floor of a real house with interconnecting rooms. This created some technical problems, but it also contributed to the effectiveness of the movie's key emotional scenes, such as the one in which Esther and her next-door neighbor move from room to room to put out the gaslights.

Minnelli felt that the whole picture should have the look of a Thomas Eakins painting. Art director Preston Ames was asked to evoke vividly and nostalgically the city of St. Louis, which was re-created on the back lot. Metro built on Lot Number 3 the façades of eight imposing Victorian houses, each surrounded by a lush lawn and beds of flowers.

The story was divided into four seasons. Minnelli introduced each segment by using the Smiths' house as an illustration, in the style of greeting cards of that era. Each card dissolves into a live-action shot of the house. Summer introduces the family and the central conflict; fall contains the Halloween sequence; winter shows the bittersweet Christmas; and spring concludes the film with a family celebration at the opening of the 1904 St. Louis World's Fair.

Meet Me in St. Louis was the first Metro picture to be shot fully in Technicolor, for which Minnelli relied on the advice of Natalie Kalmus, the studio's color consultant. Until one day, that is, when an assistant told him, "You've heard the truth about Kalmus."

"No, I haven't," Minnelli said.

"She's color blind," said the assistant.

At which point, Minnelli laughed.

Minnelli's juxtaposition of color had been praised in his stage productions, but at Metro he couldn't do anything right in Kalmus's eyes. "You can't have one sister in a red gown and another in bright green," Kalmus said. "The two colors together are wrong. The camera will pick them up as rust and greenish black." Kalmus based her judgment on trial shots of the swatches, but Minnelli stubbornly insisted that, under the changing lights, the camera wouldn't distort the colors. From then on, Minnelli relied entirely on his own instincts, and despite initial objections from Cedric Gibbons and his team, he always won the battle.

When the shoot ended, on April 7, 1943, it was clear that, despite the initially embattled production and reluctant star, the movie had an extraordinary emotional power. *Meet Me in St. Louis* became the first picture to establish Minnelli's reputation as a major talent.

Curiously, during the shoot, the star and her director forgot their initial antagonism and fell in love. This was all the more bizarre, considering that their relationship was initially distant. Judy perceived Minnelli as a strange man, moving in his own remote milieu, and he didn't trust her much as an actress, either.

Judy began to melt as soon as she watched the dailies. The same "Mr.

Minnelli" who had caused her pain accomplished what no other director had done before: He made her look beautiful, not as a girl but as a woman. Her makeup artist, Dorothy (Dottie) Ponedel, deserves some credit, too, for she rounded out Judy's thin lower lip and accentuated her dark expressive eyes.

Sharaff, who designed the costumes, also deserves credit for disguising Judy's short neck and odd figure. Ultimately, though, it was Minnelli who made each and every shot of his leading lady flattering. Although Judy never liked the way she looked onscreen, she had always wanted to look beautiful in a mature, feminine way. Now, thanks to Minnelli's efforts, she did.

Lucille Bremer, who had begun her career as a Rockette before Freed discovered her at the Club Versailles, was cast as Judy's older sister. Freed, who was enamored with Bremer, felt that she had the making of a star. Minnelli disagreed, but, knowing how important she was to Freed, reserved judgment. Ironically, when shooting began, Minnelli thought that Bremer was doing a better job than Judy, but his opinion changed quickly during the shoot.

The major coup was casting Margaret O'Brien as Judy's youngest sister, Tootie. Minnelli was sitting in Freed's office when an agent walked in with a six-year-old child.

"Margaret," the agent said, "please do something special for Mr. Freed."

Wearing kilts, the little girl marched directly up to Freed, grabbed his shirtsleeves, and cried hysterically, "Don't send my brother to the chair! Don't let him fry."

Minnelli's mouth fell open. He rushed to scripter Finklehoffe and said, "I know you're writing an audition scene with a producer. I've just seen this extraordinary little girl. You must use her—just the way she is—kilts and all." Tootie's part was then specifically rewritten with O'Brien in mind.

O'Brien turned out to be a huge success as Tootie, though Minnelli found his efforts to shape her performance enervating and upsetting. In *Journey for Margaret*, O'Brien had played a troubled war orphan, which was followed by other neurotic roles, but in *Meet Me in St. Louis,* there was no need for her to act "big," since she played a "normal" girl. It took Minnelli some time to get a natural performance out of her.

O'Brien was particularly adept at doing emotionally charged scenes. Her mother and aunt, who accompanied her on the set, would whisper something in her ear before every scene. Then, in a reaction like Pavlov's dog, she would get emotional and cry. Minnelli always wondered what precisely was whispered to evoke such an intense reaction.

On the day the company was preparing to shoot Tootie's great emotional scene, when she demolishes hysterically the snowmen in the garden, O'Brien's mother came over to Minnelli and said: "Margaret's angry at me tonight. She doesn't want me to work her up for the scene. You'll have to do it."

"Okay, but how do I do it?" Minnelli asked.

The mother said, "She has a little dog. You'll have to say someone is going to kill that dog."

"I can't do that," Minnelli said.

Since in the story it was a cold night, O'Brien was sitting inside the Smiths' house with a blanket over her shoulders. Minnelli braced himself before walking over to her.

"Margaret," he said, "there's this little dog and somebody is going to take a gun and shoot it."

O'Brien's enormous brown eyes grew even larger.

"Is there going to be lots of blood?" she asked.

"Yes," Minnelli said.

Margaret's face registered a stunned expression, but there were no tears.

Out of the corner of his eye, Minnelli could see that her mother and her aunt were staring at them. Minnelli felt they expected him to go further, be even more extreme in his instructions.

"The dog is going to suffer terribly," he said with a sinister voice. "It's going to yelp and stumble around."

Working himself up to a feverish pitch, Minnelli finally said, against his better judgment, "The dog is going to die!"

"Oh, no," Margaret screamed, tears rolling down her face.

Minnelli turned to his assistant and said, "Turn the cameras!"

Mercifully, Margaret did the scene in one take, after which she went skipping happily off the set. That night, Minnelli went home feeling like a monster. He had never done such a thing before, and vowed never to do it again. That sort of direction struck him as unhealthy and manipulative. By today's standards, it would be considered child abuse, a severe violation of children's work ethics.

In most scenes, however, such as the cakewalk number with Judy, which became one of the film's highlights, O'Brien was delightfully natural and spontaneous, and there was no need for special instructions or any manipulation.

Judy did not exactly throw herself into playing the part of Esther. Used to wisecracking her dialogue in most films, she responded to the low-keyed script with mockery of her lines. However, aware that something was wrong, she complained to Freed that she had no idea what Minnelli expected from her. Freed told Judy to trust the director. But the atmosphere on the set remained cordial at best.

Taking note of Minnelli's mannerisms, Judy developed all kinds of comedy routines to entertain the crew while he was off the set. She would play two parts, that of Minnelli and of a veteran actor, who for decades has earned a living by speaking only one line in every movie he had made.

The actor arrives for work primed for his big moment, which calls for looking up at the sky and remarking, "I think it might rain." He is anticipating another routine paycheck, but Minnelli runs him through his spot and suggests that he might consider the possibility of pausing between raising his eyes and speaking his line. The actor agrees.

Minnelli likes that better, but he then thinks it might be stronger if the actor made an effort to sound a trifle put-out at the prospect of rain. They rehearse again. Then comes a suggestion of a sneer. That's good, but maybe he should do it once more, this time with a hint of resignation as the line is spoken. Minnelli approves, but now wonders how the actor feels he should play the line. This process continues indefinitely, until the skit ends with the bit player reduced to a blathering imbecile unable to remember his own name.

Judy experienced problems with Minnelli that differed from those with her previous directors. Minnelli rehearsed a scene over and over again until he was satisfied with every detail. He would then shoot it in as few takes as possible. Shots would be taken and retaken, until each one was exactly as he wanted it to be.

Though he didn't scream at his actors, Minnelli found ways to let them know whether he was pleased with their delivery. Minnelli seemed quiet, but in fact, he was even more stubborn and insistent than Busby Berkeley, whom Judy didn't like, didn't get along with, and didn't work with after *For Me and My Gal.*

One morning, Minnelli shot the same scene numerous times, but each time, Judy failed to satisfy him. Feeling hapless, Minnelli said calmly, "We'll try the scene again after lunch." Distraught and hysterical, Judy called Freed: "Please come down. I just don't know what this man wants. The whole morning's gone by and we still haven't got a single shot. He makes me feel like I can't act." Freed comforted her. "Well, Vince is from New York, and sometimes he's a little hard to understand, but you'll get on fine with him. You'll see." With Freed's assurances, work resumed.

There was one particularly difficult scene in which the entire Smith family sat at the dinner table and talked. Each member—the father, mother, grandfather, and four daughters—had lines of dialogue. Minnelli saw the scene as a fugue, in which the actors were to play off one another with the precision of musical instruments. Each member had to join in the conversation at a precise moment and with the right inflection. Minnelli set up the dinner table on a separate set, and each time another scene finished shooting, he had everyone sit down and rehearse the dinner scene.

Minnelli didn't hesitate to call Judy back to do retakes after she thought she was through for the day. One afternoon, after finishing her scenes, she got into her car and was driving out the studio gate when the guard stopped her with a message: "Mr. Minnelli wants you back on the stage to rehearse." This was unheard of; it was like school detention. Swallowing her indignation and pride, Judy returned, and Minnelli asked that she take her place at the table. When they finished, Minnelli said, "Well, I know that when we come to shoot it, we'll still have to work on it."

Fuming as she rose from the table, Judy complained to Mary Astor, who played her mother, Mrs. Smith. "This is ridiculous." But Astor surprised her with her response: "Judy, I've been watching that man. He knows what he's doing. He's absolutely right. Just go along with it." Since it was hard to fault a veteran actress like Astor, Judy calmed down and became more obedient. Grudgingly, based on the rushes, she began to see that Astor was right.

Nearly two months into filming, the initially charged and turbid atmosphere on the set began to warm up. The invaluable lesson Minnelli taught Judy was how to be part of a larger troupe. She had always been the principal of her movies, but *Meet Me in St. Louis* was more of an ensemble piece, and Minnelli wanted her to shine—as a trouper.

In the first couple of weeks, Minnelli was not pleased with Judy's performance. Bremer, who played Rose, Esther's older sister, was reading her lines with sincerity, but Judy was mocking the script. She was not accustomed to dealing with a director as subtle, mild-mannered, yet as tough as Minnelli.

In most movies, Judy's instinctive talent and impressive memory enabled her to complete each of her scenes in a few takes, without much guidance from the director. But now she could not understand what she was doing wrong, and Minnelli, who was inarticulate and enigmatic, was incapable of telling her. "You sometimes wished he'd come out with a statement—a noun, a verb, put his words together," observed costume designer Sharaff.

Though seemingly quiet and restrained in public, Minnelli did complain about his leading lady to screenwriter Brecher. He had just learned how she entertained the crew with malicious imitations of his maddening indecision. Minnelli was also disturbed to hear about her complaints. Freed tried to assure him. "Don't worry. It'll work out. I told Judy you know what you're doing and that she should have trust in you."

"But she doesn't," Minnelli said.

Judy was also distracted with her makeup, hair tests, and costume fittings. In her first scene, she had to stand with her sisters in front of a mirror nervously primping before a party. In reading her lines, Judy failed to come across as an impressionable young girl. Minnelli told her, "I want you to read your lines as if you mean every word." He proceeded to shoot the scene several times, but to no avail. No take was good enough. As a result, Minnelli called for a break, informing the cast, "We'll shoot it again after lunch." Yet another scene was delayed.

Minnelli admired Judy as an accomplished actress—but in other films, not his, not yet. A perfectionist, he rehearsed each scene until every move was right. Judy would be ready to go before the camera, but at the last moment, Minnelli would give her new directions: Enter from stage left, not right. Turn on this word, not that. Place the key here. Judy would say, "Yes, yes, yes, Mr. Minnelli," but he wondered whether he was getting through to her, and if he was, could she possibly remember all these changes?

Minnelli treated each of Esther's crises in the story, no matter how minor, seriously. It took a long time to gain Judy's confidence, but eventually, Minnelli was able to signal his ideas to her with just a look or a tiny gesture. At first, though, he had to find the right words to get her reaction. What seemed obvious to Minnelli was perplexing to her, and vice versa.

Minnelli perceived Esther Smith as the film's thread, the one character who integrated the various songs into a more or less coherent story. Once Judy grasped Minnelli's approach, she was as brilliant in the dramatic scenes as she was in the musical ones. Alternately wistful and exuberant, she was truly endearing. When she finally put her heart into her part, Minnelli knew that they were creating together "something very magical."

Judy's relationship with John Truett, the boy next door, is established when she asks him to turn out the gaslights for her. Esther wants to get him to kiss her, but all she gets is a friendly handshake. Since it was a conventional scene with banal dialogue, Minnelli opted for pauses and silences and camera movement to eliminate much of the talk. The action flowed smoothly from room to room, but shooting took considerable preparation as lighting had to be adjusted for each of the dozen gas burners. After a day of rehearsals, Minnelli got the whole scene in the first take.

This scene couldn't have been realized without cinematographer George Folsey's fluid and mobile camera. Folsey had already established his genius in the number "The Boy Next Door," spending enormous time setting up little lights and masking them off. With *Meet Me in St. Louis,* meticulous choreography of the camera became a crucial element of Minnelli's distinctive style, his signature.

In capturing the beauty of Judy's face, Folsey enjoyed the cooperation of her makeup artist, Dottie Ponedel. Ponedel had been responsible for Marlene Dietrich's makeup at Paramount, and now she worked with Judy, whose features were not classic, to say the least. Spirited and eccentric, Ponedel was notorious for her methods. If there was no water available, she simply dipped her makeup brush in a cup of cold coffee. "What the hell," she would say.

The first day, Judy reported to makeup with her usual rubber disks, inserted to change the shape of her nose, and caps to disguise her irregular teeth.

"What are these?" Ponedel asked. "You don't need all this junk. You're a pretty girl. Let's see what we can do."

Minnelli became the first director to make Judy look and feel beautiful, and for that she would remain eternally grateful. In no other film did Judy look so beautiful. It was Minnelli's idea to make her eyes more expressive by applying white eyeliner to her lower lids.

One of the problems Minnelli faced was how to stage a love scene between Esther and John, since it was a romance that couldn't be consummated. He kicked around a few ideas but none worked. Then he wrote the scene almost as rapidly as it took to speak it. The lines were simple, but with the actors' hesitant and insecure delivery, every word and pause registered strongly.

Judy's singing voice possessed a kind of distinctive emotional throb, a quality that also benefited her dramatic lines. The town clock strikes midnight. Esther and John kiss, whisper Merry Christmas to each other, and Esther runs into the house.

For the scene in which Esther comforts a crying Tootie about their impending move, Minnelli used a music box with a monkey on it, which he had found in an old-toy store in New York. The box was to accompany Judy's rendition of "Have Yourself a Merry Little Christmas." As written, the song initially ended with the gloomy words, "it may be your last," but Minnelli requested a more upbeat line. The song, as we know it, now ends with "make the yuletide bright," and went on to become a classic Christmas melody and a staple song in Judy's repertoire.

Toward the end of the shoot, Don Loper, then a dancer and later a fashion designer, decided that Judy and Minnelli should get to know each other better on neutral territory. Minnelli first met Loper in New York, when he did a dance number in *Very Warm for May*. Loper, who was dating Judy at the time, arranged a double date for Judy and Minnelli with his friend, Ruth Brady. Minnelli, still the confirmed bachelor, consented.

On their first outing the foursome got along marvelously. A delightful companion, Judy told zany stories to her captive audience. Minnelli and Judy hit it off immediately. He was captivated by her delicious wit, acting as a willing audience for her routines. Minnelli found her self-deprecating wit disarming, and her disguised vulnerability touching. Talking about the famous Metro school, where Mickey Rooney and Lana Turner were her classmates, Judy described how "scandalized" she'd been by their behavior.

"Did you know that between classes they used to sneak behind the building for a smoke? For that matter, so did I."

Minnelli laughed heartily. He couldn't help noticing that Judy always turned the humor on herself; she was always the butt of her jokes. Occasionally, she zeroed in on the studio people. Judy told them of the times Mayer brought visitors to the set. "Do you see this little girl? She used to be a hunchback," he would say. "Look what I've made her into."

The visitors gasped in shock.

"Yes, a hunchback. Isn't that true, Judy?"

"Why, yes, Mr. Mayer, I suppose it is," Judy would say humbly.

No matter how the conversation began, the talk always turned to Judy's early days in the movies.

Minnelli himself revealed a dry humor, a sense of the absurd that Judy never knew existed. He could also do brilliant impersonations of his cast and crew, which were shocking, considering how remote he seemed to be on the set.

A week later, just before going out on another date, Loper called Minnelli, "I'm sorry, I can't make it tonight, Vince. Will you call Judy and tell her we've got to call it off?" Minnelli agreed and dutifully called Judy, "I'm sorry, our date is off tonight because Don can't make it." But Judy, in her own inimitable way, said, "Well, why don't we go out together? We don't have to have Don and Ruth along." There was nothing to prevent them from having dinner together. From then on, Minnelli and Judy usually dined alone, which had been Loper's intent all along.

As their relationship began to warm up, Judy sometimes joined Minnelli and his assistant director, Al Jennings, along with Jennings's wife,

Juanita, for dinner at one of the studio's hangouts, after which they would watch the rushes together. However, there was no hint of any romance during these dinners with Loper and Jennings.

Judy had never met a man like Minnelli. Minnelli was an artist with a style. Why, he'd even had a Japanese valet in New York! He gave her drawings by Max Beerbohm and introduced her to his large library of art books. Minnelli knew everybody in the theater and literary worlds, from Cole Porter to George Balanchine to Josephine Baker to William Saroyan. She was eager to get all the details about how Minnelli had met Harold and Anya Arlen before they were married, the evenings he'd spent with the Gershwins in New York and L.A., the witty barbs by Oscar Levant and Dorothy Parker. She bombarded Minnelli with questions about these sophisticated celebs, the New Yorkers, who differed from their Los Angeles counterparts, especially her friends from the industry, all self-absorbed and limited in culture.

Truth to tell, Judy began dating Minnelli to break away from her problematic relationship with director Joseph Mankiewicz. Switching from Mankiewicz to Minnelli was like plunging into a totally new milieu. Minnelli sensed that she was both intimidated and fascinated by his sophisticated entourage, and he enjoyed sharing his enthusiasm in a noncondescending manner. He took Judy with him to exhibits and auctions, and through him, she fell in love with antiques and porcelain.

Minnelli courted Judy with an unabashedly Old World courtesy, placing her on a pedestal. Before meeting Minnelli, she had been treated as a girl. Blessed with a wry, self-deprecating humor, Judy was unaware of the beauty within her. It was Minnelli who brought that beauty to the surface and made her feel like a desirable woman. It was he who convinced her that she was really attractive.

One night, while having dinner at the Villa Nova on the Sunset Strip, the couple contrasted their experiences as theater children. "I always have to be my best in front of the camera," Judy said. "You should know that. You expect it of me too. Well, sometimes I don't feel my best. It's a struggle to get through the day."

Minnelli was clueless as to what Judy was talking about.

"I use these pills," she confessed. "They carry me through."

"Well," Minnelli said, both embarrassed and shocked at the revelation, "as long as you don't overdo it, it's all right."

The unions, during Judy's early days at Metro, were not as powerful as they later became. Everyone put in long hours, and Judy needed help. Monstrous stories were circulating in Hollywood about how Metro's doctors had started Judy on addictive pills. Fellow actors and directors, trying to be helpful, also offered her amphetamines. Gradually, she was seeking them out to see her through long and grueling working days. Since the pills left her wide awake and unable to sleep, the doctors then offered sedatives, which precipitated a vicious cycle of uppers and downers.

Initially, Minnelli refused to believe those stories. Little knowledge existed then about the drugs' long-term effects. By the time of *Meet Me in St. Louis,* the working conditions at Metro were more humane than a decade earlier, but Judy continued to use pills heavily; she was addicted, and they were helpful.

Minnelli didn't realize that his friendship with Judy was gradually growing into a love affair. Up until then, he had evaded the whole issue of marriage. Since Judy was still legally married to David Rose, he didn't know where their relationship was going, and he didn't care much. What counted most was the fun, the joie de vivre that they had together. Minnelli refused to latch on to Judy, as other directors often did with their female stars. He wanted her to be sure of her feelings for him, and until that happened, he determined to keep tight rein on his own emotions.

There were several obstacles to matrimony. For one thing, David Rose delayed granting Judy a divorce. This much-gossiped-about delay prompted musician Roger Edens to write nasty lyrics to David Rose's song, "Holiday for Strings":

> *Oh, see the little violins*
> *Enjoying the sunshine at the shore.*
> *They're rid of David Rose, the bore,*
> *Who won't divorce his wife, and so*
> *Her life is at a standstill.*

Eventually Rose consented, and on June 8, 1944, almost three years after they had married in Las Vegas, a Los Angeles judge severed their tie.

During the spring of 1944, there was a hiatus in Minnelli and Judy's romance. Judy walked out on the affair for a final fling with her old flame, Mankiewicz. Minnelli didn't have much time to brood about it. As soon as Minnelli completed cutting *Meet Me in St. Louis,* he began working on a new musical, *Ziegfeld Follies,* with Judy as one of the stars. Though they were no longer lovers, they decided to maintain their working relationship.

Mankiewicz returning into Judy's life presented another obstacle to the marriage. The affair was not yet terminated entirely. As Minnelli observed: "Judy simply gravitated back to him just as she had toward me at the start of our affair. I theorized that Judy must have been flattered by the attentions of such a brilliant man, and intrigued by the fact that he was in analysis. It didn't alleviate my pain."

Mankiewicz finally broke up with Judy after a false pregnancy. She wanted Mankiewicz to leave his wife because she didn't like "sharing him." But Mankiewicz told her bluntly: "You ought to go out more, Judy. It's not right you sitting at the phone, waiting for me to call you." For his part, Mankiewicz never meant their affair to be exclusive. And, indeed, Judy started going out with Don Loper, Charles Walters, the dancer and choreographer, and Freddie de Cordova, all at the same time. She also slept with Tom Drake (who played the "boy next door") and complained that he was a lousy lover, not realizing then that he was gay; years later, Drake came out.

On her last date with Mankiewicz, Judy summoned her courage and told him bluntly and with pride, "Well, I took your advice and I went out, and Vincente and I are in love and are going to be married." Mankiewicz was more relieved than offended, as he had never meant to hurt her. Mankiewicz loved Judy, but he knew that he could never take their affair too seriously.

When Judy left Minnelli for Mankiewicz, he resumed the social courtship with Marian Herwood Keyes, his previous assistant who was now Irene Sharaff's costume supervisor. For a brief time, he even contemplated marrying her, hoping it would quell the rumors about him. Unaware that Minnelli had resumed his relationship with Judy, Marian was astonished when she found out about their engagement. Minnelli had never bothered to explain or to apologize. His misconduct annoyed Marian so much that she began spreading rumors around town about her status as the "unkissed fiancée," and that Minnelli's embraces were detached and dispassionate, like those between brother and sister.

By June, it became clear to Judy that her affair with Mankiewicz was over. Their final days together had been just an erotic fling before each returned to their less-than-exciting sexual partners. It was not the end of their friendship, however, and they continued to socialize after Judy's divorce from Minnelli, in 1951. "I've had my share of affairs with women," Mankiewicz later recalled. "But they only exist as affairs. Every year, as I grow older, the memory of what we went through when we did it grows dimmer and dimmer. That isn't the case with Judy. I remember her as I would remember an emotional experience that is an event."

Another obstacle to the marriage was Minnelli's homosexuality, or bisexuality, technically speaking. His sexual orientation was an open secret in Hollywood. In fact, even his close friends were astonished when they found out he was dating Judy in earnest. Minnelli's colleagues at M-G-M did not know any details of what went on in his bedroom, but most of them simply assumed that he was a homosexual who could sleep with women, but was decidedly not the marrying kind.

Judy also had heard the rumors about Minnelli's "other side," but she chose to ignore them. Her response to the whispers about her dating a gay man was rather casual. "It's not that at all!" she would say. "It's just his artistic flair, his sensitive nature!" However, Judy confided in her friends that sex with Minnelli was not exciting, a far cry from the fireworks she had enjoyed with her more macho lovers, Orson Welles, Yul Brynner, Frank Sinatra, and Mankiewicz.

Meet Me in St. Louis finished shooting in April 1944, and Minnelli asked Judy to move in to his place in early summer, about the time he began cutting the film. She was glad to give up her rented house in Beverly Hills and move in with him.

Minnelli was ecstatic when she declared that she wanted to marry him as soon as her divorce was final. He let go of his marital fears and convinced himself that Judy really needed him. Minnelli dismissed his friends' alarming stories about her emotional problems with a shrug. "We would face all problems together."

Judy celebrated her twenty-second birthday in June 1944, while Minnelli was busy editing. As a present, he gave her a metallic evening bag, for which she wrote him a most personal note: "Vincente dear, your beautiful birthday gift has changed my outlook on life. It used to be a difficult task for me to walk into a room full of people with any self-assurance. But not anymore. Now I merely hold my handbag at the proper angle, descend upon the group and dazzle each individual. Thank you for one of the loveliest gifts I've ever received. Love, Judy."

Minnelli was asked to recut *Meet Me in St. Louis* when the film proved to be too long. A Metro executive wanted to excise the Halloween sequence, claiming, "It's the only scene that doesn't have anything to do with the plot." Minnelli was flabbergasted. The Halloween sequence was the reason he had wanted to do the picture in the first place. He'd worked very hard on the scene, and it came off beautifully.

Before shooting the scene, Minnelli took the Metro kids to the costume department and spent a whole day collecting a wild assortment of clothes, the kinds people stored in old attics and closets for some special occasion. Margaret O'Brien's costume was a man's coat worn inside out, pajama bottoms, and a derby. Her face was smeared with burnt cork so that she wouldn't be as visible in the dark night.

When the new assemblage, without the Halloween scene, was run for Minnelli, he decided to keep quiet. After the screening, the lights in the projection room came back on and Freed said, "It's not the same picture. Let's put it back." Relieved, Minnelli considered it a major victory, one achieved without having to fight for it.

Instead, Minnelli cut other scenes, such as "Boys and Girls Like You and Me," a song that had been dropped from *Oklahoma!* Originally, Minnelli thought that it would develop Esther and John's affair, but their romance came through much better with the family as a counterpoint and the scene was easily excised.

Minnelli felt good about *Meet Me in St. Louis,* a film that was emotional without being sentimental. The film had human touches and wonderful characters: the crusty grandfather, the no-nonsense cook, the older sister. Minnelli particularly enjoyed directing the scene in which the husband and wife sing, "You and I," a beautiful ode to the stability of their marriage. This was the way Minnelli wished to remember his own parents, and it was the way he hoped it would be with his own wife one day.

But Minnelli didn't want a singer's voice for "You and I." In a burst of spontaneity, he asked Arthur Freed if he would dub the singing for Leon Ames. Freed's sweet croak was perfect for the song. At first, Freed sang in too high a key, but after a number of rehearsals, he did it well.

Meet Me in St. Louis was Minnelli's coming-of-age film at M-G-M. Overjoyed, Mayer conceded that his opposition to the picture had been all wrong. The reviews were equally glowing. *Time* magazine wrote: "The real love story is between a happy family and a way of living."

Eight

A Fresh Look at Old Genres:
Ziegfeld Follies and *The Clock*

MINNELLI'S NEXT MUSICAL FILM WAS *Ziegfeld Follies,* M-G-M's opulent tribute to the old-fashioned revue form. The picture was made in 1944, but it was not released till 1946. Though dismayed by his breakup with Judy, Minnelli was not too hurt to work with her again. In July, just weeks after they split, he directed her in the *Ziegfeld Follies,* a revue that included, among other numbers, an Esther Williams water ballet and Fred Astaire and Gene Kelly's first and only dance number together on film.

Minnelli was elated to work with Astaire, who he had admired in his RKO musicals. Fortunately for Astaire, an exciting musical era was beginning at M-G-M with the Freed Unit. Unlike other directors, such as Mark Sandrich and George Stevens, who had allowed Astaire to devise his own routines and then photographed them as unobtrusively as possible, Minnelli shaped Astaire's material and left on it his own imprint. For better or worse, the impromptu spontaneity of Astaire's RKO work was gone.

Despite being a new addition to the Freed Unit, Astaire was given four numbers in *Ziegfeld Follies*; other performers were featured in only one each. First seen with Cyd Charisse in a tutu during the opening "Bring On the Beautiful Girls," Astaire returns for two more ballets with Lucille Bremer.

"This Heart of Mine," about a jewel thief whose yearnings for Bremer overcome the lure of her diamonds, evokes the haunting specter of "Let's Face the Music and Dance" from *Follow the Fleet*. The number was filmed in an intriguing fashion: Rather than shoot the dance against a theatrical backdrop, Minnelli enveloped Astaire in a dizzying three-dimensional swirl of sweeping camera movements.

Astaire and Bremer then switch to the somber eroticism of "Limehouse Blues," billed as a dramatic pantomime. Playing an Asian character, Astaire catches sight of the beautiful Bremer looking with admiration at a fan in a shop window. While he contemplates how to obtain the fan for her, a group of thugs rob the shop and Astaire gets killed by random gunfire. The scene then segues into a romantic dream ballet between the duo amidst hallucinatory décor. The setting and Astaire redeem the fantasy sequence, which ends with panache. Astaire's refusal to satirize or camp-up the material lends a moving, lyrical touch to the conceptual idea.

"The Babbitt and the Bromide" is less startling as a dance piece, but of greater historic significance. It's Astaire's first and only screen collaboration with his rival, dancing ace Gene Kelly. Introduced by Astaire and his sister, Adele, years earlier, in *Funny Face,* this vignette would have been more exciting if it had contrasted Kelly's and Astaire's stylistic differences, pitting Kelly's muscular acrobatics against Astaire's elegant agility. Instead, in Minnelli's picture the duo merges styles for a mishmash spree of slapstick frivolity and lighthearted tap.

Leaving the number to his dancers, Minnelli was fascinated to watch how the two pros and competitors went about their jobs. He couldn't help noticing the cautious, guarded relationship between the pair. Minnelli regretted that Astaire and Kelly danced together only once. For him, their never working together again was both a shame and a loss for moviegoers. Minnelli tried to interest both in a future project but it didn't work.

Before he came to Hollywood, Minnelli's innovation with scenic tints and textures had startled Broadway. Astaire's color debut in *Ziegfeld Follies* gave Minnelli a chance to use his palette to dazzling effect, but his obsession with décor overwhelms the dances. (In 1945, when he was assigned to direct Astaire again in *Yolanda and the Thief,* Minnelli gladly transitioned to pure Technicolor phantasmagoria.)

The most surprising scene in *Ziegfeld Follies* was Judy's ten-minute sketch "A Great Lady Has 'An Interview,'" written by Kay Thompson and Roger Edens, which lampooned Metro's reigning queen, the stately Greer Garson. Though Edens is coauthor, this delightfully wacky sketch bears the unmistakable stamp of Thompson, who had become Judy's new mentor.

Next to Edens, Thompson was to have the greatest influence on Judy's performing style. The sketch satirizes the whole idea of stardom, which was the essence of M-G-M as a studio. Shooting the number was fun, and Judy came off extremely well, revealing a new flair for delivering biting lines. Affecting a grand manner and a pretentious accent, her Madame Crematon slithers around the set in a slinky white gown, holding a press conference in which she gives absurd answers to absurd questions. When the film came out, the sketch received excellent reviews, and Judy was gratified by Minnelli's success at revealing another facet of her multitalented persona.

MGM had already used the celebrated Ziegfeld name in two spectacles, *The Great Ziegfeld* (1936) and *Ziegfeld Girl* (1941), a melodrama with songs, which followed the fortunes of Broadway chorines, one of whom was played by Judy Garland. Thus, in *Ziegfeld Follies,* Minnelli revived the plotless revue, an extravaganza featuring Metro's roster of singers, dancers, and comedians.

With a budget of $3.4 million, a huge amount by 1946 standards, this opulent exercise in escapism was the Freed Unit's most expensive enterprise to date. The endless reshoots, recuts, and reshuffling of material was responsible for a delay of two years between the start of the production, on January 2, 1944, and the film's theatrical release, in spring 1946.

The musical was first assigned to George Sidney, then an unseasoned director. After months of shooting, Sidney asked to be released. Minnelli was summoned to take over just one day after the shoot of *Meet Me in St. Louis* ended. Minnelli wondered why Freed hadn't assigned him to direct in the first place, since he was the right director for such material, having made his reputation with chic Broadway revues.

For the sake of efficiency, several numbers and comic routines were shot simultaneously, which meant that several sequences were given to various directors, most of whom were credited in the title cards introducing their respective segments.

According to most records, Minnelli directed about half of the final movie. Some of George Sidney's work, however, remained intact, including Red Skelton's "When Television Comes" monologue. Sidney also staged "Bring on the Beautiful Girls" opener, in which circus ringmistress Lucille Ball, wearing cherry-vanilla spangles, brandishes her whip at a cage of panther ladies, all dressed in black.

More footage was shot than could be incorporated in the final version. For example, none of Jimmy Durante's sequences made it to the final print. Among the episodes shot but not used was a Fred Astaire dance to his own song "If Swing Goes, I'll Go Too," the Gershwin song "Liza," sung by Avon Long to Lena Horne, and Fanny Brice's celebrated stage and radio sketch "Baby Snooks."

Originally, Minnelli chose for Judy the "Reading of the Play" sketch, a Beatrice Lillie highlight of his 1936 revue, *The Show Is On,* but it was never shot. One of the first numbers Minnelli staged was a duet for Judy and Mickey Rooney, "Will You Love Me in Technicolor (As You Do in Black and White)?" The lyrics had an insider's jokiness: "Since you have seen my pan in a house of Westmore tan, I'm so afraid you'll put me on the shelf," quips Rooney. To which Judy replied: "You never were such an eyeful till you had a Natalie Kalmus dip."

The finale, a tableau featuring tons of iridescent bubbles on Metro's biggest soundstage, was drastically revised. The bubbles remained, but the stars, including Astaire and Lena Horne, were left on the cutting-room floor.

Principal photography on *Ziegfeld Follies* was completed in mid-August 1944, four months after Minnelli took over. Since the reaction to the first sneak preview, in November 1944, was tepid, more cuts and reshoots were ordered by Freed. Additional cuts were made after a second preview, in spring 1945. *Ziegfeld Follies* finally opened in April 1946. Surprisingly, the public responded enthusiastically to the parade of stars and musical numbers. *Ziegfeld Follies* became one of Minnelli's most commercially popular films, grossing more than $5 million.

The movie was popular with moviegoers who had not seen the fabled Ziegfeld revues. For these audiences, M-G-M re-created the show on such an opulent scale that it even outshone the showman's original efforts.

Nonetheless, lagging behind the times and industry trends, *Ziegfeld Follies* was an anachronism in 1946, and an endeavor the studio would never repeat.

The Broadway musical formula of stars and showmanship had long since been replaced by a more streamlined approach. Revues usually consist of a series of showstoppers and stage fillers. In its heyday, the best examples of the format, such as Minnelli's *At Home Abroad* and *The Show Is On,* disguised the form's mixed nature by imposing a unified stylistic concept. But no such approach marks the screen version of *Ziegfeld Follies.* The film's uneven components are linked by Minnelli's theatrical imagination, though the lack of an integrative concept only emphasized the archaic stiffness of the comic sketches and the musical's fragmented structure. The primary allure of the revue format, as Stephen Harvey pointed out, resided in the personal interplay between entertainers and the live public. On Broadway, topical satire and naughtiness sparked laughs between the production numbers. Both were discouraged, however, by M-G-M, whose middlebrow sensibility reflected the conservative taste of Louis B. Mayer and the fact that the country was at war.

Given these parameters, Minnelli resorted to vaudeville routines, such as the Victor Moore–Edward Arnold "Pay the Five Dollars." While Roy Del Ruth's staging of the "Sweepstakes Ticket" sketch at least provided a showcase for Fanny Brice's madcap virtuosity, the rest of the material, with the exception of Astaire and Garland, was boring. Paradoxically, the proficiency of Metro's craftsmanship subverts what made the form so appealing in the theater.

Though it revealed some new facets of its performers, such as Judy's sophisticated humor and Astaire's gift for mime, the magnitude of the surrounding production overwhelms spontaneity and dilutes the fun. *Ziegfeld Follies* was the first of several musicals in which Minnelli's elaborate mise-en-scène struggled hard but ultimately didn't succeed in elevating the form to new stylization. Even so, he added some cinematic energy to his already developed stage flair with color and composition, and his looping crane shots enriched the performers' choreographed routines. The stars remain at the center of the frame, but they function as one among several vivid elements, without overwhelming the whole composition.

The first Minnelli segment in *Ziegfeld Follies* is actually the fourth in the film. It is preceded by a ponderous prologue of Ziegfeld in heaven, directed by Norman Taurog and featuring William Powell in a reprise of his turn in the Oscar-winning *The Great Ziegfeld*. Astaire then introduces Lucille Ball and her whip, and there's a fragment of Esther Williams frolicking around the faux coral before she darts up among the lily pads for air.

Minnelli's staging of Verdi's "Brindisi" from *La Traviata* doesn't meet his usual standard of glamour, due to the low wattage of his performers and Merrill Pye's bland sets. The duet is sung by Marion Bell (later the star of Broadway's *Brigadoon*) and opera tenor James Melton. The soundstage is dressed with curtains and chandeliers all in the same stark white hue. Minnelli tries to distract the eye with a waltzing chorus arrayed in Irene Sharaff's hoopskirts with butterflies and pinecones, but the bland setting fails to convey a sense of romance.

The next sequence, however, is pure Minnelli. Harry Warren and Arthur Freed's song "This Heart of Mine" is a ballroom-dance ballet, telling the story of a gentleman-thief (Astaire) who crashes a society ball and woos a bejeweled princess (Lucille Bremer). After their dance, his greed clashes with his love, and as they exit, he wins both the diamonds and the girl.

Quite disappointingly, the film's conclusion is a messy bit of kitsch. Kathryn Grayson sings an undistinguished Warren-Freed song, "Beauty," shot against projected clouds in atomic hues. A blob of orange foam covers the lens as the camera segues into the aborted bubble number, in which Cyd Charisse and her tutued corps de ballet pirouette through columns of suds.

There's a Dalíesque landscape of slate-colored skies and a tilted, forced-perspective desert floor, and the mirage is populated with anesthetized voluptuaries in gold lamé gowns. Engrossed by current trends in surreal art and psychology, Minnelli had already used this element in the theater, in his design for "Words Without Music," a Balanchine ballet for the 1936 *Follies*. In the film, Minnelli gives movement to a static canvas by having his restless camera circle lunar-landscape odalisques to the off-screen voice of some Queen of the Night. Unfortunately, the movie fades out on a conventional note, with Grayson standing atop a pedestal.

Working together on *Ziegfeld Follies* reintroduced Judy to Minnelli's virtues and charm. Even in her one, short segment, he was able to endow it with the quality she most coveted: beauty. As a result, she fell deeply in love with Minnelli, all over again.

A dramatic event on the Metro lot helped to cement their relationship. On August 24, 1944, after three weeks of shooting *The Clock,* a romantic drama starring Judy and Robert Walker, was shut down. Judy and her director, Fred Zinnemann, didn't get along and the footage was vastly disappointing. Judy was desperately eager to make the picture, but Mayer saw no point in continuing under those conditions.

In a last-ditch effort to keep the project alive, Judy turned to Minnelli, who was about to take a vacation. The unexpected call from Judy was an invitation to lunch with her at The Players.

"What picture are you doing next?" Minnelli asked.

"You know *The Clock* has been canceled," Judy said. "But I have told Arthur how much I believe in it."

Minnelli understood immediately that the lunch meeting had been orchestrated by Freed.

"Would you consider directing it?" Judy then asked.

"I guess I can look into it," Minnelli said. "Let me read the script and have a look at the existing footage."

To Minnelli's dismay, each scene seemed to belong to a different picture. Much of the problem stemmed from the flat script, not from Zinnemann's direction, which was decent, if not great (Zinnemann was at the beginning of his career as well).

A few days later, Minnelli told Judy that he would commit to *The Clock* project on two conditions. First, that Zinnemann did not object to his taking over. And, second, that he would be granted complete freedom and the unconditional trust of his leading lady.

Robert Nathan and Joseph Schrank's screenplay had interesting shadings, capturing the romantic mood of Paul and Pauline Gallico's original story. But it didn't play well onscreen, and it was confusing, a jumble of different tones and moods. Minnelli could see why Metro had canceled the project. Still, he thought he could make it work.

A gentleman of the old school, Minnelli talked to Zinnemann, himself a man with good European manners. Though irritated by Judy's lack of confidence in him, Zinnemann promised not to stand in Minnelli's way. Delighted, Mayer and Freed allowed Minnelli to make whatever changes he thought necessary.

Three days after his lunch with Judy, Minnelli reported to the set of *The Clock*. M-G-M had already spent $200,000 on the film, including a full-scale replica of the interiors of Penn Station, New York. With the exception of some exteriors, shot by a second unit in New York, all the footage was scrapped. Except for the two stars, Judy and Robert Walker, the only element retained from the original shoot was the Penn Station set, where the couple meets, before embarking on a weekend courtship, and where they part at the end.

Scrapping most of the footage already shot, Minnelli started afresh. His idea was to make Manhattan an integral character in the story, which was ambitious, considering that the entire film was made in Culver City. To create the required atmosphere, backgrounds photographed by a location crew were combined with studio footage. Though New York landmarks were essential to the story, it was decided to shoot everything on a soundstage, because it would be too impractical to manage thousands of passengers at Penn Station; it also saved a lot of money. With the country still at war, the studios were under extreme scrutiny over their budgets and expenditures. Minnelli succeeded in making the viewers aware of New York as a strong influence on the relationship of the couple.

Several incidents in the script needed further revision. In a scene set by the boat pond in Central Park, Robert Walker befriends a young boy who's helping him rig the sails of a boat. The boy is convinced that his boat will be of no service in the war effort, but Walker tells him that he is mistaken. When the boy falls into the pond, and a policeman wants to arrest him for swimming, Walker and Judy pretend to be his parents. Finding this trite, Minnelli decided that when Walker attempts to befriend the boy, he would get a kick in the shins for his trouble. The problems that Walker's character has with children became one of the film's leitmotifs.

During the shoot, Judy was in particularly good shape, having found a director for a movie she really wanted to make. But Walker was a mess: His marriage to Jennifer Jones had fallen apart and he was drinking heavily. Going through a painful breakup, Walker became bitter and vengeful, since Jones was already dating David O. Selznick (who was still married to Irene Selznick, Louis B. Mayer's daughter) in a much-publicized affair. Under the influence of booze, Walker exhibited sudden, scary personality changes.

Assuming a maternal role, or that of a big sister, as she told Minnelli, Judy decided to nurse Walker throughout the shoot. On more than one occasion, Judy, Dottie Ponedel, and her publicist Betty Asher went from bar to bar looking for Walker. Once he was found, they brought him home, dried him out, and got him into shape for the following day's work. In the end, despite drinking problems and arguments with Minnelli about his role, Walker turned in one of his most touching performances.

If Minnelli and Judy began the year of 1944 in bitter conflict, they ended it on a high, cheerful note. They exchanged a midnight kiss at Jack and Mary Benny's New Year's Eve party, which was attended by many stars and studio execs. Judy's picture on the cover of *Life* magazine in December 1944 was also a major boost to her ego and morale.

Minnelli might have been inarticulate in his guidance, but he was a thoughtful and sensitive filmmaker who was able to make Judy shine. *The Clock* sealed her fate to Minnelli's. On January 9, 1945, a few days before Judy was to begin work on the musical western *The Harvey Girls*, her first picture in two years without Minnelli, the couple announced their engagement.

Despite Minnelli's fears, no one had asked why a filmmaker known for his musicals had been entrusted with a romantic drama. In fact, the press was more curious to know why Judy was eager to appear in a non-singing dramatic role. They got their answer onscreen, when *The Clock* achieved immediate success upon its release in May 1945.

For this movie, Minnelli relied more on his vivid memories of New York than on photographs or research. The city's locations were re-created using photographic plates, which were projected as backdrops in front of the actors, a technique that proved effective and inexpensive. In one scene, Minnelli blew up a small photo of Rodin's statue *The Thinker,* and placed it on the edge of a plate, giving the illusion of a museum setting. Overall, *The Clock* was so emotionally involving that critics and audiences hardly noticed its artifice.

Judy behaved extremely well throughout the shoot, but Minnelli thought she was taking the wrong approach to her acting. He had to convince her that her natural talent and dramatic instincts were sufficient. Insecure about her dramatic skills, Judy began working with a coach. She would come back from her classes with all kinds of tricks, anxious to demonstrate them to her director. Despite all of this nonsense, in the end, Minnelli coaxed a great dramatic performance out of her that was devoid of affectation.

A minor clash occurred when Minnelli was about to shoot the scene where Judy and Walker meet at Penn Station. In a typically cute Hollywood meeting, Judy's high heel snaps off and Walker comes gallantly to the rescue. Based on her extensive work with the drama coach, she limped along, as if one leg were shorter than the other.

Minnelli watched her rehearse the scene and thought it was ridiculous. "Why do you limp?" he asked. "A girl would walk on her toes in order to keep her balance." "How do you know?" Judy fired back at her director. "Because," Minnelli explained, "I have seen it happen many times with women in my family." What he didn't tell her was that, as a boy, he once wore his mother's dress and high-heel shoes.

Minnelli then told Judy to get rid of her drama coach. Surprisingly, she agreed. Having already proven she was a dramatic actress, what she really needed was stronger self-confidence and trust in her director, not a bunch of tricks.

On this picture, Minnelli volunteered to do something he had never done before, that is, write an essay with answers to all the questions Judy might have about her character. What was the girl like? The magazines she read? Her hang-ups, her favorite movie stars? He also devised a similar essay for Walker's ordinary guy. Minnelli didn't share these essays with either actor; only when asked would he offer bits of their characters' history and psychology. The exercise proved helpful to both director and actors.

The picture opens with a crane shot of Penn Station, showing hundreds of people scurrying around. It picks up a young soldier, obviously dazzled by his first visit to New York, making his way through the crowd. In this film, Minnelli opted for symmetry, a device he would develop in future movies. At the end of the story, when Alice sees the boy off, the process is reversed. The camera now follows Alice, pans back on the boom until her figure is lost in the crowd. In between these sequences, a sweet love story unfolds.

During the shoot, Robert Walker was drinking heavily, but Minnelli was unaware of the toll *The Clock* was taking on his actor's nervous system. Judy knew of the actor's drinking problems, but in tune with her humanity and discretion, she never told Minnelli about her and Dottie Ponedel's rescue missions that often ended with finding Walker drunk or passed out.

Late one night, Judy and Minnelli received a phone call from a drunken Walker, threatening to kill himself. They tried to find out his whereabouts, but he refused to say. After some cajoling, Walker agreed to come over to their house. He showed up tipsy half an hour later.

"Give me a drink," Walker said belligerently, "and make it snappy."

Minnelli fixed him a drink.

Walker then said that he hated Hollywood and its people, and that most of all he hated himself. Minnelli realized that Walker was expressing all the resentments he had been storing up inside. While Walker attacked his hosts with ugly utterances Minnelli was mum, as usual, but Judy reacted with patience. Meanwhile, Minnelli called the actor's friends to find out who his doctor was. When he couldn't reach anyone, Minnelli called his own physician.

Walker demanded more drinks, and Minnelli obeyed, though he watered the drinks down considerably. Realizing what his host was doing, Walker insisted on getting stronger drinks. Around dawn, Minnelli's doctor finally arrived, but Walker used such profanities that the doctor himself walked out.

The only "solution" was to serve the actor drinks that were stronger and stronger—until he passed out completely. Finally reached, Walker's doctor suggested he use the back entrance of the hospital and register the actor under a fictitious name. Clearly, the doctor had been through all this before. Walker was hospitalized for a long time. His life was cut short tragically in 1951, at the young age of thirty-two.

A single scene in *The Clock*, set in Central Park, established Judy as a mature actress. While she and Walker are talking about the sounds of the city, Minnelli shows a brief close-up of Walker but lingers much longer on Judy's face. Cinematographer George Folsey captured her face lovingly and expressively. For the first time, Judy revealed onscreen that special glow of hers. People who saw *The Clock* held that because of that scene it was obvious Minnelli was deeply in love with her. Not surprisingly, the shy Minnelli expressed his strongest feelings for his leading lady through his camera.

Minnelli shot the final scene, in which the lovers part, and which contained pages of dialogue, at the very end of production. A crucial decision was made on the morning of the shoot. Walker's speech would be given to Judy; it seemed nobler for her to say it. Minnelli then staged the rest of the scene in pantomime, hoping their gestures would imply that, after spending their first night together, their marriage is to endure. He instructed the couple to smile, but Walker couldn't smile when he discovered he would have to descend via nonexistent stairs to the train below. In the midst of this emotional scene, Walker had to play the old vaudevillian's trick, lowering his body as he descended, so that only his head was visible. Walker never forgave Minnelli for that humiliating bit.

When *The Clock* was released, Minnelli was overwhelmed by the positive reaction. *Time* magazine heaped hosannas: "Minnelli's talents are so many-sided and generous that he turns even the most over contrived romanticism into something memorable. He has brought the dramatic talents of his bethrothed, Judy Garland, into unmistakable bloom. Few films in recent years have managed so movingly to combine first-grade truth with second-rate fiction."

The film was so visually and emotionally arresting that it even played well without sound, as a silent picture. Minnelli was particularly pleased with the praise showered on his technical command, specifically the Penn Station crane shots. For the first time, the critics specifically acknowledged Minnelli's talent with the camera, described by one reviewer as "swooping and sailing, drifting and drooping."

At the end of the shoot, to express her gratitude, Judy sent Minnelli a present, a desk clock. In a burst of spontaneity, she wrote him a personal note:

> Darling, Whenever you look to see what time it is—I hope you'll remember *The Clock*. You knew how much the picture meant to me—and only you could give me the confidence I so badly needed. If the picture is a success (and I think it's a cinch) my darling Vincente is responsible for the whole damn thing. Thank you for everything, angel. If I could only say what is in my heart—but that's impossible. So I'll say God bless you and I love you!

Nine

Falling in Love

WHEN THE SHOOT OF *The Clock* ended on November 21, 1944, it was clear that Minnelli had succeeded in salvaging the troubled movie. James Agee, the astute *Time* critic, praised it: "*The Clock* inspires ingratitude for not being great." More important, *The Clock* accomplished what Judy had hoped for, demonstrating, as Agee noted, "for the first time beyond anybody's doubt, that Judy Garland can be a very sensitive actress. In this film she can handle every emotion in sight, in any size and shape, and the audience along with it."

Various directors at Metro had always believed that, given the chance, Judy could be a fine dramatic actress, that all she needed was a strong, visionary director to point the path for her. Minnelli proved to be that director, plus he was the one to make her look and feel beautiful. "Vincente saw something in Judy that nobody else did," said Minnelli's long-time costume designer Irene Sharaff. "I think Judy was more in love with the idea that somebody took her seriously and made her beautiful as a woman."

Judy did not realize then that her gratitude was a form of disguise for her renewed love for Minnelli. After a brief and painful detour for both, she and Minnelli again began dating. Minnelli was finally reassured that Judy not only needed him but was also in love with him.

Their romance was no longer a secret. During breaks, they were seen hugging together or engaged in intimate conversations. They were so smitten with each other that once, thinking no one was around, they began making love. Some extras, returning to the set during lunch hour, dressed as sailors for a subway scene, were astonished to glimpse the couple kissing in a darkened alcove.

The extras kept their mouths shut, but the light operators, who ate their sandwiches at work, saw the couple and gossiped about it. Within minutes, the whole studio knew what had happened in the shadowy alcove. "Is it true? Did Judy really go down on Minnelli on the subway set?" Minnelli didn't deny the reports. He enjoyed, and even encouraged, such gossip. It was good for his reputation as a bisexual.

Along with Judy's present, Minnelli received a gift from Metro, a free trip to New York City. The official purpose was for him to meet the national press at the premiere of *Meet Me in St. Louis,* so that Mayer could deduct the expenses involved, but he saw it primarily as a pleasure trip.

In November 1944, the studio organized a promotional junket to New York City. Judy and Minnelli were romantically entwined and socially inseparable, reflecting a romance that mingled fact with fiction. It gave Minnelli the chance to play a mentor, a Svengali. Though Judy had been there before, Minnelli showed her a new side of Manhattan—the theater world. Proving to be a rapt audience, Judy was thrilled when Minnelli took her to see *Oklahoma!,* her very first Broadway musical. They then visited Richard and Dorothy Rodgers, who were bowled over by Judy's talent. Judy asked Rodgers to play on the piano the songs she had sung in her films. Before long, she was singing them herself.

He also took her to the actual spots where *The Clock* was set: Penn Station, the Metropolitan Museum, the Central Park Zoo, an Italian restaurant in Times Square. Through Judy's fresh and enthusiastic eyes, Minnelli saw New York anew. Minnelli exposed her to two of New York's key facets, the sophisticated and the hedonistic, which sometimes overlapped. Born in the Midwest, and now a provincial Californian, she was eager to learn. Like all good students, Judy absorbed Minnelli's vast knowledge like a sponge.

———

When they returned to Los Angeles in early December, Minnelli continued his mentoring, ushering Judy through art galleries and antique showrooms, often on opening night; it was very important for Judy to be seen with the glitterati. Minnelli observed with joy Judy's new interest in antiques, painting, jewelry—things that had given him pleasure and that he wished to share with Judy.

Minnelli asked Judy to move in with him once again, and she willingly gave up her rented house. However, Judy's mother, Ethel Gumm Gilmore, disapproved strongly. Ethel was not prepared to let her daughter live "in sin," without a marriage certificate. Yet another inevitable argument arose between mother and daughter, this time around about Minnelli.

Before their trip to New York, and before Judy's divorce from Rose was final, Ethel had called Minnelli to deliver one of her lectures, whereupon a hysterical Judy ran upstairs and packed her bags. Accusing her mom of suffocating her, she dashed out of her mother's house and moved into Minnelli's.

A few weeks later, Minnelli received a disturbing letter from Ethel, in which she complained of how mistaken she had been about him. She had always thought of Minnelli as an honorable gentleman. From her selfish perspective, Ethel could not help but feel that a man of his age and stature was taking advantage of her young and "innocent" daughter.

Minnelli replied immediately. He wrote that he loved Judy, but could not marry her until her divorce from David Rose became final. He also confided in Ethel Judy's wish to obtain a quick divorce in Mexico. All along Minnelli objected to it, since Mexican divorces were not always recognized in the United States. Finally reassuring Ethel of his honorable intent, he repeated his strong wish to marry her as soon as possible. But Ethel simply refused to believe; it sounded too good to be true.

The couple were now eager to get married. Judy suggested eloping to Mexico, but as her divorce wasn't final, Minnelli proposed to wait. Not pleased, Ethel wrote Minnelli another long letter in which she expressed her unhappiness about their sharing the same bed together, accusing Minnelli of abusing her daughter's innocence.

It was no secret that Judy hated her mother. Ethel was a strong-willed, domineering stage mother whom Hollywood insiders believed was just like Mama Rose, Gypsy Rose Lee's mother. Mrs. Gilmore always consented to what Louis B. Mayer had determined for her daughter. Some of her "good will," as Judy told Minnelli, derived from trust, but a lot had to do with the fact that she was on Metro's payroll and her livelihood depended on getting along with Mayer.

However, it was in New York that Minnelli noticed with alarm Judy's swinging moods. He had to learn how to deal with those aspects of her personality that could not be changed. The frequent shifts from exuberance to melancholy to depression were part of Judy's nature, the cumulative result of an unhappy childhood and years of taking drugs.

Additionally, Judy was plagued by the hot temperament and deep insecurity that affects most great performers. When Minnelli's friends inquired, "Why do you put up with so much?" he simply said, "She gives me so much. I could learn to live with her occasional moments of despair." "Occasional" was the operative word, for, while she was with Minnelli, Judy could snap out of her mood.

Late one night, she confided in him: "I think I might be taking too many of those pills."

"I know," Minnelli said. "I can't put my foot down and tell you to stop. I know there are times when you're tired and when things don't go well at the studio. I can always tell when you're on Benzedrine. You think this is the best performance you've given. But you're not nearly as effective as you think you are."

Mute, Judy didn't utter a word.

"Promise me you'll stop taking them," Minnelli said. "At least try."

"You know I try," Judy said softly.

She did try. There were days when everything went smoothly, and she didn't need any pills. But then there were days when she desperately needed them just for routine functioning. Minnelli witnessed a cyclical behavior, ranging from long periods when Judy took no drugs at all, to days when life would be too much for her, and he would come home to find Judy drugged and speechless. "I'll quit tomorrow," Judy would say. "I promise." She would then recover from the periodic spells to become her natural sweet and considerate self.

Minnelli hoped that Judy would intuitively understand how much he loved her. He knew he was unable to say the right things when she needed to hear them the most. Minnelli was never good at expressing his feelings. Judy must have discussed Minnelli's inarticulateness with her friends, particularly Betty Asher. Walking into Judy's room one day, Minnelli watched her adjusting her stockings. "Darling, you have great-looking legs." Judy and Betty burst into uncontrollable laughter. It was as if he had never seen her legs before.

As a young boy in Ohio, Minnelli derived tremendous joy watching his mother dance onstage in a costume he had designed for her. It was one of his childhood's proudest moments, about which he endlessly reminisced. When he talked about teaming with Josephine Baker at Radio City, he always mentioned the dress he designed for her, which for him was the highlight of their collaboration. Though Joseph Mankiewicz was Minnelli's polar opposite in many ways, the two men shared one thing in common, they were part Svengali and part Pygmalion. And both had a passion for molding and nurturing potentially exceptional women.

"Vincente loved someone he could make beautiful, someone he could create," observed Lena Horne, herself molded by Minnelli. Minnelli loved dressing women. Up until his affair with Judy, Horne was his most conspicuous protégée. Minnelli showed Horne off to advantage onscreen, as the sensuous seductress in *Cabin in the Sky,* and also advised her about her offscreen wardrobe. As a self-educated man, Minnelli liked to impart his knowledge—which books to read, which paintings to look at, which knives and forks to use for various kinds of dinners.

Like Horne, Judy embraced Minnelli's tutorship eagerly and willingly, becoming his Galatea, though in a different way than she was with Mankiewicz. Whereas Mankiewicz instructed Judy in strictly intellectual concerns (which plays to read and what to say about them), Minnelli concerned himself with beauty, elegance, behavior and appearances in public places, pragmatic issues that the insecure Judy cared about. And whereas Mankiewicz denied Judy his undivided attention and complete emotions, Minnelli devoted his full concentration to her.

Judy's engagement to Minnelli didn't deter her from dating other men secretly. Her most ardent pursuer in the winter of 1945 was Orson Welles, a notorious womanizer and the dashing wunderkind who had created the masterpiece *Citizen Kane* at age twenty-six. An affair with Welles, who was then slim, attractive, and young (much younger, in fact, than most of her lovers), was titillating for her. It thrilled her to be able to entice Welles away from one of Hollywood's greatest sex goddesses, his wife Rita Hayworth. All in all, Judy saw Welles about half a dozen times, mostly for sex. In his rough sexual manner, and intellectual attitude, Welles reminded her of Mankiewicz, and was the opposite of her effete fiancé.

The illicit affair was risky for both of them. The jealous Hayworth came close to discovering it when she spied a huge bouquet of flowers in Welles's car. Assuming that the flowers were meant for her, Hayworth was about to retrieve them when Welles's smart secretary, who knew of his affairs and escapades, rushed out and removed the card that was intended for Judy before Welles handed the flowers to Hayworth. It was a peculiar moment, right out of a Hollywood movie, with Hayworth wondering why her unromantic hubby would bring her flowers on a routine day.

A similar mix-up almost caused a disaster for Judy. Disregarding her calendar, Judy had invited Minnelli *and* Welles to dinner on the same night. Realizing her mistake only when she heard Minnelli's car in the driveway, she rushed out the door with Dottie Ponedel before Welles could arrive. The stove was malfunctioning that night, Ponedel said, and they would have to eat in a restaurant.

Mayer had been against all of Judy's previous lovers, complaining that they were either married men, or too old for her, or both. At forty-two, Minnelli was the oldest among them, but Mayer embraced him as a son-in-law, and he was impressed with his kindness toward Judy, on and off the set. As always, Mayer's support of Judy's lovers and romances had more to do with business than genuine personal feelings.

To Mayer and other members of the M-G-M brass, the marriage was a match made in heaven. Mayer wanted the Minnellis (as he already called them) to become Hollywood's new royal couple, as the Lunts (Alfred Lunt and Lynn Fontanne) were for the New York theater. This attitude only reinforced Judy's motivation to belong to Hollywood's inner circle as a member of its cherished elite.

Rather ignorant about sexual matters, Mayer did not perceive Minnelli's rumored homosexuality (or bisexuality) as an obstacle to the marriage. Earlier, he had tried to fix up the openly gay director George Cukor with women, too, until the more courageously homosexual director told him to his face about his orientation. Like others in the industry, Mayer believed that homosexuality was a self-induced "perversion," adopted under bad influences and therefore easily discarded by dint of a strong will. Mayer held that a good marriage would straighten out Minnelli and make a real man of him, while it would also steady Judy, bringing much-needed stability to her life.

Judy's rationale for marrying a homosexual—or bisexual, as she preferred to think—was based on her desire to continue to have sexual flings with other men without feeling guilty. Unlike many Hollwood wives, she didn't subscribe to the theory that "it takes the right woman to cure a gay man." Nor was she jealous of Minnelli. For one thing, he never looked at young men when the couple was together, and God knows, there were plenty of opportunities in Hollywood, at least to look at.

In this respect, Judy was ahead of her time, a true believer in open marriages, European style. At the same time, she wanted to feel needed and taken care of by a strong and loving man, and she knew that marriage to Minnelli would provide that. In short, she was a bundle of contradictions.

Following in the footsteps of her mother, who had also married a gay man, Judy knew that protective love was more important and far more lasting than carnal passion. While Minnelli and Judy looked good together, the very idea of their marriage was laughable to some industry members, incredible to others. Some of her best friends thought that her love for Minnelli was just a whim, one that would pass with time, until she met another desirable man. They were wrong. Judy couldn't function alone; she had to have a man in her life, even if he represented a compromise.

The critics' praise for *Meet Me in St. Louis* and *The Clock* suggested to Judy that Minnelli knew what was good for her, and that he was the right director for her. Considering how the project began, and that there had been a chance it would never be completed, the success of *The Clock* brought the couple happiness and made them feel closer to each other than ever before.

Judy could never separate professional from emotional relationships, and that kind of blend—or confusion, if you will—was at the very foundation of her marriage to Minnelli. In an interview with Adela Rogers St. John, held before her marriage to Minnelli, Judy said: "I made one mistake, I don't want to make another. I love my work. I know there are girls who can give up their work and get married and just live at home. I don't believe I could. So I have to have someone that understands about me and my work and thinks it's important. Vincente is wonderful. He's the most interesting man I've ever known. I don't know yet, maybe it will be right for us. We both know that a marriage can either be the most wonderful thing on earth, or it can gum up your whole life and spoil everything. We're thinking it over."

Then, talking to the other gossiper, Louella Parsons, Judy contradicted herself and said that she still missed the applause of live audiences, and that when her contract expired, she might leave Hollywood for Broadway.

Upon reading Louella's story, the studio got alarmed as Judy had been one of their biggest bankable stars. Though they could not force her to sign a new contract, Metro decided to give her a helpful "push" by encouraging her to marry Minnelli. From the studio's point of view, Minnelli was the ideal husband. If she were happily married to an M-G-M director who would cast her in his movies, she would not be able to work on Broadway. As simple as that.

Metro had another reason for approving the union. Though Judy behaved well during *The Clock,* she was still unstable. The studio reasoned that a reliable husband like Minnelli would be a steadying influence. Mayer chose Louella Parsons to convey the corporate line to her global readers: "Everyone at M-G-M is delighted with the Garland-Minnelli alliance. They say that Judy is a different girl, happy as she can be."

As soon as they decided to get married, Judy wrote to Minnelli's parents in Florida. "We haven't met, but Vincente has told me such wonderful stories about you and the tent theater that I feel I know you and also love you." Minnelli's mom and dad were absolutely charmed by Judy's letter, as they were by her frequent phone calls, usually made when Minnelli was not around.

"I want Mr. Mayer of my studio to be at my wedding," Judy had said before marrying her first husband. But this time, Mayer not only showed up, like a father, to give the bride away, he presented the happy couple with a wonderful present—three months away from the studio for a honeymoon in New York. Their first night as a married couple would be spent on the Super Chief.

Minnelli could never remember his proposal to Judy. Did he ever pop the question, as expected? All he recalled was saying, "I wish we'd be married." By his standards, this was a far more explicitly emotional statement than what he was used to. Judy was too perceptive to miss it.

One afternoon, when Judy was leaving her dressing room, she turned to Dottie Ponedel. "Dottie, I'm going to dinner tonight with Vincente and I think he's going to ask me to marry him." "Grab him," Dottie said, "if you love him." Dottie thought highly of Minnelli and she knew he would be good for Judy.

Minnelli had dated several women, mostly in platonic relationships. However, to the outside world, he always projected the image of the confirmed bachelor. Judy never knew how sensitive Minnelli was about his unattractive looks, his shy demeanor, his stutter. Nasty jokes circulated in town that Minnelli had once told a friend that he would never dare have children, fearing that "they might look like me."

Yolanda and the Thief was conceived as the next film for Minnelli to direct and for Fred Astaire to star in. A Latin-baroque reverie, it was based on Ludwig Bemelmans and Jacques Théry's short story, which was published in the July 1943 issue of *Town and Country* magazine. Freed composed the music himself and he asked his frequent collaborator, Harry Warren, to write the lyrics.

Lucille Bremer played Yolanda—not the best choice, but she was having an affair with Freed at the time and he promised to do something "special" for her. To persuade Minnelli, Freed pointed out that Lucille had "proven" to be a congenial dance partner for Astaire in *Ziegfeld Follies*. Minnelli was to direct *Yolanda and the Thief* right after *Ziegfeld Follies*. However, because of the crisis with *The Clock,* the priorities had changed.

With a budget of $2.4 million, *Yolanda and the Thief* began shooting on January 15, 1945, and was completed on time and on budget four months later. Realizing that the story was slim, Freed encouraged Minnelli to unleash his imagination as much as possible. As a result, he responded with a mishmash of subtropical romance, paganized Catholicism, and nocturnal hallucinations about guilty desire. No M-G-M musical had ever looked so strange in its mixture of bizarre, ill-fitting elements.

Bemelmans and Théry's outline was handled with fidelity in the screenplay. *Yolanda and the Thief* takes place in an imaginary South American utopia, called Latino in the story, Patria in the film. Bemelmans had a whimsical bent, but when writing for adults, his tone curdled into faux naïveté. *Yolanda and the Thief* had a cute premise, but no solid plot or real characters to speak of.

The story concerns a descendant of the Aquaviva clan, an orphan named Yolanda. Having reached legal age, Yolanda must leave the protection of the convent to take charge of the family legacy. Though otherwise vastly different, *Yolanda and the Thief* has a protagonist similar to the one in *Cabin in the Sky*, with both films celebrating heroines whose religious convictions inspire the reformation of the errant men in their lives. Nonetheless, whereas *Cabin in the Sky*'s Petunia is blessed with a genuinely selfless devotion, *Yolanda and the Thief*'s heroine is not convincing, and her very faith is shaken.

For a purported musical, *Yolanda and the Thief* is undernourished in songs and dances. The script was polished by Freed's regular team members: George Wells, Joseph Schrank (*Cabin in the Sky*), and Robert Nathan (who worked on, among other projects, *The Clock*). The final credit was given to Irving Brecher, who cowrote *Meet Me in St. Louis,* but the combined efforts of four writers resulted in an incoherent, uninvolving narrative.

The stylized characters inhabit a never-never land in a seemingly whimsical story. The thin plot, marred by an arch and cloying flavor, concerns an American con man name Lucre who tries to bilk a convent-bred Latin heiress of her millions by posing as her guardian angel.

The role of the thief's cohort in crime was tailor-made for Frank Morgan (of *The Wizard of Oz* fame), whose character is described as "the only bank embezzler in history who successfully juggled the books and then forgot to take the money." Yolanda's dithery Aunt Amarilla (Mildred Natwick) is too wacky, as is evident in her command, "Do my fingernails immediately and bring them to my room at once," which recalled Serena Blandish, the heroine of the musical that Minnelli had longed to mount a few years earlier.

What's missing is heart, an emotional center for the surrounding giddiness. It didn't help matters that Freed's score was the weakest of any of Minnelli's musicals, apart from *I Dood It.*

The film opens with a boy-soprano chorus singing the insipid lyrics of the Patria national anthem: "This is a day for love, this is a day for song. And all together we will merrily walk along." The Angel number in *Yolanda* recalls the far superior Kurt Weill song "Speak Low" from *One Touch of Venus*.

The hero, Johnny, encounters Yolanda in the same vein. His nightmare in dance is underlined by "Will You Marry Me?" sung by Bremer. The picture's one good number comes toward the end, with a refurbishment of an old Freed tune, "Java Junction," now called "Coffee Time." Though out of synch with the movie's Latin setting, this big-band swing number is the film's only spirited sequence, heightened by Minnelli's vivacious staging.

For all the novelty in intent, *Yolanda and the Thief* misfired in execution. The biggest error was casting Lucille Bremer in the title part of a good fairy. She was simply too frosty and too old to bring it off.

Astaire's extortionist is an unpleasant character who patronizingly harangues the ingénue by preying on her innocence and religious devotion. In fact, Yolanda's crooked pursuer was the most unsavory part Astaire had ever tackled. To project underworld nastiness in his scenes with Bremer, Astaire subdues his usual ebullience, lowers his voice to a monotone, and cynically rations his charm. Yolanda's thief provides the rough outlines for a persona that Astaire would embody in the future, including Minnelli's own *The Band Wagon*—the dour skeptic resigned to solitude until a younger, spirited heroine lures him out of his introverted world to join the real world.

Astaire's most ambitious number is a surrealistic dream ballet meant to symbolize the conflict between Lucille and Lucre. It begins promisingly as Astaire wanders from the heightened unreality of the village square into the stark Dalíesque landscape of his perturbed psyche, but the number collapses under the weight of pretentious imagery and mannered choreography.

Astaire's "Coffee Time" duet with Bremer is more appealing, perhaps because of its joyous movement. A Latin-accented jitterbug, the number recaptures the spontaneity Astaire had flaunted with Ginger Rogers in their RKO musicals, and is heightened by Minnelli's ostentatious scheme of color, a dazzling white, yellow, and brown. Nonetheless, *Yolanda and the Thief* demonstrated that there were limits to Minnelli's vision and that for his fantasy to reach truly high levels he needed to be given worthier material to work with.

The previews in New York and Los Angeles went over well, but the critical reaction was negative. *The New York Times's* Bosley Crowther gave the film its most favorable notice, noting that "taste and imagination are so rare" these days that Minnelli's film stood out. However, the reviewer Howard Barnes called the film "a pretentious bore." Most reviewers dismissed the script as inane, while some were offended by the idea of a con man passing for an angel. American audiences had shown tolerance for con men but they couldn't accept Astaire playing one, and doing it so raffishly.

A modestly budgeted movie like *Yolanda* should not have failed so miserably. But it did. The public didn't accept a simple story placed in an avant-garde setting. *Yolanda* became Minnelli's first big flop, slapped with negative reviews. The notices depressed him, since they totally contradicted his expectations. *Yolanda*'s failure disheartened Minnelli, who thought that the script was witty, but it just didn't play.

From the start, Freed worried that *Yolanda and the Thief* would end up looking like a laborious collage of ill-assorted parts, full of decorated visual audacity. Indeed, the public's response was tepid since the musical was too rarefied and too exquisite for audiences who were adjusting to the end of World War II and the beginning of the cold war. *Yolanda and the Thief* became the first major flop of the Freed Unit. Nonetheless, Minnelli's idiosyncratic daring is evident, and though a failure, the film remains superior to the pointless *I Dood It,* Minnelli's previous worst effort.

On Friday, June 15, 1945, five days after her twenty-third birthday, and with her divorce from David Rose final, Judy and Minnelli got married. The wedding ceremony took place at three o'clock in the afternoon at Judy's mother's house in the Wilshire district. Metro's Irene Gibbons, Cedric's wife, designed the dress, a smoky gray jersey with pink-pearl beading to match her engagement ring. Betty Asher served as her bridesmaid, and Ira Gershwin stepped in as Minnelli's best man. Minnelli's parents were not there because his father was too ill to make the trip from Florida.

It was meant to be a small wedding, just for the immediate family and close friends. In attendance were Freed and Metro's publicity head,

Howard Strickling. Minnelli was naturally nervous. Reverend William E. Roberts of the Beverly Hills Community Church performed the service. At the end of the ritual, he held out a wooden staff that was to be grasped, as a symbol of the union, by the four people standing in front of him: the bridesmaid, the best man, and the bride and groom. All four did as they were directed.

Because Minnelli's memories of the wedding were vague, he relied in his memoirs on Ira Gershwin's recollections: "Ira swears that, at the end of the ceremony, the minister brought out a symbolic wooden staff. He asked Betty to grasp it first, then Ira, followed by Judy and me. Then, out of nowhere came an alien hand [that] grasped the staff by the knob on top. It was Louis B. establishing his territorial imperative." "We were now man and wife in the eyes of God," Minnelli noted. "But what's more, we also had the blessing of a man upstairs who in many instilled far greater dread."

For all of his sophistication, Minnelli sincerely believed in astrology. Born on June 10, Judy was a Gemini, and Geminis were known to be happy and high-spirited one moment, depressed and moody the next. Also, Minnelli had heard that left-handed people like Judy were cursed with explosive tempers, but he resolved to disregard that weakness too. None of these traits were evident during their honeymoon in New York, and Judy seemed to be as happy as she could ever be.

Shortly before the marriage, Judy began working on *The Harvey Girls,* and Minnelli began preparing *Yolanda and the Thief.* Then, out of the blue, Minnelli received a call from his aunt Amy to inform him that his mother had died. Her damaged heart had just given out.

Minnelli had to make that sad trip by himself; Judy couldn't join him, because of work. It was a long, painful journey, first to New Orleans, then on to Miami and St. Petersburg, Florida, but he arrived in time for the funeral.

Though an invalid himself, Minnelli's father held up nicely, insisting on paying tribute to his wife by going through the proceedings of a wake and a respectful church burial. Minnelli returned to Judy's comforting arms. As always, work proved to be a "healthy distraction" (in Minnelli's words) from life's sadness and tragedy.

———

Deeply in love, Minnelli was determined to make his marriage last forever. The Minnellis went to New York for their honeymoon. In the summer of 1945, New York felt like an ongoing festival. Minnelli saw the city anew through his wife's fresh eyes, sharing with her the joys of rediscovery. They were too much in love and too caught up in the buzz of the town to allow any anxieties to spoil their fun. The Minnellis rented an apartment on Sutton Place for three months, courtesy of Louis B. Mayer.

Arriving in Manhattan on the morning of June 18, 1945, the newlyweds had breakfast in their three-story penthouse whose terrace gardens overlooked the East River below. As they had planned, the pair settled in right away, pretending to be real New Yorkers.

Judy absorbed the sights, the sounds, the atmosphere like a sponge, with Minnelli as her proud and knowing guide. Minnelli sought out little Italian restaurants and bakeries he had known while living in Greenwich Village. Consciously or not, they behaved like the lovers in *The Clock*, except that unlike the screen couple they had three months, not hours, to enjoy the city.

Minnelli and Judy looked forward to a fresh start, a life free of the drugs and depressions. Judy's reliance on pills, always a sensitive and painful issue, could not be avoided in New York. Minnelli told her that he always knew when his actors were on drugs, because they were thin, nervous, and withdrawn. She did not tell him that in her family, even without pills, the women were easily irritable and hysterical as a result of weight fluctuations and slight, if also permanent, depression.

One night, as they walked along the East River, Judy asked her husband to hold her hand. She drew a bottle of pills from her purse and in a gesture of hope threw it into the dark river. Then she threw another vial of pills into the water. "I'll never take them again," she said, a victorious declaration over a cruel enemy that had afflicted her most of her life.

Minnelli was deeply moved. He knew it would be difficult for Judy not to use pills, and just hoped that the abstinence would at least last for years. He was not aware of the fears and phobias that assailed her, which none of her future psychiatrists would be able to diagnose. Minnelli knew only that Judy was the best companion he'd ever had—when she was not on medication.

"Whenever I came to New York before," Judy told the press, "I lived in a hotel for two weeks and then rushed on to another city." On this visit, for the first time, Judy was able to enjoy herself and be a woman of leisure, with money to spend, a maid, and a cook. Minnelli proved a devoted husband who took care of all of her needs except for one—sex.

On their trip to New York the previous year, Judy had met some of Minnelli's friends. Now she met the rest, including his old companion, Lester Gaba. Gaba joined them for dinner one night. At first, the conversation was strained. She could tell that Gaba was still in love with Minnelli and still completely stunned by their marriage. In fact, mutual friends reported that Gaba was not just upset by Minnelli's marriage, he was utterly crushed. Gaba knew that the relationship he had had with Minnelli, problematic as that had been, was over, and now his hope that they would maintain a close personal contact was dashed.

If Judy expressed any irritation during their honeymoon, it revolved around her still-dominant image as a child star. Judy yearned for satin pajamas and up hairdos, but the studio forcibly dressed her in blue gingham pinafores and red patent leather Mary Janes. "I'll probably qualify for Social Security and play my first love scene in the same week," she used to joke.

Minnelli's friends had planned a busy schedule of parties and shows. Judy was taken with the excitement of such spontaneous evenings. The soirées stood in sharp contrast to the predictability of the Hollywood social scene, with its lists of announced guests. Because guests had to drive long distances, events in Los Angeles had to be arranged weeks in advance, and there was little unplanned socializing.

It was in New York that Minnelli realized how deeply Judy had affected people. She projected the same warmth and friendliness offscreen as she did onscreen. Taking long walks on those summer nights, she was treated by people on the streets with love and familiarity. She finally understood why Metro insisted on maintaining her image as the world's eternal adolescent.

"Hi ya, Judy!" a truck driver called while driving. "Howza, kid?"

"Is that you, Judy?" an old woman asked.

"Yes," she giggled, "and this is my husband. His name is Vincente Minnelli, and he's a very fine movie director." Refusing to play the imperious grande dame, Judy enjoyed being approached by strangers.

An unexpected incident almost marred their honeymoon: the disappearance of their dog, Gobo (named after Minnelli's lover with the *o*'s substituting for the *a*'s in his name). When they took the cross-country train back East, they decided that only Gobo, the more neurotic of Minnelli's two black poodles, would come with them. The dog and Judy had a special rapport—it would have been cruel to keep them apart.

The Minnellis were spending an evening with friends, their car parked outside a nightclub, with Gobo in the backseat. As it was a very hot and humid night, they left the car's windows wide open. The fans, recognizing that this was Judy's car, must have frightened Gobo and he jumped out.

Minnelli and some of the fans ran in search of Gobo, but they couldn't find him. There were also periodic reports from the police. Later, as the rumors spread, people came up and reported that they'd seen Gobo at such and such location, at such and such time. Most of the reports were of course false or fabricated but for a good reason. Minnelli knew that Judy's fans were just seeking an excuse to talk to her.

After hours of frantic but fruitless search, the Minnellis returned to their apartment. But Judy was inconsolable, too hysterical and upset to fall asleep. Something had to be done. Yet even when she seemed out of control, she showed resourcefulness. She picked up the phone and called the police. "This is Judy Garland," she said, waiting for the thought to sink in on the other end of the line before explaining the problem in detail. A couple of officers hung up on her in disbelief—the real Judy Garland calling the police for a lost dog!

It was close to dawn when Gobo was found on the docks. The capricious dog didn't give up without a fight; he jumped into the river. Gobo was quickly fished out and delivered back to them. His coat covered with tar, looking like a contaminated bird, he was a sight to behold. Gobo's return was a grand emotional reunion with Judy; her cries and whimpers of relief were joined by the dog's whines.

Minnelli volunteered to wash up the dog. He took off his clothes and jumped into the tub with Gobo, but any tar he got off the dog stuck to his own skin. It took hours to clean up both of them. Minnelli wondered how successful they would have been in finding Gobo if his wife were not Judy Garland, and he was thankful that her fans had dropped everything to help.

Judy encountered the same warm attitude among the sophisticated theater crowd. Her unique brand of savage humor did the trick. Initially expecting the squeaky-clean whiteness of her sweet screen image, based on *The Wizard of Oz* and her movies with Mickey Rooney, they instead found spice and guts. Minnelli's friends were enchanted by Judy's sense of malice. Her self-effacing wit and disrespect for Hollywood captivated those who, like her, felt victimized by the system.

Judy showed that she could be just as perceptive about the theater as were New York connoisseurs. By dismissing a current show with a short aside or a cocked eyebrow, Judy proved herself a pro. For example, *Oklahoma!* was too wholesome for Judy's jaded viewpoint. She took a line from one of the show's songs as her opinion: "The corn is as high as an elephant's eye." At the same time, though she was familiar with all the tricks used by the players in *Carousel,* she was so transported by the story that she cried all the way home. Then again she could trade the most sarcastic comments. Years later she described Robert Goulet's shiny good looks as an "eight-by-ten glossy," a jibe he would suffer from.

Judy had the makings of a vagabond, a vulnerable one, and Minnelli's friends sought to protect her. She summoned her effusive charm, bowling them over with the sheer force of her personality. Judy could will people into adoring her, no matter who they were. After all, she had been doing it all her life with larger, more demanding, and paying audiences. When her self-effacing wit and genuine concern for others failed, she fell back on her greatest weapon, her incredible vulnerability. No one could resist Judy's brand of defenselessness.

The Minnellis went to see Tennessee Williams's *The Glass Menagerie*, starring Laurette Taylor in one of the greatest performances in theater history. Responding to Taylor's genius, Judy's face was covered with tears. After the show, she declared that this was the dramatic height to which every actor should aspire.

Judy was eager to meet Taylor to tell her how touched she was by her brilliant portrayal. Backstage, she was prepared to kneel at the feet of the legendary actress. But, in turn, Taylor's reaction to Judy Garland was that of a movie fan wanting to know all about her as a movie star.

Minnelli was shocked to see the severe toll that Taylor's heavy drinking had taken (though it might have benefited and made more poignant her performance as a faded Southern belle). Taylor was averse to talking about her art, but Judy refused to settle for that, demanding to know more about her approach to acting, preparations for the part, consistency of performance night after night.

Judy was thrilled to have met this singular artist. Observing the two women together, Minnelli became aware of the similarities between them, which might explain the immediate, intense bond they established. Both women brought a highly individual and tragic quality to their work. Both were victims of excess, which nearly destroyed their talents. The difference was that Taylor's drinking problems were behind her, whereas Judy's hadn't yet begun. When Taylor died the following year, Minnelli had to convey the tragic news to Judy; she was devastated.

Although they had their friends and the theater world to distract them, the Minnellis still found time to grow more intimate together. In later years, Minnelli would say that, like everyone else, they were awed by the dropping of the atomic bomb in Hiroshima, but couldn't recall where they were at the time or how they reacted to the news of the Japanese surrender. Being together, they ignored the madness on the streets, though their friends didn't allow them to isolate themselves for very long.

In New York, Eleanor Lambert took Judy under her wing, accompanying her to fashion shows. They traded tips, Eleanor cueing Judy on fashion, and Judy passing on to Eleanor her makeup tricks. (Under pressure, Judy could apply makeup quicker than any other artist on the M-G-M lot.) Both Minnelli and Judy envied Eleanor's organizational skills, her ability to work a full day at the office and then go home to host a huge dinner party.

In her efforts to play the gracious hostess, Judy emulated her friend. The Minnellis decided to entertain all of their New York friends at a dinner party. Besides Eleanor, the guest list included Moss Hart and his vivacious wife, Kitty Carlisle, S. N. Behrman, Oscar and Dorothy Hammerstein, Bea Lillie, and Harold Arlen. Judy organized every detail, down to the candles in big red snifters, placed on the tables on the terraces, but once the caterers arrived, she became a guest at her own party. Minnelli was very proud. "I think I'll keep you," he told her after the guests left. "My dear sir, you do me such great honor," she said mockingly.

The Minnellis' honeymoon coincided with New York at its most exciting. History was being made: Just days after the Minnellis' arrival, millions of jubilant New Yorkers took to the streets to welcome the triumphant General Dwight Eisenhower. In August, when Japan accepted the terms of surrender, there were more crowds and glorious parades. "Never again would that city of tall towers and even taller egos be enveloped in the New York of yesterday," observed *The New York Times* the day after Japan surrendered. In what was an exciting coincidence, a new era was beginning for the world as well as for the newly married couple.

While still in New York, Minnelli had to deny a newspaper report that he and Judy planned to adopt a child. He said they hoped to have many babies of their own—"until we have a good-sized family." That time arrived sooner than either of them had anticipated. At the end of August, about ten days before they returned to California, Minnelli took Judy to a Park Avenue doctor, who confirmed that she was pregnant.

They conspired not to let anyone know, and used the three days on the train to decide how to tell Metro the news. Metro had proven unsympathetic to Judy's previous illnesses, because they had kept her away from work. Pregnancy and childbirth might be perceived the same way—and for the same reason.

Without consulting her husband, a petrified Judy called her mother in California. "I'm going to have a baby, Mama," she said. Remembering how her mother had forced her to have an abortion while she was married to David Rose, she asked a peculiar question, "Do you mind?" To Judy's surprise, Ethel was delighted with the news. Freed and Mayer were also genuinely happy for the Minnellis. "These were our happiest times together," Minnelli would say of the first months of his marriage.

Hoping to use her once more before her pregnancy began to show, the studio speeded up its schedule of the Jerome Kern biopic, *Till the Clouds Roll By.* The picture was not so much intended as a portrait of Kern's life as an excuse for a parade of his songs to be delivered by Metro's glorious ensemble. With three songs, Judy's part was small, but Metro, hoping to lure Judy into a contract, assigned Minnelli to direct her songs and dramatic scenes. Rehearsals began on September 17, 1945, about two weeks after the couple's return from New York.

Ten

Husband and Father

ON THEIR RETURN FROM THEIR HONEYMOON, the Minnellis set out to work on what would be their first professional collaboration during their marriage. Freed was preparing a musical biography of Jerome Kern, entitled *Till the Clouds Roll By,* with an all-star cast. Judy, the studio's top singing star, was cast as Broadway's musical comedy luminary Marilyn Miller.

Less than a month after production began, in October 1945, Kern died suddenly, which forced a major rewrite of the script. In the six months it took to shoot the film, Freed lined up one director after another. Busby Berkeley, not the best choice to begin with, lasted only a few weeks. Henry Koster replaced Berkeley, but he contributed little before he, too, was replaced. In the end, Richard Whorf received solo directorial credit, a dubious achievement since the film's song-medley finale, with Sinatra in white tails crooning "Ol' Man River," was directed (uncredited) by George Sidney.

Choreographer Robert Alton was the only key member of the creative team to stay on board throughout. By necessity, with so many chefs involved, the finished film lacked a unified vision. Minnelli's sequences aside, this musical is an example of moviemaking-by-committee.

Minnelli staged Judy's sequences, and was acknowledged in the opening credits. Because of Judy's pregnancy, her scenes were the first to be shot, in October 1945, and Minnelli had to come up with some clever staging to hide his wife's condition.

Till the Clouds Roll By was the first and blandest of M-G-M biopics about Broadway's composers, a cycle that included tributes to Rodgers and Hart (*Words and Music,* 1948), Kalmar and Ruby (*Three Little Words,* 1950), and Sigmund Romberg (*Deep in My Heart,* 1954).

The story centers on Kern's courtship of his future wife, Eva Kern (played by novice actress Dorothy Patrick). It also deals with Kern's life-long friendship with song arranger James Hessler and the latter's rebellious child. But, inexplicably, the movie never mentions Kern's own daughter. At least seven writers worked on the script, the parameters to which were constricted by Freed's reverence for Kern. Kern was played by Robert Walker with a solemn dignity; as his pal Hessler, Van Heflin was mediocre, and Lucille Bremer, as Hessler's irritable daughter, was utterly miscast.

Unfortunately, there was too much story and not enough musical specialties. Since the songs were listless, the film's popular singers, Lena Horne, Dinah Shore, Kathryn Grayson, and Tony Martin, could project little personality. Only a few numbers show some vitality, such as Angela Lansbury's music hall turn.

The freshness of the three Minnelli sequences, which appear in the middle of the picture, only underlines the surrounding dullness. Judy's Marilyn Miller is first seen at the opening-night intermission of her 1920 triumph, *Sally.* The setting is essential Minnelli: the anteroom to the star's dressing room is a cherry-red chamber with white Grecian busts, each crowned by the top hats of Miller's admirers. Miller acknowledges the praise of her fans, and plans the next costume change with her dresser, while humming a new arrangement with the conductor.

In one extraordinary take, Minnelli follows Judy as she strides through the wings past the multicolored spotlights onstage toward the unlit set—a restaurant sink with dirty dishes. After checking the placement of her props with the stage manager, she gets the spotlight. In a quiet but emotional voice, she sings Kern's "Look for the Silver Lining," which Miller had introduced. The lyrics' wistfulness are underscored by her concentration on mundane tasks, keeping her hair out of her face and her sleeves out of the sink's suds.

Up to this point, every song in the film had been staged as a tableau seen from the audience's perspective, concluding with shots of their applause. But here, the public's presence is indicated only by the play of lights on Judy's face as the curtains close and she basks in applause. Approached from the performer's point of view, the sequence is about the magic of live musical comedy, the combination of professionalism under pressure and the high caliber of talent, which made both Marilyn Miller and Judy the stars that they were. In the process, Judy, in a rare happy phase, becomes a legend in the making. Unlike the other stiff performers, she comes across both as flesh and blood and larger than life.

From the intimate feeling of *Sally,* Minnelli shifts to the spectacular numbers from the Kern-Miller musical *Sunny,* with a set that represents a dazzlingly colorful circus. The sequence, which was inspired by Minnelli's childhood memories, opens with vertiginous lines in a shot taken from atop the offstage rafters, and a red spotlight is seen before the whole set is flushed with lights. The center ring, done in scarlet and white, reveals a marching band in red uniforms and gold-sprayed elephants surrounded by attendants in Indian silks. Then tightrope walkers are shown in silhouette against a big canvas, waiting for Judy, clad in white tutu, to enter.

Since Judy was four months pregnant when shooting began in October 1945, Minnelli had her sing the song and then run behind a group of extras while her double jumped on a pony for a rapid gallop around the gold-colored ring. It had to look as if the number was being done on a stage, and so a boom camera swept in to cover the action.

Minnelli was the proudest of staging the *Sunny* sequence, a number that was meant to convey the essence of circus life. His gift for blending seemingly disparate details creates a surprising visual harmony, keyed with precision to the accompanying music. As a tribute to the magic of the circus, Minnelli exploits the screen for spectacle, building toward a dizzying final image. The camera captures a spinning female aerialist catapulting herself in great arcs over the antics below. From the title song, Minnelli dissolves to a more subdued scheme for the number "Who?" in which Judy reflects another, more sophisticated facet of Marilyn Miller's rich persona.

Oscar Hammerstein's lyrics proved jovial, as Judy croons, "Whoooo stole my heart away?" to ardent chorus boys doffing their top hats one by one. Though not as elaborately staged, "Who?" prefigures Minnelli's "I'll Build a Stairway to Paradise" in *An American in Paris*. Flanked by the men, Judy glides airily down a white staircase to deliver a carefree solo. Alton's choreography is accentuated by the monochromatic chic of Minnelli's concept. The chorus is dressed in black and white, and the star in yellow chiffon is the only spot of color. "Who?" flaunts the ever-shifting mobility of Minnelli's camera. Most of Alton's numbers are stagy, but in this one Minnelli recaptures the glory of a bygone theatrical era in uniquely fluent screen terms. However, Judy felt that her pregnancy showed in the last number, a glamorous mounting with a huge chorus and spiral stairway. She felt ridiculous, running up to each man in the scene and singing the question, "Who?"

A formulaic biopicture, *Till the Clouds Roll By* was planned as yet another all-star extravaganza. How could these pictures be entertaining and realistic, Minnelli wondered, when much of the musician's work—actually composing—was visually static, not to mention the avoidance in the screenplay of any controversial personal material. It was simply not cinematic enough to show a composer sitting at a piano or talking about his songs. This is the reason Minnelli never made another musical biopicture despite their popularity at the time.

Fortunately, her songs didn't take long to shoot, and Minnelli was able to complete his work in two weeks. Judy then retired to await her baby's birth. For her, those months were the longest of being professionally inactive since she had arrived at Metro. By 1945, she had made twenty-three films, and the demands on her energy and health were excessive. Minnelli had to report daily for work at the studio, so it became Judy's responsibility to supervise the expansion of their house: the building of a nursery, an enlarged kitchen, and another dressing room.

Shortly after their marriage, Minnelli and Judy made a decision not to bring their work problems home. Minnelli felt that talking about their problems was ineffective, and it usually left both of them depressed. Besides, he was much more productive and resourceful in the morning. Instead, they would have the typical conversations that all parents have. The real challenge for two pros consumed by work was how to implement this impossibly difficult decision.

When rumors began to spread in town that Judy was suffering from a slight depression, Minnelli asked her to deny them Accordingly, she gave interviews to confirm that everything was just perfect. "Actually," she asserted to the *Los Angeles Times,* "I haven't felt much better during my whole life." Minnelli was relieved to see her well enough to sing on the radio and at a memorial for Jerome Kern at the Hollywood Bowl.

For a full year after *Till the Clouds Roll By,* Judy didn't have to worry about work and was allowed the luxury of idleness. The Metro brass was right in predicting that marriage would confine Judy to Hollywood. How could she leave her husband and baby for Broadway? In November 1946, Judy caved in to Metro and signed a new five-year contract. The studio was so eager for Judy to resume work that it canceled her old contract, which still had a year to run.

The new agreement boosted her pay from $3,000 to $6,000 a week, more than double the $2,500 a week Minnelli was making. "Judy always said that M-G-M was home," Louella Parsons wrote to her fans, "and when you get right down to it, there's still no place like home, even to a movie star."

By the end of 1946, Judy had worked at Metro for eleven years, or half of her life. She had grown up inside its protective walls, navigating through a perilous adolescence, broken love affairs, and two marriages. But she felt that while Metro protected her, it also imprisoned her. She continued to complain to Minnelli about the early-morning calls, the unrelenting pressures, the condescending attitudes. No matter how much Minnelli reassured her of her talent and stature, Judy felt that for Metro she was still the ugly duckling, Mayer's little hunchback. It would take Minnelli two years to realize that the damage to Judy's ego was permanent, beyond repair.

All of Judy's suppressed anger burst out within days of signing her new contract. Immediately regretting her decision, she believed she had turned the key in the lock to her own prison. The tensions building up in her against the studio hit the boiling point, and she told her husband, "Every day I go to work with tears in my eyes, and resistance in my heart and mind."

After Artie Shaw, Mankiewicz, Welles, and the other macho men she'd been involved with, Judy found Minnelli to be a gentleman of great taste. However, except for the brief flings with Mankiewicz and Welles, to date, she had never had a satisfying long-term sexual relationship. Sex with first husband David Rose was acceptable but the marriage didn't last long. Minnelli's approach to sex was detached and passive, clearly lacking much heat. Judy told her friends that Minnelli enjoyed the foreplay more than the actual intercourse, and she complained that he took forever to get a hard-on, and even longer to climax. The easiest way to please her husband was oral sex.

The Minnellis wanted to project to their friends and to the outside world the image of a happy Hollywood couple, gracious hosts of parties at their home and desirable guests at others'. They socialized with Kay Thompson and Bill Spear at least twice a week. At their own parties, they encouraged the guests to play intricate word games, poke fun at foreign films dubbed in English, and indulge in gossip, at which Judy excelled. The regulars at the Minnellis' house included Johnny Green, the composer-conductor, Ira Gershwin and his wife Lee, Oscar Levant and his wife June. Minnelli enjoyed himself the most when he was among his intimate clique of witty friends.

Nonetheless, Minnelli and Judy could not have been more different. He was orderly; she was disorganized. He was methodical and predictable; she was spontaneous and erratic. Every day after work, Minnelli would have only one dry martini before dinner, then retire to his library of art books and read until it was time to go to bed.

Minnelli did not care for glitzy parties, while Judy loved big events. Making sure that no journalists were around, Judy would go to those parties with an escort, often one of her gay friends, or Van Johnson, rumored to be bisexual, who was a favored companion until he got married. On more than one occasion, she didn't return home all night, crashing at one of her gay friends' houses, often with a sexual partner.

Once in bed, Minnelli would fall asleep right away and would snore so loudly that Judy couldn't sleep. She would lie there exhausted, yet wide-awake because of the noise he was making. Finally, one night, out of frustration, Judy hit him and broke his nose, forcing them to rush to the hospital in the middle of the night.

Early on, the couple decided that Minnelli would run the household, which meant paying the bills, supervising the work of the gardener and the cook, and even overseeing the dinner parties. While Judy was capable of cooking, her repertoire was limited to some favorite foods. On occasion, and rather erratically, Judy emerged from her lethargy to seize domesticity, as if she were taking on a new screen role. Her efforts were haphazard and short-lived but typically obsessive. "What pleased me most about Judy's homemaking was not that she did it well, but that she bothered to do it at all," Minnelli fondly remembered. Occasionally and surprisingly, she set out to be the model housewife. But like her husband, she had a short attention span, and her efforts came in spurts. Minnelli rationalized to himself that if he had wanted a domesticated wife, he would have married another type of woman.

Despite some growing tensions between them, these were Minnelli's happiest times. Their life together was even happy by Hollywood standards. They weren't falling prey to the *Star Is Born* syndrome, where one partner is on the way up while the other is going down. Minnelli wanted to believe that in time he and Judy would raise a whole brood of children.

Once the remodeling was completed, they settled into their Hollywood hills house, which was decorated in a lavish style. As money was streaming in weekly from M-G-M, no indulgence was too extravagant. Minnelli's friends were collecting French impressionist art, but he had no desire to invest in fine art. Instead, he continued to cultivate his passion for beautiful art books, which gave him the illusion that he actually owned the world's greatest paintings.

Up until then, Minnelli had not given much thought to his and Judy's disparate interests. Once they settled down, the Minnellis tried to mesh their markedly different personalities and lifestyles, making special effort to present to the world a balanced couple with a unified style.

Minnelli often accompanied Judy to the jewelry and antique auctions she enjoyed. Having been introduced to designer clothes by Eleanor Lambert, she also began to frequent fashion shows. She said she desired a totally new and mature wardrobe after their baby's birth.

Judy wasn't as unschooled or anti-intellectual as she pretended to be. Minnelli hoped that, as Judy matured, her knowledge would broaden. For her part, she hoped that Minnelli's shy and reserved demeanor would diminish and he would become more emotionally demonstrative and socially outgoing.

Minnelli determined that if his wife stumbled, he would be there for her. But he also was resolute not to force upon her his attitudes. He told his friends, "Why would I want to play Svengali to one of nature's already adorable creatures?" Deep down, though, Minnelli felt that Judy still had a lot of growing up to do, and he was committed to helping her achieve her full potential. Deeply in love, his motto was: "Together we would be sensible; together we would be adult. Whatever was best for her was best for me."

From time to time, Judy would get compulsions. One day she went down on her knees to scrub the kitchen floor, despite the fact that the maids had already done it. The next day, she tried out a recipe for chicken fricassee. On another occasion, she might bring home a needlepoint kit. Her close friend, the actress Sylvia Sidney, had urged Judy to take up needlepoint as a way to calm her jangled nerves.

When Judy decided to bake a cake, it was a momentous event. The effort called for compliments. "Terrific, sweetheart," Minnelli would say, as she set up the ingredients on a kitchen counter. Their cook stood beside Judy, cleaning up after her, since she used every pan in the kitchen; every surface was coated with flour when Judy was baking. Cleaning up the mess was delegated to the servants.

After dinner, the cake, whether fallen in the middle or with gooey frosting running off the plate, was brought out ceremoniously, an occasion that called for another effusive compliment.

"No, I don't think it's lopsided. I think it's delicious," Minnelli said. After one bite, he felt forced to outdo himself and say, "This is without doubt the best cake I've ever eaten."

Minnelli found Judy's need for constant approval pathological. As soon as she finished washing the kitchen floor, he had to reassure her that it was the cleanest floor in the world. If she became bored with doing needlepoint, he had to reassure her that the few stitches made were the most uniform that ever existed.

The Minnellis ran a casual household. Judy became pals with the cook, the nurse, the housekeeper, and the driver, and could not impose any discipline on them. Minnelli would come home from work to find Judy in the midst of a conspiracy with the helpers. The muffled laughter and shifting eyes told Minnelli they were keeping something from him. Minnelli thus became the ogre in the setup, the force to be reckoned with when things went wrong. Cast by Judy as the heavy, Minnelli tried to speak to the servants authoritatively, but her giggling indicated just how ineffective and absurd he was. They both would burst out laughing at his ridiculous efforts to play the housemaster.

Judy felt the most comfortable in her dressing room or the bathroom. Minnelli had designed the rooms, covering the walls in antique glass and furnishing the rooms with Victorian papier-mâché objets d'art. In her hideaway, she relaxed on her fur-covered chaise, sitting there for hours. By now she had graduated from movie magazines and romantic novels to serious fiction and biographies. She also began reading the national periodicals and, for the first time, began paying attention to film reviews. When Judy disagreed with the reviews, she became a most articulate critic, particularly when Minnelli's work was concerned.

Minnelli began shooting the noir melodrama *Undercurrent* at about the same time that Judy's physician recommended, due to her narrow pelvis, a Caesarean. To Minnelli's surprise, Judy's reaction was calm, and there was no need for barbiturates or amphetamines. She wanted a perfect child so much that she completely kept away from pills during her pregnancy.

The Minnellis told themselves a hundred times, "We don't care if it's a boy or a girl, so long as it's a healthy and happy child." But they did care, and both wanted a girl. Choosing the baby's name, however, proved to be a bigger problem. They had settled on Vincente Junior if it was a boy, but a name for the girl eluded them. Late one night, Judy nudged Minnelli awake.

"How about Liza?" she asked.

Judy knew that her husband loved the Gershwin song, and that it would be a tribute to Ira to use the title of his song for their child's name.

Minnelli readily agreed. "You know," he told Judy, "I've always wanted to name a child after my mother. Could we call her Liza May?"

"Perfect!" Judy said before drifting off to sleep.

Judy was making last-minute arrangements. By that time, the remodeling was complete, and the layette installed. Even the godparents were selected: Kay Thompson, Minnelli's longtime friend, and her husband, Bill Spear.

On Friday afternoon, March 8, 1946, Minnelli drove Judy to the Cedars of Lebanon Hospital. She experienced some of the inevitable fears, while Minnelli settled in for a long, long wait. The Caesarean section was scheduled for the following Tuesday, March 12. That morning, at 7:58, Judy gave birth to a girl weighing six pounds, ten and a half ounces. Soon after he was informed that he was the father of a baby girl, Minnelli was allowed to see Liza.

When the pregnancy was announced, many at Metro had joked, considering Minnelli's bisexuality and effeminacy, that the baby must have been the product of immaculate conception. However, physically, with her dark hair, long lashes, and big brown eyes, Liza was clearly Minnelli's baby. Upon seeing her, the proud daddy proclaimed, "My baby is the most beautiful baby in the nursery!" To him, Liza was a perfect baby with absolutely no wrinkles. Upon seeing her dad, Liza let out her first cry. Minnelli went home that night on cloud nine, telling all of his friends that Liza was "Projecting! Big!"

In the fall, after giving birth and regaining her strength, Judy invited some fan magazine reporters to the Evanview Drive house to photograph her with Liza. "She really loves water," Judy told reporters as they were watching her give Liza a bath. "I expect she'll be at least a champion swimmer." But Minnelli knew that the bath was mostly for show, since all the daily chores were handled by Liza's nurse. In fact, when the nurse took her first day off, Judy confided in Minnelli that she was terrified of being alone with the six-month-old baby.

For the next six months, Minnelli's workdays at Metro seemed interminable. Minnelli the father couldn't wait to get home to his new family.

Undercurrent, Minnelli's first try at film noir, was based on an Edward Chodorov screenplay, from a story by Thelma Strabel. Producer Pandro Berman had already cast Katharine Hepburn as the star, and she had approval of both director and leading man. Pandro was a rough guy, all business and no intellectual pretensions. His violent temper was notorious, particularly around selfish actors, for whom he had no patience.

Berman's showman instincts pointed toward Minnelli, though he was an unknown quantity with the noir genre. Minnelli was a strange choice, having done only one previous drama, *The Clock*. Hepburn's adoration of Berman, stemming from their long history of working at RKO, combined with Chodorov's friendship, made her eager to start working. "I'm sure we'll get along," she told Minnelli when they first met. To Minnelli, it sounded like both an order and a threat. He had never met anyone with such self-assurance, and she made him nervous.

This melodrama, about a young woman married to a psychopath (played by a miscast Robert Taylor), was sabotaged by the absurd casting of Hepburn as a frail, defenseless woman. During the first few weeks, the star locked horns with Minnelli. The movie required an acting style different from the one she was comfortable with. Suspense did not demand in-depth probing. Failing to find the right key, Hepburn played the part mechanically, accompanied by an elaborate musical score that was "borrowed" from Brahms.

During the shoot, Robert Taylor became totally insecure, fearing that his director was throwing all the good scenes to Hepburn and that Robert Mitchum, who was playing his brother, was stealing the show as the new star just by his sheer youth and physical presence. Though Taylor had gotten over his pretty-boy image, he was not a particularly skillful actor and it was not easy for him to disguise his charm, as his part required. The audience simply couldn't accept him as a menacing murderer.

To get "the mad dog expression," as Minnelli put it, from Taylor, he suggested that he do the long scene in the stable without blinking, hoping that Taylor's eyes would get wider and have a teary, fanatic look. They did so many takes of that scene that the effort reddened his eyes and Taylor had to be sent to the dispensary for medical care. Another device Minnelli used to increase the effectiveness of Taylor's performance was to hang a lantern and blow it in the wind to accompany the dialogue and action. The hypnotic movement of the swinging lantern compelled Taylor to act more forcefully.

For Hepburn, the problem was not Minnelli or Taylor, but Robert Mitchum. Loaned out to M-G-M, he too was miscast in *Undercurrent*, never feeling comfortable as Robert Taylor's sensitive brother. Hepburn took out her anger toward the film on Mitchum. "You can't act," she told him bluntly, in front of Minnelli and the crew. "If you hadn't been good-looking, you would never have gotten the picture. I'm tired of working with people who have nothing to offer."

Minnelli, however, was impressed with Mitchum, as he later said: "Few actors I've worked with bring so much of themselves to a picture, and *none* do it [with] such a lack of affectation as Mitchum does." Minnelli thought that Mitchum was underestimating his ability during the shoot, but Mitchum was exhausted: he was working on *Undercurrent* in the morning, on *The Locket* (at RKO) in the evening, and sometimes on *Desire Me* (back at M-G-M), in the afternoon. It was an absurd situation that continued for twenty-six days without a break.

Undercurrent turned out to be a disaster. Mitchum later referred contemptuously to the film as *Underdrawers*. With its glossy look and painted backdrops rather than real locations, the result was a fake picture. Here and there, Minnelli managed to produce the right mood, despite the fraudulent story. All along, Hepburn knew that Minnelli would much rather be working with an actress more suitable for the role, such as Ingrid Bergman, who had scored big two years before in Cukor's suspenseful noir melodrama *Gaslight*.

However, despite initial tension, Hepburn gradually grew to like and to know Minnelli both personally and professionally. Immediately recognizing Judy's shaky emotional state, Hepburn tried to be helpful and more considerate on the set with Minnelli, even when he was completely inarticulate. Not having children of her own, she took an especially keen interest in Judy's health and Liza's progress.

Though both Hepburn and Judy were under contract at Metro, they had never been close. Frequently they found themselves seated next to each other under hair dryers in the makeup department, but they seldom socialized. Minnelli often told the story of Hepburn's first visit to their house, when she took Judy's hands, looked her in the eye, and bluntly said, "You have one big trouble—your talent." It was known in Hollywood that the capricious Hepburn really cared for troubled people who were greatly talented—people like Judy.

Hepburn was the first to come to the house, when Judy was shaky or unstable, and she was always pragmatic, as Minnelli recalled: "Kate does not presume—unless there's a crisis." Extremely athletic, she forced Judy to get up early and take morning walks. Drawing on her experience with Spencer Tracy, who was frequently drunk and insomniac, Hepburn relieved Judy's sleeping problems by trying to distract her with various activities. On more than one occasion, Minnelli overheard Hepburn talking to Judy as a big sister. Like many other friends, she also tried to stop Judy from heavy drinking and drugs, but to no avail.

Eleven

The Great Debacle: *The Pirate*

MINNELLI FIRST DISCUSSED THE IDEA OF filming *The Pirate* with Judy during their honeymoon in New York, asking her to read S. N. Behrman's play, which she did right away with great pleasure.

"Let's make it into a musical," she later suggested, thinking it was her idea.

"Absolutely," Minnelli said, whereupon he called Freed in Hollywood.

At first, Freed resisted the idea, but after reading the treatment, he grudgingly agreed to produce the film. *The Pirate* was marketed as Minnelli and Judy's next big project, after the cameo role she had played as Marilyn Miller in *Till the Clouds Roll By*.

Though Behrman's play, written for Alfred Lunt and Lynn Fontanne, was the couple's only Broadway show that was not successful, Minnelli felt that its failure was caused by the particular interpretation of the stars, which he didn't like, not by the text itself. The celebrated duo played it like a farce, instead of doing it straight—the only way Minnelli believed farce should be played.

Given the success of *For Me and My Gal* in 1942, Freed urged Minnelli to find a suitable vehicle to pair Judy again with Gene Kelly. *The Pirate* seemed the right choice for both stars and director. Writers Albert

Hackett and Frances Goodrich, the husband-and-wife team, were asked to adapt the story and the dialogue for the stars' specific talents.

The film was to feature a camp sensibility, an element that hadn't been used in Hollywood films up to then. Assigned to compose the score, Cole Porter was delighted, telling Minnelli he was glad that someone in Hollywood thought he was still employable. It was Porter's idea to rename the pirate Mack the Black, a homage to one of his close gay friends.

The Pirate is a comedy of mistaken identities. Set in the Caribbean Islands in the 1830s, the story concerns a young woman named Manuela who's in love with the stories she has heard about a notorious pirate, Macoco, better known as Mack the Black, the alter ego of a man pretending to be a pillar of Caribbean society. Manuela has fallen in love with Mack, unaware that he is actually Don Pedro Vargas, a middle-aged bore, chosen by her family to marry her. Meanwhile, Serafin, a conceited actor, pretends to be Mack in order to win Manuela's love. Kelly's athletic style made him the obvious choice for Serafin, and character actor Walter Slezak was well cast as the real Mack.

The high-style comedy needed changes to satisfy the Breen Office. As played by Lynn Fontanne onstage, Manuela was already married to Don Pedro, the West Indies mayor, while daydreaming a romance with the notorious pirate. But in the movie, Manuela is a younger single woman, eager to find the love of her life.

Judy, initially enthusiastic, began rehearsals on December 2, 1946, the last day of her maternity leave. Minnelli thought that *The Pirate* would be fun, a welcome change of pace for both of them. For Judy, however, the real allure was playing for the second time opposite Kelly.

As was the norm, songs were to be prerecorded and then lip-synched during production. However, when Judy showed up for her first day of recording, on December 27, 1946, she was frail and depressed and the session had to be canceled. Judy's frequent absences caused further delays and *The Pirate* didn't begin shooting until February 17, 1947.

Minnelli conceived *The Pirate* as a totally artificial film, based on a frothy story. He transformed M-G-M's soundstages into a fanciful tropical island, drawing on his experience as an art director, and working more closely than usual with the studio's set designers Cedric Gibbons and Jack Martin Smith and costumer Irene Sharaff.

Over the years, Minnelli had built up a huge library of books, to which he turned for visual inspiration. He spent months working on *The Pirate,* researching the period's look in his library and corresponding with various experts on the West Indies. Representing a new form of screen musical, a period burlesque, *The Pirate* allowed Minnelli free rein to indulge his eclectic aesthetics. He designed exotic settings that were products of his imagination, specifically instructing cinematographer Harry Stradling to lend the film's color palette a strong surreal touch.

Unfortunately, Judy's enthusiasm for the project began to decline as soon as shooting started. To reassure his vulnerable wife, Minnelli reminded her that she had also been against—and ultimately wrong— about *Meet Me in St. Louis.* He told her that the critics would compare her to Lynn Fontanne, then the first lady of the American theater. If only she could trust him, he said, the picture would dazzle with the kind of sophisticated wit that would place her in the same league as Metro's then dominant star, their friend Katharine Hepburn.

Judy, however, was not reassured. She felt that it was the wrong vehicle for her. Moreover, she worried that Kelly, who had a flashier part, would dominate the film. Fighting her doubts, Minnelli repeated that this would be her smartest picture to date, a showcase for her wide comedic range.

Minnelli was looking forward to another lovely collaboration, hoping Judy would not have to rely on amphetamines, or consult her psychiatrists. He was confident that Judy would not only "deliver," but would also show her mettle and discipline to those Metro execs who always complained about how difficult and unreliable she was.

Minnelli's worst fears materialized during rehearsals, when he witnessed Judy's anxiety about Kelly "stealing" the show away from her. Having liked the stage production, Kelly was glad to assist Robert Alton's choreography however he could. Kelly saw *The Pirate* as a chance to take dancing closer to ballet. Judy admired Kelly as a performer and liked him as a person, but his excessive enthusiasm increased her insecurities. At first flattered by being offered the role, she now blamed her husband for encouraging her to accept it.

Pressures started to build up on the set, as Kelly recalled: "Judy had periods when she didn't show up on the set. This was the first indication that something was wrong." Minnelli was proud that ever since their marriage, Judy had been temperate in her use of pills. But now, with her tolerance lessened, the periodic spells of illness began, and Judy turned again to the pills that had sustained her during crises. Minnelli stood helplessly by, unable either to stop his wife from taking the pills or detect the pills' suppliers.

In her notorious squabbles with Metro, Judy's indomitable spirit always came through. But now she resorted to counting the exact number of days that the studio could shoot around her, reporting to work at the last possible moment that would allow her picture to finish within the allotted schedule and budget. Quite shockingly, Judy was gone for 99 out of the 135 days it took to make *The Pirate*. For the first time, she had failed the studio, big time.

During *Meet Me in St. Louis*, assistant director Al Jennings had been awakened in the middle of the night with the news that Judy would not turn up the following day. Now it was Wallace Worsley, *The Pirate*'s assistant director, who got the midnight calls. At least twice a week, Minnelli would overhear his wife telling Worsley on the phone, "I don't feel well. I won't be able to come in." Worsley finally refused to pick up the phone when Judy called after midnight with news of yet another migraine or flu.

Minnelli didn't enjoy such a luxury—he had to go to work. And in the evenings, at home, he was subjected to his wife's endless barrage of complaints. Judy's troubles were now very much his own. The routine got tiresome, and Minnelli was beginning to suffer from perpetual anxiety and sleepless nights, during which Judy kept him awake with bitching about the studio's mistreatment, which invariably turned into bickering with him.

Occasionally, they were halfway to Culver City when Judy forced Minnelli to return home. On other occasions, she arrived at the studio, worked for an hour, and then asked for the studio doctor. Judy quickly forgot her pledge to stay off pills and would appear on the set in a barbiturate stupor. After keeping the cast and crew waiting for hours, she arrived one morning in such a daze that she appeared to be sleepwalking. Then after wandering aimlessly around the set for two hours, she simply informed Minnelli that she needed to go home.

At other times, the amphetamines had the reverse effect, making

Judy high-strung and overly anxious, tense and paranoid. In a scene that called for Judy to dance around open fires, Minnelli heard his wife shouting, "I'm going to burn to death! They want me to burn to death!" Embarrassed, Minnelli watched passively as his hysterical wife was led away, crying and laughing at the same time.

Minnelli the director tried to improve Judy's performance as an actress "with judicious cutting and excision." He dropped at least two numbers that fell short of her usual high standard. But from Judy's perspective, the loss of those numbers, combined with Kelly's attention grabbing, threw the movie off balance. Instead of being the center, Judy felt that her Manuela became a secondary character.

Truth to tell, even if Judy's performance were better, *The Pirate* would have been flawed. With few exceptions, Porter's songs lacked his trademark wit, and Minnelli again allowed the sumptuous sets and exotic costumes to overshadow the slender tale. Though visually pleasant, the picture never quite comes together, being too static and lacking real energy.

Once *The Pirate*'s shooting schedule was extended, it was suggested that Judy go back to the psychiatrists for help. Minnelli wanted to strike out at the monster-psychiatrists (as he viewed them) who came between him and his wife, but he was persuaded to keep calm. He felt the unbearable pressure of being the one constant factor in Judy's life. Looking back, he confided: "If I'd loved Judy less, I could have been dispassionate enough to laugh her out of the moods that resulted in pill-taking. Sympathy that came too readily just didn't seem to help."

Minnelli drove Judy to the psychiatrist's every day after shooting, then waited for her in the car until the session was over. More often than not, Judy would leave these fifty-minute sessions with her mood unaltered, if not worsened.

The pent-up anger found its outlet at home, and the spats and bickering became more intense. Minnelli tried to control his own volatility, but the exchange of harsh words and lashing out inevitably left scars. That much hostility couldn't be contained for long under the same roof.

In an upstairs room, the Gershwins had a sofa that had belonged to

Lee's mother. When Judy and Minnelli had to be apart, Lee Gershwin was the symbolic mother they went to. Minnelli would call Lee and ask politely, "May I use your mother's couch tonight?" "Of course, darling," she'd say, her tone unruffled. As he was packing his toiletries, Judy would already be walking out the door. "I'll go," she snapped. "After all, this is your house!"

As things grew intolerable at home, either Judy or Minnelli would call up the Gershwins. One night, unable to spend the night in the same house with Judy, Minnelli called trembling and incoherent. "Can I use your mother's couch tonight?" "No," said Lee, "it's already been re-quested by Judy. Please call me tomorrow, darling, if you still need it."

Lee Gershwin recalled many a night in which Judy knocked at her door, asking for a place to sleep. Lying on that well-used couch in the Gershwins' spare room, Lee comforted Judy by stroking her arms for hours until she finally fell asleep.

The Minnellis' marriage was going through a vicious cycle. They would go about their business for several days in a row, then have recon-ciliations as stormy as their partings. Judy would be apologetic, and Minnelli would be made to feel guilty for his alleged insensitivity and lack of understanding.

Toward the end of shooting *The Pirate*, Judy was gone from the set for three consecutive days, and Minnelli was caught in the middle. As direc-tor, he should have insisted that his star fulfill her obligations, but as a concerned and loving husband, he simply couldn't do it. In his typically passive manner, he made excuses for Judy, lying to his bosses that she had the flu. Then, after a few days off, Judy would be back, performing as well as before, with the customary ebullient mood.

During those agonizing times, Minnelli became a total wreck. He kept asking himself the inevitable questions: How responsible was he for Judy's regression? How had he failed? What could be done to improve the situation? Submerging personal doubts while presenting an untrou-bled manner to the outside world became Minnelli's modus operandi.

What Minnelli failed to do was to reach out to Judy, tell her how much he really did care for her. As a result, Judy treated her upheavals as solitary battles. One anxious look or an awkward inflection would give Minnelli's thoughts away. Judy's darker side resented Minnelli's lack of faith in her. He felt that she was storing up mental ammunition against him.

As usual for him in times of crisis, Minnelli threw himself into his work with excessive determination. He observed with admiration how Kelly was putting together the musical numbers with choreographer Alton. Minnelli was developing the most intense professional association he had ever had with any actor. Their talents complemented each other's well, with one idea melding into another. "My approach is less esoteric and more gutsy," Kelly told Minnelli. "Yours is evanescent and ethereal."

As shooting progressed, Kelly, who at first staged only his own numbers, became involved in all facets of the production. No longer the newcomer he had been while making *For Me and My Gal,* Kelly was full of ideas. An increasingly paranoid Judy became jealous of the time Minnelli and Kelly were spending together. She feared that Minnelli was expanding Kelly's role at her expense, while also excluding her from any discussion. For his part, Minnelli felt that it was not necessary for her to have a voice on Kelly's role.

"You and Vincente are having a lot of fun," Judy said, pouting at Kelly. "You're both ignoring me. Well, how about doing something for me? Will you stage my numbers?"

"How about Vincente?" Kelly asked.

"No, I want *you* to do it," Judy said.

Kelly was stunned. And the episode left a puzzled Minnelli wondering, "How had we come to this state of affairs where suddenly I could do nothing right in Judy's eyes?"

Caught up in the midst of the couple's intense domestic squabbles, Kelly tried to help without offending either side. Minnelli hoped that the problem would work itself out, that Judy would realize how unreasonable she was. He was wrong: She became more paranoid and resentful, claiming that Kelly didn't need Minnelli's care as much as she did. She was jealous of what she considered Minnelli's efforts to make Kelly shine at her expense.

The close relationship between Minnelli and Kelly would come to fruition three years later, when they made *An American in Paris.* With Judy's mental state unstable, she became irrationally jealous of their professional and personal intimacy. One day, she interrupted their working session with a violent public scene, accusing them in front of the entire crew of using the picture to advance themselves at her expense.

The unspoken rift between husband and wife got deeper and deeper. Minnelli wondered how they had gotten to a point where suddenly he could do nothing right for Judy. How could he escape the limbo to which he had been assigned by Judy? Minnelli was too much in turmoil and too hurt to talk it out with his close friends, and his isolation made things worse.

Judy's addiction to drugs exacerbated her paranoia. The slightest word or glance was now perceived as a conspiracy against her. Moreover, her bouts with paranoia were not isolated incidents; they became a pattern. When Hedda Hopper visited the set of *The Pirate,* she found Judy in her trailer shaking hysterically, asserting that everyone had turned against her and that she had no friends. She claimed that her mother was tapping her telephone. "She is doing everything in her power to destroy me," Judy said. In fact, Judy became so agitated that she had to be carried from the trailer in costume and makeup and taken home from the studio in a limo.

Judy might have been paranoid but other members of *The Pirate* crew couldn't help noticing the crush that Minnelli seemed to have on Kelly. This was evident from their behavior at parties given by Kelly and his wife, actress Betsy Blair. On these occasions, Judy felt that Minnelli was standing too close to Kelly, always embracing him when they talked and looking straight into his eyes. She began to worry that her husband was having an affair with Kelly, even though the latter was presumably heterosexual and happily married.

Minnelli saw a rough cut of *The Pirate* on August 29, 1947, a week after Judy returned from Stockbridge's health center, at a special screening held for Freed, Cole Porter, and Irving Berlin. Porter's reaction was reserved, but Freed and Berlin reassured the composer that *The Pirate* was a special picture. Judy, however, shared Porter's doubts. She felt that the film elevated Minnelli's stature as an artist and displayed Kelly's athletic dancing, but it was not the career milestone that Minnelli as director and as husband had promised her. Judy became slightly more encouraged when Berlin said he liked the film, as she trusted his instincts.

Nevertheless, Minnelli's directorial skills and Kelly's and Garland's star appeal were not much help at the box office. With all the talent involved and the huge budget spent on the production, *The Pirate* was perceived as a cloddish film, no more inspired than the Broadway play had been.

Kelly was particularly disappointed with the results since it had all looked so good during the rehearsals and shooting. Kelly thought that he looked like "fake Barrymore or fake Fairbanks," but he blamed "the damned elusive camera" he had been trying so hard to tame. Kelly later observed: "Vincente and I honestly believed we were being so dazzlingly brilliant and clever that everybody would fall at our feet and swoon clean away in delight and ecstasy, that they would kiss our toes in appreciation for this wondrous new musical we'd given them. Well, we were wrong. About five and a half people seemed to get the gist of what we set out to do. And in retrospect, you couldn't really blame them. We just didn't pull it off."

Minnelli and Kelly did not have to wait long to find out just how wrong they were about the picture. The critics charged that the story lacked the lightness of a Fairbanks plot and that the dialogue had no edge to it. Minnelli was offended, particularly by one comment scrawled on a preview card: "I would have fallen asleep were it not for all the noise on screen."

The Pirate was the only picture Judy ever made at Metro that failed to yield a profit. What made it worse for her was that most critics praised Kelly's performance as a good parody of Fairbanks and Barrymore. The musical numbers were inventively staged and Kelly had some good moments. Unfortunately, with the exception of "Be a Clown," the songs were not among Porter's best, and even Judy could not improve on them.

Judy's touch with comedy was assured, but her Manuela seemed too nervous, even neurotic, with her eyes darting and her hands restless. Defying Minnelli's instructions to tone down her performance, she was too mannered, always nervously playing with the rings on her fingers, which Minnelli found distracting. Kelly attributed the nervousness to Judy's unconscious fear that the picture would not appeal to her fans.

In an industry defined by the latest success—you are as good as your last picture, the saying goes—Minnelli's triumphs with *Meet Me in St.*

Louis and *The Clock* didn't count for much. And while some saw artistic merits in *Yolanda and the Thief* and *The Pirate,* it was hard not to acknowledge the commercial failure of both pictures.

Nonetheless, over the years, *The Pirate* has developed a cult status. Looking back, it's one of Minnelli's underestimated musicals, though its particular brand of artifice and its fey eccentricity were too innovative and peculiar at the time.

After *The Pirate,* the studio did not immediately offer Minnelli a new assignment, and he did not force the issue. To maintain his emotional balance, Minnelli read scripts and again accepted the chores of conducting screen tests. He was deeply annoyed that Metro blamed him for ruining Judy's career. All of a sudden, even Arthur Freed was distant with him when they met on the lot.

The rigors of *The Pirate* marked the start of a frustrating period for Minnelli at Metro. Up until then, his rise to eminence had been steady, but the failure of this picture was disquieting. Oblivious to all matters but the work itself, Minnelli was at first slow to absorb the impending trouble.

When at length his new assignment came along, Minnelli decided to take a more emotionally nuanced approach. *Easter Parade* was a kind of Tin Pan Alley *Pygmalion*, set in New York, circa 1910. The failure of *The Pirate* had shaken his self-confidence, his determination to be innovative with each and every project. As a result, he decided to play it safe with *Easter Parade,* and to imbue it with the same emotional nostalgia that *Meet Me in St. Louis* had. Rehearsals began in September 1947 but numerous crises made it a difficult production from the start.

Minnelli was casting the supporting roles when Freed called him into his office. Looking grim and uneasy, Freed said, "Vincente, I don't know how to tell you this." Minnelli knew immediately that something was wrong, fearing that perhaps the front office had decided to scrap the picture.

Freed's words came tumbling out. "Judy's psychiatrist, Dr. Kupper, thinks it would be better all around if you didn't direct the picture."

Minnelli was utterly stunned.

"Why not?" he asked.

"He feels Judy doesn't really want you as the director, that you symbolize all her troubles with the studio."

Freed's tone was slightly kinder when he said, "It would be better if you don't do it." Minnelli and Judy trusted and confided in Freed, but now, Minnelli felt that Freed had simply given in to Judy's demand— which was actually an ultimatum.

There was nothing for Minnelli to say; the matter was settled. If their working together created emotional problems for Judy, then the "solution" was obvious, they would not work together. Minnelli would stay home with Judy and give her as much attention as needed.

Minnelli left work for the day, trying not to feel betrayed. Yet he kept wondering why Judy hadn't told him directly. Why did the message have to come through other people? Weren't married couples supposed to openly discuss such issues with each other?

Upon arrival, Judy met him at the front door with the usual kiss.

"Hello, sweetheart," Minnelli said.

He sat down to read the evening paper in his easy chair.

Liza came toddling in, and Minnelli had a few giggles over her antics.

Conversation over dinner was formal and stilted. After dinner, Minnelli read scripts and Judy settled down with a book. They were both in bed early that night. Lying together in the dark, where so many differences are ironed out, no mention was made of the catastrophic happening. Minnelli felt that Judy's reasons for demanding his departure were too obvious to ignore, too tactless to mention.

Good or bad, the doctor's advice was not an issue, and Minnelli felt wounded and betrayed. Judy never said a word about *Easter Parade* the next day, or the following week. Worse yet, Judy never acknowledged that she had in fact removed her husband from what was potentially Metro's biggest movie of 1948.

Minnelli was shocked by her silence. Despite all the miseries with Judy at home and at work during *The Pirate,* it had never occurred to him that such a thing could happen. He was replaced by Charles Walters, a former choreographer turned director. First, the Goodrich-Hackett script was given to Sidney Sheldon for a refurbish, and then Gene Kelly broke an ankle and was replaced by Fred Astaire, who was brought out of semiretirement to costar.

On the side, however, Judy had told the Gershwins that she was relieved not to work again with her husband. She felt that their problems would get worse if they continued to spend all their time together. At least now they didn't have to argue in front of the crew, and then pretend that everything was okay at home. Judy believed that their artistic relationship was getting unhealthy, and that Minnelli was pushing her in the wrong direction, particularly after *The Pirate,* which represented Minnelli's taste rather than hers. Reconstructing the past to suit her convenience, Judy went so far as to claim that, as a director, Minnelli had remade her image to fit his own fantasies.

Twelve

Scandalous Melodrama:
Madame Bovary

AFTER *THE PIRATE* and his replacement as director of *Easter Parade*, a bleak stretch followed for Minnelli. For the first time since *Cabin in the Sky,* he became idle, with no assignments in sight. Still getting $2,500 a week (from his 1946 contract), he continued to mark time by directing screen tests for M-G-M's new talent. Minnelli felt he was being punished for Judy's misbehavior. He and Judy had become victims of the intense, inseparable link between their private and professional lives.

The new, perverse "twist" now was that it was Minnelli's turn to pay for it. Ironically, Judy was showing resilience by working happily on *Easter Parade,* a project she knew Minnelli had truly desired. Minnelli was a convenient target to blame. In the studio era, directors were more expendable than movie stars because the latter had more tangible value at the box office.

However, suddenly, without fanfare or any warning, things began to change in Minnelli's favor. The phone rang at his office one morning; it was producer Pandro Berman.

"Are you interested in directing *Madame Bovary,* the screen version of Flaubert's notorious novel?"

"God, yes," Minnelli said. "When can we start?"

Berman knew that Minnelli had been inactive for a whole year, and was eager to work.

In actuality, there was no conspiracy against Minnelli. It was not unusual for directors to experience long periods of idleness. Berman's offer, more than merely welcome, dispelled Minnelli's anxieties. It was important for him to reestablish his reputation as a first-rate director of musicals as well as of serious dramas. *Madame Bovary* was a prestigious, potentially exciting project with a glamorous cast.

Minnelli hoped that Judy would share his excitement about *Madame Bovary*; she knew how difficult the forced idleness had been for him. Instead, Judy felt more dejected, complaining that she was stuck playing "dull little shopgirls" while he was assigned prestigious and challenging literary projects. Minnelli attributed Judy's bitterness to her mental anguish, but he was deeply hurt by what he perceived as unfair and irrational jealousy.

In his first meeting with Berman, Minnelli addressed some of the most crucial issues raised by *Madame Bovary*. The producer held that Flaubert's novel wasn't very visual, and that it might not interest American audiences because it was a period piece, set in the nineteenth century. Additionally, the Production Code didn't consider adultery an appropriate subject for a major Hollywood movie.

To obtain the Breen office's seal of approval, it did help that the film was an adaptation of a world-renowned novel, and that the uncensored thoughts of the characters were to be implied rather than overtly shown. Screenwriter Robert Ardrey was instructed to stay within the Production Code limitations, while trying to maintain the mood of the original work.

Madame Bovary was one of Minnelli's favorite novels. He felt a strong emotional affinity with both the fantasies of Emma Bovary, the protagonist, and the feelings of her dejected husband. As usual, Minnelli threw himself into researching various writers' interpretations of the lead character, reading essays by Henry James, Somerset Maugham, and Sigmund Freud, among others. Flaubert's novel had enthralled generations of readers, each of whom projected his or her own values onto Emma Bovary, trying to explain the motivations of this errant woman who pays for her sins of sexual and materialist obsessions. Minnelli was trying to find a new, relevant, and contemporary angle that would touch a chord with American audiences of the late 1940s.

Next to *Meet Me in St. Louis, Madame Bovary* became the film that most profoundly shaped Minnelli's development as a filmmaker. The project came at a time when Minnelli was full of personal and professional doubts. He was beginning to wonder whether art was imitating life. *Madame Bovary* tells the story of a woman whose private phantoms made daily life unendurable for herself, her spouse, and their infant daughter. Living a similarly hellish scenario in his Beverly Hills home, Minnelli later acknowledged that Judy's periodic retreats into fantasy helped shape his view of Flaubert's self-destructive and capricious Emma.

Like Minnelli's best work, *Madame Bovary* simultaneously exalted the style of Hollywood moviemaking that M-G-M, the industry's most prestigious studio, was known for, while shrewdly and subtly contesting the underlying moral assumptions of seemingly traditional fare, in this case a film that could have been seen as yet another lavish "woman's picture."

Madame Bovary could have easily been made as an "Illustrated Literary Classic," a genre that M-G-M excelled in before and during World War II with its opulent adaptations of Dickens, Shakespeare, and other famous authors, some of them starring vehicles for Norma Shearer and Greer Garson, actresses Minnelli disliked. Those pictures aimed to please romantic if provincial female viewers with pretensions to literary refinement, offering thrills that their otherwise ordinary lives lacked.

Minnelli, however, was attracted to the subversive elements of the story and the lead character. Specifically, he was drawn to Emma's doomed infatuation with the idea of love, and her vanity, which was a form of narcissism. A faithless wife and negligent mother, Emma defies all the feminine ideals M-G-M movies were promoting in their Greer Garson vehicles after *Mrs. Miniver.* Minnelli argued that if Emma earns the sympathy of the readers, it's thanks to her human lapses of judgment.

Madame Bovary was not the first film version of Flaubert's novel. Minnelli was familiar with Jean Renoir's 1934 adaptation, which he liked, but he wanted to make a different kind of movie. The book was tailor-made for Minnelli, who understood all too well how sensual deprivation and the lure of daydreams could lead to obsession, and in this case become fatally destructive. The fascinating theme of seductive fantasies, both positive and negative, is a recurrent motif in at least half of Minnelli's movies, including *Cabin in the Sky, Yolanda and the Thief, The Pirate, An American in Paris,* and *The Band Wagon.*

Berman assigned the script to Robert Ardrey, who opted for a nuanced condensation of the novel. But, worried about censorship, Berman feared that even Emma's suicide might be deemed insufficient punishment for her adultery. On screen, Ardrey suggested Emma's promiscuity, but very little was actually shown. The distancing device chosen to defuse the potentially censorable material was voice-over narration, which bracketed the story with a fabricated reenactment of Flaubert's trial for obscenity. Minnelli hoped that the Motion Picture Association of America and its Production Code would learn a lesson from the novelist's narrow-minded contemporaries.

It's hard to believe, but Berman initially planned to offer the role of Emma to Lana Turner, the studio's resident glamour queen, still described as "The Sweater Girl." But Minnelli rejected the idea as both implausible and impractical. The Production Code censors had already warned that *Madame Bovary* was trouble enough, even without Lana Turner's incendiary screen image. Minnelli refused to consider Metro's other stars, British imports Greer Garson, who was established but boring, and Deborah Kerr, who was still new in Hollywood, because both women were too refined for the part.

Over drinks with David O. Selznick one evening, Minnelli learned that his wife, Jennifer Jones, was interested in making *Madame Bovary,* a film that he had wanted to produce himself. Selznick was quick to point out Jones's recent track record: her Oscar for playing the saintly Bernadette of Lourdes in *The Song of Bernadette,* and her range, enabling her to make a radical switch from the sexy vamp Pearl Chavez in *Duel in the Sun* to the spirit of eternal innocence in the title role in *Portrait of Jennie.*

Selznick agreed to lend Jones for the film as long as M-G-M used some of his idle leading men. Hence Emma's aristocratic seducer, Rodolphe, was assigned to Louis Jourdan, also under contract to Selznick. James Mason was cast as Flaubert, affording the estimable British actor the opportunity to flaunt his impeccably musical and cultured voice. Only one leading man was cast from the M-G-M stable, Van Heflin, as

Charles Bovary. As it turned out, he was the only male player who gave a weak performance—a performance that upset Minnelli.

Minnelli shot *Madame Bovary* from mid-December 1948 to February 1949. He tried to make a stylish-looking though not extravagant picture. Minnelli re-created a nineteenth-century village at Culver City. Jack Martin Smith's set design was a model of backlot recycling. An English hamlet, with its rustic stone bridge, used in *That Forsythe Woman*, was re-dressed and emerged as the quintessentially French town square of Yonville.

Though Flaubert devoted only a few pages to the grand ball at a nearby chateau, Minnelli turned it into the picture's dramatic highlight, the occasion for Emma's illusions and Charles's forebodings to converge in music and movement. One of the last sequences to be shot, and the most complicated to orchestrate, Minnelli planned it as if it were a production number in a big glossy musical.

Indeed, for Minnelli, the picture's standout scene was the waltz, which was new to the period. In that sequence, Minnelli wished to convey the giddiness that enveloped Emma at the ball. In dramatic films, music is usually added in postproduction to the edited footage. Minnelli, however, shaped his ball scene to the prerecorded strains of the neurotic waltz he had commissioned from the noted composer Miklos Rozsa, known for his evocative scores for many noir films.

At the ball, Emma is Cinderella, outshining everybody else, only briefly remorseful over her neglect of husband and child. The music was played at an accelerated tempo, to accentuate the idea that as Emma was swirling around, the chateau's baroque mirrors and chandeliers were whirling around with her.

Unaccompanied by words, the sequence relied on camera movement to suggest Emma's dizzying breathlessness as well as to explain without dialogue why the host ordered the windows broken to give her air. This is shown while Emma's husband is in the billiard room getting drunk, oblivious to her plight.

The waltz was among the most difficult sequences Minnelli had ever staged or shot. Minnelli devised a series of 360-degree pans to convey Emma's perilous exhilaration. The scene created major headaches for the crew, but, ultimately, it represents one of the more audacious and spectacular images in a Minnelli movie, one that critics and audiences have continued to talk about for years.

As Minnelli expected, Jennifer Jones proved to be tremendously insecure and hence required constant reassurance. From the moment she
was cast, Minnelli prepared himself for Selznick's interference via his
(in)famous memos, which dissected every aspect of the production.
Selznick did not disappoint, endlessly complaining about Flaubert's psychological approach, the size of Louis Jourdan's role, and even about
Metro's makeup department's "willful attempt to sabotage Jennifer's
unique loveliness."

Selznick's visits on the set were not welcomed, either. Minnelli maintained a cordial if distant approach when Selznick arrived. In the end,
he listened to Selznick's advice only about Jones's makeup, dismissing all
other complaints, particularly those concerning her dresses. That was
one area where Minnelli was an expert, and he would not tolerate any
interference, not from a man as crass as Selznick, who had let his wife
look bizarre and act preposterously in *Duel in the Sun*. Like Cukor, who
had been fired from *Gone with the Wind*, and who loathed Selznick's
taste, Minnelli was critical of the mogul; at M-G-M, *Duel in the Sun* was
known as "Duel for My Sins."

Minnelli was aware of the similarity between his own marital situation and that described in the screenplay. Engrossed in work after many
idle months, he didn't lavish his undivided attention on Judy, as she expected. Vulnerable and troubled, Judy had always resented Minnelli's
immersion in work, and now even more so. Judy's criticism and self-pity
soured Minnelli's enthusiasm. Nonetheless, this time around, he was
determined not to let Judy kill his professional joy entirely. In fact, he
used the studio as an escape from home, putting in longer hours than
usual.

Madame Bovary's tragedy became the prototype for many of Minnelli's
subsequent domestic dramas. At the center, there's usually a hero or
heroine misfit who's burdened and tormented by life's routines, norms,
and rituals. Having experienced similar emotional struggles in his own
private life, Minnelli identified with his protagonists, male or female.

Minnelli's melodramas hold up a dark mirror to his musicals. What's
optimistic in the Technicolor musicals becomes pessimistic in his black-
and-white melodramas. As Stephen Harvey noted, *The Pirate* and

Madame Bovary made a symmetrically matched pair, in the same way that, in the 1950s, the back-to-back films *The Bad and the Beautiful* and *The Band Wagon* complemented each other by presenting two sides of the film industry. Thematically, each tells a similar story, but stylistically, they're vastly different, resulting in widely divergent films.

Like *The Pirate*'s Manuela, Emma Bovary is a woman stifled by the mores of her time. For each woman, the main allure of her impending marriage is materialistic. Both heroines fall prey to erotic longings, born and shaped by literature and popular magazines. The difference between the two women is that, as befits a hopeful genre like the musical, Manuela is liberated by her imagination, while the gravity of daily life brings Emma's fantasies to grief.

These two films depict a conflict between the urge for self-expression and the pressure to conform to societal norms. They also show Minnelli's understanding of and sensitivity to women. Arguably, there's greater intensity in a Minnelli movie when the protagonist is female. *"Madame Bovary, c'est moi!"* Flaubert famously declared, and Minnelli could have said the same, and occasionally did. Yet he also expresses empathy for the male characters with a cool irony, a detached authorial voice, as embodied by James Mason's narration.

This mode of detachment is also reflected in the way Minnelli defines Emma visually, as an alien figure, ill-matched to her surroundings. The interplay between the insider-outsider perspectives is what makes the film so intriguing.

The script of *Madame Bovary* compressed the richly dense source material. Every episode in which the heroine doesn't figure directly was omitted. For dramatic emphasis, Rodolphe enters the plot at an earlier point, before introducing Emma to the intoxicating waltz at the gala ball. Certain characters, such as Charles Bovary's mother and his first wife, are eliminated completely. Minnelli's intuition and craft preserve Flaubert's spirit, while at the same time translating it into a language and look that could be understood by viewers of the era.

"There are hundreds and thousands of women who wish they were Emma Bovary and who have been saved from her fate not by virtue but simply by lack of determination," proclaims Flaubert in the prologue's courtroom scene. These were sentiments Minnelli related to viscerally.

Though her interpretation lacked depth, Jennifer Jones's star quality, her frail beauty, and elegant poise were important factors in accentuating Emma's fatal delusions. Her life is sustained entirely on illusion, and she imagines herself the center of glamorous fantasies. At one point, Minnelli's Emma muses on "love in a Scotch cottage, love in a Swiss chalet."

Minnelli draws a number of tongue-in-cheek contrasts between Emma's reality and her fantasy life. In her grand entry in the film's first reel, she is seen graciously preparing breakfast for the young doctor who's called to see her father. In her kitchen, she is standing over her omelette pan beaming, while dressed in a long white gown! Viewers have been tipped off that this elegant domestic is not the "real" Emma, but a show intended to titillate her own vanity and dazzle Charles. In an earlier scene, where Charles is not present, Minnelli showed the girl in her usual guise, bustling around the farmhouse kitchen in a smock, with a kerchief under her chin.

The origins of Emma's fantasy life are shown in a flashback to her convent years. It's an image that held strong personal meaning for Minnelli. In her bedroom, we see the teenager lost in thought as the camera pans across her eclectic collection of framed landscapes of enchanted woods, engravings torn from books of rapt lovers, copies of fashion magazines. They are described by Mason's mournful voice-over as "images of beauty that never existed." These fetishes accompany Emma for the rest of her life, placed in the attic to which she retreats from her bleak domesticity. Just as Judy used to do.

Emma constructs a beautiful world out of scraps, and so does Minnelli as director. As part of his work, Minnelli collected clippings and objects that grabbed his eyes, and turned them into a shifting collage. Minnelli knew that sooner or later Emma must fail. If Emma's reach exceeded her grasp, it's nevertheless the subject of tragedy. Emma is a victim of her own attraction to the gaudy, the sentimental, the unreal.

Significantly, in Minnelli's version of the melodrama, Bovary's villain is an amoral interior decorator, the shopkeeper/moneylender Lheureux, who furnishes Emma's new home and adorns her. Minnelli indicts Lheureux for his malign influence on his gullible heroine with a vignette that's absent in Flaubert's novel. Out of all his new merchandise, Emma gets excited over a plaster cherub of negligible merit, prompting Lheureux to remark, "You have unfailing taste." Was he also talking about Minnelli's penchant for kitsch?

Madame Bovary is a tale of a misguided nineteenth-century housewife who is rushed down the primrose path to ruin. However, by using the device of Flaubert's trial, Metro suggested that Emma Bovary's tragic life was not the result of willful sinning by a selfish, licentious woman, but the consequence of her social environment, her upbringing, and her childish dreams. "We had taught her to believe in Cinderella," Mason's Flaubert tenderly remarks. In Minnelli's interpretation, Emma is the victim of hopeless illusions, a product of the romantic age and its ideals. She doesn't find the man of her dreams in her poor loving husband, or in her dazzling lover, or in the pitiful law clerk. In the end, all she finds is ruin and despair, shame, desolation, and death.

Minnelli kept the story moving with smooth directorial touches. However, one wishes for a better performance of Emma than the beaming and breathless one Jennifer Jones gives. Minnelli thought that Jones was too light to bring out the anguish of this tormented soul. Given the choice, he would have preferred an actress like Vivien Leigh in the part.

None of the men in the cast was distinguished, either. Louis Jourdan is not quite electric as Bovary's phony and elegant lover, Rodolphe. Van Heflin, though disappointing to Minnelli, is moderately appealing as her trusting, small-town spouse, but the script neglected to give him long scenes, mostly allowing him reaction shots; it was a passive role. A better portrait is given by Christopher Kent as Emma's weakling lover. The only actor who fit Minnelli's vision of the film was Frank Allenby as the shrewd and manipulative merchant, Lheureux.

In the spring of 1949, *Madame Bovary* was edited, scored, and dubbed. The results of the previews, which were held in Santa Monica and Pasadena, were satisfying. Audiences' reaction cards rated the film and Jennifer Jones as outstanding. Berman, however, wasn't impressed; he never found preview cards effective. Minnelli relied on Berman's personal reactions for many of the changes made after the previews.

Madame Bovary was released late in the summer of 1949, just as Judy was experiencing her most severe crisis. After finishing *In the Good Old*

Summertime, Judy began work on *Annie Get Your Gun,* but soon suffered a complete collapse.

Although *Madame Bovary* was too gloomy and fatalistic for much of the general public, the film drew on Minnelli's rare sensitivity to its source material and his vivid sense of melodrama, and it performed respectably at the box office. It was Minnelli's first dramatic film since *The Clock* to fulfill his expectations and meet his high standards, and it demonstrated Minnelli's breadth of talent, proving that his stylistic flair could enliven the most demanding and bleakest of themes.

Madame Bovary ended Minnelli's first career phase at Metro with a bang. With his private life in shambles, the solace of work was again crucial—a matter of life and death, Minnelli said. Channeling all his energies and anxieties into the making of *Madame Bovary* was not only a good idea for the sake of his sanity, it also paid off professionally. The favorable reception signaled a new, highly creative phase in Minnelli's career that would last for a full decade, up to *Home from the Hill,* in 1960.

Thirteen

Problems with Judy

MINNELLI WAS A PASSIVE BYSTANDER during Judy's struggles with M-G-M. "These were my most ineffectual times," he later admitted. Minnelli's sympathies lay with the studio, and for a while, he did his best to convince Judy that Metro cared for her. Minnelli thought he was doing the right thing, but Judy felt that her husband was reproaching her.

"You never fight for me," Judy angrily told Minnelli in one of their many arguments. All her life, ever since her father died in 1935, she had been seeking a man to replace him, a man to protect her. Judy always fell in love with older, wiser, and stronger men, like Artie Shaw, Oscar Levant, David Rose, and now Minnelli, but, in the end, all of these men disappointed her.

Judy's new designated protector was Carleton Alsop, a sometime agent and radio producer, who had taken over her career management. Alsop quickly learned that Judy's finances were as precarious as her physical and emotional health. M-G-M's accountants calculated to the penny the costs of the delays she had caused by her behavior on *The Pirate* and by her withdrawal from *The Barkleys of Broadway* for reasons of poor health, as well as the days she had spent at the Casa de las Campanas and Austen Riggs clinics. Metro's "retroactive penalties" amounted to an enormous debt of $100,000, to be deducted from her salary.

Alsop informed Mayer that he had no legal claim for such a penalty, threatening to go to court. The stingy mogul then devised another solution, giving Judy bonuses for her two songs in *Words and Music,* which would cover Metro's expense. Thrilled that she had at last found a strong and rational man to stand up against the studio, Judy asked Alsop to become her manager in all career matters.

Minnelli perceived Alsop as a father figure to Judy, who indeed nicknamed him "Pa." Unlike Minnelli, Alsop refused to bow to her neurotic tantrums. When Minnelli could not handle her, he would call Alsop in the middle of the night. "Now, goddamn it, Judy," Alsop would say, "go back to bed, or get your ass up and go to work." To Minnelli's surprise, his wife did exactly as told by Alsop.

Sane and unselfishly giving, Alsop and his wife, the actress Sylvia Sidney, had taken the Minnellis under their wing. Alsop had endeared himself to Judy at her twenty-sixth birthday party, when he asked her, "What would you like for a present?" "Well, I've never met Ronald Colman," she said. "I'd like to meet him."

As it turned out, Colman was just as eager to meet Judy. The elegant British star was carried into the party by Alsop, enclosed in cellophane and tied up with a huge ribbon. Colman's humor and wit so captivated the Minnellis that he and his wife, Benita, became their friends.

When Judy could not cope with the studio or home crises, Minnelli encouraged her to spend a few days with the Alsops. The couple brought her from Evanview Drive to their house in Beverly Hills, where they treated her like a daughter. Recalled Sidney: "I thought it would be absolutely criminal if somebody didn't do something to preserve that talent." Alsop fought Metro over Judy's salary suspension, while Sidney played the good Jewish mother, cooking all of her favorite foods, and introducing her to some new Jewish delights. Then, as soon as Judy felt she could again cope with life, she'd call Minnelli to come and take her back home.

In February 1949, in the midst of their marital crisis, *Look* magazine sent journalists to M-G-M to photograph all the stars currently working at the studio. The stars sat for the historic occasion of Metro's silver anniversary, with over a thousand international distributors and salesmen in attendance. The night before, Judy drove Minnelli crazy with questions about what to wear; she really wanted to look good.

Standing around while waiting to be told what to do, Judy noticed Katharine Hepburn, who was clad in her usual casual shirt and black slacks. Hepburn came over and disarmed Judy with her witty observation: "I knew I'd be badly dressed, and I knew you'd be badly dressed. The only difference between us is that you took the time."

Minnelli was happy that Judy was able to sustain her schedule on *Easter Parade*. Unfortunately the calm didn't last long. Relations turned particularly bitter one day, when Minnelli snatched away Judy's pills. At the end of February, she announced that they were separating.

In the spring of 1949, their marriage entered its last days. Minnelli rented for Judy a second house on Sunset Boulevard as a getaway place. "We're happier apart," she told the gossip columnist Louella Parsons when she called for an update.

Minnelli was pleased that despite the turmoil Judy recorded the entire score for *Annie Get Your Gun* during the week of March 25. Her voice was strong and vibrant for Berlin's humorous songs, and just as tender for his more romantic ballads. But when shooting began, she again became insecure. Portraying the gun-toting Annie was a stretch, a role different from any she had attempted. Judy confided in Minnelli that she was intimidated by the need to play a character so intimately associated with the robust Ethel Merman. Minnelli guided Judy, recommending that she stress the vulnerable and sympathetic aspects of Annie more than the powerhouse Merman had done. He believed that with his help Judy could put her singular stamp on this classic Americana role.

Broke financially, Judy put pride aside and requested a loan from Mayer. "By all means," said Mayer. "The least we can do is pay for your hospital bills." But when Mayer called studio executive Nicholas Schenck for approval, the latter was not so generous. Mayer promised to pay her bills out of his own pocket if Schenck refused, but in the end, Schenck came through.

When Mayer asked Alsop what should be done about Judy, the latter said, "Why don't you get her away from all the sycophants and the doctors who give her these pills?" On May 27, 1949, Judy, accompanied by Alsop, boarded the Super Chief for Boston. Unlike the previous rehab centers she had checked into (Las Campanas and Austen Riggs), the

Peter Bent Brigham Hospital, which she entered on May 29, was not a psychiatric clinic but an ordinary hospital. Judy was put on a regime to restore her weight and energy and to treat her depression and addiction to drugs. She was prescribed three big meals a day, recreation time, an early bedtime, and so on. Judy had to relearn how to eat and sleep like a normal person.

Alsop felt that Judy should see a neurosurgeon, not a psychiatrist. He warned the doctor, "She's wily and can outcraft you. She has this jungle intelligence, this animal cunning. It's like trying to help a drunk across the street. He stumbles and weaves, and as soon as he's on the other side, he straightens and laughs at you."

When the psychiatrist told him that he had never treated a star before, Alsop retorted, "You can't work on the premise that you'll change her into Mrs. Vincente Minnelli, housewife. She is making half a million dollars a year."

Shortly after being admitted, Judy demanded to leave the institution. Alsop refused, claiming, "It's not your money. It's the studio's." In one of his visits, Alsop found Judy under the bed in her room, screaming in agony. He immediately called Minnelli in panic. "Just be a son of a bitch and get her out," Minnelli demanded. Alsop later said that he had never spoken so cold-heartedly to anyone in his life as he did to Judy.

One day, Alsop proposed to take Judy to a visit at Children's Hospital, a center in Boston for rheumatic children. Judy protested. "I can't go, it's too soon." Nevertheless, Alsop dragged her out physically. As soon as they arrived, however, and Judy noticed how thrilled the children were to see her, she melted. "I loved feeling I could help somebody else for a change," she later told Minnelli.

Relaxed for the first time since her honeymoon with Minnelli, Judy attended baseball games and enjoyed weekends at the Ritz Carlton Hotel with the Alsops. Sylvia Sidney, who was performing in summer stock outside Boston, came to visit her a number of times.

Minnelli was urged to keep quiet—and to make himself scarce—so he called Judy only occasionally. In contrast, Frank Sinatra, with whom Judy had a brief fling during her relationship with Minnelli, called her every day and visited once or twice. Sinatra filled her hospital room with flowers, perfume, records, and a phonograph.

In June, Minnelli arranged for Judy to go to New York to see Liza.

He sent their daughter with her nurse to celebrate her mother's twenty-seventh birthday. During Liza's visit, he called every day from Los Angeles to get a report from the nurse. After a few days in Manhattan, Judy and Liza traveled to Cape Cod for a vacation. When her visit was over, what Liza remembered the most, and talked about endlessly with her father, was the heartbreaking farewell.

Judy spent much of that summer at Peter Bent Brigham Hospital, where she was treated for, among other things, barbiturate and amphetamine withdrawal. During her recovery, Minnelli came several times to visit her. When she was released, they tried to resume their marriage, but the ensuing months brought only a temporary reprieve.

Minnelli was able to detect a dangerous status game during Judy's psychiatric sessions. One analyst would offer an interpretation of her behavior based on a current theory, which would later be supplanted by yet another psychiatrist with his own trendy theory. Initially, he had faith in each psychiatrist, hoping for some kind of miracle cure, praying that one of them would finally understand the real source of her problems. Judy, on the other hand, had no faith at all, and made no secret of her reluctance to really cooperate with her doctors. It took Minnelli a while to realize that Judy was lying to them all the time.

As he couldn't solve Judy's psychological problems, Minnelli had tried to help in professional matters, advising her how to interpret her songs in *Easter Parade,* based on Irving Berlin's music, for which her talents were most suitable. The title song already had a successful history, and the new songs showed great promise, too. Roger Edens did an excellent job of adapting the Berlin songs into manageable arrangements, which Gene Kelly could sing despite his limited vocal range. For Judy, however, Edens opened the songs up since her voice was staggering and limitless.

Judy's spirits were significantly better after the success of *Easter Parade.* The film had been such a huge hit that Metro was eager to reteam Judy with Fred Astaire. The delays and expenses caused by her erratic behavior were now all forgotten. Like *Easter Parade,* the new project, *The Barkleys of Broadway,* was a story about a theatrical team, this time set in a contemporary locale. Pleased with his work on *Easter Parade,* Metro put Charles Walters at the helm.

However, mentally and physically exhausted, Judy found it impossible to go through the process of making another film. Dangerously thin, she was now down to eighty pounds, and on most days, she couldn't get out of bed. Metro asked Ginger Rogers to step in, reteaming her with Fred Astaire for the first time in years. Minnelli stayed home for a few days to console Judy after she lost the part.

Judy felt that the only thing she represented to M-G-M was box-office. The paternal feeling Metro's execs held for her was tied directly to the profits she generated. Nothing Minnelli said could dissuade her from believing that the studio's "genuine" affection was a calculated way to get her to perform. As far as Minnelli was concerned, Judy, feeling betrayed, was wasting enormous time and energy scheming all kinds of revenge plots against the studio. Unfortunately, instead of lashing out, the anger turned inward, seething uncontrollably, threatening to destroy her. These were Minnelli's most frustrating times as a husband, because Judy simply refused to listen to him.

Gradually, Judy began to hate their Evanview house, too. In arguments, she charged, "It's your house!" claiming that she needed another home. Judy's psychiatrist also felt that it would be good if she could occasionally get away. Minnelli offered to take a year's lease on a house at 10000 Sunset Boulevard, and for the next few months, they alternated living in the two houses. During their periodic separations, Judy went over to the Sunset house and Minnelli stayed at Evanview. The good-natured and tireless Alsop functioned as their intermediary, and they continued to have dinners together at least two or three times a week.

Though Judy had agents to represent her, eventually they all had thrown their hands up in frustration. For a while, no one represented Judy until Alsop sidetracked his own producing career to help. Selflessly and single-handedly, Alsop dealt with the studio as well as with the Minnellis' hopelessly tangled finances.

In order to pay back the amount that she "owed" for her illnesses and absences, as well as the wasted preproduction expenses on *The Barkleys of Broadway,* Judy did a number in *Words and Music* for which she was paid $50,000. Mayer proposed to give her another $50,000 if she'd do a second number. Having already done "Johnny One Note," Judy teamed up with Mickey Rooney for a duet, "I Wish I Were in Love Again."

Weight problems had always plagued Judy. Whenever she was at an optimal weight, she was emotionally stable. But the changes in her weight were radical. In the first song, Judy hardly casts a shadow, then for the second song, she came back looking much heftier.

Judy began her next picture, *In the Good Old Summertime,* in reasonably good shape. But as soon as the pressures of daily shooting mounted, her weight began to rise and fall, and her figure changed from one extreme to the other.

With so many problems at home, Minnelli felt he couldn't be efficient enough to direct a major film, though he needed the distraction of work. To compensate, he grasped at minor assignments thrown his way, directing screen tests at Metro, reading scripts, offering oral and written reactions to producers and directors who requested them—in short, doing what he had done as a novice director, a decade ago.

Minnelli was not paranoid; he never felt that Metro was out to get him, or that he was being kept idle because he had fallen from grace. He never felt that the studio had written him off as a director, or relegated him to being Judy's caretaker. It was Judy who thought that Minnelli should sacrifice his career for her. He was prepared to do it, for a while. It seemed a small price to pay as her illness took hold, and her mental health declined. If he could only believe that Judy would be able to function again, normally . . .

Minnelli tried to keep up his own strength for Judy to draw on, but he was vulnerable too. Long after the flop of *The Pirate,* his self-assurance continued to be at a low ebb. With Judy's future in jeopardy and his at a standstill, a triple disaster—professional, emotional, and financial— loomed large. Minnelli was still drawing his weekly paycheck from Metro, but he worried that they would not be able to live comfortably for a long time.

Metro had bought *Annie Get Your Gun* for Judy, paying the highest amount ever spent on a property. Busby Berkeley, who had worked with her before, was assigned to direct, but she refused to work with him. Judy could be malevolent toward other people, but she could never understand the animosity others felt for her, based on lost jobs and pictures delayed or canceled due to her erratic conduct. Charles Walters, with whom Judy always got on well, was brought in.

After Judy completed the prerecording of her songs for *Annie Get Your Gun,* the shoot was about to begin. Judy was in terrible condition, with her weight down to ninety pounds, and yet, in desperation, she continued to take pills. Occasionally, Minnelli took the pills away from her, which made her all the more angry and violent. For the next few days, she treated him in a contemptuous manner.

There was no way that Judy, so physically weak, could keep up with the production schedule. On June 16, 1950, Mayer demanded that Judy come in the next day, a Saturday, for an hour's rehearsal.

However, pleading illness, she stayed home. Though it was only the first day Judy had missed entirely, and involved only a few hours of work, the studio used it as an excuse to suspend her. Within hours, a telegram arrived at her home from Metro's New York corporate office. Obviously, it had been written in advance. With a shaky voice and trembling hands, Judy handed it over to Minnelli and asked him to read it out loud. Trembling himself, Minnelli read: "This is to notify you that, for good and sufficient cause, and in accordance with the rights granted to us under provisions of Paragraph 12 of your contract of employment, you are no longer . . ." Judy had been summarily fired.

Minnelli realized immediately that this action was different from the previous suspensions. The first thing to do was to put the distraught Judy to bed under heavy sedation, which he did. By Monday morning, Judy was steady enough to participate in a crucial conference, orchestrated by Alsop and attended by Minnelli and Judy's secretary, Myrtle Tully.

They all agreed that Hollywood was not the only place where Judy could work. New York City's Broadway and London's Palladium presented viable options for a singer of her caliber. There was also the relatively new medium of television. (Sometime later, as soon as NBC heard about Judy's ordeal, the network offered Judy a contract. A telegram from NBC's top executives read: "Cheer up, Judy! We all love you.")

On June 19, 1950, on Monday afternoon, shortly after Alsop drove to Culver City to obtain a reversal of Judy's suspension, Judy ran into the bathroom and locked herself in. "Leave me alone, I want to die," she screamed, as Minnelli and Tully ran after her. When she refused to open the door, Minnelli broke it down with a chair. Judy had scraped the edge of a piece of smashed glass across the right side of her throat. "I didn't want to live anymore. I wanted to hurt myself and others," she later said.

When Alsop called from Metro with the bad news that Judy's dismissal was final, he was subjected to much worse news. "Get over here as fast as you can!" screamed the frantic Minnelli. Rushing back, Alsop found a hysterical Minnelli on the verge of collapse. Alsop slapped Minnelli hard across the face, which forced an immediate return to his senses.

Hiding the bundled-up Judy on the floor of Alsop's car, the two men drove to the Sunset Boulevard house, where her doctor, Francis Ballard, was already waiting. After examining her neck, Dr. Ballard told them that Judy was not seriously harmed. Slightly scratched, her throat required just a Band-Aid. "I had done more damage to myself when shaving," Alsop wryly observed. Alsop's humor was very much needed, considering the absurdity of the situation.

Someone must have tipped off the newspapers, because they all quickly used the incident as a front-page headline. "Judy Garland Cuts Throat Over Lost Job," noted the *Los Angeles Mirror.* "Judy Garland Slashes Throat After Film Row," headlined the *Los Angeles Times.* The stories continued for the next several days, each trying to outdo the others in analyzing Judy's downfall. "Hollywood Heartbreaks—Story of Fame, Fortune and Despair," wrote one, listing the names of all the actresses ruined by Hollywood, including Frances Farmer, who was confined to an asylum.

At first no one realized the consequences for Judy's mom, whose career was basically to "keep Judy in line." Ethel was shocked when her salary as a studio consultant ended with her daughter's suspension. For all these years, Ethel had pretended not to know that her salary depended on Judy's employment. Trying to react to the disclosure with pride, Ethel was nevertheless offended that the studio could calculate precisely what her "worth" was in monetary terms.

Finally, the studio borrowed Betty Hutton from Paramount as a replacement. George Sidney was brought in to direct, and Charles Walters, like Minnelli before him, was let go. Secretly, Minnelli believed that Judy's suspension was justified as a lot of money had already been spent on the picture.

In actuality, Minnelli was not so much a "broad-minded" husband (which is how he perceived himself) as an indifferent one. He was now eager to bring the marriage to an end. To the cynics in Hollywood, it was inevitable that when Judy broke with Metro, she would also break with Minnelli. She could not separate the two. Wasn't their marriage, just like their movies, a product of M-G-M?

Minnelli would remain under contract to Metro for twenty-six years, longer than most directors of his cohort. Outlasting three regimes, those of Louis B. Mayer, Dore Schary, and Nick Schenck, Minnelli became the quintessential Metro director. While his talent was a major factor in keeping him at Metro, there was no denying that Minnelli's remarkable durability at M-G-M was at least partly due to his diplomatic behavior and seemingly passive manner; Judy believed that he was passive-aggressive, and she was probably right.

Judy accused Minnelli of being married to the studio. It devastated her that not once during their marriage did he stand up for her against Mayer. Minnelli knew that his wife needed a stronger man than himself to lean on. Though sensitive and understanding, Minnelli realized that he was simply inadequate to cope firmly with her problems. "It was an indictment I couldn't ignore," he later acknowledged. "I obviously failed Judy."

Drugged and depressed, Judy sometimes stayed in bed for days, allowing only the maid or the cook to tiptoe silently into her room. Judy consumed enormous amounts of alcohol, usually vodka or Blue Nun or German white wine; her thermos contained mostly vodka with a bit of grapefruit juice.

Judy felt confident only when surrounded and held by a strong man she could trust. "Only you could give me the confidence I so badly needed," she had written Minnelli after *The Clock*. When her confidence in Minnelli vanished, so did her marriage, her career, and her emotional stability.

Judy believed that her husband had failed her, but in fact they had

failed each other. Judy's hysterical temper, suicide attempts, and paranoid crises wore Minnelli out completely. He was tired of living this way.
If they stayed together, he realized, their lives would always be shaped, if
not dominated, by her problems. Minnelli could never accept Judy's glee-
ful confession that she had lied to her psychiatrists. As far as he was
concerned, Judy had not really tried to get well, and he found it impossible to forgive her.

Minnelli and Judy finally realized that their marriage was taking a toll
on their beloved daughter. On December 7, 1950, the couple announced
their separation and intent to divorce. Three days before Christmas,
Judy left the Evanview Drive house. "It was characteristic of the quiet,
gentle Vincente that he never said a word when Judy walked out," wrote
Louella Parsons. "Perhaps Vince was too easy and too gentle with her."
Although they were to remain friends, for Liza's sake, occasionally one
or the other would slip in a disparaging remark. "Oh, Vincente," Judy
would say with sarcasm, "the man with the perfect taste and flawless
manners."

Minnelli believed they were divorcing for Liza's benefit, rather than
staying married for her benefit. "I opted for sanity," he later said. "Liza's
well-being would be better served, if she had one stable parent living
apart from his mate, rather than having two emotionally wounded parents living together."

Judy's divorce suit came before Superior Court Judge William R. Mc-
Kay on March 29, 1951. Dressed in black and white, Judy gave a surprisingly reserved and calm testimony: "When we were first married, we
were very happy. We had many interests in common, and many mutual
friends. But sometime later, without any explanation, my husband withdrew himself and shut himself out of my life. I had to appear in public
without him. It was very embarrassing. Finally, I didn't go anywhere
myself because it was too difficult to explain his absence. I was terribly
lonely. I frequently became hysterical. I had to go under a doctor's care. I
just couldn't understand his attitude. My husband lacked interest in me,
my career, my friends, everything."

Her testimony of mental cruelty was hard for Minnelli to take. Admittedly, Judy was impossible to live with. But Minnelli, who continued

his homosexual liaisons discreetly throughout the marriage, was hardly an ideal husband. Though Minnelli was upset by Judy's dismissal, the truth was that he had done nothing to help in the growing dispute between his wife and her employers. Judy told their friends that Minnelli "just looked the other way."

Judy was granted custody of Liza, provided that the girl spent half of the year with her father. This arrangement would be managed in such a way as to avoid undue regimentation in Liza's life. Division of the estate was not an issue since the Minnellis were virtually broke, having spent most of their money on psychiatrists and medical bills. Minnelli agreed to pay $500 a week child support while Liza was with Judy, and to be responsible for his daughter's medical bills.

Despite their impending divorce, Judy continued to seek Minnelli's advice. Shortly after the divorce, she drove up to Evanview Drive with her pianist-friend Buddy Pepper to show Minnelli a preview of her new act. In fact, it was Minnelli who suggested that Judy, often referred to as the greatest entertainer since Al Jolson, include in her concert one of Jolson's standards, "Rock-a-bye Your Baby with a Dixie Melody." Listening to her singing, Minnelli found Judy's voice not only better than ever but also more profound and mature.

Judy appeared at the Royal Dublin, on July 2, 1951, at the conclusion of her British tour. She had not seen Liza for three months. Minnelli consented to her request to see their five-year-old daughter in England. Minnelli reasoned that Liza had too often witnessed her mother ill or depressed, and that a visit to London would balance her memories, offering the girl an opportunity to observe her mother at her most triumphant.

A week in England, followed by an ocean voyage back home, would do a lot of good for his daughter. Minnelli was right. When Liza got back, she seemed happier and full of adventurous stories about her mom and her bizarre, eccentric friends.

Fourteen

An American in Paris

THE EARLY 1950S WERE A PERIOD OF crisis and change in Hollywood, particularly for a studio like Metro. First, its parent company, Loew's Inc., had been ordered to divest itself of its theater chains, just as Paramount, RKO, and Warner Bros. had. Then, hundreds of Hollywood professionals were fired or blacklisted as a direct result of the second round of investigations by the House Un-American Activities Committee. Moreover, a new threat came from the medium of television, which was quickly changing the face of American popular culture, replacing film as the dominant medium of entertainment by being accessible, free of charge, in American living rooms. Threatened from various directions, Hollywood had to come up with solutions, some of them related to its organizational structure, while others involved the development of new genres, such as big historical epics that viewers couldn't see on the small screen.

In 1950, after leading Metro for a quarter of a century, Louis B. Mayer lost his power and was forced to resign. Dore Schary, Metro's vice president of production, took over his job, and was tasked with re-activating the studio's sagging production slate. *Madame Bovary* was one of the first projects to be green-lighted by Schary.

Minnelli remained aloof from the executive changes that rocked Metro, pretending they would not affect his destiny. His forced sabbatical after *The Pirate* had occurred during a sharp decline in the studio's output, but M-G-M couldn't afford to let an expensive contract director like Minnelli go unused for too long.

Some filmmakers distrusted the new regime, but with Schary's pledge to maintain high artistic quality, Minnelli was happy to oblige. After a lengthy one-on-one meeting he was quickly swept up in the studio's accelerating pace. In fact, the new decade would become much busier and more significant for him than the one during his wartime and early postwar years.

In 1950 and 1951, Minnelli completed two comedies, *Father of the Bride* and its sequel, *Father's Little Dividend,* and one major musical, *An American in Paris.* He also began preproduction on *Huckleberry Finn,* a film that would not materialize, and added one long sequence to the musical *Lovely to Look At* (1952).

While Minnelli was busy preparing *Huckleberry Finn,* Mervyn LeRoy, a versatile director who had worked in every genre, was shooting *Lovely to Look At,* a film with songs by Jerome Kern, for producer Jack Cummings, sort of a remake of RKO's *Roberta* (1935), which had starred Irene Dunne, with Fred Astaire and Ginger Rogers in supporting roles.

When the project was initially discussed, Minnelli argued that there was no point to redoing the story—unless the musical took a new approach. Needing product, the studio went ahead with the picture. However, as was often the practice, LeRoy was summoned for another production while the shoot was in progress, and Minnelli was asked to stage the picture's musical climax.

Most of the picture was done when LeRoy left, and Minnelli concentrated on the musical's finale, an opulent Kern medley and fashion parade. Loathing idleness, and amused by the chance to upstage LeRoy, one of Metro's most respected directors, Minnelli consented, forgoing screen credit for his job.

In lieu of credit, Minnelli asked for more time and a larger budget to shoot the musical numbers. After discarding the preliminary set sketches, Minnelli gathered his associates and worked on that one segment for three weeks. The *Lovely to Look At* finale is only a footnote in Minnelli's career, but it had his customary dazzling energy. Up to the finale, the film is inferior to its 1935 predecessor, but then it bursts out with spark and vision.

Jack Cummings was a less demanding producer than Freed, and LeRoy was a curious choice to direct since he had no extensive experience with the musical genre. As a result, Minnelli had to work with LeRoy's leftover sets, which he disliked. Minnelli managed to subsume the score, the cast, and Adrian's costumes within dizzying tints and geometry. M-G-M's obsession with fashion shows nearly stranded good films, such as *The Women* and *Easter Parade,* but Minnelli replaced the couture with a whirlwind montage of hues. A tableau of lavender shifts to aqua, then to turquoise and white for Adrian's costume parade.

Minnelli didn't like LeRoy's footage, which lacked personal style and polish, and dismissed completely the art department's sketches for his sequence. He was glad to shoot the long fashion show that concludes the musical, willingly forgoing credit, knowing that LeRoy would take responsibility for the overall lackluster production.

Though LeRoy had used Kern's music in his 1935 movie *Sweet Adeline,* he showed no particular sensitivity to musical numbers. In contrast, Minnelli's interest in kinetic compositions that integrated dance, music, color, and movement is on full display in this sequence. In his dazzling vision, each section of the fifteen-minute sequence has a distinctive color scheme. Letting loose his imagination, Minnelli builds a flamboyant climax that stands in sharp opposition to LeRoy's drab and boring sequences.

The opening shows a group of people in red coats (one of Minnelli's two favorite colors) arriving at a salon door, where emcee Red Skelton is introduced in white tie and tails, surrounded by chorines in white chiffons. The men hand him a black top hat and cane, and the viewers are treated to a banal bit of dialogue: "Please enter, priestesses of beauty."

A tableau of lavender shifts to aqua and then turquoise, through which designer Adrian parades his dazzling costumes, bathed in unnatural light. The second part, the fashion show, is done in a mixture of mauve and green. As if in a harlequinade, the characters, dressed in mauve, move pillars, lighted from within, to form sharp vertical compositions. The dancers emerge from doorways in the center of a wall, and the section concludes with a long take that climaxes with the introduction of Ann Miller. Minnelli's color combination might have been in-spired by Leon Bakst's inventive designs for the Ballets Russes. Green plant leaves are wrapped around pyramids of light on the purple cloths, forming the domino masks worn by the harlequin figures.

The third part changes the color scheme to a dazzling mixture of red and green, and a float of metal-like constructions that recalls the spiky objects framing the "Limehouse Blues" number from *Ziegfeld Follies,* with a jewel thief and one of his society lady victims, just as in "This Heart of Mine." The dances are performed by Marge and Gower Cham-pion, whose numbers included a dance to "Smoke Gets in Your Eyes," with Marge in a red dress. Unlike Astaire's jewel thief in "This Heart of Mine," who was clad in white tie and tails, Gower Champion is in black, looking more like a burglar. The couple's dance ends in high style with a chase through the concentric arches. The color scheme changes again, as the fashion show resumes with yellows, as well as reprising the blue and mauve of the second section.

In one of the most impressive camera movements, the pavilion moves forward and down the steps, along with a model parading under it. When the first model leaves, a second moves under the pavilion, and the figures supporting the pavilion turn, as does the next model. The mov-able pillars are supported by figures clad in stylized medieval armor, making it impossible to determine their gender; they seem androgy-nous.

As usual, Kathryn Grayson sings in a terribly shrill voice, but she wears a beautiful gown, white with gold trim, against a background of one pavilion, and is joined by Howard Keel, who's also in elegant white tie and tails. The other couples, dressed in similarly spectacular fashion, emerge in one long take that zigzags across the screen. Still in his tails, Skelton lifts Ann Miller in a green dress. Marge and Gower Champion return, with Marge in a scarlet gown and Gower in white tie and tails, to perform to a jazzy arrangement of Kern's "Yesterdays." Minnelli's cam-era swirls around, and *Lovely to Look At* reaches its glittering if also distracting finale.

Quite predictably, neither art director Cedric Gibbons nor Jack Cum-mings, the producer, liked Minnelli's contributions to the movie be-cause they were too showy, too grandiloquent, calling attention to themselves. This, however, was precisely the intent of Minnelli, who, violating his own ideal of the "integrated musicals," now succumbed to excess for its own sake.

As 1951 ended, Minnelli was involved in two important projects. The first was a behind-the-scenes melodrama about moviemaking, initially called *Tribute to a Bad Man* and later renamed *The Bad and the Beautiful,* to be shot in the spring of 1952. It was to be followed by an Arthur Freed musical, *The Band Wagon,* also about showbiz. Both films would become signature Minnelli pieces, representing the very best of his efforts.

Minnelli's first film under M-G-M's new regime was planned to be a modest comedy, *The Skipper Surprised His Wife,* starring Robert Walker. But something more promising came along thanks to Pandro Berman, the producer who earlier had rescued Minnelli from a year of inactivity by assigning him to *Madame Bovary.* After that film's artistic and commercial success, Berman offered him a more interesting comedy, *Father of the Bride,* a picture that would start the most prolific and accomplished decade in Minnelli's career.

Pandro Berman was one of Hollywood's most eclectic and discerning producers. After a brilliant career at RKO, Berman moved to M-G-M, where he made such hits as *National Velvet* and later *Ivanhoe,* both starring Elizabeth Taylor. As a producer, Berman combined two rare qualities: shrewd practical instincts and great rapport with artists, particularly those behind the camera. Next to Freed, Berman became the producer with whom Minnelli worked most frequently at Metro, where he mounted most of Minnelli's comedies.

Berman owned the screen rights to Edward Streeter's 1949 bestselling novel, *Father of the Bride.* Frances Goodrich and Albert Hackett, who'd written *The Pirate,* were asked to work on the script. The idea of doing a comedy based on a more realistic and contemporary domestic setting appealed to Minnelli. Besides, he could finish *Father of the Bride* quickly, before moving on to a much bigger production, "the Gershwin picture," as it then was referred to, before it was titled *An American in Paris.*

Despite the excitement, initially, the casting of *Father of the Bride* proved to be problematic. Jack Benny had told Dore Schary that he would like to play the lead, the stern father, Stanley Banks. Without consulting anyone, the new studio head just said, "Great, we'd love to have you on board." However, Berman was upset and disappointed. He told Schary: "Jack Benny is a wonderful personality, but he simply won't do. We don't even have to ask Vincente. I can predict his response."

Schary requested that a screen test of Benny be made, confident that once Minnelli saw the results, he would change his mind. Minnelli, however, did not like the test, and decided to approach M-G-M top executive Benny Thau.

"Who do you have in mind?" asked Thau.

"Only one actor would do," Minnelli said. "Spencer Tracy."

"That's out of the question," Thau noted. "Spence has absolutely refused to do the picture. . . ." Assuming uncharacteristic courage, Minnelli asked, "Is there any reason why I can't talk to Spence about it myself?"

"Certainly," Thau said. "If you want to talk to him as a friend."

In his campaign to recruit Tracy, Minnelli decided to involve his long-time companion Katharine Hepburn, whom he had befriended during the making of *Undercurrent.* Hepburn, who was also close to Judy, invited the couple to their house for dinner, although Minnelli came alone, while his wife stayed with their baby, Liza.

"With you," Minnelli told Tracy bluntly, "this picture could be a classic of a comedy."

That brief sentence did it. Tracy consented without even reading the script. He had been aware that other actors were being considered for the lead, and assumed that Minnelli wasn't interested in him. It was to protect his ego that Tracy spread the rumor that he had refused to do it. Though at the peak of his career, Tracy still needed to be courted by directors. Minnelli's act of diplomacy succeeded, and as a result his stature was elevated both within and beyond the studio as a firm director who fought for and succeeded in getting the right cast for his pictures.

Minnelli knew instinctively that Tracy was ideal for playing the disgruntled father, and that casting Benny would have turned the comedy into a showcase for the usual Benny shtick. He persuaded Tracy that only he could give the role the necessary gravitas and resonance.

Once Tracy was on board, the rest of the cast fell into place. Minnelli chose the young Elizabeth Taylor as the bride, and Joan Bennett as her chic, matronly mother. The two actresses looked alike physically, having similar coloring and complexion.

As for the couple, Joan Bennett and Tracy had shown chemistry on-screen in earlier teamings, such as the melodrama *Me and My Gal.*

There was no friction whatsoever on the set of *Father of the Bride,* and the shoot became the shortest and smoothest experience Minnelli had on any Metro picture. Initial work on the film began while Judy was making *Summer Stock,* which would become her last picture at M-G-M before getting fired.

A gentle satire of the nuptial rites of upper-middle-class suburbia, *Father of the Bride* was a perfect film for a studio that celebrated the idealized American family under the guise of being "typical." Berman hoped that Minnelli would bring to *Father of the Bride* the same charm and resonance that had marked the folksiness of *Meet Me in St. Louis.* Like that film, *Father of the Bride* was basically plotless, but one with a strong premise, several poignant vignettes, and some sharp situations and characters.

Delighted with the cast and script, Minnelli began shooting on January 16, 1950, and finished exactly a month and a day later. This was an extremely efficient shoot for a major M-G-M production. Minnelli credited cinematographer John Alton, a veteran of B-pictures who was used to working fast, for getting the texture right and doing it quickly.

As Stephen Harvey pointed out, there are significant similarities between *Meet Me in St. Louis* and *Father of the Bride.* In both, a domestic setting and family epiphanies give the films a more shapely structure. The Smiths and the Bankses are both defined by their upper-middle-class existence. In both stories, the home is the arena where the important events happen, and in both, each family member plays a narrowly defined role based on society's mores. While the earlier film looks back nostalgically to the turn of the century as an age of stability, *Father of the Bride* is a Truman-era product that promoted a return to traditional family values after World War II. Not surprisingly, *Father of the Bride* became the prototype for many TV sitcoms of the 1950s and early 1960s.

M-G-M labeled the Bankses a "typical" family, but there was an undertone of smugness and elitism to them. Though seemingly ordinary, the characters belong to a higher social class than that of average movie-goers of the time. Stanley Banks, or Pop, is the breadwinner, and his wife, Ellie, combines immaculate grooming with feminine practicality. While their teenaged sons, Tommy and Ben, play peripheral roles, the family's favorite is clearly Kay, nicknamed Kitten, soon to be the bride. Kay wishes to replicate her mother's life, as if no changes have occurred in women's roles since the 1940s.

Minnelli used Beverly Hills' North Alpine Drive as a model for Everydale, USA, with white colonial-style houses on a tree-lined street. Like most M-G-M movies, *Father of the Bride* dilutes the more specifi-cally Scarsdale look of Streeter's book, though it presents a suburban community as an exclusive enclave. In Kay's speech about the Dunstans, her in-laws, she says that "they're as good as you and Mom," which was meant to reassure audiences that they, too, were as legit and desirable citizens as the Bankses.

Still, not everything is as smooth as it appears to be, and Minnelli's intimations of middle-class trouble are evident throughout the film. In the course of the story, Stanley is insulted by the catering staff, berated by his wife, and half-trampled at the wedding rehearsal. He can't even find relief in slumber, where terrifying visions of himself ruining the Protestant rites on the happy day shatter his sleep. As with *Meet Me in St. Louis,* the buoyant spirit of *Father of the Bride* collides with its latent, darker subtext.

Minnelli would never again look at the American family with such fond cheerfulness. In later films, he would be much more critical and cynical, as is evident in *Some Came Running,* with its dysfunctional fam-ily and adulterous father, and *Home from the Hill,* with its repressed, emasculating matriarch. Minnelli's later melodramas would show that Metro's depiction of the nuclear family in the 1940s and early 1950s was a product more of myth than reality.

But in 1950, as someone who himself had lofty ambitions in his youth, Minnelli sympathized with the Bankses, including their class snobbery. "I always used to think that marriage was a simple affair," Pop says at the beginning, echoing Minnelli's earlier opinion about that institution. The ensuing story shows how wrong Pop and Minnelli, the husband and father, were about marriage and family.

Kay's wedding reception is an example of claustrophobic giddiness. The film shows middle-class weddings as occasions of ostentatious materialism. Stanley asks, "What are people going to say when I'm in the gutter, because I tried to put on a wedding like a Roman emperor?"

The Bankses' social status suffers one blow after another. The Dunstans (played by Moroni Olsen and Billie Burke), turn out to be more sophisticated than the Bankses assumed; they've got a white (rather than black) servant. And Ellie's dignity is shaken when a snotty caterer (Leo G. Carroll) observes, "Little cakes and tea sandwiches is what we usually serve for children's parties."

The comedy's most vulnerable character is Stanley Banks, the benevolent patriarch. A quintessential Minnelli screen hero, Stanley is thrust helplessly into situations he doesn't relish and cannot control. The poignancy derives from Banks's series of humiliations—he loses his most cherished person and gets to pay for the privilege. Though Banks is the narrator, he lacks authorial power; in fact, he's the last person to know what's going on.

Banks doesn't even know which suitor his daughter will marry. Minnelli presents a montage of close-ups: a nerd, a chinless egghead, a scowling radical, a rubber-jointed bebopper (Spike Lee would borrow this montage for his parade of foolish men courting Nola in *She's Gotta Have It*). The lucky winner is Buckley (Don Taylor), a bland, muscled man holding a tennis racquet.

Spencer Tracy's moral gravity and pragmatic approach were assets for the role. It was refreshing to see him playing a victim for a change, the stoic who loses his dignity before utterly collapsing. Tracy wasn't a light farceur, but he was good at projecting offhand details that humanize the character. At one point, he toys with a rice-filled shoe as he surveys the wreckage after the festivity. Tracy's grave gaze, his gruff, narrating tone, and underacting stood in contrast to the shallow perkiness and high energy of other Hollywood comedy actors, such as Jack Benny and Danny Kaye.

Minnelli imbues the comedy with disquieting undertones. Shot in black and white, the film has a shadowy texture. Stylistically, it qualifies as a suburban comedic film noir. More than half of the film takes place at night, when the family succumbs to the worst nightmares a family could have—wedding bills, serious doubts about Kay's groom and their in-laws, and endless arguments over just about any topic.

Minnelli instructed composer Adolph Deutsch to avoid the kind of schmaltzy score that usually manipulates audiences' feelings. The first half of the movie contains no music at all, and the second uses minimal music. It comes from the story, what film scholars call diegetic sound, like a church organ at a wedding. Moreover, the prenuptial sequences are not accompanied by any music. Much like Bernard Herrmann's score for Hitchcock's darker movies, Deutsch's sustained theme is the discordant score that frames Stanley's hallucination of the ceremony, a Gothic sequence even by standards of Minnelli's screen nightmares.

In Streeter's book, Stanley's bad dream is mild and innocuous, amounting to being dressed in clothes that don't fit. But, significantly, in Minnelli's film, the nightmare is much harsher, showing a man who's completely lost, debased, and out of control. Punctuated by the silent screams of the throng, the sequence consists of an almost surreal collage of superimposed images. Stanley is not an unthreatening and unthreatened dad, like Leon Ames in *Meet Me in St. Louis*. He's more like Margaret O'Brien's Tootie, with anxieties that are real and primal.

In the end, however, as in most Metro films, a semblance of equilibrium is restored, but on a different level. The movie ends as it begins, showing Banks exhausted, sunk in his armchair amid the wreckage left by the wedding party. "Nothing really changes, does it?" he says, before taking his wife into his arms for a waltz, with the music playing "Goodnight, Sweetheart."

The film's last shot is particularly impressive. Stanley and Ellie dance, while the fluid camera retreats in reverse dolly shots. The couple is framed from a distance, just as the couple were at the ending of *The Clock*. The camera then pulls back through the length of the house and out the French windows into the dark garden.

The studio execs realized that *Father of the Bride* was going to be a success as soon as they watched the first dailies. Halfway through production, Metro announced the making of a sequel, *Now I'm a Grandfather,* later renamed *Father's Little Dividend,* to be directed as a quickie by Minnelli.

Released in May 1950, *Father of the Bride* became a smash hit, earning

$4,150,000 in domestic figures, thus becoming the year's sixth top-grossing film. At Oscar time, the film was nominated for Best Picture, Best Actor, and Best Screenplay, but Minnelli was denied a nomination from his colleagues at the Directors Branch. Did the movie's charm look too easy to appreciate? It would take another year before Minnelli would get an Oscar nomination, for *An American in Paris*. Even so, after the failure of *The Pirate* and the moderate appeal of *Madame Bovary, Father of the Bride* was much-needed proof of Minnelli's commercial viability, as well as an equally desired boost to his ego.

By any standards, *Father's Little Dividend* was a quickie. Minnelli spent three weeks preparing the movie, which began shooting on October 9, 1950, and ended twenty-three days later.

A pale imitation of the original, *Father's Little Dividend* opens the same way as the first picture, with Stanley Banks (Spencer Tracy again) sitting in his armchair and tying his shoelace, while confiding to the public his adventures ever since his favorite daughter, Kay, got married. Stanley's new worry is becoming a grandfather, an unpleasant reminder of his advancing age and declining faculties. Although Stanley fumes, his wife, Ellie, is jubilantly preparing for the baby; with her maternal instincts reawakened, she feels the baby makes her useful again as a family member.

Minnelli repeats other devices from the former film, some successfully, others less so. In lieu of a montage of gentlemen courting Kay, we see a photo album of grandfathers Stanley has met in his life. There's also a display of conspicuous consumption, in the baby shower sequence. And, of course, the Dunstans again try to upstage the Bankses for their grandchild's attention.

Stanley has to actually confront his worst fear, humiliation, rather than imagining it or dreaming about it in a nightmare. He loses the baby during a walk in the park. His anxiety is alleviated only when he finds out during the christening that his name has been bestowed on his grandchild.

Scenes of Kay and Buckley fighting invariably end with predictable apologies and embraces. There are also solemn speeches in the manner of Sunday school preaching, as when Stanley says, "When the time comes, you mothers seem to have a courage and a strength you never knew you had."

Despite its shortcomings, the film is appealing because of the rapport among the cast members. Unlike the previous film, which belonged to Tracy, the sequel belongs to the mother and daughter, thus restoring the gender balance that was slanted toward the father in the first picture.

Bored by the routine script and formulaic situations, Tracy mugs more than he acts, falling back on mannerisms. In later years, companion Hepburn said that Tracy more or less phoned in his performance. On the other hand, Joan Bennett, displaying her specialty, a brittle kind of matronly elegance, makes the most of her reveries on the pleasures of having large families with male grandchildren.

Taylor's Kay is more fragile, contemplative, and mature than she was in the first film, playing a kind, gentle foil for Tracy as he reminisces on the early months of parenthood, when he feared that his wife's affections would be squandered on Kay. While Kay's account of her obstetrician's ideas is boring, she is better in extolling the fortitude of primitive women, who keep their babies "slung on their backs for the first two years of their lives. . . . You would carry them around on your back, while you were doing your housework, and then when it got hungry, you'd swing it around and feed it and then swing it back again. It gives the baby a wonderful sense of security."

Minnelli's professionalism is evident, but his imagination flags, reflecting the speed with which the picture was made and his genuine lack of interest in it. Though it was made on the same budget as its predecessor, the sequel feels cheaply produced, with underwhelming art direction and other production values. Minnelli directs with minimum visual fuss.

There are more lengthy medium shots than usual in a Minnelli movie, again a result of functionalism and laziness rather than style. Camera movement is saved for Stanley's agitation as he wanders in panic in the neighborhood, searching for the missing baby carriage, retrieved by a local cop while he refereed a kids' soccer game. In place of the wistful elegance of the first picture's ending, here Minnelli fades to credits with a more facile and economical style. Minnelli gives the baby, Stanley Banks Dunstan, in christening clothes, a likable star-like close-up.

In short, this movie lacks the ideas, energy, and snap of the original. There's no novelty or dramatic urgency, and the only reason it was made was to make money, as is the case with most Hollywood sequels.

The three public previews yielded the expected results. Lawrence Weingarten, one of M-G-M's top executives, wrote to Dore Schary after the first preview: "Looks like this one will pay the rent." Indeed, the comedy grossed $3.1 million against a production cost of $941,437.

The film opened at Radio City Music Hall in April 1951, less than eleven months after the premiere of *Father of the Bride*. It was a pleasant surprise when the Directors Guild of America honored Minnelli with its quarterly award that spring.

Three years passed between *The Pirate* and Minnelli's next musical, *An American in Paris*. In those years, Arthur Freed made *On the Town*, whose exuberant tone didn't suit Minnelli's temperament. Two of the Freed Unit's musicals, *The Barkleys of Broadway* and *Annie Get Your Gun*, were planned specifically for Judy, though she didn't make either of them. Metro's other musicals, *Take Me Out to the Ball Game*, a Gene Kelly–Frank Sinatra vehicle, and Esther Williams's *Pagan Love Song*, were perceived by Minnelli to be routine, and he was relieved that Freed didn't put pressure on him to make either of them.

Meanwhile, the studio green-lighted a George Gershwin musical. M-G-M thought that *An American in Paris* was a good project for Minnelli and Kelly, if Freed kept a tight watch on the set and didn't let the duo get too carried away and waste time as they had done on *The Pirate*.

The project began in late 1949, when Minnelli first discussed with Freed a musical based on Gershwin's work. Freed had a vague notion for a musical about an expatriate Yank living in Paris, with only one clear concept: The film was to conclude with a smash finale, a full-length ballet to be danced to Gershwin's suite "An American in Paris." Because the Irving Berlin medley, *Easter Parade*, was a big hit, and the British import *The Red Shoes* had an unexpected success, studio executives thought that there might be a large public for dance-oriented musicals.

Ira Gershwin was easily persuaded to provide new lyrics and revise old ones, as needed. Freed wanted Alan Jay Lerner, then Broadway's brightest talent, to shape the narrative. Unlike Betty Comden and Adolph Green, whose forte was satire (as demonstrated in *Singin' in the Rain* and *The Band Wagon*), Lerner showed a preference for higher-brow material, like *Love Life*, with music by Kurt Weill, or *Brigadoon*, with choreography by Agnes de Mille. Lerner's specialty would be in adapting classy literary works, such as George Bernard Shaw's *Pygmalion*, which became *My Fair Lady*, and Colette's *Gigi*.

A Francophile, Minnelli identified completely with his hero, Jerry, an American painter in Paris. Arguably, no Hollywood director was as knowledgeable about French art and letters as Minnelli. His work often sought to evoke the light and color of his admired French painters. A project like *An American in Paris* also had a sentimental value, a personal reminder of Minnelli's friendship with the Gershwins, and a tribute to George, who had been dead for over a decade, with only the 1945 film *Rhapsody in Blue* to showcase his legacy.

Minnelli had the requisite taste and knowledge to execute a ballet that would become a kaleidoscopic collage, sort of a brief history of French painting. In the end, it would run almost seventeen minutes and cost nearly half a million dollars—a staggering amount, equal to the entire budget of a modest film.

For the story, Lerner devised two romances. One between Jerry, an artist studying in Paris under the G.I. Bill, and his patron, Milo Roberts, an older expatriate heiress interested in Jerry both personally and professionally. The second romance is between Jerry and a young Parisienne, Lise Bourvier. Initially, Jerry is unaware that Lise is the fiancée of his close friend, music hall star Henri Baurel; Henri had sheltered the orphaned Lise during the war.

Minnelli thought that the story was uninspired, but there were other compensations, prime among which were Kelly's acrobatic dancing, Gershwin's melodic music, and the picturesque Parisian setting.

Jerry's caustic pal, pianist-composer Adam Cook, a perpetual expatriate living in Europe on the largesse of foundation fellowships, was tailored for Gershwin's crony and Minnelli's buddy, Oscar Levant. "We thought of no one but Levant for Jerry's sidekick," Minnelli later said. "Including him in the film lent the enterprise a legitimacy, though he would have blanched if I'd told him that."

For the part of the older woman, Milo, Minnelli tested Anne Sargeant and Mercedes McCambridge (fresh from her Oscar win for *All the King's Men*), but he didn't like either and settled on Nina Foch.

Henri Baurel was intended as a comeback role for Maurice Chevalier after his long absence from the American screen. However, the French star was dropped from consideration due to M-G-M's fear of controversy about his alleged collaboration with the Nazis during the Occupation. Instead, Georges Guétary, a veteran of French musicals who had appeared with Nanette Fabray and Pearl Bailey in the Broadway musical *Arms and the Girl,* was chosen. Minnelli's initial doubts about Guétary were dispelled after watching his emotional rendition of "I'll Build a Stairway to Paradise."

The main casting challenge was to find the right actress to play Lise. Kelly said he remembered meeting a seventeen-year-old ballerina named Leslie Caron, whom he had seen in a ballet. Kelly was then sent to Paris to conduct a test of Caron. When he returned, the decision was positive, despite Caron's lack of acting experience. She was immediately offered a long-term contract that catapulted her to stardom, with films in the future like *Lili* and Minnelli's own 1958 musical, *Gigi*, among them.

Preston Ames, a former architecture student in Paris, was to design the sets. Metro's designers often found working with Minnelli frustrating, because he was full of paradoxes, aggressive yet inarticulate, demanding but unclear or unspecific. However, from their very first collaboration, Ames and Minnelli got along well. Ames would go on to contribute to every musical Minnelli made at M-G-M. Adrienne Fazan, whose sensibility was also in synch with Minnelli's, was hired as editor.

An American in Paris, however, marked Minnelli's first clash with a cinematographer. His wish for visual nuance and detailed mise-en-scène didn't suit Alfred Gilks's style; no matter what the emotional texture of a scene, Gilks tended to flood it with light, an aspect of film production Minnelli knew particularly well.

Minnelli asked to replace Gilks with John Alton, who had just shot for him the more stylized black-and-white *Father of the Bride.* More of a film noir specialist, Alton had not worked much with color cinematography, but Minnelli believed this was an asset because Alton would not be confined by preconceptions of what was possible (or impossible) to achieve in Technicolor.

John Green, then head of M-G-M's music department, assembled the score before delegating much of the more routine work to orchestrator Saul Chaplin. Minnelli spent weeks with Freed, Kelly, Ira Gershwin, and Chaplin, looking for those songs that would best fit Kelly's choreography and Lerner's script. Some songs carried special resonance: "Our Love Is Here to Stay," used as a romantic duet for Kelly and Caron, was Gershwin's very last song, left incomplete by his death. And the mock-Viennese number, "By Strauss," had been written for Minnelli's last Broadway revue.

Oscar Levant's piano rendition of "Liza," and a second duet for Kelly and Caron to "Somebody Loves Me," were never shot. Other songs were recorded and photographed but cut after the first preview. "I've Got a Crush on You," one of Kelly's favorites, was deleted, as well as two of Guétary's songs.

Curiously, no one paid attention to the fact that Caron was a decent dancer but could not sing at all. Thus, instead of performing with a borrowed voice, as was the custom, Minnelli decided to keep her silent during the musical interludes. He handled Caron's scenes so sensitively that, when the movie was released, few film critics noticed Caron's lack of singing. *An American in Paris* became M-G-M's, and the era's, only major musical to feature an all-male score.

Preproduction accelerated in the spring and early summer of 1950. At this point, it was still unclear whether the musical would be shot in Paris. For authenticity's sake, Minnelli rooted for Paris, pointing out that Metro's other big releases of the year, *King Solomon's Mines* and *Quo Vadis?*, were both shot on location, and became blockbusters partly because of that. Kelly supported Minnelli, citing the success of *On the Town,* a musical that benefited immensely from its New York locations.

In July 1950, two weeks before shooting began, Metro determined that the company would go to Paris for several weeks of location work. In the end, however, the studio chose not to take risks, and instead, re-created Paris on its back lot. Under Ames's supervision, facsimiles were constructed of portions of the Left Bank; a Montmartre street below Sacré-Coeur; the quay behind Notre Dame; the Café Bel Ami near the Seine, and so on. Some of these sets would again be used in Minnelli's films, such as *Four Horsemen of the Apocalypse*. Peter Ballbusch, a second-unit director, was sent to Paris to shoot some exteriors, which were later inserted, such as the opening montage depicting Milo's residence in the Hotel Ritz.

Despite Minnelli's disappointment, shooting the film on the studio lot liberated him and his creative team, particularly where executing the complex ballet was concerned. The real city of Paris would have to wait to be used by Minnelli until 1958, when he shot the musical *Gigi* there. In designing a dreamlike Paris with lights and canvas, Minnelli relied on his bold imagination and huge collection of art books. Like the paintings the movie evokes, Minnelli's soundstages had both a distilled magic and mystery about them.

No single sequence in this or any other M-G-M film could rival the "American in Paris" ballet for its delirious abstraction and dense texture. The music and choreography were meant to convey the city's "essence" as perceived by Minnelli. In conception, the piece combined a uniquely exuberant American energy with a specifically Gallic flavor, a cross-cultural style that for some was refined—and for others was no more than kitsch.

Shooting began on August 1, 1950, and proceeded smoothly throughout. Most of the script and musical numbers were done in six weeks. The production then closed down to allow Kelly to work out the details of the climactic ballet.

While the sets were constructed and Kelly worked on the choreography, Minnelli directed *Father's Little Dividend*. During that shoot, Minnelli was restless, brimming with ideas; he couldn't wait to get back to his pet project.

While making *An American in Paris,* Lerner and Minnelli quickly developed a shorthand communication with each other. As Lerner recalled, "Vincente spoke falteringly and vaguely, but in a manner that had nothing to do with logic. I always could feel what he meant more than I understood the words."

Calling Lerner from California one day, Minnelli tried to explain that he needed some kind of speech to lead into the ballet, which would relate the movie's love story to the art of Dufy, Toulouse-Lautrec, and all the other French painters whose work was inspired by the ballet's scenic backgrounds.

"Nothing too long," Minnelli said. "Just a short speech. You know what I mean."

Lerner did not know. "When do you need it?" he asked.

"Not right away," Minnelli said. "I'll be home tonight. Could you phone it to me? We're shooting it tomorrow."

It was a challenge, a short speech to sum up a two-hour story that at the same time would serve as an introduction to Dufy and Toulouse-Lautrec and a ballet. Lerner knew that Minnelli must have thought it possible, or else he would not have asked him. He then sat down and wrote what he thought Minnelli wanted. A few hours later, Lerner phoned and read the text to Minnelli.

"Perfect," Minnelli said. "Thank you." And that was that.

In later years, despite the fact that Lerner saw *An American in Paris* many, many times, he was still not certain what exactly the speech said. But if Minnelli said it was perfect, that was all that mattered. In fact, no one to this day has ever said: "What on earth is that speech all about near the end of the film?"

One thing Freed insisted on from the start was that there would be no concert music in the movie. "I don't want any lulls in this picture," Freed told Levant, who would play the piano. Freed wanted Levant to play only a medley of Gershwin's songs. The Freed Unit was redefining the movie musical, and he wanted to ensure that the story would be as strong as the music, and at no point should the action stop just to showcase a star turn or a big production number.

The ever-opinionated Levant felt differently. After the meeting, Levant walked into Minnelli's office and collapsed into a chair. He then blurted out his idea, that Minnelli film him playing all the instruments in the orchestra in a performance of the third movement of Gershwin's Concerto in F. At the conclusion of the scene, Levant would be seen sitting in a box seat cheering his own performance. "That's a marvelous idea," Minnelli enthused and embraced the concept.

Lerner said, "I wrote into the script the basic idea that Guétary at this point describes Leslie to Oscar. It was Vincente's idea, not mine, that in describing her, Guétary and Levant misunderstood each other. But in terms of the script, I indicated that Leslie should be introduced in a dance at this point. I left it open for Minnelli to figure out how precisely to do it."

Lerner wrote that when Henri starts talking about Lise, her image should be reflected in a mirror. Since she was a dancer, it was important to show her dancing before showing her doing anything else. Stylistically, that was very important. The audience had to accept Lise as a dancer. They were used to Gene Kelly as a dancer, but as Leslie Caron was a newcomer, it was important to see her dance early on.

Minnelli suggested that "Embraceable You" would be a good song to use at that point. And it was his idea to show Caron in a montage of different period settings. "It sounds terribly simple," Kelly said, "but it was a brilliant idea, the kind that choreographers can really use."

An American in Paris exemplified the virtues of the studio system, specifically, the cooperation among the various talent groups. Once completed by Ames, the designs were executed by George Gibson and Keogh Gleason. Minnelli's regular collaborator Jack Martin devised the black-and-white scheme for the Beaux Arts Ball that precedes the ballet. Conrad Salinger orchestrated the score that had been assembled by Green and Chaplin.

As solo choreographer, Kelly shaped the dances with his own ideas, which were fully embraced by Minnelli. Both the medley to "Embraceable You," which introduces Leslie Caron, and the staging of Guétary's "I'll Build a Stairway to Paradise," reflect Minnelli's and Kelly's intimate collaboration, based on their complementary ideas of how to stage musical numbers for the camera.

Their seven-page continuity called for a glorified production of a ballet that was a mini-musical in its own right. In fact, filming the ballet took longer than the entire shooting schedule for *Father's Little Dividend*. Minnelli began shooting the ballet on December 6, and after a short break for Christmas, finished on January 8, 1951.

What made the ballet special was Minnelli's visual conception, which keyed each sequence to a different color scheme and architectural style. Some of the segment was actually shot by Kelly while Minnelli was busy with *Father's Little Dividend*. Kelly's choreography provides the basic movement, but it was Minnelli who turned it into a masterful whirlwind of color and movement, endowing the numbers with propulsive energy.

Irene Sharaff, who had created the costumes for *Meet Me in St. Louis* and other musicals, was instructed by Minnelli to design about five hundred costumes for the ballet. Sharaff's sketches served as blueprints for Preston Ames's set designs. The main challenge faced by the art department was how to render the Dufy/Renoir/Utrillo/Rousseau/Van Gogh/Toulouse-Lautrec sketches onscreen. While sculptor Henry Greutert designed a Place de la Concorde fountain à la Dufy, Minnelli and Alton devised the specific lighting for the sculpture.

When it was screened for the first time to Metro executives, some felt that the picture needed to move faster toward its happy ending and that the ballet slowed things down. But Minnelli argued that the ballet should stay as is, since vast energy and money had already been spent on it. The final cut was ready in May 1951, after a reshoot of Kelly's number "I Got Rhythm," with another cinematographer, Hal Rosson, and a drastic reduction of Minnelli's black-and-white bacchanale.

In the ballet, Minnelli conjures up the eloquence of silent film, using images for sensuality and emotion. For almost seventeen minutes, not a single word was uttered, a stylistic decision that reflected Minnelli's long-standing belief that words presented unnecessary barriers between the images and the emotions they convey.

The film that began as a series of shots of Parisian landmarks (the Eiffel Tower, Place de la Concorde, and so on) concludes as a film-within-a-film filled with impressionist paintings of similar landmarks. The title of Gershwin's tone poem is also the title of the movie and its dream ballet. As a composer, Gershwin transcended the boundaries between Europe and America, theater and film, concert hall and music hall. A hybrid artist, Gershwin served as role model for Minnelli.

In the movie, Jerry searches furtively for an elusive love, symbolized by an intensely red rose. Like the rose, and like Lise in "Embraceable You," the beloved is a projection of the dancer's desire. Only the rose can give color to Jerry's world; only with his beloved can he dance in a world of impressionist color; without her, his world is black and white.

Minnelli's smooth transitions between individual impressionist settings utilized cinema's unique dimension of time to evoke the painting's unique dimension of space. Minnelli's shifting light, inventive dissolves, and twirling mirrors create a space that has no parallel in the physical world, reflecting the mental world of his imagination.

As Kelly searches for his beloved, he is tempted by lures that mirror temptations in the plot. Milo lures Jerry with her money, a temptation that turns artists into gigolos. A quartet of female Furies (two in red, two in white) try to distract him from his quest. A parallel quartet of soldiers momentarily snag Kelly with the quest for light amusement, but he deserts them when he catches sight of the beloved. At the end of the ballet, Jerry feels that he has lost her forever. He stands alone, holding the symbolic rose of his longing in the black-and-white sketch that began his reverie.

Minnelli and Lerner resolve the film's narrative before the ballet. It's remarkable how quickly the film ends after the ballet. The camera follows a trail of cigarette smoke to a smoking face, revealing that Henri has overheard Jerry's farewell to Lise. The final reunion of Jerry and Lise concludes the film after a sequence of pure visual imagery and music. The painter finally grasps the rose.

The ballet's duration of sixteen minutes and thirty-seven seconds is the culmination of all the frames, mirrors, and psychological projections that had preceded it. Some believed that the ballet was responsible for the film's winning the Best Picture Oscar. Moreover, after 1951, ballet became a staple for the musical genre: No prestigious musical could do without a dance. However, in both concept and audacity, no other film's ballet can compare with the dominant one in *An American in Paris.*

Minnelli not only saw dancing within painting, but dancing through paintings. At times, it feels as if the paintings themselves dance. For Minnelli, the ballet was an American renewal of the spirit that produced Gershwin's music in the first place. Gershwin, like a whole generation of American soldiers and painters, went to Paris. The difference between them is that, unlike Gershwin, Jerry decided to stay in Paris to paint.

On another level, the dream ballet celebrates the mythic union of America and Paris, of music and painting as art forms. The old France of Henri Baurel steps aside so that the American Jerry Mulligan can marry the young France of Lise. As in every M-G-M film of the era, the final credit reminded viewers that the film was "Made entirely in Hollywood, U.S.A." Specifically, *An American in Paris* serves as a declaration of faith, sort of a bridge between Hollywood and Paris, reflecting the optimistic zeitgeist of the postwar era.

After the ballet, the fade-out is brief and anticlimactic. Jerry looks down the street as Lise descends from a taxicab, after bidding adieu to Henri. The lovers race into a stairway of thirty steps to paradise, with Kelly going downward as Caron goes upward. They embrace at mid-landing, before descending quickly together. In a final shot, Minnelli pans upward to a sapphire Paris skyline, an image he would return to at the end of his 1958 melodrama, *Some Came Running*.

When the film was released, the critical response was favorable, but not ecstatic. Kelly and Caron were praised, but some critics lamented the lack of dramatic continuity. Minnelli was disappointed that *An American in Paris* was regarded as just another M-G-M musical, albeit one with a classier score and more innovative ballet.

Nonetheless, the movie became a box-office hit, grossing more than $8 million. At Oscar time, *An American in Paris* received eight nominations, mostly in technical categories, though Lerner's script garnered a nod. Minnelli finally received his first directing nomination, thus becoming the first filmmaker to be nominated for a musical since Michael Curtiz, for *Yankee Doodle Dandy,* in 1942. The Best Picture nomination was also a first for producer Freed.

Few people in the industry expected *An American in Paris* to win the Best Picture. Within Metro, some execs favored the movie over the other M-G-M nominees, the historical epic *Quo Vadis?* and the modest war drama *Decision Before Dawn,* which was unexpectedly nominated.

The frontrunners of the 1951 Oscar race were Elia Kazan's *A Streetcar Named Desire* and George Stevens's *A Place in the Sun,* prestige dramas based on respectable literary sources. The New York critics divided their prizes between these films, with *Streetcar* winning the top award. Each film represented a facet of the new Hollywood, bent on tackling mature themes seldom before seen on the big screen. Insiders expected Oscar night to turn into a back-patting session honoring the industry's newfound maturity and daring.

When *An American in Paris* opened in October, the critics liked Gershwin's music, Kelly's innovative choreography, and Caron's charm. Kelly said he wasn't disappointed when he failed to earn an Oscar nomination. However, he later rationalized the snub in a way that indicated he was indeed hurt: "There is a strange sort of reasoning in Hollywood that musicals are less worthy of Academy consideration than dramas. It's a form of snobbism, the same sort that perpetuates the idea that drama is more deserving of awards than comedy."

Hosted by Danny Kaye, the 1952 Oscar show took place on March 20, at the RKO Pantages Theatre in Hollywood. The Academy's Board of Governors had earlier voted Gene Kelly an honorary Oscar for his "versatility" and "brilliant achievements in the art of choreography on film." Kelly, who was in Germany, asked Stanley Donen, his codirector of the upcoming musical *Singin' in the Rain,* to accept the statuette on his behalf. Minnelli, who was in the audience, was offended that Kelly had not asked him.

The Best Picture Oscar was presented by the veteran industry leader, Jesse Lasky. Opening the coveted envelope, Lasky exclaimed, "Oh, my! The winner is *An American in Paris.*" The roars that had greeted Freed when he accepted the Irving Thalberg Memorial Award were not repeated when he returned to the stage for the second time. With a big smile on his face, Freed said, "I'd like to thank M-G-M, a great studio with real courage and leadership."

Joy was certainly not universal when *An American in Paris* was announced the winner. Gossip columnist Sidney Skolsky called it a "shocker" and suggested a recount. *The New York Times*'s Bosley Crowther fumed, perhaps forgetting that he had placed the musical on his ten best list. He wrote: "It was unbelievable that the Academy had so many people so insensitive to the excellence of motion-picture art that they would vote for a frivolous musical picture over a powerful tragedy," revealing his favorite, *A Streetcar Named Desire.*

But the *Hollywood Reporter* justified the Academy's choice: "The dissenters have had plenty to say. They're saying 'It was a frame. A studio the size of M-G-M has too many votes and they can swing an award.' That's a lot of hogwash. The best picture ALWAYS wins and it's made no difference whether that best was from the largest or the smallest studio."

M-G-M greeted its unexpected success with an ad that depicted Leo the Lion, the studio's mascot, looking at the Oscar with an apology, saying: "Honestly, I was just standing In the Sun waiting for A Streetcar."

The fact that M-G-M won Best Picture soon after the departure of Louis B. Mayer indicated that the new management knew what it was doing. However, Alan Jay Lerner recalled in his memoirs that one of the toughest obstacles was convincing the studio to allocate $400,000 for the climactic ballet, the musical's most celebrated moment. Though Dore Schary later took credit for that decision, everybody in the industry knew it had been Mayer's doing.

In the 1950s, Minnelli was becoming increasingly aware of his stature among critics, particularly the French ones in the influential magazine *Cahiers du Cinéma,* and of the commercial appeal of his films abroad. Hence, he was delighted to read about the opening of *An American in Paris* at the prestigious Empire Theatre in London, and the box-office records set on the film's opening day, which surpassed those of such recent hits as *The Great Caruso* and *King Solomon's Mines.*

The critical response was equally laudatory. *The Sunday Times* wrote: "Minnelli's movie may make fresh converts to the American musical, and the ballet is surely destined to become a classic. There are only a few moments that are not enjoyable, but Leslie Caron is a charmer with a face mischievously memorable."

Minnelli requested clips of these reviews and then proudly thanked some of the theater owners in person. Moreover, in a letter dated January 28, 1952, to Mr. D. Torrington in Rag Office, a philanthropical organization in Manchester, he wrote: "We who contributed to the making of the film hoped that it might in some measure bring joy, beauty, and an hour's surcease from the cares of the world. We are honored if our picture can be of any aid in assisting such a worthwhile cause as children's charities. Our respective causes are not so far apart—to make life a little easier."

This reflected Minnelli's basic philosophy of the entertainment function of Hollywood movies, a philosophy that led him to steer clear of "message" and "social problem" films. And it also expressed his attempt to get as much joy out of his parental role as possible, since he had no companion in his life. Which meant that once again Liza became the sole focus of his off-screen attention and happiness.

One day, during the filming of *An American in Paris,* Minnelli brought Liza to the set. As they were driving home from M-G-M after a long day at the studio, Liza suddenly said, "Daddy, I want you to direct me!" Minnelli's mind was preoccupied, so at first he didn't grasp his daughter's request. He reassured Liza that he would direct her in a scene when they got home. But Liza's protests continued. "No, no, I want you to direct me! I want you to get mad at me and shout at me just like you get mad at other people." Liza was expressing a childhood dream that would materialize two decades later, when her father directed her in *A Matter of Time,* in 1976.

Liza remembered vividly those studio days, particularly the drives home, when she had her dad just for herself. Liza thought she had his undivided attention, though more often than not, he was distracted, or still bothered by the day's problems. It always took Minnelli time to forget his worries and truly relax.

Liza later recalled, "I used to be at the studio so much. I especially loved the musical numbers. I didn't quite understand the drama, but the musical numbers I thought were wonderful. I used to see how people would change their delivery, after Daddy talked to them. I wanted to know if I could do that and to show off for him. I always wanted to be perfect for him."

Years later, Liza told columnist Rona Barrett, "I really had a weird life, but it was a great life. We laughed a lot, but nobody wants to hear about that." Indeed, during Liza's childhood, all the gossip was about the negative aspects of her parents' marriage, particularly its damaging effects on her upbringing. "Some people think reality must be constantly depressing," Liza said, "but I think reality is something you rise above."

After the divorce, according to the custody agreement, Liza was to spend six months with her mother and the other six with her father. At the young age of five, Liza inhabited two entirely different showbiz worlds, Judy's and Minnelli's, shuttling uncomfortably back and forth between them.

Minnelli went out of his way to please Liza whenever she was with him. Like many divorced fathers he tried, out of both guilt and love, to make Liza's life special, accommodating each and every one of her wishes and whims. "If I spoiled Liza outrageously, it was done to achieve a balance with the starkness of her life with Judy," he rationalized. "Much as Liza loved her mother, Judy represented duty and worry. I required nothing. As a result, I shared Liza's most carefree times."

When Judy moved to New York, Liza stayed on with Minnelli in Los Angeles. In fact, she adapted better to her father's bachelor life than he himself did. Lee Gershwin reproached him: "Vincente, I love Liza dearly, but she is very spoiled. It's your fault, you know. Judy is the disciplinarian with her and tries to instill some character in her. But you, you give her everything. You're nothing but a puddle of love. For her own sake, Liza should be disciplined. If she's not, you mark my words, she's going to grow up being a commuter to an institution." At which point, all Minnelli could do was shrug his shoulders and say, "I know, I know I should, but I just can't help myself."

Minnelli and Judy showed their love for Liza in different ways, based on their contrasting values and different personalities. Minnelli's love was undisciplined and uncoordinated, dispensed without any reason or formality. For him, Liza was a Hollywood princess living in an ivory tower, to be handled kindly and with respect. Liza often said, "My father treated me like a lady, he dealt with me on a feminine level. To do that to a little girl is the most valuable thing that can happen."

Liza relished her father's new status as a bachelor. In his personal life, Minnelli was passive and ineffectual yet extremely kindhearted, bringing Liza up to the best of his abilities. Overwhelmed by an all-consuming love, Minnelli imparted to Liza his fine artistic sensibility, his creative talents, and his gifts as a low-key raconteur (unlike her mom who was a high-key raconteur).

By the time Liza was five, Minnelli had already taught her the Cole Porter song "Love for Sale," and other sophisticated ballads. Minnelli's selection of reading material for Liza was equally mature. "My father read to me about Colette and her men, when other children were being told about Heidi and her goats," Liza recalled.

Now that he was divorced and Judy's problems no longer consumed his energies, he did everything to prevent Liza from being subjected to humiliation. He couldn't bear anyone hurting his little girl. One Halloween, Minnelli designed a costume for Liza, as a young witch, assuring her that it would frighten people to death. Despite his reassurances, Liza was laughed at. Minnelli insisted that the laughter expressed fear, but Liza was terribly offended. It was only when he took her to Gene Kelly's house, and Kelly pretended to be terrified by her costume, that Liza calmed down.

Minnelli the father relished telling anecdotes about his slavish devotion to Liza. When Liza was four, he drove for hours to take her to the Ice Capades. When they finally arrived, Liza said she didn't like her dress. Undaunted, Minnelli drove all the way back home, waited patiently while she changed into another costume, and then drove back to the event. By the time they arrived, two hours later, the Ice Capades show was nearly over. Minnelli didn't care; he had proven his genuine concern and deep love for Liza. For the rest of her life, Liza would search (in vain) for another man whose love would match her father's.

By necessity, Minnelli's time with Liza revolved around the studio. Zsa Zsa Gabor, who appeared in *The Story of Three Loves*, an episodic film for which Minnelli directed one of the three segments, recalled, "We would film at M-G-M and I would look up at the boom and see this tiny little girl with enormous brown eyes staring down at me. It was a sad and touching sight."

Needing to work yet eager to please and entertain his daughter, Minnelli often entrusted Liza to the care of studio makeup artist Charles Schramm. According to Schramm, Minnelli was facing the classic dilemma of a divorced father: "Liza would come down to the makeup department, and I would give her some clay to work with. She was just a little girl being taken care of by her father's secretary, because there was no one else to look after her."

Minnelli's bond with Liza was unshakable, as much a product of his guilt as of his love, but it also reflected Minnelli's own loneliness, his longing for a soul mate. Liza perceived her dad as a special, even magical man.

Liza observed with curiosity the rare occasions when her father lost his temper on the set. She recalled, "He'd take me on the set when he was directing, and he'd yell a lot." But later, at night, he couldn't remember his yelling. As Liza recalled, she would say, " 'Daddy, you yelled so badly today.' And he'd say, 'I did? When? Why did I do it?' He didn't yell for effect, he yelled to get things done. I never felt intimidated. He'd never put me in that position."

Liza was often bored on the set, but she tried to conceal it from her father. She liked watching the musical numbers, though at that time she had no interest in acting. Occasionally, Minnelli would offer some tips on acting, stressing that "no matter what, always, always listen to the director." In the future, Liza would never forget her dad's advice, clinging to his wisdom as a talisman.

Guarding him passionately and jealously, Liza behaved like a grown-up woman fearing the loss of her lover. Minnelli recalled that at Liza's sixth birthday party, a little girl came over and sat on his lap. "I hugged and kissed her," he recalled, "and I didn't notice that Liza was watching, but then she came over and punched me on the nose. It was so completely unlike her. The attitude was, 'That was for nothing. Now watch it!' "

But to everyone else, it was very much like Liza. Minnelli just refused to believe how jealous Liza was of any attention he gave other people, a situation that would worsen when he remarried and had a second daughter, in 1954.

Though it may sound strange, Minnelli was an ideal noncustodial father. As the most tangible proofs of his loving care, he created special costumes for Liza. Every year, Minnelli designed scaled-down versions of outfits made originally by Adrian or Irene Sharaff. The costumes were replicas of those worn by actresses in *An American in Paris* or *The Band Wagon,* and they symbolized his love. They helped create a fantasy world to which he and Liza could—and would—retreat during hard times. Minnelli photographed Liza in her costumes, which she looked at over and over again, occasionally sharing them with her friends.

Liza spent many long days on the set of *The Band Wagon.* Years later, in her tribute revue, *Minnelli on Minnelli,* she said she was unable to single out a personal favorite among her father's films. However, she loved one scene in *The Band Wagon,* in which Fred Astaire sings and dances ecstatically after having his shoes shined. That scene demonstrated to Liza her father's belief in the universal need for "a little magic." Liza asked fashion guru Halston to design a wardrobe for her that would make her look like a female version of Astaire.

Liza said that watching Astaire in *The Band Wagon,* in 1953, motivated her to become a professional dancer. She began taking dance classes at the school of Nico Charisse, actress Cyd Charisse's husband. Liza improvised to records, singing and dancing with her friends, Amanda Levant and Gayle Martin. By that time, she had already mastered her mother's stage routines. Occasionally, Liza belted out in full volume and great intensity Judy's songs, like "Button Up Your Overcoat," using a pinecone as her microphone.

Observing Liza with equal measure of fascination and alarm, Minnelli had mixed feelings about his daughter's displays, but he kept them to himself, hoping they were only a passing phase, part of the growing pains of a girl without a live-in mother.

He also felt great concern about Liza's "double" personality. When she was with her father, she was outgoing and friendly. When at school, or by herself, Liza was sour and somber, just like her moody and temperamental mother. Minnelli didn't know what to make of it. He wondered whether he should consult a psychiatrist, a profession he disliked and distrusted immensely after the awful experience he had gone through with Judy.

Fifteen

Minnelli's Masterpieces:
The Bad and the Beautiful and *The Band Wagon*

HAVING JUST PRODUCED A HIT, *An American in Paris,* Dore Schary was keen for Minnelli to direct another picture quickly. M-G-M wanted a similar kind of musical starring Leslie Caron and offered him *Lili,* but this time around, Minnelli felt assured enough to decline. As the first solo vehicle for Caron, Helen Deutsch composed a fable-with-songs about a provincial French waif who joins a traveling carnival. Minnelli was the obvious choice, but the turf was too familiar. Instead, *Lili* was assigned to Charles Walters, who by then had become used to picking up Minnelli's rejects. When *Lili* proved to be an unexpected commercial hit, Minnelli regretted his decision, which had been based solely on artistic considerations.

Minnelli had recently read a script titled *Tribute to a Bad Man,* which had been kicking around the studio for some time.

"You really want to do that?" Schary asked in a state of disbelief. "That's the story of an out-and-out heel."

Minnelli disagreed. "No, I don't think it is. I think anybody like Jonathan Shields, who has the charm to get people to work for him and get involved with him, must have the charm of the world."

Schary then asked, "Who could play such a monster?"

Minnelli was ready with an answer. "Only one actor, Kirk Douglas."

Minnelli believed that Douglas was the only star who could effortlessly combine tough harshness with easy charm. Douglas was the kind of actor who didn't have to portray strength; it came naturally to him. The challenge would be for him to get the character's smooth charm right.

Unbeknownst to Minnelli, Schary approached Clark Gable (still labeled "The King"), whose popularity as M-G-M's reigning star was beginning to decline. Quite expectedly, Gable turned it down. Douglas, in contrast, thought that the script was wonderful, and relished playing a "bad" movie mogul. When M-G-M announced that Lana Turner was the "beautiful" of the title, the papers were filled with gossipy items, such as "When would these two get together?"

It was no secret that Douglas's character was partly based on, or at least inspired by, Orson Welles. Despite differences in age and aesthetic sensibility, Minnelli and Welles shared some elements. Both became famous as young directors in the New York theater in the 1930s. Both moved to Hollywood and began making movies in the 1940s, and both collaborated with producer John Houseman. In later years, Minnelli would tell *Cahiers du Cinéma* that Welles was the Hollywood auteur he most respected because of his brilliant, audacious style.

Some saw the comically pretentious Jeffrey in *The Band Wagon*, an artist who tries to direct a musical version of *Faust*, as a fictional synthesis of Welles and Minnelli. And as several critics pointed out, the two directors' personalities converge again in *The Bad and the Beautiful*, a steamy Hollywood melodrama that was inspired by, among other sources, *Citizen Kane*.

Welles's former associate, John Houseman, who had recently become an M-G-M producer, came across a short story by George Bradshaw, "Memorial to a Bad Man," which was published in the *Ladies' Home Journal*. Based on the life of Jed Harris, the tale concerns the death of an unscrupulous Broadway director. The director's lawyer invites his former collaborators to the funeral, where each one recalls how they were first seduced and then betrayed by him. Anticipating his colleagues' hostility, the dead man defends himself in his will, claiming that he had taught them important lessons that helped make them successful. As a last request, he begs them to collaborate on producing a play in his memory. Amused by this presumptuousness, and still fascinated by him, they agree to work on the play. The story ends on an ironic note, with their speculation on the bizarre future project.

Bradshaw's tale was interesting because of its multiple-perspective narration, which recalled *Citizen Kane,* and the film's narrative structure was also similar, including the equivalent of a "Rosebud" symbol and Kirk Douglas's Oedipal confusion. However, instead of adapting the story as a satirical exposé, Houseman opted for a glossily made, intensely emotional melodrama. He proposed to change the setting from Broadway to Hollywood, and to tell the story of a producer (rather than a director), someone like David O. Selznick. Houseman said he was tired of theatrical stories with protagonists patterned after Broadway's Jed Harris. He also wanted to avoid a film that might seem too similar to *All About Eve,* another cynical multiple-perspective narrative about the theater world, written and directed by Herman Mankiewicz's brother, Joseph.

In the 1950s, Hollywood movies were becoming more self-reflexive, examining their own past with a peculiar mixture of nostalgia and cynicism. A whole cycle of films, including Billy Wilder's *Sunset Boulevard,* George Cukor's remake of *A Star Is Born,* Joseph Mankiewicz's *The Barefoot Contessa,* and Robert Aldrich's *The Big Knife,* appeared. Though less troubling, and more in tune with M-G-M's conservative image, *The Bad and the Beautiful* represented one of the highlights of that cycle.

Houseman asked Charles Schnee, a former financial partner in his Mercury Theatre, to write the script. Drawing on "Memorial to a Bad Man," and ideas taken from a second Bradshaw story, "Of Good and Evil," published earlier in *Cosmopolitan,* Schnee created the character of Jonathan Shields, an independent producer who's in decline. In the first draft of the script, Shields makes a call from London to three of his former associates—a director, an actress, and a writer—to ask them to participate in his new, comeback film.

At first, they all refuse. In flashback, they recall how they were first courted and then abused and betrayed by Shields. Shields pretended to love the actress Georgia, when, in fact, he was sleeping with another woman. Shields attempted to gain control over the writer's work by arranging a secret (and fatal) affair between the writer's sexy wife and the studio's Latin lover. All three, who have since pursued successful careers, claim they'll never work for him again. The ending of the movie is ambiguous, however, showing the trio as they eavesdrop on Shields's call to his assistant Pebbel, curious to learn more about the new project.

Minnelli's interest in the project made it easier to mount a big glossy film in the mode of M-G-M's prestige ensemble productions of the 1930s, such as *Dinner at Eight* or *Grand Hotel*. The cast members' names jump out one by one during the credit sequence, unfolding to the rhythm of David Raksin's bombastic music.

Helping to devise the final script, Minnelli had to handle a "list of suggestions" that were meant to avoid accusations that the fictitious character of George Lorrison, Georgia's father, was based on John Barrymore. Hence, while it was all right to show a love scene in a bedroom, such a love scene should not be too reminiscent of any specific love scene associated with Barrymore. And it was all right to have a recording of excerpts from a Shakespearean play, but Minnelli could not choose one too closely associated with Barrymore.

For Minnelli, *The Bad and the Beautiful* was about the tawdry absurdities and operatic splendors of the bizarre dream factory known as Hollywood. In his picture, the characters are less conniving, greedy, and corrupt; they are more frustrated dreamers who, despite disappointment, still yearn for the art, glamour, and sophistication that movies afford. Having experienced moments of exhilaration, they relish any chance to re-create and relive those moments.

To highlight those ironies, Minnelli requested some changes in the script. The original draft was a hero-as-heel story, a Kirk Douglas screen specialty, as established by his previous films, including *Champion* and *Ace in the Hole*. Shields was originally drawn as a villain who stepped on everybody's shoulders to get to the top and lacked any human qualities or redeeming graces. By contrast, Minnelli's conception emphasizes his charm, flamboyance, and, above all, the sheer magnitude of his talent. Minnelli argued that greater attention to psychological realism, accentuating his charisma and gifts, would discourage the audience from making a quick and harsh judgment of Shields.

In the end, Minnelli's picture was milder and softer than the script. Initially, it contained two darkly comic scenes that illustrated Shields's unpleasant character. In the first, Shields accepts an Oscar for a film he has produced called *The Faraway Mountain* and pays lavish tribute to his dead father, but barely mentions the work of the film's fledgling director. This scene was actually shot, but was later dropped from the final cut, because it didn't fit.

The second scene, which wasn't filmed, occurred at the end of the story, with Shields in a Paris hotel, aware that the people he once betrayed are eavesdropping on his call to Hollywood. Pretending to be unaware of their presence, he apologizes for what he did to "three fine people that he loved." Then, in the midst of outlining his idea, he deliberately breaks off the connection. Leaning back in his chair, he awaits a return call while talking to his press agent. The phone starts to ring and the agent reaches for it, only to be told by Shields, "Let it ring for a while."

In contrast to the script, the completed film ends on a more ambiguous but also a more clever note. The three characters gather around a telephone in an outer office, eavesdropping on Shields's conversation with Pebbel. The audience doesn't see Shields. He is, as the scholar James Naremore has observed, an "absent presence," an image mediated by memory, an overheard voice. Shields's collaborators, standing in for the real audience, indicate their endless attraction to the alluring magic of showbiz.

The film's most celebrated scene was a flashback depicting Georgia's drive after visiting Shields late at night and finding him with another woman. Stumbling outside, Georgia leaps into her car. Stunned and terrified, she begins to drive faster and faster down the Pacific Coast Highway, until she goes berserk. Sobbing and screaming, she disregards the steering wheel and oncoming traffic, until she spins out of control and lands on the roadside, miraculously safe.

Instead of presenting the drive as a montage, cutting back and forth between Georgia's reactions and her car, Minnelli shot the entire drive in a single take, cutting away from it only once to show Georgia's shoe pressing on the accelerator.

Minnelli also dispenses with music, the customary device for increasing the impact of such scenes. The scene's intensity derives from Lana Turner's intentionally hysterical performance, the striking sound effects, the visual effects of the flashing lights, and the swirling camera movement, which by now has become Minnelli's distinctive specialty.

To accomplish this effect, Minnelli attached Georgia's car to a vast turntable on the back lot, which made it rock from side to side. Mounted on a dolly, the camera sweeps in little arcs around Turner, viewing the action from over her shoulder, or looking into her face. As lights rake across the screen, Georgia becomes a blur of white mink and rhinestones. While screaming, she closes her eyes and releases the steering wheel. Her cries are punctuated by various sounds: the rain on the windshield, the stroke of the wiper blades, and the horns of the passing traffic. The car spins and rocks wildly. There's more traffic, more horns, then soft sobs, rain, and windshield wipers.

After the flashback ends, there's a fade-in to a close-up of Georgia in the present. Dressed in widow's black, framed by a veil and a dark fur stole, she's lit by a ring of diffused light. "I told you I'd never work for him again," she says in a cool manner.

The sequence was so effective that Minnelli tried it again ten years later in *Two Weeks in Another Town,* when Kirk Douglas and Cyd Charisse go for a drive in a red sports car. But the later version is just movieish, lacking the brilliant photography, unceasing movement, and emotional power of the original 1952 sequence.

Various critics have pointed out that the "auto hysteria" gains much of its strength from the context: The vaguely dizzying scene inside the mansion raises the stakes by employing "silent movie technique." The frantic drive provides a cathartic release of tension. Georgia's behavior is chaotic and violent, and at the same time, she is the epitome of artifice, a movie star sitting in a studio mockup of a car.

While Minnelli produced powerful emotions and sexually charged feelings, he also offered audiences the vicarious experience of being amused and awed at Hollywood's fabricated magic. The car scene is a manufactured play of light and sound that's formally exciting. The noted critic Andrew Sarris once observed that Minnelli's art can transform "corn into caviar," and, indeed, in this instance, the thrill derives from the unusual combination of dramatic reality and fabricated art.

Moreover, Minnelli succeeded in creating a dual response. He makes the viewers feel toward the movie what Georgia feels about Shields, and at the same time he encourages the audience to take a more detached and ironic approach.

For the *New Yorker* critic Pauline Kael, however, *The Bad and the Beautiful* was no more than a hysterical piece of Hollywood self-analysis, a film that becomes a satire in spite of itself. As an overloaded, glossy melodrama, the film was a piquant example of what it purports to expose: luxurious exhibitionism. And yet even Kael acknowledged (perhaps reluctantly) the undeniable emotional power of the film.

In a memo to Dore Schary dated July 9, 1952, Houseman raised objections to the film's title: "Having been lulled and flattered into acquiescing to *The Bad and the Beautiful,* this morning's lead in Hedda Hopper's column has jolted me back into manhood and common sense. Mr. Hughes' latest pictorial melodrama at RKO is called *Beautiful but Dangerous.* I take it that knocks out *The Bad and the Beautiful* once and for all. I admit that there is much to be said against the words bad man, because of its Western connotations." Houseman therefore suggested a meeting between the title department, Minnelli, and Schnee to deliver a substitute for *A Tribute to a Bad Man,* one that would retain the word *Tribute* and the irony of the original title.

There were also deliberations on whether to shoot the picture in color, as was becoming more common in Hollywood, or in black and white. Houseman wrote to Schary on January 11, 1952: "At the preliminary production meeting, I was shocked at the complete surprise with which everyone greeted my assumption that this picture was to be in color. You will recall that a strong preference for color was always indicated. Minnelli very definitely shares our feeling that color would immeasurably enhance the picture. As precedent, may I cite *A Star Is Born* and your own *Singin' in the Rain,* both about the picture business, in which the use of color for the human story is contrasted with the black-and-white of the film they created. It is not a question of wanting a color picture just for the hell of it. We all feel it is very much to the advantage, if not essential, to this particular picture."

Shooting on *The Bad and the Beautiful,* M-G-M's production number 1581, began with an exterior of the cemetery, scene 7, then the cemetery gate, scene 8, then an exterior of Jonathan's estate, scene 10, and an exterior of a Hollywood club, scene 25. The four scenes, each taking one fourth of a day, were completed to Minnelli's satisfaction. From that day on, the shoot proceeded rather smoothly.

Previews were held at the Bay Theatre in Pacific Palisades on September 18, 1952. Howard Strickling reported that most of the 160 responses were outstanding or excellent, and only one poor. While Kirk

Douglas got the highest scores for his performance, Barry Sullivan and Gilbert Roland received the lowest.

When *The Bad and the Beautiful* opened, savvy critics understood the film's self-reflexivity, its insider's look at Hollywood. "Perhaps the sharpest film made about Hollywood," wrote the *Los Angeles Times*. "The film has *What Makes Sammy Run?* and the bitter flavor of *Sunset Boulevard* and *All About Eve,* and like the latter, it is told in flashbacks by Shields' victims."

Eighteen months passed between the completion of *An American in Paris* and the beginning of Minnelli's next musical, *The Band Wagon*. During that period, Minnelli did not sit idle. He worked for almost a year on a song-and-dance project that didn't materialize, *Huckleberry Finn*. It was to be M-G-M's second version of the Mark Twain classic; the first, *The Adventures of Huckleberry Finn,* had been filmed in 1939 with Mickey Rooney.

The new *Huckleberry Finn* seemed ill-fated from the start, but no one wanted to admit that. In 1946, the *Meet Me in St. Louis* team of Sally Benson, Hugh Blane, and Ralph Martin wrote a new script and original score for the project, but their efforts didn't impress Freed and the project was postponed. Freed resuscitated the idea in 1950, with a new team that included scenarist Donald Ogden Stewart (who won the 1940 Adapted Screenplay Oscar for Cukor's *The Philadelphia Story*) and composer-lyricists Burton Lane and E. Y. Harburg.

Hollywood was then under the second round of the House Un-American Activities Committee's investigations on alleged Communist infiltration of the industry. Stewart and Harburg, who were known for their leftist sympathies, completed their work in May 1950, but it soon became clear that their work would not be used. On January 18, 1951, M-G-M's legal department confirmed that Stewart and Harburg had been relieved of their duties, seemingly because of other commitments. Sadly, their Hollywood careers ended abruptly.

Two weeks after *An American in Paris* finished shooting, Minnelli was assigned to direct *Huckleberry Finn*. Minnelli cast child contract player Dean Stockwell as Huck, and wanted Danny Kaye and Gene Kelly to play his roguish traveling companions. In June 1951, Minnelli went to

New York to confer with Alan Jay Lerner on script revisions, and work with Irene Sharaff on the visual design and costumes, always crucial ingredients of every Minnelli production.

Rehearsals began in August, while Kelly was still busy as choreographer, codirector, and actor in *Singin' in the Rain*. Minnelli rehearsed Kelly's routines with assistant dance director Ernie Platt for three weeks, while the sets were being constructed. On September 21, to Minnelli's bafflement, the production was shut down. The obstacle this time was Kaye's commitment to do another picture for Samuel Goldwyn.

The project was doomed. Truth to tell, both Kelly and Kaye wanted out. Kelly was exhausted from his triple duties on *Singin' in the Rain,* and he didn't care much for the new score. The studio proposed to resume production in six months, which conflicted with Kelly's plan to take advantage of a legal loophole that allowed Americans to work abroad tax-free for eighteen months.

Having done a lot of research, Minnelli felt that M-G-M had lost an opportunity to explore another vivid facet of Americana, of a kind he had first assayed in *Meet Me in St. Louis.*

The studio went out of its way to find a new project to justify Minnelli's $3,000 per week salary. In the end, they settled upon a curious fantasy without music called "Mademoiselle," which formed the center of an omnibus film, *The Story of Three Loves.* Hollywood has made only a few successful omnibus films, a genre that was always more popular in Europe. There were anthologies based on classic short stories, such as Somerset Maugham's *Trio,* or Max Ophuls's *Le Plaisir,* a homage to Guy de Maupassant.

Veteran producer Sidney Franklin initially asked Minnelli to direct another of the film's three short tales, "Why Should, I Cry?" But one was enough for Minnelli, and the latter was given to Charles Walters, a regular replacement for Minnelli.

Shot on the back lot, the anthology consisted of "Mademoiselle," set in Rome, "The Jealous Lover" in London, and "Equilibrium," with a Paris setting. Favoring old-fashioned fare with an all-star cast, Franklin assembled an international troupe. Theater director Max Reinhardt's son, Gottfried, directed "The Jealous Lover," a pale variation of *The Red*

Shoes, with James Mason playing the Anton Walbrook role, and "Equilibrium," starring Kirk Douglas and Pier Angeli.

Planned for Leslie Caron, "Mademoiselle" was based on Jan Lustig and George Froeschel's short story, "Lucy and the Stranger." The heroine, a wistful governess of an American boy on holiday with his family in Rome, recites poems by Verlaine to her seven-year-old charge, Tommy, who can't wait to become a grown-up. When an old sorceress grants his wish for one evening, a transformed Tommy awakens to Mademoiselle's charm. Ricky Nelson, already popular on TV, played the young boy, and Farley Granger the mature Tommy. Zsa Zsa Gabor was cast as a worldly barfly who vamps the hero before his date with Mademoiselle.

Ethel Barrymore flaunted an imperious delivery as the fairy godmother, Mrs. Pennicott. For Minnelli, working with Barrymore, long a grande dame of the New York theater, was the major reason for doing the film. Enchanted by Barrymore's energy and professionalism, he accepted all of his star's suggestions, the good and the mediocre ones. For her first scene, Minnelli placed Barrymore in an Italian Gothic villa, basking in velvety Roman twilight. The actress later reported that no director, not even her friend George Cukor, had treated her with such respect or presented her with such loving admiration.

By the late 1940s, Minnelli had gotten used to the workings of Metro's art department, and vice versa. Aging and in decline, stubborn art director Cedric Gibbons now fully accepted Minnelli's status as the studio's most brilliant director and accommodated most of his wishes and whims. Indeed, *The Story of Three Loves* offered a luscious if bizarre series of matte shots by special-effects master Warren Newcombe, who re-created the Roman Forum and Caracalla Baths, while back-projection was used to illustrate Farley Granger and Leslie Caron's carriage ride through the city.

There was always much recycling of ideas, images, sounds, sets, and objects in Minnelli's movies. For example, Miklos Rozsa's "new" score for his segment borrowed motifs from his waltz for *Madame Bovary.* And this film's park setting would be used as a substitute for New York's Central Park, where Fred Astaire and Cyd Charisse take a ride in *The Band Wagon,* Minnelli's next picture.

With such smooth collaboration, "Mademoiselle," the first segment to be shot, was done very quickly by Minnelli standards, requiring only three weeks, and wrapping up in February 1952. However, the entire anthology was costlier and took longer to finish than anticipated.

Not knowing what to do with their inflated artsy production, M-G-M kept it on the shelf for more than a year. *Three Loves* finally opened at Radio City Music Hall in March 1953, after *The Band Wagon,* even though that musical had been shot first. The public response was tepid, and the movie turned out to be a commercial failure.

Even so, Minnelli imbues "Mademoiselle" with some touches of lyricism and whimsy. Fables like this one succeed or fail on their charm, and "Mademoiselle" simply lacked charm. The settings are photogenic, and some of the close-ups appealing, but overall, it's a stalled film, marred by a sumptuous but fake look.

Skeptical viewers wondered why a young boy in a Roman hotel would read gloomy Gallic poetry. Granted the wish to become a man of twenty-five, he accidentally encounters the fey governess still weeping over Verlaine. The tuxedoed transient succumbs to her thrall, and soon the two somnambulists proclaim love, in slow verse and slow motion, drifting across the screen like lost souls.

Like *The Clock,* the movie brings together two lonely innocents in a city of strangers, but the emotional urgency that propelled *The Clock* eludes Minnelli here. Despite high production values, and Minnelli's camera caressing Caron and Granger in their romantic scene, the segment is lifeless. Fleeting seconds in the segment transport it to the Eternal City of Minnelli's imagination, for a change a dream without a ballet. There is a succession of soft frescoes of nocturnal Rome, a giddying overhead shot of Farley Granger running down a gaslit alley, dwarfed by an equestrian statue, a shot recycled out of *An American in Paris.*

The appearance of Ethel Barrymore halfway through the story is refreshing, injecting much-needed energy. Like *Gigi*'s Aunt Alicia, Mrs. Pennicott is the star of her miniature domain. With her, the story's high-flown literary sentiments give way to an astringent comedy. Barrymore is a Minnelli type of witch, an elegant fairy godmother who presides over crumbling baroque archways and sunken Roman pediments.

Barrymore's grande dame reveals how she subdued the overweening German governess who blighted her own youth: To achieve the spell that would liberate him from Mademoiselle, the boy must invoke Mrs.

Pennicott's name on the stroke of eight. When Barrymore utters the line, "I love to hear it pronounced, it intoxicates me," the veteran star, by turns vain and seductive, gets a chance to show off her deliciously rich theatrical voice.

Though "Mademoiselle" was a minor assignment to fill Minnelli's idle weeks in between more important projects, the segment touched a personal chord. Mrs. Pennicott personifies an essential Minnelli theme: the power of imagination to overcome the mundane daily life. As Minnelli himself grew older and dissatisfied with his personal life, he relied more and more on fantasy as an escape from harsh reality.

"Mademoiselle" may be seen as a first draft for Minnelli's final picture, *A Matter of Time,* yet another fable about an aged eccentric countess (played by Ingrid Bergman) who introduces a frustrated innocent (Liza Minnelli) to the lure of dreams, a topic that was also explored in *Gigi.* The idea corresponds to Minnelli's real-life role in transforming young women, like Lena Horne, Judy, and his own daughter, into sophisticated society ladies. Unfortunately, the supernatural and comic relief elements in "Mademoiselle" were supplanted by pathos and nostalgia in the 1976 picture.

Neither "Mademoiselle" nor *A Matter of Time* sustains the transcendent artistic quality Minnelli hoped to convey. However, each film featured thematic motifs and visual imagery that recur throughout Minnelli's work. In his swan song, a reclusive old lady enveloped in the sapphire light of a Roman dusk contemplates the mysterious promise of the darkness to come. Placed against the context of his own life, the film couldn't have been a more personal one. By 1976, Minnelli's professional glory had receded into memory, like the amorous exploits of the ravaged countess.

As the shooting of *The Bad and the Beautiful* was coming to an end, Minnelli was already preparing Freed's first film since *Singin' in the Rain.* The new work was to be a backstage musical with songs by Howard Dietz and Arthur Schwartz. Freed liked to create musicals around anthologies of composers' works, and the Dietz-Schwartz catalog held particular appeal. A man of many talents, along with being a famous lyricist, Dietz was also M-G-M's vice president of publicity. However, Dietz and Schwartz had never written a successful book musical—their specialty was the revue, a format that had lost its appeal in Hollywood.

One of their songs from *At Home Abroad,* the first Broadway show that Minnelli staged, had originally been written for *The Band Wagon,* but it didn't make the final cut. Dietz and Schwartz set the era's standard for escapism, their shows serving as showcases for such stars as Clifton Webb, Libby Holman, and Fred and Adele Astaire, who had made their final joint appearance in *The Band Wagon,* in 1931. In 1949, Twentieth Century–Fox had produced *Dancing in the Dark,* a film that used some of the *Band Wagon* score, with the nonsinging stars William Powell and Betsy Drake.

Just as the Gershwins' jazzy exuberance suggested Gene Kelly in *An American in Paris,* the moody sophistication of the Dietz-Schwartz score called for Fred Astaire, for whom the project was planned as star vehicle.

As much as Minnelli liked Kelly, he secretly favored Astaire, not only for his bravura skills and natural elegance, but also for his European demeanor and expressive philosophy. Astaire's ability to escape mundane reality into the perfect fantasy world of dance, stood in contrast to Kelly, who, energetic as he was, tries to accommodate and adjust to this world by making it slightly more magical through dance.

Minnelli's big challenge was to find a semblance of a plot, even a slender one, which could effectively contain the gloriously melodic score and accommodate the star. Writers Betty Comden and Adolph Green concocted a backstage yarn about—what else?—the making of a Broadway musical. The premise was formulaic, even banal, but the witty dialogue and inside jokes lifted the text several notches above the routine.

Like Minnelli's Hollywood movie à clef, *The Bad and the Beautiful, The Band Wagon* was sparked by its allusions to actual showbiz personalities. The protagonist, Tony Hunter, was a heightened portrait of Fred Astaire, whose own career was in decline in the 1950s. Astaire played an aloof, middle-aged hoofer out of sync with the times.

In Minnelli's opinion, Astaire was to the American film musical what Chaplin was to silent comedy. Like Chaplin, Astaire used a trademark, the top hat and cane that identified him immediately and effectively.

Hence, as a tribute, in the film's opening image, Minnelli uses a close-up of a top hat and cane. There was no doubt in Minnelli's mind that Astaire should flaunt his trademark in the film's very first scene.

The inspiration for the character of Jeffrey Cordova was partly Orson Welles, partly playwright George S. Kaufman, and especially the pretentious actor José Ferrer, who had directed and starred on Broadway in *The Shrike* and had won (some think undeservedly) the Best Actor Oscar for *Cyrano de Bergerac.* The real-life model for Hunter's costar Gabrielle Gerard was the French ballerina Zizi Jeanmaire, who made her American screen debut in the Danny Kaye vehicle *Hans Christian Andersen.*

Under pressure from Minnelli, Freed agreed to discard his working title for the musical. Instead, Freed chose *The Band Wagon,* which summoned up the memory of Astaire's 1931 stage triumph of the same name, and deepened the movie's resonance as a valentine to the legendary dancer. Minnelli consciously set out to direct a backstage musical that would capture the bygone magic of Shubert Alley.

A young, novel cast was selected by Minnelli for the musical. The only familiar face was Oscar Levant, whose malingering offscreen personality meshed with the role of the comic-neurotic Lester Martin. As Levant's partner, Minnelli cast vivacious Broadway leading lady Nanette Fabray.

Cyd Charisse is considered to be Astaire's most sensuous and technically expert partner, and indeed, *The Band Wagon* is almost inconceivable without Charisse. However, obtaining the okay to cast Charisse was not easy for Minnelli. For years, she had only decorated M-G-M musicals, and had never been entrusted with a starring role. While *The Band Wagon* exposed her lack of acting abilities, it also showed what a great dance personality she was. Minnelli later insisted on casting Cyd Charisse as Kirk Douglas's seductress flame in *Two Weeks in Another Town.* This time, however, Minnelli fell flat on his face as the reviews panned the performance of Charisse who really was no match for an actor of Douglas's caliber.

For Jeffrey Cordova, the musical's most colorful part, Minnelli's first choice was Clifton Webb, a comedian who began his career as a dancer. Webb declined the role because of its small size, but he recommended the British actor Jack Buchanan, who was then virtually unknown to

American viewers. Buchanan's wit, energy, and stature made him an ideal foil for Astaire.

The film's backstage setting was flexible enough to contain a wide range of Dietz-Schwartz songs. When production began, in September 1952, there were about twenty songs, out of which a dozen made it into the final cut. Freed asked the team to write a new number, a rousing anthem à la Irving Berlin's "There's No Business Like Show Business." The duo came up with the boisterously melodic "That's Entertainment," a song that epitomized the spirit of the M-G-M musical and was used as the title of a series of nostalgic musical-anthology films that included footage from many Minnelli movies.

Due to their overlapping duties as art directors, Oliver Smith and studio veteran Preston Ames clashed severely on the set. On more than one occasion, Minnelli had to mediate between the bickering artists in front of the cast and crew.

The studio felt that cinematographer George Folsey succumbed too readily to Minnelli's time-consuming attention to detail, and decided to replace him with Harry Jackson halfway through the shoot to speed up the production.

To grant greater authenticity, Minnelli imported two Broadway artists with no prior movie experience: choreographer Michael Kidd (of *Guys and Dolls* fame) and designer Oliver Smith (*On the Town*). Kidd, who favored working with Stanley Donen over Minnelli, later recalled: "Stanley Donen had the imagination to understand what I was talking about. Many directors wouldn't have had the slightest idea, because they're not trained dancers. There'd be no point in telling them anything. From my point of view, I'd rather work with Stanley than Vincente."

According to Kidd: "Vincente was a difficult person to communicate with. He was not very articulate, he would leave sentences unfinished. He had a great love of the visual aspects of moviemaking. He was originally a set designer, and people used to complain all the time, 'He shoots the scenery.' "

Unfortunately for Kidd, "Vincente was not one to engage in collaborative work." While choreographing *The Band Wagon,* said Kidd, "If I came up to Vincente with an idea, he would say, 'Just a minute, just a minute, just a minute. Let me think about it.' He wouldn't engage in conversation about it. I don't mean to detract from Vincente's creativity in any way. Vincente was very artistic. But when it came to a dance number, his thinking and mine were not always the same."

In contrast, Kidd appreciated Donen's process of give-and-take. "Vincente would not welcome disagreement or reveal what was on his mind, whereas Stanley would always say what he was thinking, and was very clear and methodical. Vincente may have had an idea of what he wanted, he kept art books and cutouts from magazines as examples of what visuals he had in mind, but when it came to talking, Vincente kept pretty much to himself."

Other problems involved Buchanan, who was ill much of the time, and Levant, who exasperated Minnelli with his constant complaining, on screen and off. In retaliation, Minnelli would cast Levant as a psychotic in his 1955 mental-asylum melodrama, *The Cobweb*.

Quite uncharacteristically, Astaire proved to be problematic too. Astaire was known for his pessimistic outlook on life. As a youngster, Astaire had been dubbed by his sister Adele "Moaning Minnie." A perpetual worrier, Astaire was concerned about Kidd's unconventional choreography as well as about Cyd Charisse's height, which was inserted into the script as an inside joke. Even more disturbing to Astaire were the obvious parallels between himself and the fictitious Tony Hunter. How could he not be, in a movie about a performer's advancing age, dour temperament, and fear of growing stale and overextending his welcome?

Things got worse, when Minnelli became too absorbed in his work to pay sufficient attention to his leading man. One day, just like in the story, in a rare burst of temper, Astaire stormed off the set, while Minnelli was rehearsing "I Love Louisa," though he scarcely noticed that Astaire was absent. Hours later, Astaire returned and apologized profusely for his unusual conduct, to which Minnelli just said, "Oh, that's perfectly all right, Fred, I am used to it. I drive everybody crazy."

The Band Wagon was made back-to-back with *Singin' in the Rain*, co-directed by Gene Kelly and Stanley Donen, the rising director who presented a threat to Minnelli's dominance as Freed's most brilliant director of musicals. As the crowned genius of the Freed Unit, Minnelli was generally handed the high-profile projects—with budgets to match.

Stanley Donen, on the other hand, was relegated to the category of the brash young kid. Producer Joseph Pasternak held Donen in higher esteem than Arthur Freed did.

Interestingly, except for *Meet Me in St. Louis* (1944), Donen didn't like Minnelli's musicals, because of their "sloppy" stories. Which, ironically, was Minnelli's complaint about other directors' works! Vocal about his opinions, Donen claimed that most of Minnelli's musicals had no sting or energy. He much preferred the Disney animated musicals. In Donen's films, the characters are more realistic and recognizable, life's livers and enjoyers rather than beholders and survivors, which allows for action, movement, and energy. Unlike Minnelli's characters, Donen's don't have to retreat into memory, dream, or hallucination to stabilize or enhance their dreary reality. In fact, there are few Donen musicals that contain daydreams or visions.

Given the emphasis Metro placed on musical numbers, Donen's advisory role was considered pivotal to the studio's operations, whether the problem with a film required shooting a quick take on the spur of the moment or conceiving an elaborate production number. Donen's anonymous assists continued even after he began getting director's credit on his own pictures. A scene of Donen's might show up in a movie credited with direction by Minnelli, George Sidney, or Charles Walters. This was Donen's reason for refuting the auteur theory, claiming "You can never be too sure when you read a movie's credits who really should get credit for what."

As manifest in the contrast between *Singin' in the Rain* and *The Band Wagon,* there were major differences in visual strategy between Minnelli and Donen. Some critics prefer Donen's bold, no-nonsense, more "realistic" style to Minnelli's impressionist visual mode. For camera technique, Donen proved his agility with horizontal tracking and crane shots, as opposed to Minnelli's tendency to track forward or back. Donen's camera tries to always keep up and promote the story and its performances, whereas Minnelli doesn't mind pausing and arresting the story flow if a spectacular sequence or grand performer is involved.

After the first preview of *The Band Wagon,* Minnelli was elated. He immediately sent a handwritten note to Oliver Smith, who was out of town:

"The preview last night was the most exciting I've ever been connected with. Your work has dazzled everyone. Couldn't have been produced without you. Come back immediately." This was followed by a telegram to choreographer Michael Kidd: "You were the hit of the evening last night. I couldn't be prouder of you. Congrats. Vincente."

As expected, *The Band Wagon* opened on July 10, 1953, at Radio City Music Hall to rave reviews. Bosley Crowther wrote in *The New York Times*: "That wonderful talent for satire which Betty Comden and Adolph Green possess, and which was gleefully turned upon the movies in their script for last year's *Singin' in the Rain,* is even more gleefully let loose upon the present-day musical stage in their book for *The Band Wagon.*" Praising all the talents involved, in front and behind the camera, he went on to enthuse: "This literate and witty combination herein delivers a show that respectfully bids for recognition as one of the best musical films ever made."

Two days later, Minnelli received a telegram from M-G-M's offices in New York that read: "*The Band Wagon* did $23,332 on opening day, the best business of any M-G-M picture except for *Ivanhoe,* which grossed $24,000. However, it bested *Showboat* ($22,001), *The Great Caruso* ($20,400), and *King Solomon's Mines* ($17,000)." A telegram in the same spirit was sent from Howard Dietz: "Dear Vincente. Clean sweep of notices and smash business at Music Hall. Everybody acclaiming your 'Girl Hunt' ballet. Love and kisses, Howard."

Three weeks later, Howard Strickling reported enthusiastically from New York: "Music Hall wound up gross of third week was $156,742, for a 21-day cumulative total of $483,245." By comparison, the other hit musical, *Singin' in the Rain,* grossed $178,405 and $462,172, respectively. Figures were also provided for *An American in Paris* ($148,937–$471,050), *Show Boat* ($157,774–$486,962), and *Ivanhoe* ($170,516–$520,773).

In the end, the triumphant result and overall impact of *The Band Wagon* justified the long, arduous, and expensive production. Most historians consider the film to be one of Minnelli's two or three masterpieces. It is my second-favorite musical of his, after *Meet Me in St. Louis.*

Eddie "Rochester" and Lena Horne in *Cabin in the Sky* (1943), Minnelli's first film musical. *Courtesy of the Academy of Motion Picture Arts and Sciences*

Eleanor Powell, Red Skelton (right), and Jimmy Dorsey and his band in *I Dood It* (1943), arguably Minnelli's worst picture. *Courtesy of the Academy of Motion Picture Arts and Sciences*

Family tensions in *Meet Me in St. Louis* (1944): patriarch Leon Ames, refusing to eat, has left the dinner table despite pleas from his wife (Mary Astor, center) and daughters (Judy Garland, at right, and Lucille Bremer). *Courtesy of the Academy of Motion Picture Arts and Sciences*

Judy Garland delivers her famous Christmas song by the window in *Meet Me in St. Louis*. *Courtesy of the Academy of Motion Picture Arts and Sciences*

Robert Taylor threatening his fragile wife, played by Katharine Hepburn, in Minnelli's noir melodrama *Undercurrent* (1946). *Courtesy of the Academy of Motion Picture Arts and Sciences*

Fred Astaire (right) and Gene Kelly perform "The Babbitt and the Bromide" in *The Ziegfeld Follies* (1946), a number Astaire had previously done with his sister, Adele, in the Broadway musical *Funny Face. Courtesy of the Academy of Motion Picture Arts and Sciences*

Lucille Ball as the ring mistress with a bejeweled whip makes the panther girls cower in the dazzling Merry-Go-Round number from *The Ziegfeld Follies. Courtesy of the Academy Motion Picture Arts and Sciences*

Jennifer Jones in a white gown and her admirers in *Madame Bovary*, all reflected in a mirror, one of the recurrent motifs in Minnelli's work. *Courtesy of the Academy of Motion Picture Arts and Sciences*

Spencer Tracy in anxiety mode in the comedy *Father of the Bride* (1950). *Courtesy of the Academy of Motion Picture Arts and Sciences*

Gene Kelly and Lesley Caron performing the long, spectacular ballet in the musical *An American in Paris* (1951). *Courtesy of the Academy of Motion Picture Arts and Sciences*

Gene Kelly (right),
Oscar Levant (cen-
ter), and Georges
Guétary as the three
pals in *An American
in Paris*. *Courtesy of
the Academy of
Motion Picture Arts
and Sciences*

Kirk Douglas and Lana Turner in the noir melodrama *The Bad and the Beautiful* (1952). *Courtesy of the Academy of Motion Picture Arts and Sciences*

Fred Astaire and Cyd Charisse in the romantic "Dancing in the Dark" number in New York's Central Park in *The Band Wagon*, Minnelli's 1953 musical. *Courtesy of the Academy of Motion Picture Arts and Sciences*

Astaire and Charisse in a virtuoso dance sequence in *The Band Wagon*. *Courtesy of the Academy of Motion Picture Arts and Sciences*

Lucille Ball cooking eggs in *The Long, Long Trailer* (1953), Minnelli's broadest and most popular comedy. *Courtesy of the Academy of Motion Picture Arts and Sciences*

Richard Widmark rips down the drapes in his psychiatric clinic in *The Cobweb* (1955), a quintessential Minnelli melodrama revolving around an aesthetic decision about curtains. *Courtesy of the Academy of Motion Picture Arts and Sciences*

Kirk Douglas holding a portrait of himself playing Van Gogh, in the biopic *Lust for Life* (1956). *Courtesy of the Academy of Motion Picture Arts and Sciences*

Douglas as Van Gogh and Anthony Quinn as Paul Gauguin in *Lust for Life*, a role for which Quinn received his second Oscar for Best Supporting Actor. *Courtesy of the Academy of Motion Picture Arts and Sciences*

hn Kerr (left) is taught to walk "like
real man" by his roommate (Darryl
ickman) in the drama *Tea and Sym-
thy* (1956). *Courtesy of the Academy of
otion Picture Arts and Sciences*

Deborah Kerr caresses Kerr on the grass,
helping him to deal with his troubled sexuality
in *Tea and Sympathy*. *Courtesy of the Academy
of Motion Picture Arts and Sciences*

Gregory Peck (left)
and Lauren Bacall as
the newlyweds argu-
ing about masculine
nd feminine lifestyles
ith Jack Cole, stand-
ing in for Minnelli's
type of effete man, in
he comedy *Designing
Woman* (1957). *Cour-
tesy of the Academy of
Motion Picture Arts
and Sciences*

Leslie Caron as the naughty defiant girl and Louis Jordan as her gentleman caller in *Gigi* (1958). Minnelli won his only directing Oscar for this musical, which received a total of nine Academy Awards, including Best Picture. *Courtesy of the Academy of Motion Picture Arts and Sciences*

Leslie Caron being groomed by her aunt (Isabel Jeans) on how to look and behave as a well-bred courtesan in *Gigi*. *Courtesy of the Academy of Motion Picture Arts and Sciences*

Minnelli accepting the Best Director Oscar for *Gigi* from presenters Gary Cooper and Millie Perkins. *Courtesy of the Academy of Motion Picture Arts and Sciences*

Dean Martin (center) introduces his girlfriend (Carmen Phillips) to Frank Sinatra in the small-town melodrama *Some Came Running* (1958). *Courtesy of the Academy of Motion Picture Arts and Sciences*

Patriarch Robert Mitchum (left) instructs his young, sensitive son (George Hamilton) how to be a man in the melodrama *Home from the Hill* (1960), arguably Minnelli's last good picture. *Courtesy of the Academy of Motion Picture Arts and Sciences*

Mitchum, his legitimate son (Hamilton, center), and his elder, illegitimate son (George Peppard, at right) represent three models of manhood in *Home from the Hill.* Note the erect position at which Mitchum holds his hunting rifle. *Courtesy of the Academy of Motion Picture Arts and Sciences*

Kirk Douglas and Daliah Lavi in a nocturnal scene, shot on Rome's Spanish Steps, in *Two Weeks in Another Town* (1962), the disappointing sequel to Minnelli's masterpiece *The Bad and the Beautiful*. *Courtesy of the Academy of Motion Picture Arts and Sciences*

Elizabeth Taylor and Richard Burton, then the most famous couple in show business, in a scene from *The Sandpiper* (1965). *Courtesy of the Academy of Motion Picture Arts and Sciences*

Vincente Minnelli escorting his daughter Liza to the Academy Awards presentation. She had been nominated for Best Actress for her performance in *The Sterile Cuckoo* (1969). *AP*

Sixteen

Minnelli Loves Lucy

MINNELLI WAS FINISHING UP *The Band Wagon* when producer Pandro Berman approached him with an idea for a new comedy, *The Long, Long Trailer,* starring Lucille Ball and Desi Arnaz. Two years after *Father's Little Dividend,* Minnelli was offered another Frances Goodrich–Albert Hackett script, adapted from the novel of the same name by Clinton Twiss, yet another book that satirized middle-class America.

It was Lucy, Berman's old flame, who asked for Minnelli as director. She wanted to make a big-screen movie that would exploit her comic television persona but not be totally imitative of it. To accommodate Lucy's busy schedule, Minnelli shot the movie in the summer, during the couple's hiatus from the popular show *I Love Lucy.*

The screenwriters focus the comedy on a housewife who almost drives her hubby crazy. Like *Father of the Bride, The Long, Long Trailer* uses dark humor to deal with middle-class anxieties, both material and emotional. However, because of its star, the film has a more anarchic tone and sharper satiric edge than the two *Father* movies.

At this phase of his career, Minnelli was enamored of the flashback structure, which he had used to great advantage in *Father of the Bride* and *The Bad and the Beautiful,* and which he would continue to use in other comedies, such as *Designing Woman.* The film begins on a dark, rainy night, showing Desi Arnaz wearing a trench coat and a snap-brim hat, narrating the events in a flashback to the manager of a trailer park.

On the surface, this cozy fantasy about marriage depicts American life on the road as fun. All of Minnelli's comedies, as James Naremore has suggested, follow the same pattern. The narratives first deflate or criticize the American dream, then embrace and honor it, and finally reestablish the old order with slight revision. This is, in essence, the classic Hollywood paradigm of balance, imbalance, and balance again.

Both as director and person, Minnelli could be warm and generous yet extremely demanding. He had an abstracted air about him that concealed a keen disciplinarian. Blessed with an instinctive flair for movie rhythm—for what really works on the screen—he displayed his knowledge of how to blend throwaway wit with more serious anxieties and darker overtones, and the result was another quintessentially Minnelli—and M-G-M—picture.

The difference between the *Father of the Bride* films and *The Long, Long Trailer,* as Stephen Harvey observed, reflects the shifting relationship between Hollywood and television as competing entertainment industries in the early 1950s. In the three years since *Father of the Bride* was released, the balance between the two mediums had changed. If *Father of the Bride* was a big-screen comedy with legit movie stars in a story that led to numerous small-screen imitations, *The Long, Long Trailer* tried to lure the growing TV audiences back to the movie theaters with the small screen's most beloved star at the time, Lucille Ball.

At first, Hollywood tried to ignore the competition with TV. In fact, M-G-M's stars were not allowed to appear on television, not even to promote their own movies. The studios were concerned about the possibility of dissipating—and losing—too much of the stars' glamour when seen on the home screen, without makeup and costumes, and with no prearranged script.

Unlike Paramount and Fox, M-G-M resisted widescreen. In 1953, M-G-M trumpeted stereo sound, then magnified screens and 3-D, as a challenge to TV's smaller, black-and-white screen. Berman himself produced *Knights of the Round Table*, M-G-M's first CinemaScope adventure.

Minnelli liked to follow his more somber and complex pictures with lighter comedic fare that was less expensive and took less time to shoot. This became a career pattern that would continue throughout the next decade. Hence, after the dark melodrama *The Cobweb,* Minnelli made *Designing Woman,* and after that comedy, he went back to melodramas with *Some Came Running,* made in the same year as the musical *Gigi.* In the 1960s, too, Minnelli alternated melodramatic movies like *Two Weeks in Another Town* with comedies on the order of *The Courtship of Eddie's Father* and *Goodbye, Charlie.*

When Minnelli first met Ball, she told him that she loved the idea of a big-screen comeback. Movies still held an edge over TV in prestige, if not in earnings or audience size. After two decades in Hollywood, Lucille Ball was still a second-stringer, and the public still thought of her as Bob Hope's foil in mediocre Paramount movies. At age forty, Ball was not young when *I Love Lucy* premiered in 1951, and the time was ripe to give Hollywood another try before it was too late for her as a big-screen persona.

As for Arnaz, he had fared in Hollywood even worse than Ball, appearing mostly in B-pictures. The couple envisioned their potential return to Hollywood stardom as a coup, and that they would achieve it in a movie directed by M-G-M's most distinguished filmmaker was even more seductive and prestigious. Blessed with a shrewd instinct for comedy, Minnelli encouraged the Arnazes to tackle the tailor-made roles with their special, slightly vulgar brand of farce.

Shooting began on June 18, 1953, and for Minnelli, it was a pleasant reprise of the smooth process he had experienced with the two *Father* pictures. Though *The Long, Long Trailer* involved outdoor locations, Minnelli shot it in under four weeks, benefiting from his stars' habit of working rapidly, efficiently, and for long hours.

There was no interference, or much communication, from Berman, for a simple reason. The producer was in London supervising *Knights of the Round Table,* while Minnelli shot *The Long, Long, Trailer* at Culver

City. During this time, Minnelli had only one argument with the studio. Aiming to distinguish its picture from Lucy's weekly TV series, Metro's executives toyed with the idea of shooting the picture in 3-D to convey more vividly what they described as Lucy's "dizzying redhead."

The studio was then in the process of dropping the saturated-looking Technicolor in favor of the less complex and expensive Ansco Color (later called Metrocolor). Minnelli disliked Ansco's duller spectrum, which to him made women's faces seem "dirty." Still in London, Berman defended his director, but M-G-M insisted and Ansco remained. Minnelli relented, though a more urgent fight, ironically in favor of Ansco, would occur two years later during preproduction for *Lust for Life*.

The Long, Long Trailer unfolds as a collection of anecdotes about the wacky misadventures of a middle-aged couple during a long trek across the country. The "trailerites," Tacy and Nicky Collini, are like Mr. and Mrs. Thoreau on wheels, vagabonds who decorate their caravan with hanging copper planters called "ferneries."

The couple is less cartoonish than their TV sitcom personas, the Ricardos. Tacy's zany housewife notions lead to one domestic disaster after another, and her "feminine" schemes clash with Nicky's bullish, masculine common sense. He explodes in Spanish, while she has a lot of "splaining" to do.

The big trick was to keep the trailer moving forward, while giving the movie some tension and momentum. Like the *Father* movies, *The Long, Long Trailer* starts at the end of the saga, with a dismayed Nicky relating in flashback all of the miseries he's endured on the road with his wife. The screenwriters used a narrative structure similar to that of Minnelli's other comedies. Under his helm, *The Long, Long Trailer* became a slapstick tribute to male passivity, in which the breadwinner is entrapped by the caprices of his energetic wife, like Stanley Banks's.

In real life, Lucy, 42, and Desi, 36, were not much younger than the book's author and his wife, on whom the novel was based, but the script casts them as newlyweds, which was not exactly credible. As a character, Nicky is a Latin amalgam of Stanley Banks and a luckless bridegroom, surrounded by nuptial revelry. Tacy likes life on the open road, while Nicky is more earthbound. In the end, their very marriage is threatened by their slapstick honeymoon.

Minnelli goes for a bumpy journey with the couple, but the movie is basically one long gimmick that lacks the appeal of the *Father* films, and the more nuanced characterization of Minnelli's other comedies. As a result, Minnelli crams the movie with visual gags, allowing his actors to play tug-of-war with the décor. By design, the film's biggest prop is the forty-foot trailer, a farcically malevolent force that literally dwarfs its owners. Minnelli turns its interior into the setting for a Marx Brothers riff on claustrophobia, in the manner of *A Night at the Opera.*

Before the ride begins, Minnelli stuffs the bride's nuptial gifts and personal belongings into one crammed space that recalls other busy rooms in his work. Happiness eludes the male protagonist when he is most expected to celebrate. Thus, like Spencer Tracy's engagement party scene at the bar in *Father of the Bride,* Desi Arnaz spends his wedding night pushed into a corner, mixing drinks not for his wife but for other mobile-home neighbors.

The movie intentionally recycles many of Lucy's classic slapstick routines from her TV show. A night in the forest, meant to be romantic, instead ends with a fall in the mud for her. While a cheery Arnaz navigates the road, she prepares the evening's "gourmet" meal, a disastrous enterprise, marked by flying utensils and overflowing flour.

In most of Minnelli's movies, movement, through dance or other gestures, signals romance and magic, but here the camera merely records the script's low-farce nature. Rather consciously, Minnelli pays tribute to his own work. Always loyal to his secondary and character actors, Minnelli cast Moroni Olsen (the father-in-law in the *Father* movies) as a trailer-park manager who reunites the bickering Collinis. *The Clock*'s Keenan Wynn plays a stoic traffic cop, and Marjorie Main, *Meet Me in St. Louis*'s bumptious housekeeper, was cast as an intrusive neighbor who turns their wedding night into a wild party.

Halting traffic in a town square, the trailer pauses in front of the marquee of a theater showing *The Band Wagon.* Later on, Tacy tells Nicky a gloomy movie plot that sounds a lot like the noir melodrama *Undercurrent.* Minnelli also recycles some of the sets of his old movies. The trailer's no-contest tussle with a rickety Victorian house recalls *Meet Me in St. Louis.*

Overall, the film is a warm and friendly yet critical take on the pursuit of material happiness in 1950s America. While *Father of the Bride* satirizes the rituals of suburban life, *The Long, Long Trailer* ridicules mobile technology, underlining the newer, more rootless middle-class existence. Both products and victims of the electric age, the newlyweds meet at the christening of a new freeway, then again at a mobile-home fair that advertises industrial American products. The weight of the goods almost causes their trailer to tip off the road and down a mountain cliff; at one point, the overstuffed trailer literally threatens to collapse.

Though the Collinis praise the joy and freedom of the open road, they are actually crushed by it. Gradually, their trip becomes an experience much less pleasant than the mundane, boring life they were trying to escape from. For a refined aesthete like Minnelli, the new technological world might be more efficient, but it represented a crass and tacky way of life. He views life on the highways as a kitschy version of modern industrial life. Against turquoise skies, the trailer park even features a swimming pool for transient homesteaders, and the trailers sport upholstered, built-in sofas and gleaming appliances.

As Stephen Harvey noted, detachment and stylization are strategies that lend wit to the basically banal story, and Minnelli benefits from treating the story as a broad farce. Even so, Minnelli's personal touches can help only up to a point, and *The Long, Long Trailer* still remains one of his lowest confections, one of his few escapist comedies to reflect a concession to the mass public's vulgar taste.

Initially, Metro feared that Lucy and Desi's fans would be reluctant to pay money to see them on the big screen, when they could get them for free in their living rooms. Nevertheless, the public embraced the feature-length romp, which premiered in February 1954 at Radio City Music Hall, and grossed more than $4 million in domestic rentals, making it even more profitable than the already popular *Father* movies.

After the success of *An American in Paris*, Freed signed Alan Jay Lerner to a three-picture writing contract. The first of these films was the 1954 film version of *Brigadoon,* with Gene Kelly and Van Johnson, to be directed by Minnelli. In the end, Lerner was vastly disappointed with the picture, which he found "quite wooden." Lerner later recalled, "That was unfortunate. Arthur Freed was the producer, and he was, and for all I know, is the best producer that ever was. But it was one of those mistakes, putting it on a sound stage instead of doing it in Scotland. I suppose it takes genuinely talented people to do something really bad."

The Band Wagon marked Minnelli's tenth year as Freed's most valued director and was a highlight for the Freed Unit, still one of the most celebrated production groups. In contrast, *Brigadoon* signaled the end of an era of sustained creativity for Freed. Until now, the consistent success of Freed's musicals had withstood the changes that shock Hollywood during the postwar years. However, due to TV's increasing prominence, movie audiences declined rapidly, and many theaters were converted into supermarkets. Also, the studio system was in decline, and Freed was no longer free to sign fresh talent from New York to long-term contracts.

At Metro, the production schedule shrank considerably, particularly in the number of musicals made. It was not just economics that led to the genre's decline. Minnelli's misfortune as a filmmaker was that he had arrived and matured in Hollywood rather late. His career would have benefited had he been there in the 1930s, like George Cukor, who made some of his best movies during that decade.

The Freed Unit viewed itself as the last creator of classy musical entertainment. As such, it struggled against the rise of mass fare such as the rock 'n' roll movies in the mid-1950s, with new stars like Elvis Presley. The style that made Minnelli's musicals lavish began to fade in the wake of Metro's new policy of playing it safer. Trying to guess the tastes of the fickle public, Hollywood increasingly relied on pre-sold Broadway hits rather than on the in-house development of original musicals.

Samuel Goldwyn and Twentieth Century–Fox had already grabbed the rights to the most prestigious Broadway hits, *Guys and Dolls* and a few of the Rodgers and Hammerstein musicals, respectively. M-G-M followed their lead, picking up whatever was left. Of the six musicals Freed was yet to produce at Metro, four were adaptations of stage hits. Almost in vain, Minnelli would point out that, despite the "safety" of Broadway imports, three of M-G-M's most popular 1950s musicals were conceived directly for the screen, *Seven Brides for Seven Brothers, High Society,* and his own *Gigi,* all Oscar-nominated or Oscar-winning pictures. The studio, however, countered with the argument that those were the exceptions rather than the rule.

Vulgar as it was, *The Long, Long Trailer* made money, which cannot be said about Minnelli's next film, *Brigadoon,* which turned out to be one of his weakest musicals, both artistically and commercially. The third collaboration between Alan Jay Lerner and Frederick Loewe was mediocre, indicating creative slowdown in the acclaimed duo's work. This operetta in kilts was a surprise hit of the 1946–47 Broadway season, when Celtic whimsy seemed to be in (*Finian's Rainbow* was also on the boards).

As early as March 1951, M-G-M had announced that Gene Kelly and Kathryn Grayson would star. But Kelly's European commitments stalled *Brigadoon* for two years, by which point the studio's contract with Grayson had lapsed. The studio then decided to cast Moira Shearer, the dancer-actress of *The Red Shoes*' fame. However, *Brigadoon*'s uncertain schedule made the Sadlers Wells Ballet, of which Shearer was a member, nervous and unwilling to commit. Having lost Shearer as his ideal Fiona, Minnelli settled for Cyd Charisse.

The Scottish writer Iain F. Anderson broke down the script, scene by scene, with comments. Though preproduction began in late 1952, the actual shoot was pushed back to January and February of 1954. *Brigadoon* became another quick production for Minnelli, and the studio was able to conduct its first preview at the Encino Theatre on June 4, 1954.

Apart from concerns about the narrative and casting problems, no one could have anticipated problems from the Production Code. In a memo dated November 2, 1953, Joseph I. Breen complained: "This material seems unacceptable, as it deals with the effort of Meg to seduce Jeff, which is made to seem highly romantic and hence is completely in violation of Code requirements." Then, in a February 2, 1954, memo, objection was raised to a line of dialogue by an incidental character in a New York bar: "Once you've driven a foreign car you'll never drive anything else." The Code was concerned about the hostile reaction of the American automobile industry, and the "anti-patriotic" line was revised.

Although Kelly and Minnelli were not entirely "in sync," to use Kelly's words, in terms of their musical conception, they nonetheless entered into a conniving relationship when the shoot began in December 1953. The duo improvised around the Lerner script as they went along, changing dialogue, "touching it up." When Lerner heard about this via the studio grapevine, he stormed into Freed's office, and then, fuming, he stalked onto Stage 15. Confronting the offenders, Lerner said, "I know I can write better than anybody on this set. So, if you want anything changed, ask me." After that, there were no further changes.

Lerner held that *Brigadoon* was one of Minnelli's least vivacious efforts, despite the potential offered by CinemaScope. Only the wedding scene and the chase that follows reveal Minnelli's unique touch. Before shooting began, Freed rushed to inform Lerner that "Vincente is bubbling over with enthusiasm about *Brigadoon*." But, evidently, his heart was not in this film. Early on, Minnelli made a mistake and confessed to Kelly that he really hadn't liked the Broadway show.

As a film, *Brigadoon* was curiously flat and rambling, lacking in warmth or charm, and the direction lacks Minnelli's usual vitality and smooth flow. Admittedly, Lerner's fairy-tale story was too much of a wistful fancy. Two American hunters go astray in the Scottish hills, landing in a remote village that seems to be lost in time. One of the fellows falls in love with a bonnie lass from the past, which naturally leads to some complications.

Minnelli thought that it would be better to set the story in 1774, after the revolts against English rule had ended. For research about the look of the cottages, he consulted with the Scottish Tourist Board in Edinburgh. But the resulting set of the old highland village looks artificial, despite the décor, the Scottish costumes, the heather blossoms, and the scenic backdrops.

Inexplicably, some of the good songs that made the stage show stand out, such as "Come to Me, Bend to Me," "My Mother's Wedding Day," and "There But for You Go I," were omitted from the film. Other songs, such as "The Heather on the Hill" and "Almost Like Being in Love," had some charm, though not enough to sustain the musical as a whole.

Moreover, the energy of the stage dances was lost in the transfer to the screen, which was odd, considering that Kelly and Charisse were the dancers. For some reason, their individual numbers were too mechanical. What should have been wistful and lyrical became an exercise in trickery and by-now-predictable style. With the exception of "The Chase," wherein the wild Scots pursue a fugitive from their village, the ensemble dances were dull. Onstage, Agnes de Mille's choreography gave the dance a special energetic touch, whereas Kelly's choreography in the film was mediocre at best and uninspired at worst.

It didn't help that Kelly and Charisse made an odd, unappealing couple. While he looks thin and metallic, she seems too solemn and often just frozen. The rest of the cast was not much better. Van Johnson, as Kelly's friend, pouts too much. As Scottish villagers, Barry Jones, Hugh Laing, and Jimmy Thompson act peculiarly, to say the least.

Most theater reviewers could not understand "the secret charm" of *Brigadoon* when the whimsical musical had played on Broadway. Was it the dancing, the music, the décor, or the blend of all these elements that made it enjoyable? As for the movie version, *The New York Times*'s Bosley Crowther summed up the general opinion when he described it as "pretty weak and synthetic Scotch."

One minor reward for the film's otherwise lukewarm reception was the Box Office Blue Ribbon Award, conferred upon Minnelli when the National Screen Council voted *Brigadoon* the "month's best picture for the whole family." Unfortunately, that family audience decided to stay at home, and M-G-M declared a financial loss by year's end.

If *Brigadoon* represented a professional low for Minnelli, his personal life was suddenly and unexpectedly enriched. Two years after his divorce from Judy, Minnelli began dating Georgette Magnani.

In 1953 Christiane Martel, a seventeen-year-old half-French, half-Italian, was named Miss Universe and offered a contract at Universal. Christiane's parents were apprehensive about their daughter traveling to Hollywood alone, so they sent her twenty-two-year-old sister, Georgette, along as a chaperon. Shortly after her arrival in Hollywood, Minnelli met Georgette at a party and immediately became smitten with her.

Minnelli was bowled over by Georgette's statuesque, dark looks and "French" charm. Glamorous enough to be a movie star, Georgette shocked Minnelli when she refused his offer of a Hollywood screen test, which he was more than willing to shoot himself.

Minnelli soon realized that, unlike Judy, Georgette was stable and efficient, the ideal wife for a single father who was raising a difficult and demanding nine-year-old daughter like Liza. Minnelli and Georgette were married in a modest ceremony on February 16, 1954, while he was directing *Brigadoon*.

While spending time on the set of *The Long, Long Trailer*, Liza had befriended Madge Blake, who played Lucille Ball's aunt. After meeting Liza, Madge wrote a letter to Minnelli that reveals a great deal about his daughter. When Madge asked Liza where she went to school, Liza didn't answer. Madge, a teacher herself, assumed that Liza had been instructed not to talk to any strangers, but it turned out that Liza simply refused to talk about her formal education, because she was not getting much schooling.

Minnelli had always been concerned with Liza's scholastic skills and academic interests. To that extent, he became Liza's teacher, or rather mentor-tutor, since his approach went far beyond transmitting knowledge or skills. "I was always Daddy's girl," Liza later recalled. "Daddy was so supportive and patient, he made me feel the prettiest girl in the world." Minnelli was everything to Liza, and, until his marital status changed, Liza was everything to him.

In April 1955, Georgette gave birth to Christiana Nina, affectionately nicknamed Tina Nina. One of Georgette's first visitors after Tina Nina's birth was Judy, who came with plenty of gifts for both mother and daughter. As Georgette remembers, "Vincente was in another world. He was a dreamer. But Judy was then happy with Sid Luft [whom she had married after Minnelli], so she had no reason to be jealous that I was now married to Vincente."

Having to compete for her father's love and attention, Liza didn't like Georgette or Tina Nina. At first, she was careful and shrewd enough not to show her true feelings in front of her father. However, from the start, Tina Nina and Liza were destined to be lifetime rivals for Minnelli's affection. As far as Hollywood was concerned, Minnelli had only one daughter, which was the way Liza wanted it.

Liza ignored her half sister from early childhood onward. Tina Nina recalled, "My earliest memories of Liza are of her waiting for Daddy every night. When he arrived, she showed him what she had learned during the day, the new songs, the new steps. Liza was very talented, very hyperactive, and full of energy. She had such big brown eyes, always searching for something."

As a father, Minnelli had beautiful costumes made for both of his daughters. Liza loved her wardrobe, particularly a long red strapless dress. As Tina Nina remembered it, "We always played make-believe games, sang songs, and read books together. Daddy always had the most wonderful art books. He always told us stories. He would never say no to anything we wanted, and he would never spank us. He spoiled us both.

"He never told me if I ever did anything wrong. I remember him asking me where I wanted to go to lunch. When I said it didn't matter, he said, 'I really want to please you. Even if you have to flip a coin, you have to make a decision, because later on, when you're older, some young man will ask to take you out and he will want to please you and he will want to know.'"

One night Minnelli invited the veteran actresses Ina Claire and Lillian Gish to his house for dinner. Liza was already starstruck. "As soon as you leave the house," Minnelli warned his lady friends, "she'll be giving an imitation of both of you. She's fascinated with actresses." Indeed, barely seconds after they left, Liza gave dead-on impersonations, mimicking Claire's mannerisms and Gish's unique way of speaking down to the littlest detail in a way that had Minnelli in stitches. How could he be angry at his Liza when she had so much talent?

Georgette recalled: "I treated Liza as if she were my only daughter. When her father was around, she was very sweet to me, but when he was out of the room, she would say terrible things to me. I wasn't thin. Liza would look at me and say, 'You aren't really as fat as everyone says you are.' She was not nice." Georgette tried to disregard Liza's barbs and to be sensitive to her loneliness: "I took care of her when she was sick. But when Minnelli came home, she would lie to him and complain bitterly that I'd left her alone all day."

Liza was simply angry with her father for having another daughter. In her mind, that was very different from Judy having another daughter, because her mother was a woman. She had a special relationship with her father, whom she adored. Until Liza got married, and even afterward, Minnelli was the most important man in her life.

Occasionally, Liza refused to eat with the rest of the family because she would not share her father with Georgette and Tina Nina, whom she perceived as outsiders. Georgette felt that Liza was putting on an act to get her father's undivided attention and monopolize his time: "Vincente always treated Liza like a star. He saw her as a star, because she really was very talented. He gave her everything he could. But when she couldn't get what she wanted, she would cry and scream."

A down-to-earth woman, Georgette quickly realized that her marriage to Minnelli was fraught with obstacles. Liza was just one problem. Georgette was unnerved by Minnelli's preoccupation with his work. He would get up in the middle of a meal and disappear to his study, where he would spend hours reading before going to bed, by which time Georgette was sound asleep. For various reasons, he seldom went to bed at the same time that she did. This was an old Minnelli way of avoiding intimate personal or physical contact with his wives.

Additionally, the marriage was plagued by financial problems since Minnelli had never been responsible with money. Georgette was the one to arrange a pension from Metro for him, and to insist that the family live on a fixed budget. Terrified that Liza, whenever she had tantrums, would leave him, Minnelli, instead of reproaching her, would rush out to the most expensive toy stores and buy anything she wanted. He would then come home and sheepishly hide the toys' price tags, and sometimes the toys themselves, from Georgette.

Minnelli took his entire family to France, Georgette's country, while he was directing *Lust for Life*. A year and a half later, Minnelli returned to France to shoot *Gigi*. Between those visits to France, his marriage fell apart. Minnelli was never really in love with Georgette, though he considered their daughter to be "the brightest spot in our marriage." When Minnelli returned to Los Angeles, Georgette remained in France. Months later, she came back to the United States to take custody of Tina Nina and move to New York.

When Minnelli was writing his memoirs, in the early 1970s, Liza pointed out that the book lacked any mention of her childhood perception of him. As a result, he invited his daughter to contribute to the book, hoping she would recapture her childhood vividly and accurately. Liza's two pages in the book focus on the years between Minnelli's divorce from Judy, when she was six, and his remarriage, when she was eight. She recalls staying in her father's house, in a room decorated to accommodate "a passing fairy princess." Her father's room smelled of "tobacco, warm colors, and thinking of all kinds."

Liza recalled her Metro days, when her father was working with Astaire and Charisse, of dinners alone together, of talks about Paris and the writer Colette. The essay ends as she and her dad part, with Liza being whisked away by Judy's driver as she says, "good-bye-good-bye," a word she had always hated.

In his autobiography, Minnelli notes: "I smothered Liza with love. If I spoiled Liza outrageously, the fairy-tale quality of our relationship achieved a balance with the starkness of her life with Judy. Much as Liza loved her mother, Judy represented duty and worry. I required nothing but love." The relationship with Liza was based on Minnelli's need to spoil her, and it also had a strong element of escapism, or the allure of magic, as he put it.

When Lorna Luft, Judy's first child with Sid Luft, was born, Liza was almost (but not quite) prepared to share her mother with another child. With her father, however, Liza always came first and her hold over him remained unchallenged. She reacted to all of her stepmothers with anger and rebellion, believing that they had annoyingly and unnecessarily taken her place in her father's heart.

Liza was used to getting her own way with her dad, who capitulated to each and every whim of hers. Georgette remembers, "As a child, Liza would want people to love her, but she was just as set on getting her own way. I tried to be very diplomatic, but it was useless trying to discipline Liza. If she didn't get her own way, she would have terrible tantrums, screaming fits like a nervous breakdown."

Intelligent and very strong, Liza knew how to manipulate her father to get what she wanted, when she wanted it. Minnelli felt guilty about Liza, fearing that if he didn't make her happy, she wouldn't want to stay with him. He gave parties for her friends, and let Liza stay up and watch movies until midnight. When she had problems falling asleep, he would read her stories until she finally did.

Georgette employed a gourmet cook, and, instinctively grasping that meals were of vital importance to her stepmother, Liza retaliated. Jeanette, the nanny, was terrified of upsetting Liza. When Liza demanded to eat her meals in her room, Minnelli allowed her to do so. "Liza's room was decorated in white and she would eat all the food with her hands. When she had finished her dinner, the wallpaper was smeared with grease, the bed cover drenched in ketchup, chocolate stains everywhere. I think she did it on purpose."

On March 29, 1955, just a few weeks before Tina Nina was born, Judy gave birth to Joey Luft. Liza embraced her half-brother, but she couldn't cope with another sibling produced by her beloved father. Liza was not happy that her dad had a new life with a second family. From the moment Tina Nina was born, Liza would cling to her status as Minnelli's "only" daughter, especially in public.

Minnelli could not blame Liza. While Judy suffered from drug dependency and weight problems, and swung from alcohol to depression, he was the only constant and positive factor in Liza's life. Minnelli knew that Liza deeply resented sharing him with another daughter—or wife.

Liza suffered only for a few years, since Minnelli and Georgette divorced in 1959, after five years of marriage. Tina Nina then went to Mexico to live with her mother and grandparents. After the divorce, according to the custody agreement, Tina Nina spent two months out of the year with her father in California. Her visits often coincided with those of Liza, who lived six months with her dad.

Although Tina Nina was nine years younger than Liza, she learned early on never to mention Judy to her. "The subject of Judy was a very delicate one," she recalled. "Daddy and Liza would say things to each other like, 'Mama did this in that movie,' or, 'Remember when she sang that song.' And Daddy told me that Judy was a wonderful person. He never talked badly about her, ever.

"I always thought of Liza as my sister and Daddy did everything he could to encourage our relationship." When Tina Nina was in Mexico, she wrote letters to her father, which he would then read to Liza, sometimes over the telephone, word by word. Years later, Liza told Tina Nina that she really hated it when their father called to report about Tina Nina's comings and goings.

Minnelli noticed that Liza was particularly jealous when Tina Nina was in the house. Sometimes, Liza pretended to be sick so that her father would take her into her room and comfort her. Tina Nina remembered Liza lying in bed and crying, " 'Daddy, you don't care about me. You only care about Tina Nina.' I felt so guilty." Liza was simply used to having Minnelli to herself all the time. Tina recalled a day when Liza was taking a picture of their dog and simply refused to include Tina in it.

Aware of what Liza went through with her mother's ups and downs, Tina Nina felt compassion for her sister. Liza's life was erratic, to say the least, living with Judy for half of the year, during which time she was expected to help her mother through her various problems. Tina recalled: "Liza was much closer to Daddy than I was. Daddy was her stability, and Liza was practically in love with him. She worshipped him and he worshipped her. He didn't have a family other than an aunt. He was alone and she was alone. They only had each other."

Seventeen

Up and Down: Contract Director

GREEN MANSIONS, BASED ON W. H. HUDSON'S NOVEL, was going to be Minnelli's next musical project. Despite the disappointing result of *Brigadoon,* no one at M-G-M bothered to think about the similarities of the two films or consider that *Green Mansions* was another supernatural romance, this one set in a forest. The only difference was that, for the movie to look right, it needed to be shot on location. Minnelli, quite enthusiastically, began research into what he believed would be the magical setting for Rima, the Bird-Girl of Hudson's Edwardian dream.

In June 1954, Minnelli set out on his first business trip abroad at Metro's expense. The extensive itinerary included Mexico, Cuba, British Guiana, Peru, and Venezuela, countries that were explored in the company of reliable production designer Preston Ames. The discomforts of the trip, compared with shooting on soundstages, became quickly apparent, but Minnelli was entranced with the vibrant and changing colors of the rain forest. The crew shot plenty of raw footage, which they planned to use for future reference.

Back in Hollywood, Minnelli and Alan Jay Lerner worked on the story of a white man's love for a sylvan sprite possessed of eternal youth. Brazilian composer Heitor Villa-Lobos was asked to compose an orchestral score that would synthesize the rhythms of tropical birdsong.

In September, Freed suggested that Minnelli try out his ideas in a filmed run-through that would also serve as an audition for Pier Angeli. Edmund Purdom, a male ingénu, was to play opposite Angeli. Minnelli ordered his set decorators to drape cascades of rubber-cement spiderwebs on all the branches left over from the *Brigadoon* set. The production was slated to start in 1955. However, neither Angeli's test, which took two weeks to shoot, nor Lerner's script were good enough to persuade Freed that this fable would translate into an entertaining film.

After spending most of 1954 on *Brigadoon* and *Green Mansions,* which never materialized, Minnelli was ready to focus on something more modest yet substantial, a film called *The Cobweb.* Like *The Bad and the Beautiful, The Cobweb* set out to reveal the inside workings of a sheltered, closed society, and, like it, the story centers on people whose professional careers compensate for emotional problems, specifically lonely, frustrated domestic lives.

Eager to work with him again, John Houseman had no trouble persuading Minnelli to join forces. Since their last collaboration, *The Bad and The Beautiful,* Minnelli had directed two musicals for Freed and the Lucille Ball farce, *The Long, Long Trailer.*

By the end of the year, switching from a musical to a melodrama, Minnelli was already busy at work on "our mental film," as he labeled *The Cobweb.* Like Houseman's other projects, *The Cobweb* was a star-laden ensemble picture that aimed at classy entertainment, but one with presumably broader appeal. The cast displayed a new generation of actors, including John Kerr, who was being touted as "the next James Dean."

The film was based on the novel by William Gibson (writing under the pseudonym William Mass), who got firsthand knowledge of a private mental hospital during his wife's work as a staff member of the Menninger Clinic. The adaptation was done by John Paxton, whose scripts for *Crossfire* and *The Wild One* had shown sensitivity to explosive, socially relevant melodramas.

Minnelli felt that it was imperative to establish a definite city name as the film's locale, rather than leaving the locale nondescript, and M-G-M opted for Riverwood, Nebraska. The casting director was amused when, in the name of authenticity, Minnelli had asked him for "Patients needed—Types," providing a list that included "a dignified, thin old man; a skinny young girl who's starving herself to death and is fed intravenously; a baby-faced girl, the bizarre mind type; a very fat, cheerful young man; a fat and morose man who's always dressed in robe and accompanied by a nurse; a Don Juan type; and a blonde football the Princeton physical type."

Gibson supported all the changes recommended by Minnelli and the screenwriters. All along Minnelli held that the film's impact would depend on the intense directness with which the audience could identify with the characters. In the book, the doctor's wife suffers from frigidity, aggravated by menopause. A decision was therefore made to subject the doctor to the tensions of a more normal marriage.

The Cobweb became a personal film for Minnelli in more ways than one. The psychiatric setting held a perverse fascination for him, after his years of nursing Judy as she spent time in various institutions, including Menninger.

The bizarre plot and some of the characters touched a chord, and played to his idiosyncrasies. The film's central conflict was particularly close to Minnelli's heart. The hostility between the clinic's patients and the warring staff erupts over a seemingly trivial aesthetic matter, the choice of new drapes for the lounge. But for an aesthete like Minnelli, the issue was not trivial at all; it was essential. Décor reflected not only aesthetics but deeper values and moral issues too.

The production had to be delayed because of adaptation and casting problems. Paxton was forced to eliminate the homosexuality of one inmate, and had to turn the central romance between an art therapist and her married boss into a repressed, guilt-ridden affair that ends with the husband returning to his wife.

To achieve greater accuracy, Minnelli brought Gibson to Hollywood to rework the dialogue, and to supervise the construction of the sets. In the end, despite much effort, Minnelli was dissatisfied with the shooting script—and the final cut.

Another problem was caused by the casting, which resulted in the first big rift between Minnelli and Houseman. Initially, the film was to star Robert Taylor as the chief doctor, Lana Turner as his neglected wife, and Grace Kelly as the woman between them. By late fall, however, when the script was finally ready, Taylor and Turner were working on other pictures.

Relieved that he would not be working with Robert Taylor, for whom he had little respect, Minnelli was glad to settle on Richard Widmark, though he had reservations as to whether Widmark could segue from his villainous roles in film noir, such as his stunning debut in *Kiss of Death,* into more mainstream melodrama. Minnelli hoped that pairing Widmark with Gloria Grahame, whom the director had befriended when filming *The Bad and the Beatiful,* would show the actor's softer side. He was wrong, and Widmark was not convincing as a doctor or troubled husband.

Houseman hoped to get James Dean right after *East of Eden* for the key role of Stevie, the tormented teenager. But Dean balked at the low fee he was offered, and John Kerr was signed, based on his appearance in the successful Broadway production of *Tea and Sympathy.* Minnelli would later cast Kerr in his movie version of that play. Then, a month before shooting began, Grace Kelly, exhausted from making four consecutive films, bowed out. Minnelli had to quickly replace her with Lauren Bacall, an actress with a strong physical presence but decidedly limited talent.

Minnelli cast his friend Oscar Levant, notorious for his real (and imagined) neuroses, as the mother-fixated Mr. Capp, who in the book was homosexual. He wished to keep the gay character intact, but it was a battle he could not win. A similar situation had occurred several years earlier with Edward Dmytryk's *Crossfire,* in which the book's homosexual soldier was changed to a Jewish one. It would take another decade for Hollywood to depict homosexuals on-screen, in movies like *Suddenly, Last Summer* and *Reflections in a Golden Eye.* Minnelli, like Cukor and other gay directors in the 1950s, would never have the opportunity to deal explicitly with this theme himself.

Houseman persuaded Lillian Gish to make her first screen appearance in years, as the asylum's reactionary administrator, Miss Inch. Minnelli clashed with Houseman again when he proposed Charles Boyer as Richard Widmark's antagonist, a psychiatrist in decline because of his excessive drinking and womanizing. Houseman thought that Boyer's Gallic charm and heavy accent would add an unnecessary note to the already overburdened script, but he grudgingly conceded when Minnelli simply refused to consider any other actor.

As soon as casting was completed, both Minnelli and Houseman realized that their main challenge in elevating the film's stature was how to overcome the lackluster box-office appeal of their chosen ensemble, which didn't include name actors or certified stars. Times were changing, and given severe competition from TV, stars were becoming much more important in positioning feature films in the theatrical marketplace. Hitchcock, a contemporary of Minnelli, absorbed the new reality right away and all of his 1950s movies were cast with major stars of the caliber of Cary Grant, Jimmy Stewart, Grace Kelly, and Kim Novak.

In *The Cobweb*, Widmark portrays a clinical psychiatrist, Stewart McIver, torn between his own family of wife, Karen, and two children, and the surrogate family that he cultivates in his clinic with attractive staff worker Meg (Lauren Bacall), and disturbed adolescent artist-patient Stevie (John Kerr).

Meg and McIver ask Stevie to design new drapes for the clinic's library as a therapeutic exercise, not realizing that Stewart's wife (Gloria Grahame) and a matronly bureaucrat at the clinic (Lillian Gish) already have assumed responsibility for doing it. This plot device generates several intricate familial, social, and professional conflicts, none of which, in Minnelli's opinion, was resolved satisfactorily. Irony abounds, for at the end, the library still remains without drapes.

Minnelli began the seven-week shoot in early December 1954. For this, his first dramatic feature in CinemaScope, he relied on veteran cameraman George Folsey, whose work on *Meet Me in St. Louis* he continued to admire. Folsey's bravura style, with his noted edgy tracking shots, was so striking that Minnelli would use him again for the boar hunt sequence in his 1960 melodrama, *Home from the Hill*.

Minnelli's most dynamic visual touch is evident only in the climactic sequence of Stevie's escape from the asylum. For this scene, Minnelli needed even more neurotic music than Miklos Rozsa provided in his waltz for *Madame Bovary*. He therefore asked for more dissonant brasses from composer Leonard Rosenman, who had established a name for himself a year earlier with his wonderful score for the James Dean film, Elia Kazan's *East of Eden*.

Throughout, Minnelli was apprehensive about a sprawling saga that contained too many incidents and subplots for a two-hour feature. As originally shot, the film was burdened with the excessive running time of two and a half hours. On this occasion, Minnelli's penchant for long takes and atmospheric detail was not appreciated, and he found himself in serious conflict with his producer. Anticipating studio pressures, Houseman demanded severe cuts. When Minnelli refused to cooperate, Houseman asked editor Harold F. Kress to step in. Upon seeing the final cut, and dismayed by Houseman's violation of trust, Minnelli accused him of willful interference that undermined his authority.

As expected, Dore Schary sided with Houseman. M-G-M previewed *The Cobweb* at the Encino Theatre on April 19, 1955, to mixed results. Though most of the comments were positive, there were occasional nasty remarks, such as "Why don't you buy Venetian blinds and have the conflict done with." Times were changing, and viewers in 1955 were not necessarily more sophisticated but they were certainly more demanding about getting their money's worth at the movies, since TV provided good entertainment free of charge.

In the end, Minnelli couldn't bring to *The Cobweb* the same vigor or style that had envigorated *The Bad and the Beautiful* four years earlier. Even so, despite its lack of forceful style, *The Cobweb* was a highly personal film. Minnelli interweaved themes from his previous works, specifically the artist as an outsider, careers as compensation for personal disappointment, the struggle between maintaining individualism (at the price of loneliness) and the need to conform and integrate oneself into a larger community. The film's underlining motif was social and emotional isolation, which marked each of the characters, including members of the professional team.

The Cobweb was also marred by a lack of authenticity. The clinic we see on the screen doesn't resemble any remotely realistic mental institution. The group scenes play out like Minnelli's customary party scenes, a nervous mix of chatty cosmopolitans and flinching wallflowers. Take the brief encounter between Karen and her husband's young charge, in which they discuss the symbolism of flowers and the tormented genius of Les Fauves. "Isn't it enough that they have color and form?" Karen says. The gladioli on the backseat of Karen's station wagon inspire Stevie to brood over the artist André Derain's deathbed cry, "Some red, show me some red . . . and some green!"

The picture's domestic scenes are more harrowing than the climax at the clinic. *The Cobweb* was the first Minnelli melodrama to reflect his ever-growing cynicism about family life in the affluent 1950s. His future domestic melodramas, *Tea and Sympathy, Some Came Running,* and *Home from the Hill,* center on presumably respectable and happy couples who actually loathe each other and are miserably unfulfilled.

Some film scholars, like Thomas Schatz, consider Minnelli's melodramas, *The Cobweb, Tea and Sympathy, Home from the Hill,* and *Two Weeks in Another Town,* as examples of a distinctive genre, the male weepie, that follows the narrative strategy of exploiting superficial plots to camouflage more serious or deeper social criticism. Whether Minnelli examines an angst-ridden familial relationship in a mental hospital (*The Cobweb*), on a boarding school campus (*Tea and Sympathy*), a small town (*Some Came Running*), or within a foreign-based Hollywood production (*Two Weeks in Another Town*), his melodramas trace the search for the ideal family. In most of these features, Minnelli contrasts the protagonist's "natural" or biological family with a professional group that's the equivalent of, and functions as, a surrogate family.

In *The Cobweb,* the emphasis on family interaction is highlighted by the fact that McIver is a Freudian psychoanalyst who doesn't get along with his wife or son. "Why don't you analyze my Oedipus complex or my lousy father?" Stevie asks McIver early on in the film. To which the psychiatrist later responds, "I'm not your father, and I won't run out on you like your father did." As good a surrogate father as McIver is on the job, though, his performance of domestic skills and his demonstrations of feelings on the home front are lacking, to say the least. He doesn't communicate with his wife either verbally or sexually, and he is a complete stranger to his own children. When McIver's daughter, Rosie, is asked at school what she wants to be, she replies, "One of Daddy's patients."

The McIver household in *The Cobweb* is the setting for a misbegotten marriage. By day, it has the sterile upscale hominess of a W. J. Sloane window display. By night, it shifts to a gothic atmosphere. Minnelli makes sure to place the doctor and his wife in the shadows of their respective bedrooms, while the children are in the background. The solemn little boy plays chess against himself, whereas the girl wants to be a mental patient when she grows up. Compared to this troubled family unit, the hospital represents harmony and sociability.

Minnelli's bleak take on the story was so persuasive that the Production Code imposed a reconciliation and happy ending. A scrawled legend in yellow, superimposed over Karen's chintz drapes, now an improvised bed for the prodigal inmate, announces: "The trouble was over." But the film builds up for a catharsis that never occurs. The mixture of psychosexual angst and textile whimsies was right up Minnelli's alley, as a filmmaker and as a person who had worked as a decorator and experienced firsthand mental illness at his home with Judy.

The Cobweb enjoyed tremendous publicity. The studio's advertising department came up with: "After blasting the nation with its *Blackboard Jungle* bombshell, M-G-M follows up with a smashing, all-star production, *The Cobweb,* a forbidden subject that will be the talk of America. For the first time, the screen dares to reveal the secrets of the psychiatrist's couch in that strange mansion on the hill they called 'The Castle.'"

Minnelli identified with the story's young patient, Stevie, and his quip: "You can't tell the patients from the doctors." A decade later, when Kirk Douglas told Minnelli about his plan to adapt *One Flew Over the Cuckoo's Nest* to the screen and play the lead role (eventually played by Jack Nicholson in an Oscar-winning turn), Minnelli was quick to point out that *The Cobweb* was the first film to show the fine line between sanity and madness, and that at times there really are no differences between the inmates and therapists, since both characters are troubled.

Consider the following charge made by John Kerr's patient to his psychiatrist: "You're supposed to be making me fit for normal life. What's normal? Yours? If it's a question of values, your values stink. Lousy, middle-class, well-fed, smug existence. All you care about is a paycheck you didn't earn and a beautiful thing to go home to every night." Minnelli was completely sympathetic to the patient's point of view, particularly with regard to the middle-class notion of normalcy, which he protested and contested in both his personal and professional lives.

After the film opened at Radio City Music Hall, the critics were divided in their response. *Variety* chided M-G-M for making a movie too tasteful and restrained for its harrowing subject matter. Other reviewers dismissed the movie as trivial. In the end, *The Cobweb*'s domestic rentals of $1.5 million didn't recoup its budget, and M-G-M deemed it a failure.

In hindsight, neither the artistic nor the commercial results justified the film's arduous production process and the behind-the-scenes arguments. Soon Minnelli himself forgot the spat with Houseman. Just weeks after their nasty fights and exchange of harsh words, some of which were, quite uncharacteristically, conducted in public and reached the press, the two men were immersed in what would become the most challenging project of Minnelli's career to date, *Lust for Life,* a film about Van Gogh, an artist he had always worshiped.

Before *Lust for Life*, however, Minnelli was forced to make a quickie. Freed owned the stage rights to a musical adaptation of *Kismet,* which was a smash hit on Broadway. This Arabian Nights pastiche had already enjoyed a long life on stage and screen. The original drama, by English playwright Edward Knoblock, had impressed theatergoers before the First World War. Two film versions appeared in 1920 and 1930, and in 1944, M-G-M created a lavish version as a Ronald Colman vehicle, with Marlene Dietrich as the sultan's mistress. Nine years later, composers Robert Wright and George Forrest turned Charles Lederer and Lutor Davis's straight play into a stage musical.

George Forrest and Robert Wright had previously collaborated on *Song of Norway,* adapted from themes by Edvard Grieg. Most theater critics thought that *Kismet* was kitsch, but a newspaper strike prevented the nasty reviews from spreading to the public, so they had no effect on the show. The musical's principal merits were Alfred Drake's star turn and the melodic score by the Russian composer Aleksandr Borodin. Songs like "Stranger in Paradise" and "Baubles, Bangles, and Beads" dominated the airwaves, and the show ran for two seasons.

When Freed first talked to Minnelli about *Kismet,* Minnelli said, "I hated the show, I don't want to do it!" Freed was so astonished by his strong distaste that Minnelli had to explain that he had a low opinion of the show because it was corny and witless. Freed had never heard Minnelli express his opinion so harshly and bluntly.

A few days later Minnelli was summoned to Schary's office for a tête-à-tête behind closed doors. Ten minutes later, when Minnelli left the office, he had lost the battle on *Kismet,* but for a good cause. In return for directing *Kismet,* Minnelli was promised the Van Gogh project, now titled *Lust for Life,* with a larger than usual budget, on-location shooting, and unrestricted artistic freedom.

Set in Baghdad, *Kismet* is a fable about how the magical powers of the street poet Hajj are abused by the scheming Wazir to advance his own stature. The poet is an opportunist who fixes things so that his daughter, Lalume, can wed the Caliph and he can be sent to a romantic oasis.

In his casting, Minnelli was forced to rely on M-G-M contract players and second bananas. The baritone Howard Keel was chosen to play Hajj, Lalume went to Dolores Gray, whose screen test Minnelli himself had shot; the young Caliph and Hajj's daughter, Marsinah, were played by Vic Damone and Ann Blyth, respectively. The villainous Wazir was played by Sebastian Cabot, a good British stage actor, then unknown to American audiences.

Jack Cole was assigned to choreograph *Kismet*'s musical numbers, based on his work on the Broadway and London stage productions. Minnelli and Cole knew each other well from their days at Radio City Music Hall, but they had different tastes that needed to be reconciled into a unified vision.

Visually, Minnelli opted for an almost monochromatic look, "like Olsen and Johnson in Baghdad but very beautiful and chic." The model for the film was *The Pirate,* a sort of fairy tale done tongue-in-cheek. The film was meant to look like a Persian painting, with surreal skies and gold clouds.

While Minnelli worked with Preston Ames on the sets and with Tony Duquette on the costumes, Cole began rehearsing the dances. Most of the songs from the Broadway show were retained, including "Stranger in Paradise," "Baubles, Bangles, and Beads," "The Olive Tree," and "This Is My Beloved." "Nineveh," the first dance number Cole choreographed, was exciting, but it caused a rift between Johnny Green, who worked on the scoring, and Cole, who was known for his short fuse and scathing tongue. In the end, Freed settled the dispute in Green's favor.

By early 1955, Minnelli was already in pre-production on *Lust for Life,* a film he was eager to make. Which explains why Minnelli had little interest in *Kismet* as the picture went into production. As a result, what was meant to be a farcical fairy tale became heavy-handed, grim, and listless. There was no real fun in the movie. Even the usually vital Cole failed to inject sophisticated humor into his dance routines. Bored, restless, displeased with the cast, and already preoccupied with *Lust for Life,* Minnelli paid more attention to the décor than to the performers, most of whom he disliked.

Minnelli was given half of his usual time to direct *Kismet.* As a result, he embarked on the most demanding schedule he had faced since *An American in Paris,* planning two films at the same time, and then shooting them back-to-back on two different continents.

Kismet began shooting on May 23, 1955, and ended two months later. Once again Minnelli was drafted to concoct glitzy tableaux out of routine material, with a third-rate cast. As always, Minnelli relied on his professionalism, though he couldn't conceal his contempt for the corny material. Usually, Minnelli was meticulous in working out every camera composition, but this time, as a result of carelessness and rush, he uncharacteristically printed the first or second takes. The timetable was too tight to afford rehearsals with the actors, who soon were exhausted by the pace. Four days before *Kismet* was completed, Minnelli flew to London to join Houseman, who was in Europe scouting locations for *Lust for Life.*

In *Kismet,* Minnelli uncharacteristically opted for a literal translation of the stage play, with the actors reciting in stiff "Arabian" syntax. Most musical numbers end routinely, with Dolores Gray or the showgirls posing. The film was made for the undemanding fans of exotica. Here and there Minnelli displays personal touches, but they are trivial, like throwing a yellow silk across the screen.

Only one sequence, "Night of My Nights," set at dusk on the evening of the Caliph's nuptials, was nearly spectacular. White steeds and courtiers in pastel silks parade across the screen, bearing a cornucopia of Duquette's swankiest accessories: sparklers, canopies, and temple altars. This scene recalls Minnelli's own costume tableaux in Marshall Field's display windows, and the *Scheherazade* suite, his first art-direction job at Radio City Music Hall.

After Minnelli's departure for France to start shooting *Lust for Life,* Stanley Donen was brought in to finish *Kismet.* Production closed on July 22, 1955, at a cost of $2,692,960. The studio held two sneak previews, which yielded only moderate response. One preview card noted that *Kismet* is "as good as Lana Turner's pictures!"—whatever that meant.

Kismet premiered on October 8, 1955, at Radio City Music Hall, on a double bill with the annual Nativity pageant. The New York press response was no more than cordial, and the box office receipts were equally disappointing, about $2,920,000.

Kismet was one of Minnelli's least personal films, and in the view of this writer, one of his two or three weakest pictures. It seemed that Minnelli was using ideas from an old scrapbook, but without his distinctive signature or his soul. *Kismet*'s commercial failure reinforced Minnelli's initial loathing for the project, except that in this instance he really didn't care as a big, exciting project was ahead of him.

Eighteen

Personal Films: *Lust for Life* and *Tea and Sympathy*

MINNELLI REGARDED *Lust for Life* as the toughest challenge of his career. It was the most visually evocative film he had made about a subject he was passionate about: Van Gogh as an uncompromising artist. *Lust for Life* was the first and only movie Minnelli initiated during his lengthy tenure at M-G-M; all the other films were planned for him by Freed, Pandro Berman, or other producers. Minnelli's plea to make the film was helped by Dore Schary's wife, who was an art lover, particularly of Van Gogh. As usual, it was easier for Minnelli to go through the executives' wives, when business was concerned.

A personal film, *Lust for Life* deals with the creative impulses and emotional isolation of Van Gogh as an artist. On this production, Minnelli's work was totally unhampered by the studio. Except for a few scenes (one showing Gauguin arriving in Arles) that were later eliminated, the released film reflects Minnelli's singular vision and the cut he submitted.

Not surprisingly, when asked to single out the favorite of his movies, Minnelli always cited *Lust for Life*. His second choice was *The Band Wagon,* and his third *The Bad and the Beautiful.*

Minnelli felt a special emotional affinity with France's cultural legacy, particularly its paintings, as he demonstrated in the grand ballet finale in *An American in Paris.* For *Lust for Life,* as an artist and painter himself, Minnelli used color as both a psychologically and artistically expressive tool.

Making this biopicture, Minnelli's first foray into one of Hollywood's most popular genres, was an exhilarating experience from start to finish. Shooting on location, in the actual landscapes where Van Gogh had worked and lived, Minnelli felt liberated from the studio's interference and from his own self-imposed constraints. As Stephen Harvey noted, *Lust for Life* became a turning point in his career, after which he began working in a freer, more improvised style, one that blended his subjective imagination with a more realistic approach to his stories in terms of time and place.

Compared with his other self-reflexive films, *The Bad and the Beautiful* and *The Band Wagon*, both of which center on show business and artistic types, *Lust for Life* was the grimmest and most revealing of Minnelli's portraits of artists. Placing his own artistic pulse at the center, *Lust for Life* reflected Minnelli's compulsive zest for work, and his long-held belief that commitment to art (and creativity in general) should be carried out to the exclusion of all other matters.

Irving Stone's fictionalized portrait of Van Gogh, first published in 1934, was purchased by M-G-M in 1946 after a new edition had become a bestseller. At one point, the studio had considered filming it with Spencer Tracy. In 1952, the unexpected popularity of John Huston's *Moulin Rouge,* a lush, Oscar-winning biopic about Toulouse-Lautrec, featuring José Ferrer in the lead and an innovative visual design, made a film about Van Gogh a more attractive and pragmatic project.

Moulin Rouge set a precedent for future films about artists in its impressive attention to detail and meticulous reproduction of its specific locale, Paris. Nominated for Best Picture and Director, the film deservedly won two Oscars: Color Art Direction by Paul Sheriff and Marcel Vertes, and Color Costume Design by Vertes. Hence, from the start, *Lust for Life* was positioned not just as a major M-G-M production, but also as a serious Oscar contender.

It's doubtful that *Lust for Life* would have been made without the success of *Moulin Rouge.* In addition, Van Gogh became popular with American students of the 1950s. Producer John Houseman was happy to report that reproductions of Van Gogh's *Sunflowers* decorated many students' dormitory rooms across America.

Casting the lead role of Van Gogh was easy. Kirk Douglas, who by then had become Minnelli's favorite Hollywood actor, was ideal to play the part by virtue of both his physique and temperament. As Minnelli recalled, "Once we got the green light to proceed with the picture, there was no question if Kirk would play Van Gogh. No other actor was even considered for the part."

There was another reason for choosing Douglas. In 1955, Douglas announced that Bryna, his production company, would be launched with a film about Van Gogh to be directed by Jean Negulesco and starring himself. Douglas recalls: "I got a call from M-G-M and they said, 'Guess again. We own *Lust for Life*.' The Bryna fantasy was over."

After reading Norman Corwin's scenario, M-G-M and Douglas came to an agreement. The film represented a reunion for Douglas with producer Houseman and director Minnelli. The three men had worked together harmoniously on *The Bad and the Beautiful*. By that time, the tensions and disagreements between Minnelli and Houseman on the set of *The Cobweb* were long forgotten.

Douglas offered to forgo his entire salary for *Lust for Life* in exchange for a single Van Gogh painting, but the studio turned him down. "I can afford to play Van Gogh," Douglas quipped to the press, "but I can't afford to own him."

Minnelli's main problem was to locate the dramatic locus of Van Gogh's rich, diffuse life, since the tale could go in any number of different directions. The last thing Minnelli wanted was to do one of M-G-M's conventional biopictures, which followed a formula, particularly when they concerned suffering artists or performers.

Robert Ardrey (who had written *Madame Bovary*) and Daniel Taradash (who scripted the Oscar-winning *From Here to Eternity*) declined to work on the film, claiming that the story was too internal and emotional to be effective as big-screen entertainment. Norman Corwin, who had recently written *The Blue Veil*, a 1951 Jane Wyman melodrama, was not exactly the most natural choice for such a task, but he was one of the studio's fastest, most prolific writers. It was Corwin's idea to focus the story on Van Gogh's lifelong conflict with his brother Theo.

To achieve greater clarity, Minnelli had suggested a more dramatically unified profile. Relying on Van Gogh's letters to Theo, Corwin stripped away Stone's character of a seductive young woman who appears in the artist's hallucinations, opting instead for a more straightforward account of his life. Changing the book's sentimental conceit, specifically the female figure who brought to the surface Van Gogh's dark inner demons, Corwin instead adhered more accurately to the historical record of the painter's life.

In the new conception, Van Gogh emerged as a sensitive artist who suffers rejection and abuse in all of his relationships. *Lust for Life* made Van Gogh's neurosis a direct result of society's hostility toward the artist's identity as an outsider, and presented his creative genius as a special gift. Minnelli liked Corwin's approach, which was based on a thorough examination of the painful correspondence between the siblings. However, since the letters were the property of Theo Van Gogh's surviving son, who threatened to sue if the script contained direct quotes from them, the dialogue had to be extremely cautious in paraphrasing the brothers' words.

New technology presented another major problem. Metro insisted that *Lust for Life* be shot in CinemaScope, which in Minnelli's view was not suitable for the reproduction of Van Gogh's work. Minnelli needed to find an effective way to fit Van Gogh's canvases into the frame. He wanted the dramatic scenes to resemble as closely as possible Van Gogh's own paintings.

Arguing against the use of a widescreen format, Minnelli went to New York to persuade studio executive Arthur Loew to opt for the old-fashioned Academy ratio, which was squarer and closer to the paintings' dimensions. Loew countered that, no matter how the movie was shot, it would be projected in CinemaScope across the country. Though not exactly accurate, Loew's argument was enough to convince Minnelli that he had lost the battle.

Then there was the problem of film stock. CinemaScope, at the time, was almost inseparably tied to Technicolor. In the 1950s M-G-M had abandoned the more expensive Technicolor in favor of Eastman Color, which didn't require special cameras. Minnelli disliked Eastman because it was unable to register a subtle shade of yellow, a color crucial to Van Gogh's palette, as well as being Minnelli's favorite hue, dominating the design and composition of most of his color films. Eastman was simply too bright and colorful for a film about a great artist.

For this film, Minnelli preferred the more subdued tones of Ansco Color. On this point he was insistent and finally was able to convince the studio. Having fallen out of fashion, however, Ansco had halted the production of their film stock, and it was difficult to find at photographic supply warehouses. In the end, Metro was able to find enough stock to shoot the film, using the last remaining inventory, and a special lab had to be opened to process it.

With Minnelli's help, the studio pleaded with various art collectors, including actor Edward G. Robinson and the Moscow Museum of Modern Art, to allow them to use Van Gogh's paintings. In the end, however, those chosen for the painter's studio in Arles were fakes. Other paintings appeared in close-up inserts of Van Gogh at work. Minnelli also sent a crew to several galleries to take still photographs of Van Gogh's canvases.

Houseman hired the Museum of Modern Art's impressionism expert, John Rewald, to serve as consultant. Two other artists were hired to execute the ersatz Van Goghs: one furnished the completed paintings, the other doubled for Douglas in the painting scenes.

Minnelli had no problems persuading M-G-M to shoot *Lust for Life* on location. For this picture, the natural landscapes were essential to convey the details of the artist's work. As a result, the crew went to the coal mines of the Belgian Borinage and to the Dutch countryside, as well as Paris and Provence, where Van Gogh spent his final years.

Unfortunately, because Minnelli was still busy with *Kismet* until midsummer, and the fields and vineyards were ripening under the sun, Houseman decided to shoot the script in reverse order, with the company moving north as the weather grew colder. Before principal shooting began, cameraman Joseph Ruttenberg flew to Arles to film the orchards in bloom, and Minnelli was very pleased with his footage.

This time around, Minnelli was more careful not to adorn what was essentially a somber and downbeat story with glossy entertainment values. In fact, Paris featured only peripherally in the film, with a few outdoor scenes that depict artists at work. Instead of showing the Parisian nightlife, as *Moulin Rouge* did, *Lust for Life* offers Van Gogh's own work and personality.

Van Gogh is usually portrayed as a womanizing artist who wanders around Europe socializing with prostitutes and sneering at Degas for painting "feminine" art, such as ballet dancers. In Minnelli's film, there's only a brief love affair with Christine, a working-class prostitute and mother. More important, Minnelli refrains from the Hollywood clichés in depicting artists. He refuses to show Van Gogh as a "sensitive" or "bohemian" artist, suggesting that there was nothing urbane about him, his life, or his work.

Structurally, the film concentrates on four phases of the artist's life: the black-and-white drawings from the mining district of the Boringe; the Dutch drawings and paintings of rural labor in the Hague; the impressionist landscapes of Paris; and the portraits and nature paintings of southern France.

Lust for Life was one of Hollywood's most impressive color films. Minnelli asked cinematographers Frederick Young and Russell Harlan to devise a different color scheme for each of the four phases of Van Gogh's career. In the film's scheme, the coal-mining scenes were dominated by gray; the Dutch sequences by bluish green; the Parisian episodes by bright red; and the concluding section, which became Minnelli's favorite, not least because of its color, was in sunny yellow.

Minnelli was interested in bringing the viewers closer to Van Gogh's work, showing, as he wrote in preparation for the film, "all the brushstrokes and even those places where he'd squeezed paint out of the tube onto the canvas." As a result, Minnelli pans the camera across the paintings or zooms in on significant details, like the sunlight in the late paintings.

Continuing his lifelong exploration of visual style, Minnelli deliberately goes for an extravagant approach that draws on strikingly swirling patterns of light and color, pushed to the extreme. Visual excess had marked some of Minnelli's previous films, but not to such an extent. In this picture, excess became more prominent through hysteria, reminiscent of the intense, melodramatic mode of *The Bad and the Beautiful*.

Judy Garland had been the first to observe that beneath the calm façade of Minnelli's personality, there was neurosis and even hysteria that he chose to express in his work rather than his personal life. Like other Hollywood directors, consciously and subconsciously, Minnelli channeled his neurotic anxieties and inner demons into his film work, particularly in his melodramas, a genre that has a built-in bias for excess and hysteria. Digging beneath the surface of Minnelli's more cheerful films, his comedies and musicals, one finds another realm that's deeply disturbing, often expressed in nightmares, such as the one in *Father of the Bride*.

Van Gogh's darker feelings are heightened by Miklos Rozsa's music, which in intensity resembled the waltz he had composed for the ballroom sequence in *Madame Bovary*. By now, Rozsa had become Minnelli's most reliable composer for melodramas, and it's useful to think about *Lust for Life* as an intense melodramatic biopic

The film is replete with thrilling montages of Van Gogh's canvases spread across the sets. Minnelli shot exteriors in the actual places where Van Gogh had lived and worked. This meant that the wheat fields and vineyards of Provence had to be filmed in the summer, before the harvest. Minnelli shot some of the outdoor sequences in ways that approximated how Van Gogh's famous paintings were created. To accomplish this effect, Minnelli often poses Douglas in the foreground, laboring over a painting that duplicates what we see in the background.

Going to the actual locales and striving for accurate detail, the film supports a more realistic style than previous Minnelli movies, most of which were studio-bound. *Lust for Life* depicts Van Gogh's painting as the expression of a lonely, tormented, and decidedly not romantic life. Minnelli's deliberate aestheticism complicates these matters, creating a tension with the film's sense of realism. James Naremore has claimed that *Lust for Life* deconstructs romantic ideas about art, and at the same time offers a complex account of a romantic personality. Though what constitutes a romantic personality, or romanticism in general, is a matter of interpretation, my repeated viewings of the film suggest that Van Gogh is a much less romantic and more deeply tormented and complex persona.

Yet, both thematically and stylistically, the brand of realism presented by Minnelli in *Lust for Life* is that of a heightened or stylized realism. This may sound like a contradiction of terms but it's not. Minnelli perceives Van Gogh as a complex figure who chose art as a quasireligious vocation, a tragically underappreciated artist who refused to adapt to bourgeois life and felt a spiritual affinity with nature. The film sees violence and excess as the keys to Van Gogh's personality, treating him as a primitive artist with uncontrollable emotions.

However, like other Minnelli films, *Lust for Life* ends on a more positive note that suggests light and brightness. No matter how dark Minnelli's movies are, either as a result of the strictures of the time, dictates of the Production Code, or the moral climate of the studio he worked for, he opts for resolutions that are more hopeful and upbeat than the stories that precede them. These resolutions could be seen as compromises on Minnelli's part rather than genuine expressions of his artistic impulses.

Consistent with Minnelli's artistic vision and his own effete personality, *Lust for Life* rejects Van Gogh's more established masculine image, instead endowing him with some feminine traits. In fact, the unsympathetic portrait of Paul Gauguin's machismo makes the contrast with Van Gogh's sensitivity even stronger. Minnelli thought that Anthony Quinn's natural animalistic sensuality was right for Gauguin, and would work well against Douglas's more complex, contradictory persona—equal parts macho brutality and vulnerability.

Minnelli identified completely with Van Gogh as an artist who's bound by both personal and social forces. He could particularly relate to the contradiction between Van Gogh's artistic ideals and the harsher social conditions under which he worked. Moreover, Minnelli is keenly aware of the story's ironies, the most poignant of which is the fact that Van Gogh didn't sell any of his work during his lifetime. Another poignant irony lies in depicting Gauguin's sneers at Millet (and other painters of the time) for painting "calendar art," unaware that both he and Van Gogh would become the ultimate calendar artists. It's hard to tell how the phenomenon began, but from the 1960s onward, one could find Van Gogh's calendars in many college dormitories.

Amusing episodes occurred on the set, such as the day Anthony Quinn claimed to have heard Gauguin speaking to him. After hearing the voice, Quinn turned his head but saw nothing. He placed a wine bottle, which had mysteriously disappeared, back on the table. Then, a deep voice warned him again, "Don't do that."

This time Quinn answered, "Why not?"

"Because *I* would never do that," the voice said.

"Oh, you wouldn't?"

"No, I would not."

The crew thought that Quinn was out of his mind, because he was carrying on a lively conversation with himself.

"Tell me," Quinn said, "who are you that I should care what you would do with this little flower?"

"Ah," the voice said back, "you know who I am."

Quinn then realized that he had been visited by Gauguin's spirit.

Two days later, Quinn had an early call for a scene with Kirk Douglas. Minnelli asked them to sit twelve feet from each other and paint, so that he could show the contrasting styles of their characters.

Satisfied with the rehearsal, Minnelli proceeded to shoot, when Quinn heard Gauguin's voice again, telling him: "You're holding the brush wrong."

Quinn thought that it was Minnelli or Douglas talking to him. "You guys say something?" Quinn asked, looking up from his canvas. Minnelli and Douglas shrugged.

"I'll be a son of a bitch!" Quinn shouted, kicking the stool he was sitting on, unable to dismiss the voice but unable to accept it either.

"Tony, what is it?" Minnelli asked, realizing that his actor was in turmoil.

"I can't tell you, Vincente, I'm ashamed." Quinn didn't want his director to perceive him as a temperamental actor given to emotional outbursts. Nor did he want to appear foolish when Douglas walked over to see what the fuss was all about.

"Ashamed of what?" Minnelli asked.

"Jesus Christ, it's too fucking embarrassing," Quinn, now shaking and sweating, said.

Minnelli tried again. "Tony, look, we've got a scene to shoot. If something's troubling you, whatever it is, we'll figure it out." Minnelli was his usual calm self, and Quinn decided to tell him, though he didn't want the others to hear. He put his arm around Minnelli and walked him off to the side.

"Shit, Vincente, Gauguin is here talking to me."

"He is?"

Quinn nodded.

"And what is he telling you?" Minnelli asked.

"He's telling me I'm not holding the brush right."

"Ah." Minnelli nodded, looking at Quinn and laughing joyously. "Oh, a ghost? Well, wonderful! Wonderful!" Minnelli laughed again, this time louder.

"Tony's had a visit from Mr. Gauguin!" Minnelli told the crew. He turned to Quinn and slapped him on the back. "So, where is your friend? Introduce me!"

To Minnelli, it was a miracle that Gauguin's spirit visited his set, not something to question or deny but to cherish and nurture. From then on, Quinn felt that Gauguin was always present on the set. Quinn later believed that Gauguin was responsible for his winning a second Oscar for *Lust for Life* (the first one was for *Viva Zapata*).

A few years later, Minnelli ran into Quinn at Le Dome restaurant. "How is Gauguin?" he asked the actor.

"I still hear his voice from time to time. He really liked the picture," Quinn said.

"Keep it going," Minnelli said with a smile.

Minnelli enjoyed the intimate rapport he was increasingly cultivating with Kirk Douglas, his leading man. Douglas expressed his views of Van Gogh, and how certain scenes should be played and shot. Since Minnelli liked and respected Douglas, he readily accepted most of his ideas. In between takes, Minnelli and Douglas were always seen working on the next scene to be shot, mapping and blocking the space, discussing the right tone of voice to use, and so on.

Douglas became as involved in this movie as Gene Kelly had been in the three films Minnelli made with him. *Lust for Life* represented Minnelli's most harmonious collaboration with an actor since his work with Gene Kelly on *An American in Paris* and *Brigadoon*. Upon arrival in Arles to begin shooting, Minnelli immersed himself completely in the production, with Douglas as his willing ally. Minnelli and Douglas spent long hours studying Van Gogh's paintings, visiting the museums that had the originals. Their extensive research helped them understand the specific way in which Van Gogh used his creative urge and channeled his ferocious energy into his art.

Minnelli perceived Douglas as "the only possible choice to play Van Gogh, due to his physical appearance and potentially violent temperament." In real life, Douglas, like Van Gogh, was fierce in his loves and hates. Working with Douglas on *Lust for Life* became Minnelli's most rewarding and stimulating collaboration. Douglas couldn't have cared less about whether he looked handsome or projected an appealing image. Throughout, he was dressed in dowdy clothes, with his famous dimple hidden behind a fuzz of red beard. After the shoot, Minnelli was ecstatic when praising his actor in public: "Kirk is blessed with tireless energy, a willingness to try anything and a complete disregard for his own looks."

Douglas's enthusiastic devotion rubbed off on the entire crew and cast. Minnelli hoped that Douglas would finally win an Oscar for his performance. Douglas had been nominated twice before, and his most recent, nomination, for *The Bad and the Beautiful,* had been a particularly unpleasant and painful experience, since it was the only one of the film's six nominations that didn't win the Oscar.

For Douglas, *Lust for Life* was a wonderful experience. Aware that Minnelli could be impatient with actors, he felt like the teacher's pet. As he recalled, "I always seemed to do the right thing; Vincente looked with pleasure on everything I did. Was it because we had worked together successfully in *The Bad and the Beautiful*? I don't know. But it was a wonderful feeling for me to have supportive looks from a demanding director."

At Oscar time, *Lust for Life* was nominated in four categories: Best Actor, Screenplay (Norman Corwin), Color Art Direction/Set Decoration (Cedric Gibbons, Hans Peters, and Preston Ames; Edwin B. Willis and F. Keogh Gleason), and Supporting Actor (Anthony Quinn, who won). Minnelli was deeply disappointed that his colleagues at the Directors Branch failed to nominate him for an Oscar. In fact, the 1956 movie that swept most of the Academy Awards, *Around the World in 80 Days,* could not have been more different from Minnelli's. And the same can be said about Cecil B. DeMille's *The Ten Commandments,* which was nominated for the Best Picture and won several Oscars.

Deborah Kerr, the star of Minnelli's next film, the melodrama *Tea and Sympathy,* which was even more personal for him than *Lust for Life*, felt the same way about her director as Kirk Douglas had. Kerr, who was represented by Minnelli's agent, Bert Allenberg, wrote to him from Toronto, where she was touring with the play *Tea and Sympathy*: "Above all, the film needs a sensitive and compassionate person to make it, and that is why I am so thrilled at the prospect of your doing it. I wish we could do it in color, and incorporate all the atmospheric feeling of spring and things about to flower and all that romantic and artistic nonsense!"

Robert Anderson's drama told of a young man named Tom, a student at a boys' school who's accused of being homosexual because of his interests in tennis, music, and poetry, instead of more masculine sports and dormitory bull sessions. Tom's housemaster, a latent homosexual himself, is married to Laura (Kerr), a woman who shares many interests with the boy. In a generous gesture, she gives herself to him to prove that he's a real man and not a "pervert," as his father and classmates charge.

In a thoughtful letter to Minnelli, Anderson explained the goals of his text: "I've always seen the play basically as a love story, which never would have had a happy ending except for the persecution of Tom. That is the irony of the story, that Tom is persecuted in a sense for his love for Laura, but the persecution brings about fulfillment of the love." For Anderson, the play's meaning was that "we must understand and respect the differences in people," but also "the whole concept of what manliness is." Referring to the famous rape scene in *Gone with the Wind*, Anderson wished to "attack the often movie-fostered notion that a man is only a man if he can carry Vivien Leigh up a winding staircase."

However, not many of those ideas were manifest in Anderson's final script, which remained vague. The Breen office insisted that the film include a prologue and epilogue, to show that Laura is punished for her sexual transgression. In the minds of the censors, retribution was required. At one point, it was suggested that Laura pay for her adultery by taking her own life. Minnelli was angry, but being typically passive, he just gritted his teeth.

Anderson's play reflected the anxieties that prevailed in American culture of the 1950s. Written and produced during the height of the McCarthy era, *Tea and Sympathy* channeled anxieties away from the political arena into a more personal one. In the play, homosexuality substituted for, or was equated with, communism as one more form of social deviance. Anderson created an allegory about innocent, conscientious people accused of being "different," if not utterly deviant. Tom was "basically normal," just slightly different from the other boys.

On Broadway, praised for its candor and meanings, Elia Kazan's production featured the most notorious curtain line since *A Streetcar Named Desire*. In that scene, Deborah Kerr's Laura says, while unbuttoning her blouse: "Years from now ... when you talk about this ... and you will ... be kind."

In the 1950s, Broadway's thematically daring productions seemed too risqué to Hollywood, an industry still constricted by the Production Code. Nonetheless, Kazan's striking stage production did impress Dore Schary, whose politics were more progressive than those of his predecessor, Louis B. Mayer, and he determined to do the picture as faithfully as possible. A week later, Schary was informed by Metro's New York office that the Loew's theater chain would be reluctant to exhibit a movie like *Tea and Sympathy* without the seal of approval of the Production Code Administration (PCA).

First, PCA's top officials, Geoffrey Shurlock and Jack Vizzard, were invited to see the play at Metro's expense. After seeing it, they told Schary that in its present form *Tea and Sympathy* was unacceptable. They particularly objected to the ending, which they found to be a "justification of adultery."

The play's homoerotic tone was also too unsettling, since the Code "forbids even the inference of sex perversion." Schary promised that the film wouldn't discuss the issue of homosexuality, instead centering on the more acceptable problem of the boy's "nonconformity." It took three years of negotiations to reconcile the onscreen portrait of illicit romance between the headmaster's wife and one of her husband's students.

Schary was hoping to further sanitize and soften Anderson's already compromised finale. There was a touch of irony and déjà vu when Schary asked Minnelli, "Couldn't Laura's husband interrupt the couple at the crucial moment?" As preposterous as that sounds for a movie's coda, this very episode had happened in Minnelli's own life, when Judy caught him in compromising positions at least twice, once with a bit player and once with their gardener. Minnelli decided to keep silent. All along, despite threats from the Production Code Administration and the Catholic Legion of Decency, Minnelli planned to adapt the play as faithfully as possible.

Tea and Sympathy was inconceivable without Deborah Kerr, a major box-office draw and the ideal protagonist, having played the role for years both on Broadway and on tour. As was evident in Kerr's other screen roles, the actress projected the era's definitive portraits of sensitive, conflicted, and tormented women, a trend that began with her being cast against type in *From Here to Eternity,* a role that was initially offered to Joan Crawford.

Though he would later regret it, Minnelli decided to cast lesser-known actors from the stage production, such as Leif Erickson, as Kerr's coarse, latent-homosexual husband, and John Kerr, as the sensitive kid. John Kerr had proved cooperative in Minnelli's *The Cobweb,* and Metro still hoped that he might become a youth star in the mold of James Dean.

In the old studio system, viable careers like Minnelli's did not have long breaks off work. Projects often overlapped, with two films running at the same time. Pandro Berman talked to Minnelli about *Tea and Sympathy* before he left for Europe for *Lust for Life.* The project was greenlighted just as Minnelli was celebrating New Year's Eve of 1955. It was a nice way to begin the new year.

Berman and Minnelli had enjoyed great rapport in their previous collaborations. Berman knew that, apart from George Cukor, no Hollywood director was more suitable for comprehending and depicting on screen the boy's neurosis and predicament. After all, Minnelli himself was effeminate, an aesthete who embodied values that collided with Hollywood's more macho sensibilities.

The production couldn't begin shooting on time because of John Kerr's other engagements, and Minnelli's back-to-back shoots of *Kismet* and *Lust for Life.* Moreover, major work still needed to be done on the script. As expected, the suggestion that the schoolmaster's persecution of Tom was motivated by his own latent homosexuality was taken out.

Minnelli was delighted with Anderson's scrupulous euphemisms and carefully placed expressions of contrition and remorse. But his optimism proved premature since Shurlock still objected to Tom's fear of homosexuality and to Laura's adultery, which was a clear violation of the Code. The script was then sent back to Anderson with new instructions of how to satisfy the censors.

After months of agony, Anderson turned the whole story into one long flashback, recalled by Tom as he reflects on his past during a ten-year class reunion. When Tom encounters his former schoolmaster, now a lonely man, the latter hands him a note from Laura. In this letter, she debunks Tom's nostalgic account of their affair in his first novel. In reality, Laura wrote, the affair shattered her husband's life and damaged her self-respect, forcing her to go into seclusion.

Minnelli didn't like Anderson's "new resolution," which negated everything that preceded it. But he knew that without it, M-G-M would impose an even more fraudulent finale. As the studio hoped, the new ending met the Code's requirements. During these endless, exhausting maneuvers, Minnelli was in the South of France shooting *Lust for Life*, but he insisted on getting daily updates about the censorship ordeal.

The first cut of *Lust for Life* was assembled in mid-January 1956. An exhausted Minnelli took a six-week break, his first paid vacation in years. He decided to go to Paris, his favorite city. Upon his return, Minnelli spent one more month with Anderson polishing the script and fixing the still-remaining problems, particularly the ending.

After two years of hassles, *Tea and Sympathy* began shooting in the spring of 1956. Its seven-week schedule was the shortest of any of Minnelli's dramatic features, not to mention his musicals, which always took much longer. Compared to the logistical problems of *Lust for Life*, reconstructing a New England campus on Metro's back lot was an easy task. Apart from a few days of location work at a California beach and a country club, the film was shot on the comfy studio soundstages, with all the fakeness that involved.

Curiously, the visceral thrills of Minnelli's more flamboyant pictures are totally missing from *Tea and Sympathy*. Minnelli simply couldn't find a satisfying way to open up the stage melodrama. Occasionally, he draws contrasts between the comforting interiors of Laura's home and the tense exterior scenes of Tom's harassment by his classmates.

In its intensity, but not visual impact, only one sequence, the school's homecoming bonfire, brings to mind the Halloween sequence in *Meet Me in St. Louis*. Minnelli turns Tom's humiliating failure with the town trollop, which was alluded to but not shown on stage, into the film's cathartic moment, one that subjected a reluctant Tom to masochistic agony.

After the previews, the censors demanded a cut of six lines of dialogue in Laura and Tom's love scene; the studio whittled it down to four lines. Then the Catholic Legion of Decency claimed that, unless an epilogue were amended to stress the boy's guilt as well, *Tea and Sympathy* would receive a C (condemned) rating. M-G-M and Minnelli had no choice but to submit to all of these pressure groups.

Tea and Sympathy opened at Radio City Music Hall to good reviews, and Minnelli was praised for his "quiet and compassionate" treatment. Still, of all of Minnelli's 1950s dramas, *Tea and Sympathy* is the most outdated and artistically disappointing. This is perhaps because the movie was so grounded in that particular decade's anxieties: the risk of lives being ruined by unjust accusations, the fear of nonconformity by individuals who don't fit in with the lonely, mass crowd to borrow David Riesman's concept. Unlike the play, the film does not portray Tom as effeminate or homosexual, just terribly shy, awkward, and sensitive—all suspect attributes for men in a moral climate that embraced rigid sex-role differences.

However, discerning viewers could still feel Minnelli's relish in exposing the macho bullies who make Tom's life miserable. Tom's schoolmates are depicted as masculine hysterics, packs of roughhousing and bare-chested adolescents, noisy, messy, and immature.

The older males are also ridiculed. Tom's father (Edward Andrews) is a coward, and Laura's husband, Bill, too much of an extrovert. Minnelli's disdain for Bill's boorishness is so obvious that viewers wondered what on earth attracted a woman like Laura to such a brute in the first place. Rough sex? Sheer masochism? Loneliness after the death of her first husband? The stigma of being a young widow?

The students' attitudes are of course misogynistic. In the climate of the school, which is a microcosm of American culture, normalcy demanded that boys be different from men, and that men be different from women. Real "fun" for the guys resides in the victory bonfire and pajama fights, in which the seniors strip the pajamas off the new boys. Tom's nightclothes remain intact until his roommate, Al, out of pity, saves Tom's honor by ripping his pajamas to shreds. Minnelli regards these rituals as rigid and silly at best, and appalling manifestations of macho behavior at worst. Absurdly, what separates masculinity from femininity is the juxtaposition of crew cuts and team sports with Tom's tousled hair and love for classical music.

The movie's most daring scene is the one in which Laura confronts Tom's chum Al, asking him how he would react if she spread innuendos about him. "How easy it is to smear a person," Laura notes. "One whispered allusion" to suspicious characteristics and a person is blackballed. However, the portrait of collective tyranny is blunted by Anderson's tentative text, with its dialogue sanitized by the Code's demands. The worst name the persecutors call Tom is "Sister Boy," not even a "sissy."

Minnelli finds some humor in these rites of passage, notably in the scene in which Al demonstrates to Tom how a "real man" should walk. Significantly, Minnelli sets the scene in the school's music conservatory and it is played to Beethoven in the background. This act becomes yet another personal moment for Minnelli, whose own languid, effeminate gait was mocked in Hollywood when he first arrived from New York. Minnelli was still shattered by recollections of the malicious gossip about his wearing light makeup, which in New York was more acceptable.

But Minnelli fails to liberate the film from the inherent constraints and stiff conventions of the source material. Despite several outdoor scenes, the film looks as if it were shot completely on the back lot. In fact, the prep school's main hall is the same red brick Victorian house where the inmates of *The Cobweb* resided.

Having played Laura for many months on the stage, Deborah Kerr strained to bring freshness to her screen interpretation, and her performance is at once too ladylike and stilted in mannerisms and inflections. Looking back, she thought that Minnelli was "extremely sensitive to the subject," and that the only thing that diffused his film was his "tendency to make his movies too beautiful pictorially, which might have softened and lushed it up a little."

Novice John Kerr also fails to register much anguish on screen. Laura and Tom's long-awaited clinch generates no sparks. While his awkwardness and insecurity were appropriate, Kerr suffered from a limited vocal range. In Minnelli's opinion, Kerr gave exactly the same performance in *The Cobweb* and in *Tea and Sympathy*. And, as he predicted, John Kerr never became a leading man or star.

Minnelli tries to compensate for the compromised ending, which he despised, with an elaborate visual scheme, based on his belief that *Tea and Sympathy* should tell its story entirely in specific colors and tonal relationships. Though he had experimented with symbolic coloring before, it was never so explicit. *Tea and Sympathy* integrates words and images in intriguing associations of three colors: yellow, blue, and the resultant green when these two are mixed.

Take, for example the different colors associated with Laura's personality evolution. In the first scenes, Laura's color is yellow, a color meant to suggest her kindness and gentleness. Minnelli frames her with yellow curtains in her kitchen (a place she spends little time in, despite being a housewife), where she's surrounded with yellow kitchen bowls. Later, Minnelli places her on a yellow chair in her living room.

In contrast, all the male characters in the movie are associated with blue, but with different shades of blue, which correspond to varying degrees of masculinity. Young and old, those dressed in dark blue are clinging desperately to their boyhood. Significantly, Minnelli dresses Tom in a blue suit when he goes to the town's whore. Verbally, too, Tom articulates Minnelli's feeling when he says, "Put me in a blue suit and I look like a kid." In the course of the film, Tom wears blue pajamas, blue trousers, blue shirts.

Later on, when Laura goes to visit Ellie, the whore, she brings her a bouquet of yellow roses from her garden, unmistakably wrapped in blue paper. Though vastly different, the two women immediately connect on an emotional level. Lonely and hungry for sex and love, both are interested in Tom's sexuality, albeit for different reasons. Ellie renders sexual services for pay, whereas Laura would offer her body as a sacrifice rather than a sexually gratifying act.

As the story unfolds, Minnelli disperses the colors of yellow and blue so that they blend into variant hues associated with the different phases of the characters' emotional states. In weaving yellow and blue motifs throughout the film, Minnelli formulates new intra-textual, inter-textual, and extra-textual references to the characters' internal psychology.

For example, one scene begins with Laura in her garden, while Tom is seen singing a love ballad from the window of his room. When they later meet at the garden, Laura says that her garden needs blue (the color of masculinity). Is she talking about the garden or about her sex life? Probably both. We get the impression that her marriage is sexually dry, perhaps even asexual. Tom later responds by giving Laura a package of blue seeds, which he places none too discreetly on the dashboard of her blue-green car. His seeds are to be planted in Laura's garden. Significantly, she's the one to take the customarily male prerogative and become the sexual aggressor, or at least the initiator.

Tom comments on Laura's "green thumb," green being the mixture of yellow and blue, and she realizes that fecundity has blossomed after her arrival at the school. Green symbolizes blue's need for yellow, and yellow's need for green. When Tom is about to leave for his visit to Ellie, Laura is dressed in a green evening gown. As noted, Tom is in a blue suit, a boy forced to wear a man's uniform, as dictated by society's rigid masculine codes.

It's no accident, as David Gerstner noted in his astute analysis, that the "seduction" scene takes place in a relatively neutral territory, outdoors in the woods, at night, while Laura is wearing her green dress. The framing of the scene, specifically the lighting, makes it look both vague and surreal, as if the act takes place in a neverland of dreamlike desires. That scene could be read as one of Minnelli's fantasy sequences in a musical. The association of colors is more than a neat scheme or distracting balancing act. For Minnelli, colors have specific narrative, emotional, and artistic resonances. He relies on the viewers' perception of visual images, based on the conscious and subconscious cultural values they associate with specific colors.

Despite its interest as a sociological reflection of the era's various anxieties, *Tea and Sympathy* is a severely flawed picture. Ultimately, the film's overt condemnation of hypocrisy and bigotry becomes as unconvincing as its own phony finale.

Deborah Kerr, too, conceded that the imposed ending was fake. In the theater, in the final scene, brilliantly staged by Kazan, the lights focus on Laura in the boy's room as she tries to comfort him with words. She hesitantly leaves the room and the boy buries his face in his pillow, a typical gesture in 1950s movies, in the manner of James Dean in *Rebel Without a Cause*. A few seconds later, Laura comes back into Tom's room and, standing by his bed, utters her infamous curtain line, "Years from now . . ." She then begins to undo the top button of her blouse as the lights fade out, leaving the audience stunned and bewildered.

On Broadway, it was an electrifying moment. One could practically hear the whole audience gasp with shock as a woman of Laura's age, thirty-five, is about to sleep with an eighteen-year-old boy to prove that sex isn't as horrible as he thinks after his failed visit to the prostitute. Though exactly the same line is used in the movie, Minnelli couldn't replicate the power or subtlety of the original finale.

The film's other main problem is the acting. Most of the Broadway cast contacted Minnelli about parts in the film. They felt that the long months they had performed the play gave them a certain proprietary interest and expertise. The actors knew the play well, perhaps too well. Having performed it hundreds of times to different kinds of audiences, they had shaded the delineations of their characters to the last, smallest detail, and didn't think they needed much coaching from Minnelli.

For his part, Minnelli paid too much attention to their advice. He felt that it might have been too late for him to suggest a new, fresher approach that was more suitable for the big screen. It was a mistake Minnelli came to regret as he watched Deborah Kerr's overly studied and calculated performance.

An unanticipated problem occurred on the set when John Kerr disagreed with Minnelli about how to play the scene showing his abortive attempt to prove his manhood with the town's whore. Minnelli thought it was crucial to the story, but the actor assumed that his character's impotence had already been established, and that he should begin as a sexual aggressor who's unable to perform at the last moment. Norma Crane was brilliant as Ellie, the prostitute, and after the scene was shot, John Kerr had to concede that Minnelli was right.

Interestingly, the liberal European press could not understand what the censorship fuss was all about. Compared with *Lust for Life, Tea and Sympathy* seemed to them like a tempest in a teapot. Years later, Minnelli saw a French production of *Tea and Sympathy* with Ingrid Bergman in the lead. Ironically, it had been difficult to get the drama produced in France, because the French producer felt there was not enough conflict. The French producer shrugged and said, "So what if the boy thinks he's a homosexual, and the headmaster's wife gives herself to him to prove that he's not. What's the problem? What's the big deal?" Watching Ingrid Bergman's more "normal and healthy" (as he put it) approach to her part, Minnelli saw the humor in the play for the first time, something missing from the American stage production and from his own screen version.

When *Tea and Sympathy* was released, it received warm notices from the critics, mostly because of the subject matter. M-G-M hoped that the film's controversial status would elevate its visibility and arouse the public's interest. However, neither a success nor a failure, *Tea and Sympathy* did decent business at the box office, earning $2,184,558 in domestic rentals, against a budget of $1,818,688.

In fact, Minnelli thought that Bosley Crowther made a fool of himself in a *New York Times* article titled "Loosening the Code": "That long-time obstruction to morally controversial material in American films is slowly and quietly being loosened to accord with what is a change in social attitudes. And the industry is much better for it, as is certainly the medium of films." Crowther reported that a committee of industry executives was making a thorough survey of the Code's restrictions and consequences, with an eye to the possible elimination of some of its more unrealistic prohibitions and pieties. There were already indications that the Code was "sensibly relaxed to permit the resolution of complications that might have been forbidden a few years back."

Crowther went on to praise the studio system's operations. In spite of the PCA's refusal to tolerate the conclusion of *Tea and Sympathy* without a compensating moral commentary, M-G-M went ahead and bought the play for the screen and asked Anderson to contrive an ending that would satisfy the Code. He eventually came up with a device that put the play into a time frame. The new "poignant" postscript suggests that Laura has paid for her sins, and offered a moral judgment of adultery.

This minor addition was accepted by the Code as an adequate touch of "moral value," to compensate for the plot's adultery. For Crowther, the censors' willingness to be appreciative of the drama's integrity was wise, since the final picture was "a very tender and disturbing show of the troubles that agitate its characters, and it is played with dignity and sensitivity."

So much for critics' honesty and liberal opinions, Minnelli thought to himself, confiding to his friends that *Tea and Sympathy* was "suffocated" with dignity and sensitivity. In future tributes and retrospectives of his work, Minnelli would ask the programmers not to include the film, because it continued to cause him embarrassment.

Designing Woman began as a sketch by Metro's costume designer Helen Rose, and was meant to be a small, quick movie. However, because of its subject matter—the meanings of manhood and styles of masculinity—it became a personal film as well, right up Minnelli's alley and unintentionally a logical follow-up to *Tea and Sympathy*. The essence of Rose's story was lifted from George Stevens's 1942 comedy *Woman of the Year,* a popular movie that became famous thanks to its first teaming of Katharine Hepburn and Spencer Tracy, who launched a lengthy filmic collaboration and an actual lifelong romance.

The "new" film concerns a sleek designer (Lauren Bacall, in the Katharine Hepburn role) and a rumpled sportswriter (Gregory Peck, in the Spencer Tracy role) who wed in haste, only to realize their "irreconcilable differences," and the incompatibility between her chic friends and his crass cronies. Complications arise with the reappearance of the groom's old flame, a musical star. More than the tale itself, the studio liked the snappy title, hoping that with the right stars *Designing Woman* would be a commercial success.

George Wells was assigned to flesh out a full-length script to suit Metro's star, Grace Kelly. But Kelly's popularity and busy schedule forced one production delay after another, and Minnelli had to wait until Kelly finished shooting *High Society* and *The Swan*. Kelly's *Rear Window* costar, Jimmy Stewart, agreed to appear in *Designing Woman* on the condition that Kelly would. Initially, the film was to be directed by Joshua Logan, then fresh from the success of the movie *Picnic*.

What began as a modest remake of *Woman of the Year* soon became one of Metro's high-profile pictures when Grace Kelly announced her plan to marry Monaco's Prince Rainier and retire from Hollywood. Schary refused to believe her, but two months after her wedding, Kelly declined to return to Hollywood. After Kelly's defection, the film lost Stewart and Logan as well. Undaunted, Schary tried to assemble a new cast of comparable prestige.

Minnelli, who was a better choice than Logan for such a light and whimsical tale in the first place, decided to cast Gregory Peck against type as the groom, though he was hardly skilled as a comedian. Peck, who had recently made heavy dramas such as *Moby Dick* and *The Man in the Gray Flannel Suit,* found it a refreshing change of pace. His deal guaranteed leading-lady approval, and he fully supported Minnelli's choice of Lauren Bacall, with whom he was friendly.

Bacall had replaced Grace Kelly once before, on *The Cobweb.* Though not flattered to be a replacement once again, Bacall needed to work after a long and intense period of taking care of her dying husband, Humphrey Bogart.

As the vamp, Dolores Gray substituted for the original choice, Cyd Charisse. For the heroine's choreographer pal, a neurotic, effeminate, and artsy type, Minnelli selected choreographer Jack Cole, even though he had never acted before Cole was also asked to choreograph the film's dance numbers, as he had done for *Kismet.*

Designing Woman received a glossy treatment from cameraman John Alton, who had just shot *Tea and Sympathy,* designer Preston Ames, who furnished the requisite Manhattan glamour, and Helen Rose, who was in charge of the elegant costumes. Shooting began on September 10, 1956, and concluded ten weeks later, with only two exterior locations, at the Newport Beach harbor and the Beverly Hills Hotel.

Aiming to recapture the sleekness of Hollywood's 1930s and 1940s screwball comedies, the film had the glossy look of studio-manufactured entertainment. *Designing Woman* emphasized high production values at the expense of an original screenplay. However, in one of the Academy Awards' inexplicable choices, George Wells's second-rate script was honored with Best Original Screenplay, in a year that saw competition from Fellini's *I Vitelloni, Funny Face, The Tin Star,* and *Man of a Thousand Faces.*

The story features a gallery of types familiar from 1930s comedies: tart-tongued working women, Runyonesque gangsters, scrappy editors, and so on. The plot's gimmick is also a throwback: Protagonist Marilla (Bacall) gets angry not at the prospect of an actual affair between her husband and the voluptuous dancer Lori Shannon, but at his past affair with Lori.

Minnelli's relaxed tempo and droll sense of chic sustains the movie, even though it lacks that zesty wit and energy of the old comedies. Minnelli saturates the screen with glamour, which contributes to the fluffy, pleasurable fare.

Mike and Marilla first meet around the pool of the Beverly Hills Hotel. After marrying, they move into her Park Avenue apartment, with its chic white sofas and bleached antiques. Marilla wears black jersey sheaths of her own design. Early on, she's seen pacing in her studio, contemplating which white chiffon to choose for her collection. The sets and costumes represent a gaudy blend of Danish Modern and French Provincial. Marilla is a Minnelli-type heroine, a woman of refined taste; a Modigliani hangs over her marble fireplace.

Meanwhile, mobsters threaten Mike's life to squelch a hot story. But they are soft-spoken gangsters, respectful of the ladies; the worst they can do is to punch Mike's nose. They are certainly not as dangerous as his spurned fiancée, Lori, who dumps a dish of spaghetti into Mike's lap at lunch.

Miscast, Peck is too squeaky-clean and well groomed to play a working journalist. Since neither Peck nor Bacall are deft at physical farce, the slapstick that Hepburn and Tracy, or Cary Grant, could do effortlessly falls flat here. There are mildly funny scenes, such as the one in which Marilla nearly collapses at a boxing match, or Mike's parody of choreographer Randy's body language (a scene similar to the one in *Tea and Sympathy,* when the effeminate Tom is taught how to walk like a "real" man).

Occasionally, Minnelli resorts to low-comedy tricks. Mike's self-appointed bodyguard, Maxie (Mickey Shaughnessy), is a paranoid pugilist who sleeps with his eyes open and is comatose when awake. When Marilla expresses distaste for the fighter's profile, Mike says, "He has a nose. It's inside." This bit feels like a tribute to Aldo Ray's role in George Cukor's 1952 comedy, *Pat and Mike,* with Tracy and Hepburn; it's no coincidence that the name of Peck's character is Mike.

Minnelli gives *Designing Woman* a visual playfulness, with energetic camera movements and other visual flourishes. Once again, his flamboyant touches turn a stale comedy into more lavish and polished fare.

One scene stands out: Beverly Hills, as seen through Mike's hangover, is a psychedelic landscape of chartreuse palms against pinkish skies. In another scene, a series of close-ups punctuate Marilla's realization that the girl in Mike's torn photo is Lori, the star of the show she's designing.

Minnelli's favorite prop, the mirror, is the focus of an elaborate camera setup. When Lori pauses to adjust her makeup, Marilla's reflection is seen, wearing one of Minnelli's red, red suits. She easily upstages Lori. The camera tracks backward as Marilla bursts into the restaurant, while Lori examines the bride in the background.

Lori's career as a TV entertainer allows for a musical number to be included in the film, and it is staged with some verve and wit. For Dolores Gray's big moment, Minnelli employs two choruses. During a run-through of "There'll Be Some Changes Made," the star belts out her song and makes love to the camera. Running between two sets in a dash, she changes from a great lady in pastels to a siren in sea-foam lamé, while studio minions fiddle with her accessories. The TV camera and microphone underscore the song with rolling movements of their own.

As Stephen Harvey noted, the film served as yet another demonstration of Minnelli's philosophy of paying attention to detail, whether he's creating art or kitsch. Despite all the references to classic screwball comedy, the movie carries Minnelli's singular signature. He invests the script's stock situations with personal motifs, establishing a link between *Designing Woman* and his other films. *Designing Woman* climaxes with a free-for-all sequence, a sly wink at the "Girl Hunt" ballet from *The Band Wagon,* and ends by foreshadowing the bloody fun fair that will feature in his 1958 melodrama, *Some Came Running.*

The brawl pitting Mike and Maxie against the bad boys takes place in one of Minnelli's favorite, and frequent, settings, a stage-door alley, on the night of a premiere. If *The Band Wagon* turns hoofers into stage gangsters, *Designing Woman* transforms a hoods' rumble into a dance routine. Marilla flails about until she's suddenly catapulted into a dark corner under a heap of cardboard refuse. She's left with a woozy head, a smudge on her cheek, and her husband at her side. (In *Some Came Running*, Minnelli would re-create this image in a serious way, with no humor, as Shirley MacLaine's hapless Ginny lies crumpled in the alleyway before a gloomy fade-out.)

The choreographer Randy's triumph over the macho men is used by Minnelli as a poignant commentary on masculinity. Though a secondary character, Randy is a key figure, who relates to Minnelli's own personality as an aesthete. *Designing Woman* deals in a comic way with issues of gender and sexuality that Minnelli had earlier probed in *Tea and Sympathy* and would continue to examine in his future films, such as *Home from the Hill.* There's a clash between Mike's blunt, macho world and Marilla's artsy trendy female set. While she dislikes the masculine exclusiveness and taste for bloody sport among his cronies, Mike is sickened to learn that her pals include an "excitable type, known on his labels as Mr. Chris."

The two milieus collide, and both sides get their satirical treatment, when Mike's poker game is scheduled to take place in their Park Avenue apartment on the same evening that Marilla hosts a reading of the show she's about to design. While the men mutter profanities over their cards, the women giggle with laughter over such cliché theatrical lines as "Aunt Agatha, she's done it again."

As in *Tea and Sympathy,* Minnelli's sympathies are clearly with the underdog and the misunderstood. When Mike maligns Randy's manhood, the dancer is forced to show photos of his wife and kids as evidence that he's straight. Randy, like Minnelli, has visions of dream ballets. And Minnelli, like Randy, carried around his own photos of his wives and daughters, ready to display them on demand to prove his heterosexuality. Having always embraced outsiders and misfits in his movies, Minnelli was suspect, no matter how many times he got married. In the 1950s, effeminacy was a more serious violation of the norm than membership in the Communist Party. Minnelli wanted to show that real men could wear Capezios.

With few exceptions, in the 1950s, no filmmaker would dare flaunt his homosexuality. Even openly gay directors, such as George Cukor, had to be discreet about their lifestyle. Though it was an open secret, Cukor never dared to have a live-in relationship. And both Minnelli and Cukor were aware of how the career of James Whale had suffered as a result of—what was, from Hollywood's perspective—his outrageously flamboyant gay lifestyle.

Minnelli skewers a virile code that equates imaginative and personal conduct and values like his own with deviance or outright perversion. In Minnelli's movies, creativity goes beyond sexual orientation, and the protagonist-artists always get the last laugh. It's no coincidence that in *Designing Woman* it's Randy's fancy footwork that wraps up the plot.

Nineteen

The Height of His Career: *Gigi*

AFTER TWO DECADES OF HEADING Metro's most successful musical unit, Arthur Freed was given an independent production company on the lot, and M-G-M agreed to finance his projects. *Gigi* was the second film, after Rouben Mamoulian's *Silk Stockings,* to be produced under the new agreement. The studio allocated *Gigi* a budget that was not to exceed $1,800,000, a modest amount for a film to be shot entirely on location in Paris.

In the two years between *Kismet* and *Gigi,* Minnelli had made three commercially successful movies: *Lust for Life, Tea and Sympathy,* and *Designing Woman.* He also made uncredited contributions to the remake of Somerset Maugham's *The Painted Veil,* titled *The Seventh Sin*, after the departure of its initial director, Ronald Neame.

After *Kismet*, *Gigi* offered Minnelli an opportunity to show his value to the new Metro regime. Like many of Minnelli's musicals, its appeal was based on a combination of winning ingredients: an original score, multinuanced characters, and a bittersweet love story that balances sentiment and irony. Above all, it was set in Minnelli's favorite time and place, fin-de-siècle Paris.

Gigi concerns a schoolgirl raised by courtesans to assume her place in society as a kept woman. Under pressure, Freed urged Minnelli to stress the innate virtue of *Gigi*'s heroine and the moral lesson conveyed in the film's ending. Indeed, the famous song about the charms of young girls, "Thank Heaven for Little Girls," was decidedly outré in 1958, and by today's standards, with our sensitivity to issues of child abuse and pedophilia, it might be considered shocking and probably would be censored by the Motion Picture Association of America, which assigns ratings to new releases.

The beginnings of *Gigi*, which became Minnelli's best-known and most commercially successful movie, actually go back to December 1951, when writer-producer Joe Fields obtained the screen rights to Colette's scandalous novella. Shortly thereafter, Fields met with Arthur Freed to discuss turning the story into a musical under the helm of Minnelli. However, after Freed saw a previous French film version of *Gigi,* he described it to Minnelli as "just a nice little film," and more or less forgot all about it.

In November 1953, Freed took Minnelli to see the Los Angeles production of Anita Loos's stage adaptation of *Gigi,* starring Audrey Hepburn. Freed liked it a lot, but Minnelli remained indifferent. Minnelli was familiar with the 1948 French film adaptation and the 1951 Broadway production. Minnelli also knew that *Gigi* would not meet with approval in Hollywood's moralistic climate of the 1950s. Colette's sophisticated vision didn't conform to the Production Code's rigid, outdated strictures.

Undaunted, Freed submitted the novella to the Production Code office for approval. Objections were immediately raised about a film, in which, as the PCA put it, "all the characters participate, or did participate, or intended to participate, in a man-mistress relationship."

A year later, in December 1954, Loos told Freed that she was working on a Broadway musical version of *Gigi*. With his interest in the project rekindled, Freed set out to kill the musical version by paying Loos and producer Gilbert Miller a compensation fee of $87,000.

In February 1956, Freed arrived in Philadelphia, where *My Fair Lady* was playing a tryout engagement. He reminded Alan Jay Lerner that he had completed two projects of his three-film contract, and thus might want to consider *Gigi* as the third. Both Freed and Minnelli, who had just been persuaded to direct, wanted Lerner, but Lerner couldn't commit, as he was completely absorbed in *My Fair Lady*. There were other reasons for his hesitancy. Disappointed by the results of *Brigadoon,* and frustrated that *Green Mansions* was never made, Lerner was reserved when approached by Freed about the new proposal. Among other objections, he mentioned that his partner Frederick Loewe had never before written directly for the screen. But Freed didn't give up.

In August, Lerner, now the famous lyricist-librettist of Broadway's biggest hit, made two conditions before signing on to *Gigi.* First, he demanded that the part of Gaston's uncle, Honoré Lachaille, be built up and that every effort be made to cast Maurice Chevalier. And second, he asked that Cecil Beaton design the costumes and sets. Freed and Minnelli consented to both conditions right away.

When Lerner finished the first draft of *Gigi,* he was already aware that he had written a text that was too similar to *My Fair Lady.* But Freed told him, "Stop trying to be different. You don't have to be different to be good. To be good is different enough." Lerner faced another problem: How to get Loewe to compose the music, which would occupy the whole winter of 1957.

In the meantime, supported by Lerner, Minnelli decided that *Gigi* should not only be shot in Paris, but that the score should also be composed there. Paris was perceived to be an inspiration, as well as a crucial place to get the right ambiance for the musical.

Few people in Hollywood realized Lerner's crucial role behind the scenes. In March 1957, Lerner was sent to London to persuade Audrey Hepburn to play the lead, but she turned it down. Minnelli then proposed Leslie Caron; Lerner, however, was disturbed by her thick French accent, even though she had made a number of Hollywood movies, including *An American in Paris.* Minnelli wanted Dirk Bogarde to play Gaston, but the British thespian was unavailable and Frenchman Louis Jourdan got the part instead.

Meanwhile, the entire production had acquired a more pronounced Gallic flavor than initially intended. For all concerned, Chevalier was deemed more important than Caron or Jourdan. Chevalier's name still meant a great deal. His cabaret performance in Los Angeles at Ciro's became the "in" thing to see and, equally important, at which to be seen.

Minnelli, like other celebs, attended the show several times, each time imagining how Chevalier would look and sound in *Gigi.* After seeing the show for the third time, Minnelli finally plucked up his courage and asked, "Would you, Monsieur Chevalier, be interested in starring in a film of the Colette story 'Gigi'?" Minnelli was not aware that earlier Freed had sent Lerner to Marne-la-Coquette to talk Chevalier into playing the crucial role of the old-time charmer. To everyone's surprise, the notoriously "difficult" Chevalier accepted the role without making any preconditions.

Minnelli hoped that Lerner would restore the delicate tone and subtlety that were missing from Anita Loos's version. He proposed to eliminate completely Gigi's mother, who was seen as a redundant character, from the script. Lerner concurred, and the result was an amusing gag: Mamita, a bit player at the Opéra-Comique, is heard but never really seen.

Lerner expanded the role of the dapper old reprobate, Honoré Lachaille, who had only a tiny part in Colette's story as Gaston's father and Madame Alvarez's former lover. In the movie, Honoré became Gaston's uncle as well as the film's narrator, something like a confidant to the audience. Honoré mediates between Gigi's world and the viewers by addressing the camera directly. The part was inconceivable without Chevalier, whom Lerner idolized; he still lamented Chevalier's absence from *An American in Paris.* The three songs assigned to Chevalier fit him like his white gloves. The only change Chevalier made was in the prop department. He didn't like the straw hat proposed by Minnelli, and instead asked for a series of elegant top hats to match the long frock coats he would wear.

But the production still lacked a leading lady. Audrey Hepburn, who was then shooting *Funny Face,* continued to decline the part. Minnelli suggested that Lerner fly to London and talk to Leslie Caron, who was performing onstage at the West End. Unenthusiastic at first, Caron expressed concern about again working with an inarticulate helmsman like Minnelli, after the exasperating experience during *An American in Paris.*

Hermione Gingold was a good choice for Madame Alvarez, and for Aunt Alicia, the retired courtesan who "trains" Gigi, Minnelli wanted veteran Broadway star Ina Claire, whereas Freed favored Irene Dunne. Both were accomplished singers, but had retired from the screen. Two weeks before production began, the part was given to the British actress Isabel Jeans, a piece of compromise casting as far as Minnelli was concerned.

Freed scheduled the location work for midsummer, when it was presumably easier to work in Paris. On this film, Minnelli worked with his usual collaborators: cameraman Joseph Ruttenberg, editor Adrienne Fazan, and song arranger Conrad Salinger. One of M-G-M's staff musicians, André Previn, who had worked on *Kismet* and *Designing Woman,* was to conduct and supervise the score. The new, significant addition to the team was Cecil Beaton as production designer, and Preston Ames was to create the interiors in Culver City under Beaton's supervision.

All the preproduction elements seemed in place when Minnelli, Freed, and Beaton arrived in Paris in April 1957. Not wasting any time, the three immediately began scouting locations. For inspiration, Minnelli emulated the caricaturist Sem for the Palais de Glace and Maxim's scenes, Constantin Guys for the opening sequences in the Bois de Boulogne, and Boudin for the later scenes on the Trouville beach.

Minnelli continued to explore with excitement all of Paris, sections of which he intended to reconstruct for the movie. Minnelli and Freed had to convince the officials of the Palais de Glace that no damages would be done to its main floor. Then Minnelli cajoled the curator of the Musée Jacquemart-André into thinking that using its interior for Gaston's house was an honor and would not harm its priceless contents. Deploying his feeble diplomatic skills to the max, Minnelli also talked the owners of Maxim's into closing the restaurant for four days of shooting.

In May 1957, Minnelli and Freed joined Lerner and Loewe in Paris, where the duo worked on the score and script. Minnelli was given three luxurious months to feel his way through Paris, select the right locations, and confer on the script.

Minnelli urged Freed to report to Benny Thau about the wonderful songs that were being written. Obediently, Freed wrote: "We heard the first four songs and they are equal at least to their writing for *My Fair Lady,* the freshest writing I have ever heard in a screen musical." However, when Thau heard that there was no finished script yet, he sent Minnelli an alarming letter requesting him to speed things up, while adhering to the budget.

Optimistic, Minnelli responded: "There has been no accurate budget yet, because many of the songs that affect whole sections are not yet written. I do not think this will take long as Alan works very fast. More than half the picture will be done here. When we get back to Hollywood, our only sets will be the three apartments and a few process shots that will involve only our five principals."

Unfortunately, a heat wave broke out in Paris, where air-conditioning was then practically nonexistent. On a particularly humid day, in Lerner's suite on the top floor of Hotel Georges V, Minnelli, Howard Dietz, Freed, and Beaton heard the first rendition of the Alan Lerner-Frederick Loewe score. When it was over, Dietz shook Freed's hand and said with a smile, "Arthur, this will be the most charming flop you've ever made." But there was no further discussion.

In July 1957, the rest of the crew arrived in Paris. The songs were pre-recorded to André Previn's piano accompaniment. Shooting began during what turned out to be the hottest summer Paris had known in years. The opening and closing sequences were set up in the Bois de Boulogne, where girls strapped into corsets fainted, fake trees collapsed, and costumes wilted.

Despite his initial rapport with Minnelli, Chevalier caused some extra anxiety. Minnelli had been warned that Chevalier was known for chewing up and spitting out the directors he didn't like. However, after the first day of shooting, Minnelli received a note from Chevalier that read, "If I were a sissy, I would be in love with you." Minnelli read the note three times, but decided to keep it to himself, lest it be misunderstood.

Location shooting continued through mid-August, with the scorching sunlight penetrating the glass roof of the Palais de Glace, making lovely configurations on the ice rink below, but also melting the ice. In the midst of this commotion, nobody bothered to ask Jacques Bergerac, who played Zsa Zsa Gabor's skating instructor, if he could skate. Well, Bergerac could not skate, and Minnelli was forced to photograph him from the waist up.

Shooting then moved to Chez Maxim. Key scenes with numerous extras were set in the famous restaurant, whose rich décor was in red, one of Minnelli's favorite shades. Though he had only four days to shoot there, Minnelli displayed his usual pyrotechnical camera movements.

Joseph Ruttenberg didn't share Minnelli's enthusiasm for shooting at the famous restaurant, because its rooms were too small to maneuver the camera. However, despite difficulties, the lenser did capture the beauty of Maxim's array of Art Nouveau mirrors. Unfortunately, the mirrors reflected not only the lights but the camera as well. Ruttenberg resolved that problem by setting up tiny bulbs beneath the faces of Maxim's patrons, thus giving them a footlight-like quality, and black scrolls were painted on some of the mirrors. The crowds and the heat made the scenes at Maxim's a challenge to shoot. The style chosen was based on Sem's paintings, complete with beak-nosed grisettes and Renoiresque cocottes, ripe and rosy, despite the discomfort the actresses felt beneath their corsets.

Other unanticipated headaches ensued. Minnelli was bitten by a swan in the Jardin de Bagatelle and consequently was in excruciating pain for two days. When he recovered, unpredictable weather canceled the location shoots in Trouville.

Lerner always thought that Minnelli's genius resided in his "faultless" sense of style. As a composer, he found each frame of Minnelli's films to approximate a complete work of art. Nonetheless, the time and effort it took to realize Minnelli's vision could be maddening to someone like Lerner, who worked fast and was extremely articulate. Minnelli could spend hours arranging the flowers the way he wanted them, while the actors and extras were kept waiting and waiting.

Minnelli had a thorough knowledge of music, lyrics, comedy, and drama, and no one could construct a musical number with as much skill and imagination. When Louis Jourdan sings "Gigi," the camera wanders all over nighttime Paris, constantly refreshing the eye without ever interfering with the flow of the song. The scene, with Jourdan pacing up and down in silhouette in front of a shimmering fountain and being shaken into a decision when a horse and carriage, also in silhouette, pull up short to avoid hitting him, is among the most memorable effects ever filmed, displaying the unique Minnelli touch.

"I am devoted to Vincente and love working with him," Lerner later said. "His gentleness, however, can be very deceptive. Frequently I would have a suggestion, he would listen appreciatively, nod, agree, thank me, and then shoot the scene exactly as he intended. But invariably, he was right."

Shooting the musical on location made *Gigi* an expensive and exacting project. The studio's continuous pressure to wrap the production speedily, cramming in a dozen locations in less than a month, was too demanding for Minnelli, who was known for his slowness in setting up elaborate tracking shots and booms, all of which were made more complicated than usual by the variable Parisian weather.

For four weeks, beginning August 5, *Gigi*'s troupe moved all over the city. Minnelli chose the cozy Place Furstenberg on the Left Bank as Gigi's quarters. Aunt Alicia lived on the Avenue Rapp, and Gaston's family scenes were shot in the Musée Jacquemart-André. Gaston's song about his feelings for Gigi was done in front of the Tuileries fountains and Pont Alexandre III. "Thank Heaven for Little Girls," the film's opening and finale, and the Battle of the Flowers, were shot in the Bois de Boulogne. For the fin-de-siècle mood, Minnelli chose the Palais de Glace at the Rond Point of the Champs-Élysees. Both were in bad shape, and needed to be restored.

In the midst of the shoot, Minnelli faced a marital crisis. Georgette, who was in Paris with him, decided to return to California. A few weeks later, she asked for a legal separation. Sad as he was, Minnelli immersed himself in work as compensation.

Worse yet, out of the blue, M-G-M's Benny Thau called from Hollywood, instructing the company to return home due to the fact that *Gigi* was already half a million dollars over budget. Indeed, in late August, M-G-M pulled the plug, and Thau ordered Freed to finish the film on the lot. Minnelli never got to Trouville to shoot Gigi and Gaston's scene by the sea. As a result, the rest of what was shot was vastly uneven, with back lot swans standing in for the Jardin de Bagatelle.

On September 13, 1957, shooting resumed in Hollywood, with California's Venice Beach standing in for Trouville. "I Remember It Well," with Chevalier and Hermione Gingold, was shot on Stage 11 at the Culver City studio. To save time and money, Minnelli used a crude back-projected sunset for the their famous duet. Unfortunately, it didn't match the authentic fading light of the intercut beach scene.

The interior of Gigi's and Mamita's apartment was re-created for "The Night They Invented Champagne," a number that was choreographed by Charles Walters. A horrified Beaton, surveying it all, later confided in his friends: "All the scenes taken in Hollywood were very damaging. Suddenly, it looked like Hollywood instead of France."

André Previn conducted and recorded Conrad Salinger's orchestrations before rerecording Leslie Caron's numbers, with Betty Wand providing Caron's singing voice. Work on the remaining interior scenes went smoothly, and the shoot wrapped up on October 30, 1957.

The film's title also proved problematic. After *Lili* and *Gaby,* M-G-M was nervous about giving yet another film a Gallic name, particularly since both the earlier movies had also starred Leslie Caron. In the meantime, the working title was *The Parisians,* named after one of the songs. However, publicity head Howard Dietz insisted that *Gigi* must prevail, due to the novella's literary caché and the audience's familiarity with the source material.

More trouble occurred on January 20, 1958, when *Gigi*'s first preview took place at the Granada Theatre in Santa Barbara. One woman wrote angrily: "I am the mother of a very nice girl, but this movie contributes in a major way to the decline in the morals of the young and not so young." M-G-M's top brass expressed strong concerns about the musical's remote and cynical tone.

It didn't help that Lerner thought that some of Previn's orchestrations were too bombastic. Both Lerner and Loewe were displeased and were vocal about their criticism. "That's not the film we wrote," Lerner and Loewe complained to Minnelli quite bluntly. The duo asked for many changes, such as a different ending, different shots for some scenes, slower tempos for the song "The Parisians," and Louis Jourdan's soliloquy. But M-G-M refused to pay for the expenses involved, as *Gigi* was already way over budget.

After a few trims, a second preview was held, to scarcely better results. *Gigi* was now deemed an entertainment for the sophisticated but not suitable for the general public that had embraced M-G-M fare for decades. Lerner demanded major changes, and when the studio balked, he offered to pay for them out of his own pocket. In the end, M-G-M's president, Joseph Vogel, approved an additional budget of $300,000 for nine days of retakes. The changes were finally agreed upon but executed without Minnelli's supervision.

Minnelli was already in London, about to begin shooting the British-flavored comedy *The Reluctant Debutante.* The changes were also done without the approval of Beaton, who had to return to London for stage work. Before his departure, Beaton made sure to put down in writing all of his complaints, particularly about the color balance in some scenes. To soften the harsh, unfriendly tone of Beaton's memo, Freed changed the word "complaints" to "suggestions."

The studio expected its expensive directors, like Minnelli, to shuttle from one picture to another, without any break. Minnelli, whose new contract paid him a weekly salary of $4,250, had thus been dispatched to Europe to work on *The Reluctant Debutante* two weeks before *Gigi*'s first preview.

In Minnelli's absence, Charles Walters and cinematographer Ray June took over, substituting for Ruttenberg, who had also joined Minnelli's new project. There's still dispute over exactly what Walters reshot, or how much of his footage appears in the final cut. Lerner credits "I Remember It Well" and "The Night They Invented Champagne" to Walters, but M-G-M records don't support his claim. Walters did reshoot segments of the title number, but editor Adrienne Fazan later restored Minnelli's version.

Louis Jourdan's close-ups during the song "She Is Not Thinking of Me" were probably done by Walters; Minnelli wouldn't have interrupted the sweeping panoramas of Maxim's with such obvious cutting. Gaston's climactic marriage proposal scene was also directed by Walters, as was the rendition of "The Parisians," when Lerner complained that Minnelli's version was too brisk for the lyrics to be intelligible.

Despite all the admiration for Lerner's witty dialogue, *Gigi* was still seen as being too similar to *My Fair Lady*. Both stories take place at the beginning of the twentieth century, and both center on the shaping of a wild yet innocent girl by an initially misogynistic and arrogant man who then falls in love with his creation. Maxim's echoes the Ascot opening day scene in *My Fair Lady*. Gigi's ball gown recalls Eliza Doolittle's transformation. The similarity between the two works prompted some critics to dub the musical "Eliza Doolittle Goes to Paris." Minnelli also borrowed from his own work, asking Leslie Caron to sing "Say a Prayer" to a cat on a bed, just as Judy Garland sang "Have Yourself a Merry Little Christmas" to Margaret O'Brien in *Meet Me in St. Louis*.

Honoré's character bears similarity to *My Fair Lady*'s Colonel Pickering, the hero's elder buddy. And while Henry Higgins distrusts women because he has never known any, Gaston has known too many, and of the wrong kind. Both Higgins and Gaston argue with themselves, contrasting their emotions with their reason. Gaston's soliloquy is the equivalent of Higgins's "I've Grown Accustomed to Her Face."

In melody and theme, many of *Gigi*'s songs also recall *My Fair Lady*. *Gigi*'s "Say a Prayer for Me Tonight," sung when she goes out with Gaston, was actually written for Eliza, but cut from *My Fair Lady*. Nonetheless, if *An American in Paris,* Lerner's first Freed-Minnelli script, was more in the vein of typical M-G-M musicals, *Gigi* was a more innovative work, different in tone and sensibility.

The self-containment of the story, which unfolds within Madame Alvarez's cramped flat and her sister Alicia's hotel, was a challenge successfully met by Minnelli. But despite many distinctions, *Gigi* lacks the flowing rhythm of Minnelli's other great musicals, such as *Meet Me in St. Louis,* perhaps a result of his excessive reverence for Colette's story and Lerner's script. *Gigi*'s fidelity to Colette's ideas is impressive, but the film is less cinematic than *The Band Wagon.* Carried away by the era, Minnelli put too much effort into re-creating the milieu in a painterly way.

As Stephen Harvey noted, Minnelli records the terms of transaction, following Colette's focus on a barter system in which female sexual compliance is exchanged for male financial protection. In words that were too harsh and candid to be uttered by a heroine in a 1958 Hollywood musical, Gigi says: "To take care of me beautifully means that I should go away from here with you and that I should sleep in your bed, and when it's over and done with, Gaston Lachaille goes off with another lady, and I have only to go into another gentleman's bed."

Indeed, *Gigi* takes place in a cynical world defined by calculated ethics. With Hollywood's dwindling self-censorship, Minnelli was free to explore themes that had always intrigued him. Minnelli's personal convictions are defined by his empathy with Gigi. In this and other respects, *Gigi* is a quintessential Minnelli musical, based on a delicate interplay between seductive images and their underlining emotional anxieties. It's the kind of delicate interplay that also defined Minnelli's personal life. Judy Garland always said that Minnelli's calm, reserved surface was a camouflage for strong inner tensions.

A feminist streak runs through most of Minnelli's movies, both musicals and melodramas. Like other Minnelli heroines, Gigi is schooled to stifle her feelings as payment for an easy, paid-for life. Minnelli's melodramas depict the clash between the need for self-determination and the

confines of domesticated marriage, and they often pose bleak alterna-
tives. In *Undercurrent,* the submission of Hepburn's wife had damaging
effects, too. In *Madame Bovary* and *Tea and Sympathy,* the heroines' defiance of conventional codes of behavior turn them into outcasts who pay
a heavy price for their deviance; the former dies, and the latter is ban-
ished into oblivion.

If Minnelli's musicals are more cheerful and hopeful than his melodramas, it's thanks to the genre's ideological bias. The musicals feature
heroines who still can shape their own fate without paying a heavy price.
Marriage may be the solution for them, but it's a negotiable arrangement
that takes into account women's terms as well. It's noteworthy that in a
Minnelli musical, a happy ending means finding the man who wants a
real partner and a suitable companion, not a trophy or traditional wife,
and although the story may upend the usual moral code, the dilemma
remains unresolved.

Most of Minnelli's heroines fret at the prospect of ordinary domestic
life. Gigi is a spontaneous girl whose free-spirited ways must be tamed
before she matures. Like *The Pirate*'s Manuela, Gigi is urged by her elders
to be sensible—that is, to become a desirable object in a man's world. At
first, Gigi obediently savors Alicia's wisdom, but then she learns that
what's required of her is a double form of deception. With submissive
devotion, she can trick a man like Gaston. She tries to be compliant, but
she is repulsed by Gaston's pledge of love and promise of a kept life.

Minnelli isn't impervious to sensual pleasures, and it's his bemuse-
ment at these double-standard mores that gives *Gigi* its edge and sparkle.
Minnelli shows that a kept life could be alluring, which makes a cynic
like Aunt Alicia seem like the embodiment of calculated good sense.
Similarly, because of his age and experience, Honoré knows how ephemeral everything in life is, both its joys and sorrows. Like Alicia, Honoré
is motivated by self-preservation, and the best way to achieve that is to
keep moving and show zest and energy. This makes his reunion with
Madame Alvarez, their renewal of long-discarded vows at Trouville, all
the more touching, recalling the reconciliation scene between husband
and wife in *Meet Me in St. Louis,* when they sang "You and I."

Of all Minnelli's movies, *Gigi* proves the most forcefully that style is
a goal in its own right, that style is a way of life, and for many critics,
artifice is *Gigi*'s one and true subject. Yet Minnelli, being an artist,

knows better than other directors about the hard work, skills, and commitment—and also the joy and gusto—that go into creating magic and style on the screen.

The visual design of *Gigi,* like that of his other works, was inspired by the artists Minnelli admired: Boudin for the seascapes, Seurat for Paris on its leisurely Sundays. The drawings of the caricaturist Sem were adapted for the opening credits. Other inspirations derived from Lubitsch's 1930s Hollywood musicals starring Chevalier, *The Smiling Lieutenant* and *The Merry Widow,* light escapist concoctions whose magic transported audiences to a bygone era. In *Gigi,* Minnelli brushed the dust off of Lubitsch's antirealist world and blended it into his own film vocabulary.

The opening sequence at the Bois de Boulogne sets the tone for the rest of the film. Minnelli's camera shows a wooded alley in which the bystanders form a human frieze of elegant languor, their parasols and walking sticks perched at the requisite angle. He gives each figure its own idiosyncrasies, cutting from matrons to Amazons to ingénues with dyed Titian coiffures. It's a lovely portrait of a time and place when style ruled supreme.

Then there's the first glimpse of Gigi, an outsider who has not been civilized yet. Larking about with her books, she throws the seemingly placid and balanced setting into chaos. Leslie Caron as a misfit suits Minnelli's overall plan. She easily overcomes the problems of playing a teenager (Caron was older by a decade). She endows the role with a vivacious, irresistible charm, a schoolgirl whose spirit is too rebellious to conform to her allotted position in the rigid hierarchical structure.

Beaton was well aware that it would be Colette's own world that he would have to re-create, and by degrees he began to see *Gigi* through her avid eyes. The colors and the atmosphere should be hers, not his. Little girls in tartan dress, in *broderie anglaise* with black boots and stockings, and bejeweled ladies sipping at Maxim's or airing themselves in all manner of *équipages* in the Bois.

Together with Minnelli, Beaton drove to the Musée Grevin, to the skating rink, to the Parc Monceau and other landmarks. "This is where Gigi might have lived!" Minnelli mused, pointing to a tall seventeenth-century house overlooking La Cour de Royan. Then an *art moderne* building suggested Aunt Alicia's apartment. Gaston, with his sugar-merchant parents, most likely would have inhabited the grandiose Victorian mansion that now housed the Musée Jacquemart-André. As a result of the extensive trip, Beaton's interiors are lush: Honoré's café-au-lait Art Nouveau digs, the reddest room for a Minnelli heroine, the gaudy set pieces.

It's Minnelli's depiction of Paris that gives *Gigi* its special if artificial glamour. Stanley Donen's *Charade* offers a touristy view of Paris, as do most Hollywood pictures set there, with the obligatory picturesque cityscape of the Eiffel Tower, the Louvre, and Montparnasse. Minnelli, however, goes for those architectural elements that serve best as props for his story and characters. For example, statues of mythological rape loom over Gigi as she ponders the Parisians' sex drive, and the Beaux Arts fixtures of the Pont Alexandre III are seen when Gaston expresses his feelings about the "new" Gigi. If *Brigadoon* tries to make the synthetic look real, *Gigi* attempts something more intriguing, shaping actual landscapes into its own brand of art.

The characters' shifting moods derive from Minnelli's gifts for painting with light: the cobblestones washed blue by the moon; Gaston as a dapper black silhouette against a sapphire sky and liquid-diamond fountain. The stateliness of the group portraits in the Bois is more striking because Minnelli frames them with real chestnut trees in the sunshine.

If *Gigi* suffers from stylistic lapses, it's because of the forced retreat into the studio for some exterior shots. One of the film's weakest scenes is set in a backlot outdoor café, where Chevalier croons two choruses of "I'm Glad I'm Not Young Anymore." It's one of Minnelli's few movies that occasionally feels like an overly studied work. Even so, the blend of French literature, old Broadway, and Hollywood traditions defines Minnelli's freewheeling instincts. *Gigi* flaunts a particular beauty unmatched by any other Hollywood musical, and remains Hollywood's most endearing reverie of an age mostly known from French paintings.

After Fazan's final editing, and a rerecording of Jourdan's soliloquy, *Gigi* was previewed twice more, to better results. *Gigi* finally opened on May 15, 1958, as a reserved-seat attraction at the Royale Theatre, a legit house in New York's theater district. In November, the movie changed theaters and continued a first-run engagement that lasted more than one year.

In the end, *Gigi* became the biggest hit of all the Minnelli-Freed collaborations, a morally ambiguous story staged in an alluringly sumptuous style. As Stephen Harvey noted, the film reflected the technical powers of high-gloss Hollywood, a summation of the classical era. But Minnelli never forgot that the movie was made in an atmosphere of suspicion and pessimism, initially undermined by threats of censorship, reduced budgets, and overall skepticism.

Heavy campaigning resulted in getting *Gigi* into the prestigious Cannes International Film Festival as its closing-night attraction. However, quite predictably, the French press was divided. The more elitist Gallic critics complained about Hollywood's audacity at filming such a quintessentially French work, but the more popular press, such as *France Soir* and *Le Figaro*, praised the musical and Minnelli, who was in addition, always popular with the auteurist critics of *Cahiers du Cinéma*.

Back home, *Gigi* became the year's most honored film. Minnelli received the highest accolade from his colleagues at the Directors Guild of America. The film was then nominated for nine Oscars, mostly in the technical categories. Though none of the actors received a nod, Maurice Chevalier received an Honorary Oscar from the Academy.

At Oscar time, *Gigi* won in every category in which it was nominated. Minnelli received the first Best Director Oscar ever given to a musical filmmaker.

(The year 1958 represented a peak in Minnelli's professional career, and one of his busiest. Later that year, *Some Came Running,* opened in L.A. at the end of December to qualify for Academy Award considerations. The film garnered four nominations, including Best Actress for Shirley MacLaine.)

Metro was pleased by *Gigi*'s huge international success. By 1962, its worldwide rentals amounted to $9,965,000 against a budget of $3,447,000, a profit of $4 million. In 1966, the film was rereleased theatrically and had another successful domestic run.

When he finally saw the picture, in 1959, Maurice Goudeket, Colette's widower, gave Minnelli an unusual commendation: "My heartiest congratulations on *Gigi*'s great success. I was personally enchanted, and feel that Colette would have been equally thrilled by the delicate and faithful way her unforgettable story has been handled." For Colette's fans, *Gigi* came as close as possible to the spirit of the source material. Minnelli infused the musical with a vivacity that was specific to Gigi's world.

Although Minnelli and Freed were to make only one more musical together, *Bells Are Ringing*, in 1960, that pale transfer of the Broadway show would be a nominal coda to their careers. In many significant ways, *Gigi* was the grand finale, the last of the great M-G-M musicals, and the film for which Minnelli was most widely praised during his lifetime. After his death, though, *The Band Wagon* replaced *Gigi* as his acknowledged masterpiece, largely due to the reevaluation of his career by the auteurist critics.

Minnelli's next film, *The Reluctant Debutante,* was based on William Douglas-Home's sly drawing-room comedy about the last group of British debutantes to be presented to the queen before the archaic ritual was abandoned. On a superficial level, Douglas-Home's satire of the London social season and the toll that it takes on one debutante's father sounded like a British version of *Father of the Bride.*

The plot centers on Lord Jimmy Broadbent, a rich, witty international banker married to Lady Sheila and father to Jane, his young daughter from a previous marriage. Rex Harrison, fresh from the stage success of *My Fair Lady*, and his new wife, comedienne Kay Kendall (who had done a delicious turn in George Cukor's *Les Girls*), were cast in the leads.

In June 1955, producer Pandro Berman recommended that M-G-M acquire the rights to what he saw as "a comedy with class." Although the play was a success in the West End, on Broadway it had only 134 performances, a fact ignored by Berman. Three years passed before the film began shooting. Fearing that upper-crust whimsy might not appeal to American audiences, Berman wanted to change the text. To that extent, he asked Frances Goodrich and Albert Hackett, of the *Father of the Bride* films, to transpose the play to New York. The writers, however, declined, claiming that what made the work special was its distinctly British flavor.

Kenneth MacKenna's associate in the story department, Marjorie Thorson, proposed turning the movie into a fish-out-of-water story about an American father and daughter engulfed in London's hectic social scene. Julius Epstein, the Oscar-winning cowriter of *Casablanca* fame, was hired to do the adaptation. "To soak up atmosphere," Berman sent Epstein to London and to the famous Josephine Bradley's school for debutantes. In fall 1957, while Minnelli was wrapping up *Gigi,* Berman showed him the first draft of the script. Upon reading it, Minnelli protested that the transatlantic move neutered the play's charm.

Minnelli then flew to New York to approach Rex Harrison and Kay Kendall. Harrison was intrigued by the project and liked the idea of working with his wife. He told Minnelli, "We would love to do it, but the script is no good." In fact, Harrison loathed the script even more than his director did. Minnelli reassured the couple that the revised screenplay would restore the flavor of the original. Douglas-Home was called in for rewrites, which he continued to do throughout production.

Even so, Berman felt that, to appeal to American audiences, Lord Jimmy's daughter and her love interest needed to be American. However, the casting of all-American Sandra Dee was so implausible that the script needed to explain that her character was Harrison's daughter from a previous marriage. A Universal contract actor, beefcake John Saxon, was chosen to play David, her aristocratic, bongo-playing beau. Accordingly, Saxon became the new Duke of Positano through his mother's side of the family! Angela Lansbury, who lived and worked in Hollywood but was still associated with being British, rounded out the cast as Kendall's chum and confidante.

Dee played a typical Minnelli ingénue, a "worldly innocent," or "a restless misfit," like Esther Smith in *Meet Me in St. Louis*, Kay Banks in *Father of the Bride*, and Gigi. However, in real life, Dee was so uneducated and unpolished that she projected the innocent simpleton much better than the worldly sophisticated daughter of such savvy parents as Harrison and Kendall—the trio made one of the most incongruous families to be seen onscreen. Since Dee was of working-class origins, she had to be coached in upper-class diction and demeanor. Upon learning of David's lineage, Dee had to exclaim one of the comedy's most preposterous lines: "Oh, darling, what a lot of housekeeping!"

The film had to be completed by the spring of 1958, to accommodate Harrison's commitment to appear in the London stage production of *My Fair Lady*. A Swiss resident for tax purposes, Harrison couldn't go to London to shoot the film, and was not eager to go to the United States, either. Hence, five months after he left Paris, Minnelli was back in the City of Lights to shoot a movie with an Anglo-American cast and Franco-American crew.

Minnelli hoped to spend three weeks of location shooting in London, but, under the circumstances, he again resorted to matching actors against back-projection footage. All in all, it took seven weeks to shoot *The Reluctant Debutante,* from mid-February to early April.

During the shoot, there were some unpleasant experiences. Minnelli was shocked to learn that André Previn's theme music for *Designing Woman*, which he had never liked, would be recycled for the title sequence of *The Reluctant Debutante*. While in Paris, Minnelli heard another piece of bad news, about the attempts to tamper with his cut of *Gigi* after the first disastrous preview.

As if these professional problems were not enough, there was also bad news on the personal front, when Minnelli's estranged wife Georgette decided to file for divorce. Though disappointed, Minnelli realized that they had drifted apart and didn't have much in common. After his painful experience with Judy Garland, he resolved never again to let his marital problems interfere with his work, which was always the best solution in times of crisis.

On top of it all, Minnelli himself was not well, slowly recovering from an upper respiratory infection and a kidney stone that needed to be removed. Due to his ailments, shooting was delayed by two days, after which everything resumed normally.

When the shoot was over, Minnelli flew to *Gigi*'s world premiere in New York and then to California, to supervise the cutting of *The Reluctant Debutante*. It was a busy time for him, as he was already engaged in preproduction for his next feature, the melodrama *Some Came Running*.

The Reluctant Debutante was a commercial failure. But Minnelli was considerably proud of his work, perceiving it as an exercise in high style, if nothing else. The giddy spirit is underlined by a skillful cast that turns a verbose script into a speedy movie. Working without a reliable art director for the first time, Minnelli turned Paris soundstages into a Hollywoodized London, filling the wide screen with his signature plush textures and glittering light. Once again, there are references to his earlier work; for example, the local dance band plays the popular song "The Boy Next Door" from *Meet Me in St. Louis*.

The appeal of Minnelli's comedies always depended on the talent of the cast. Spencer Tracy and Lucille Ball inhabited worlds that viewers could relate to. *The Reluctant Debutante* was a drawing-room comedy with a smooth façade, replete with uniquely theatrical and British expressions like "darling" and "divine." However, its British milieu and humor were foreign to American viewers accustomed to watching *I Love Lucy* and *Father Knows Best* on television. In fact, Cukor's farce, *Les Girls,* made the same year with a Cole Porter score and also starring Kendall, failed as well, despite its innovative visual scheme and campy tone.

Significantly, *The Reluctant Debutante* was the only Minnelli film about the upper class, featuring aristocrats who unabashedly enjoy their privileged status. It's one of his purest and airiest comedies, though it lacks any political subtext. Unlike other Minnelli comedies, there's no commentary on marital discord, material excesses, or the inner workings of the male or female psyche.

The CinemaScope frame gives *The Reluctant Debutante* some formal style, as when Sheila and Jimmy anxiously search through the crowd for their offspring. Minnelli's tracking shots accelerate the pace. The film's running sight gag is the couple frozen in frustrated mid-gallop as the band strikes up "God Save the Queen." A delirious montage sums up the effects of the social whirl on the stoic family: While the lovelorn Jane pouts, Sheila shows her spunk on the dance floor, and the exhausted Jimmy seeks sustenance while trying to stay conscious.

Minnelli respected Harrison's generosity in the film, serving as the serene foil to Kendall's perpetual agitation. Harrison projects a slightly morose, sulky tone, even when he talks about poached eggs. However, the major reward for Minnelli was the joy of getting to know Kendall, who was already famous for her boundless charm and indefatigable energy. Determined to grant Kendall the royal treatment, Minnelli asked Pierre Balmain to design chic costumes for her in his favorite hues of yellow and red. Minnelli wanted Kendall to look really beautiful, and different from her previous appearances. Arguably, the film's most striking image is Kendall's grand entry in a red suit and slouch hat.

Minnelli was an expert at suiting his comedies to the tempos and tempers of his stars, as evidenced by Spencer Tracy's stolid work or Lucille Ball's frenzy. In this film, Kendall is the driving force that keeps the tale spinning. Deservedly compared to Carole Lombard, one of America's greatest screwball comediennes (who also died young), Kendall was a delicious player whom Minnelli described to his friends as "a glamour queen with the soul of a clown."

Kendall's clipped, fluty voice was suitable for genteel and subtle repartee, and her elastic frame for low, physical comedy. Leaping from one imagined crisis to the next, Kendall can't keep still for a moment. If Ball brought an athletic approach to physical comedy, Kendall turns slapstick into choreographed ballet, while never losing her ladylike cool. Watching her stepdaughter with "Mr. Wrong," Kendall takes a swift dive downstairs, only to land with her coiffure intact!

Minnelli enjoyed working with the Harrisons, as he later recalled: "Kay would be raucous and vital and lovable, and when the day's work was over, everyone would want to take her home." To Minnelli, the Harrisons represented the ideal couple: "I found Rex wonderfully attentive to Kay, but gave it no special thought. Kay was equally devoted to him." Reflecting their offscreen happiness, their onscreen chemistry occasionally makes the sharply uneven comedy sparkle. Moreover, the Harrisons seemed to enjoy the marital bliss that Minnelli had always wanted but never achieved.

The production was great fun for Minnelli and his stars, and the three of them spent a lot of time running around together. The Harrisons had a lovely time behaving like teenagers, on and off the screen. Since Minnelli had shot segments of *An American in Paris* and *Gigi* in Paris, he knew the city well by now and loved to show off his favorite sights. When the film wrapped, Minnelli was exhausted. It was one of the few times when he violated his otherwise strict work code and partied wildly during a shoot.

Just before shooting began, Kendall had been rebounding from a sudden debilitating malady. A doctor from the American Hospital in Paris examined her and concluded that she was entirely recovered from gastroenteritis. In what became one of showbiz's best-kept secrets, only Harrison knew that his wife was dying from leukemia. The lethal disease would take her life eighteen months later, at the age of thirty-three Minnelli thought that Kendall's death was a major loss not just for Harrison, but for the film world as well, as her brand of comedy was unique.

For Minnelli, the film's novelty was the idea of parents who behave like kids, and kids who behave like adults. It's a theme to which he could relate easily, as his own daughter Liza, now eleven, was already behaving like a little woman to him—and a prima donna to everyone else.

Unfortunately, the movie suffered from the theatrical limitations of its source material, since the play on which it was based took place mostly within the Broadbents' residence. You could say that *The Reluctant Debutante* was outdated even before it was made. In hindsight, it feels more archaic than most of Minnelli's other comedies of that era.

The Reluctant Debutante premiered at Radio City Music Hall in August 1958. The film's opening day became the second-highest take for a Metro release in Radio City's history, but soon afterward the box-office receipts declined rapidly. Hoping that the film would be more popular abroad, Metro arranged for an elegant London premiere, but the British press was even more hostile and the viewers more indifferent than their American counterparts.

Twenty

Master of Melodramas:
Some Came Running and
Home from the Hill

IN THE SPRING OF 1958, upon returning to the United States from the French shoot of *The Reluctant Debutante,* Minnelli immediately plunged into his next ambitious project. M-G-M had bought the rights to James Jones's novel *Some Came Running* even before the book was published. The property was hot: Jones's striking literary debut, *From Here to Eternity,* was a bestseller that became a successful Oscar-winning film directed by Fred Zinnemann. *Some Came Running* was touted as a thinking man's *Peyton Place,* the melodrama that had become a popular film that was better than its literary source, Grace Metalious's sleazy potboiler.

Convinced that there was a vivid melodrama in Jones's book, Sol C. Siegel, who had taken over Dore Schary's job as head of production, decided to supervise the production himself. John Patrick, who had scripted the musicals *High Society* and *Les Girls,* and Arthur Sheekman, were asked to turn the 1,200-page novel into a 120-page script, which was an arduous task.

Minnelli suggested consulting the book's author, whom he had not met, for the script, but he was discouraged by his bosses, because Jones had developed a reputation as a tough and uncompromising man. For Minnelli, however, he was "a fine, but rather ashamed writer who insisted on putting in his book whatever made him a writer." Which meant everything.

Minnelli found Jones's hero, Dave Hirsh, a conflicted writer, utterly compelling. Indeed, Dave fits perfectly into Minnelli's gallery of tormented male artists, just as brutal as Kirk Douglas's producer in *The Bad and the Beautiful,* and just as sensitive as Gene Kelly's painter in *An American in Paris.* All three, like other Minnelli heroes, were ultimately dreamers dissatisfied with their bourgeois surroundings and hypocritical middle-class morality.

Moreover, at least half of Minnelli's protagonists are creative professionals who undergo some kind of moral or existential crisis before embarking on a journey of self-discovery. Most of the artists in his movies, younger or older, experience doubts about their identity and occupational worth (at least as far as mainstream society is concerned), even in musicals, such as Fred Astaire's Tony Hunter in *The Band Wagon,* or Dean Martin's blocked writer in *Bells Are Ringing.* They are all troubled men, some motivated by religious convictions, such as Douglas's Van Gogh in *Lust for Life* or Richard Burton in *The Sandpiper,* some neurotic types on the verge of a nervous breakdown, such as all the inhabitants in *The Cobweb* and Douglas's character in *Two Weeks in Another Town.*

For the role of Dave, Minnelli wanted Frank Sinatra, whose film stardom had risen quickly after winning a Best Supporting Actor Oscar for *From Here to Eternity*, which established him as a dramatic actor, and a Best Actor nomination for Otto Preminger's *Man with the Golden Arm,* in which he played a drug addict.

Minnelli had wanted to direct Sinatra in a musical ever since he saw him in George Sidney's *Anchors Aweigh,* in 1945. Then, on the set of *Till the Clouds Roll By,* in which Sinatra had a cameo, he and Minnelli barely crossed paths. Whenever they ran into each other at parties, they would reiterate their wish to work together, but they couldn't find a project that interested them both. Now under contract to M-G-M, Sinatra was excited that his first film for the studio would be *Some Came Running,* to be helmed by Minnelli.

The studio put pressure on Minnelli to work quickly, which resulted in a tight schedule of six months, from script development to screen release. From the beginning, the film was considered to be Oscar material, and Minnelli knew that the film would need to premiere in December in order to qualify for Academy Awards considerations.

Minnelli spent the months of June and July casting the roles of the low-lifes and provincials of Jones's novel in preparation for a midsummer location shooting. As Sinatra's companion, gambler Bama Dillert, Minnelli chose Dean Martin, who had just made an impressive dramatic debut in *The Young Lions,* opposite Marlon Brando, after the split with his comedy partner Jerry Lewis. Minnelli thought that Martin's languid irony and smooth charm were major assets for playing a laid-back gambler.

However, casting Shirley MacLaine as the wayward female lead, Ginnie, a dim-witted slut with a heart of gold, happened in a serendipitous way. MacLaine, under contract to Hal Wallis, had impressed in her debut, Hitchcock's noir comedy *The Trouble With Harry.* But then on loan out to Mike Todd, she played a Hindu princess in *Around the World in 80 Days*, which Minnelli disliked. Despite her unconventional looks, Minnelli thought that MacLaine's youth and eccentricity could lend poignancy to Ginnie. He also knew that she was trying to get out of her contract with Wallis, who had cast her in one preposterous role after another.

Sinatra first spotted MacLaine on TV on *The Dinah Shore Show.* Watching television together with Minnelli one night, Sinatra suddenly said, "Look, Vincente, here's our Ginnie." Wearing a tight black leotard, MacLaine belted out a poor song. Sinatra felt that "the cuteness, the strength, the humor, everything we wanted in Ginnie, was wrapped up in that one package." And this was the kind of role MacLaine had been waiting for, a tragic, morally deficient heroine who latches on to Sinatra's would-be-novelist, Dave Hirsh.

Some Came Running became a turning point in MacLaine's career. Other than Hitchcock, Minnelli was the most distinguished director she had worked with. An expert on décor, color, and costume, Minnelli knew exactly how MacLaine should look for the role. It was crucial that she be made up to look vulgar.

On the Saturday before shooting began, MacLaine's makeup test arrived from Hollywood. Minnelli thought that the makeup she was wearing that day was dreadful—simply bland. Although few directors, gay or straight, would apply makeup to their leading ladies themselves (even George Cukor never did that), Minnelli decided to do the job himself. Unabashedly and unself-consciously, Minnelli knelt down in front of the young actress, who was bewildered, and put rouge where shadows should be. Her childish face was made up to look cheap, as a small-town floozy.

Minnelli then requested color shots of MacLaine standing in a motel's driveway, and arranged for them to be quickly developed. While looking as shabby as needed, MacLaine's pretty face was not completely tarnished. For Minnelli, Ginnie represented the pathos and failure of sex, rather than the triumph that would be implied if a sex bomb had been cast in the role. He totally embraced Sinatra's idea to change the story's violent ending and make Ginnie, rather than his character, the accidental victim of an assassin.

The women in the film were put up in a hotel in Madison, Indiana, where much of the movie was filmed, while Sinatra and Martin, like the characters they played, rented a house together for the duration of the shoot. Sinatra was bothered by obsessive female fans who camped outside his door, trying aggressively to meet him.

Many of Sinatra's and Martin's friends from Hollywood and Las Vegas dropped in to visit for card games and drinks, and some of them brought hookers from Chicago with them. The poker parties sometimes went on until dawn. To Minnelli's consternation, the two men would report to the set hungover and bleary-eyed, barely remembering their lines. The experience brought back bad memories from the set of *The Pirate,* the last time Minnelli had encountered unprofessional behavior, and from none other than his wife.

It didn't help that there was no rapport between actors and director, and that Sinatra and Martin didn't take guidance well. For their first scene together, Minnelli told them, "Your meeting is like two gamblers who have not seen each other for a long time," but they didn't get it. Minnelli then said, "It's like two women who had been call girls and later married Hollywood producers." *That* they understood right away, and did the scene perfectly.

Minnelli later said, "I saw both sides of Frank. He can be vicious. If he's affronted, he becomes a rooster in a cock fight." But he also learned that on the set Sinatra was a doer, not a talker: "Frank adores doing things his way. He doesn't like to tell you what he wants to do—he just does it."

For their part, both Sinatra and Martin found Minnelli to be too prim and proper for their taste. The members of the so-called Hollywood Rat Pack were annoyed by "the artsy-fartsy," as Martin nicknamed their director, who took a long time to set up each and every shot. They resented spending hours on a single shot just because Minnelli wanted a Ferris wheel to be seen in the background, or a vase to be shot holding the right kind of flowers.

On a number of occasions, Sinatra fumed and threatened to walk out. Filmmaking was boring enough without having to sit around for hours to do numerous takes of what amounted to just one brief scene, and not always an important one. At one point, Sinatra left the set and didn't return until the next day, forcing Minnelli to shoot around him.

Later, deeply upset, Sinatra talked Martin into abandoning the film altogether. Martin decided to join Sinatra because he knew that there was no picture without him. They flew to Los Angeles, where producer Sol Siegel tried to persuade them to resume their work. Sinatra complained about Minnelli's interminable takes and waste of valuable time on minutiae. Siegel sensed that Sinatra was just bored and tired of hanging around a provincial town like Madison, with nothing exciting to do at night. Reluctantly, Siegel approved one week's vacation for his capricious but indispensable stars, who were then at the height of their popularity as Rat Packers.

Sinatra, who had had a brief affair with Judy Garland during her marriage to Minnelli, now could understand much better her complaints about her passive-aggressive husband. After the weeklong respite was over, Sinatra and Martin returned to Indiana to finish the picture—not exactly promptly, but at least it was done.

Minnelli held that "the audience had to be knocked out by the characters' vulgarity." To that end, he decided to use the image of a jukebox as inspiration for the settings, which he garishly lit in primary colors. He always thought that the film's French title, *Comme un torrent* (Like a Torrent, or Like a Storm), captured better its essence than the vague American title.

Sinatra's and Martin's complaints notwithstanding, Minnelli's colleagues agreed that his mise-en-scène in this picture was exuberant. The emphasis on the conflicted passions and ambivalent feelings of its characters makes *Some Came Running* one of Minnelli's most effective and popular melodramas, in which he examines all stereotypes of the American middle class by contesting them. Observing the suffocating Midwestern life of his elder brother, Frank (Arthur Kennedy), Dave is so disgusted that his cynicism permeates the tone of the entire film. Dave's search for a real home—his desire for familial identity—reveals that the notion of "home" might be a myth rather than reality.

A far cry from *Father of the Bride, Some Came Running* offers a critical anatomy of the new moral disorder of the American middle class. The central theme of individual identity shapes the film's conflicts, most of which derive from Dave's hatred of his brother's duplicitous, bourgeois mores. The film also provides a critique of misogyny, exposing masculine norms that result in the tragic, sacrificial death of Ginnie, the movie's one innocent woman.

Dave is the link between two worlds, each defined by a distinct set of characters and values, conveyed in locales that are vastly different. Smitty's bar, where Dave and his cronies congregate, is contrasted with the country club, where the snobbish French clan and Dave's bourgeois brother socialize. If the former setting is full of life (and smoke) and seedy, the latter is clean, cold, and stale.

Melodrama's moral clarity is founded on principles of differences of class, sex, race, and so on. The film's two worlds clash, unable to become a unified whole. Gwen French (Martha Hyer) is depicted as an alternative to Ginnie, and Dave is forced to make the "right" choice between the two women. *Some Came Running* provides an image of the idyllic life that must first be destroyed in order to be later reestablished on new principles, reflecting a better social order.

In the movie's final shot, at Ginnie's burial on a hillside, the camera moves gracefully over the cemetery to reveal an unobstructed view of the river far beyond. It's the first time in the film that Bama takes off his hat, and respectfully so. In this composition, a tentative harmony is suggested. But in the foreground, we see tombstones, just as we will see Wade Hunnicutt's tombstone in the final shot of Minnelli's next film, *Home from the Hill*. The two shots are meant to be vivid reminders of the heavy price paid to achieve some semblance of social order and stability.

The movie's opening shots show natural landscapes through the window of a moving bus. As Dave rides the bus, we see the Great American Outdoors, mountains and rivers, which then give way to the monotonously boring sight of the story's Indiana locale. Dave Hirsh's moral odyssey begins literally with a physical journey. He is returning to his "home" to uncover his origins and heritage. Dave's Army uniform lends him individual identity, but not for too long. Once the uniform is removed, he's like an orphan in his home town, out of one institution (the military) but with nowhere to go, no real family to return to, and no career to speak of. There's nothing remotely stable in his new existence, other than the bottle and sex.

In his novel, author James Jones had trouble clarifying the perversities of people who are in love. While he fully examined his characters' world with detail and skill, making them vivid, he didn't articulate what made them tick, what drives them to behave the way they do. In this and other respects, Minnelli's taut, more focused movie improved upon its source.

As the cool, lonely, and skeptical Army corporal, Sinatra is riveting, loosely casual with a bottle, bull's-eye sharp with a gag, and shockingly frank and impertinent in his womanizing tendencies. The principal object of his attention is the schoolteacher, played by Martha Hyer. She wants to help him out with his creative writing, but he is more interested in livelier game.

Martin is also engaging as the genial professional poker player who adopts Dave as a pal. Martin's comically hard-boiled simplicity is impressive, and so is his delivery of suitable lines. Of course, his boisterous pot-walloping with Sinatra and MacLaine came naturally to him.

In a tougher, straighter role, Arthur Kennedy does a crisp and trenchant job of exposing his character as the measly and rather pathetic boob he is. Leora Dana conveys the pettiness of his wife, and Betty Lou Keim is touching as their young daughter, who is learning the first (sleazy) facts of life—specifically, that her father is a hypocrite and an adulterer, who carries on with and impregnates his admiring secretary. Their fast trip to Lover's Lane disillusions Keim, encouraging her to engage in a fling with a traveling salesman.

New York Times critic Bosley Crowther complained that the struggles with the demons of sex and love, represented in each character in various measures, are never made meaningful or clear. Sinatra is quick to offer marriage to a curiously ambivalent Hyer, but is nothing loathe, when rejected, to marry the impossible MacLaine.

Minnelli dismissed Crowther's main criticism that the tale was so garbled that screenwriters Patrick and Sheekman had to resort to a melodramatic shooting to bring it all to a tolerable end. Totally misunderstanding Minnelli's ironic approach, Crowther wrote, "Minnelli, who kept it flowing naturally to this point, has to hoke it up with grotesque action and phantasmagoric stuff with colored lights, which isn't consistent with the foregoing excellence of design in color and CinemaScope."

In 1959, Minnelli was at an all-time career peak. The Oscar sweep of *Gigi*, including his directing award, and the critical and commercial success of *Some Came Running*, solidified his position within M-G-M and the industry. Happily and proudly, he threw himself into making another melodrama, *Home from the Hill*, a film that many critics consider to be his purest contribution to a genre that flourished in Hollywood in the late 1950s, perhaps for the last time before being appropriated by television, which turned them into soap operas.

The revelation of hidden secrets and anxieties in small-town America was a popular theme in melodramas of the 1950s, such as *Peyton Place*, often based on popular novels that unveiled corruption and decadence. *Home from the Hill* was M-G-M's latest foray into the then-popular Southern family melodrama.

Though based on different source materials, *The Long Hot Summer*, *Cat on a Hot Tin Roof*, *The Sound and the Fury*, and *Written on the Wind* share similar locales and characters: old plantation houses, randy or cranky patriarchs, insecure and neurotic sons, and nymphomaniac or morally loose daughters. Their stories disclose ugly skeletons in the families' closets, such as adultery, drunkenness, police arrests, and insanity. In most of these melodramas, be they set in the Deep South, New England towns, Texas hamlets, or California suburbs, the stories are about insensitive and boozy fathers, sexually frustrated or repressed wives, and misunderstood or rebellious boys.

Along with *Some Came Running*, *Home from the Hill* represents the finest of Minnelli's lurid melodramas, a flamboyant yet deeply emotional and incisive exploration of family life at its most dysfunctional, a far cry from *Father of the Bride*. Though in its basic setting and plot, *Some Came Running* deploys some of the genre's basic elements, it was *Home from the Hill* that assembled all of the genre's thematic and visual conventions. One of Minnelli's very best, overall, it's a more personal melodrama than *Some Came Running*, due to the fact that it deals explicitly with different models of masculinity.

For Minnelli, melodrama as a genre was more of a challenge to direct, and more fun to watch, than serious drama. He fully embraced what he considered the format's quintessentially defining elements: the exaggerated emotionalism, the sentimental contrivances in the narrative progression and resolution, the excessive felicity of plot for the sake of plot, the improbable degree of violence, and, of course, the emotional catharsis.

Asked why melodrama was one of his favorite genres, Minnelli said, "There's no denying there's a lot of melodrama in life, it's heightened drama, taking things to histrionic extreme. Audiences can relate to it because, at one time or another in their lives, they experienced extreme crises and emotions."

Naturally, Minnelli easily could relate to the shapeliness of melodrama as a narrative form, its fundamentally affirmative mode, and its almost limitless aesthetic opportunities in terms of design and color. The Minnelli melodrama takes as its guide the moral necessity of showing the essential rightness of the social order, as fragile as it is, and how easy it is to corrupt and destroy that order. For him, melodrama shows the continuous, painful efforts, not the successes, of social institutions to regulate all forms of sexual repression and moral digression in order to maintain stability and the status quo, namely capitalist patriarchy.

Minnelli appreciated but didn't like the British mode of melodrama, as expressed in the works of Lindsay Anderson and Tony Richardson, which was too timid and repressed to possess the audacity of genuine art and the intensity of real emotions. He was quick to point out that it is no coincidence that British melodramas such as *Look Back in Anger, Room at the Top, Saturday Night and Sunday Morning* were all in black and white, in sharp contrast to the American melodrama of the late 1950s, directed by Douglas Sirk, Richard Brooks, Nicholas Ray, and himself.

William Humphrey's *Home from the Hill*, his first novel, was set in east Texas, where he was born. Having previously adapted Faulkner's stories for the film *The Long Hot Summer*, the husband-and-wife team Irving Ravetch and Harriet Frank Jr. wrote a script that updated the period from the 1930s to the present, and inserted a more reconciliatory conclusion. As with *Some Came Running,* Minnelli thought that the writers had actually improved on the novel. (Ravetch and Frank soon became Hollywood "experts" on the South, as seen in future films such as *Hud, The Reivers, Conrack,* and *Norma Rae,* most of which were directed by Martin Ritt and were reasonably successful, both artistically and commercially.)

The studio first thought of casting Clark Gable in the role of the patriarch, but Gable was unavailable. Minnelli was relieved to learn this, since by the late 1950s Gable had become too lazy and lethargic as an actor. In addition, Gable, almost two decades older than Robert Mitchum and with an essentially gentler screen persona, would not have been capable of Wade Hunnicutt's violent temper and strong physical activities, such as hunting, not to mention his extramarital affairs.

Minnelli had first worked with Mitchum in *Undercurrent,* in which he was terribly miscast as Robert Taylor's sensitive brother. Though only forty-two when *Home from the Hill* was shooting, Mitchum was to portray a paterfamilias with two grown sons. "Gray up my hair and let me play granpas," Mitchum quipped. "Maybe they'll stop plaguing me with work." When Minnelli promised that there would be lots of time off, Mitchum, who had heard that the Mississippi location was excellent for fishing—one of his cherished hobbies—agreed to take the part. However, despite Minnelli's promise, Mitchum found himself working extremely long days without any break.

Captain Wade Hunnicutt, the ferociously macho head of a wealthy Texan family, is married to Hannah (Eleanor Parker), an embittered, sexually withdrawn wife, and is the biological father of mama's boy, Theron (George Hamilton), and the unacknowledged father of the older, illegitimate son, Rafe (George Peppard).

The movie chronicles the destructive legacy of one divided family. Wade and his disdainful wife use Theron as a pawn in their marital conflicts and power games. In the book, Wade had many illegitimate offspring, but in the movie, the scripters combined them into one composite character, Rafe. The resilient Rafe serves as a dramatic contrast to Theron, the legitimate but pallid Hunnicutt heir.

Captain Hunnicutt tells his son Theron: "You're my next of kin—legal, legitimate, born in marriage, with my name and everything that goes with it. And that's the way of the world. There are the ins and the outs, the haves and the have-nots. You're lucky, you've got yours."

Rafe, the bastard depicted as a victim of society, is a staple in such melodramas. He is Theron's masculine counterpoint, Wade's illegitimate son who has inherited all of his father's characteristics and is therefore loved by him. *Home from the Hill* is as much about Rafe's search for legitimacy as it is about Theron's search for masculine identity. Theron's failed effort to find a place within the family hinges on his discovery of Rafe's illegitimacy. The two searches are inversely related: Theron takes Rafe's place as social outcast, and vice versa.

Theron is legally his son, but Hunnicutt doesn't feel connected to him because he's a mama's boy. But, in the end, Theron is the active agent of this reconstitution of the divided family, purging the corruption and seeing that justice prevails—specifically, that Rafe gains legitimate recognition from his father.

Hannah has refused to sleep with Wade ever since she learned of Rafe's existence. She has agreed to stay with Wade on one condition, that Theron be exclusively her son, thus turning him into an overly sensitive and insecure mama's boy. At the center of the melodrama is the very survival of the family by transmitting the right values and proper inheritance, and assigning the suitable identities to all the family members, legitimate and illegitimate, within the symbolic and social order of society.

In the film's opening scene, Wade, the hunter implied in the title, returns from the hill. The hunt is the film's metaphor for masculinity, and it divides the male characters into masculine versus nonmasculine, the hunters versus the hunted, the strong versus the weak, the protectors versus the protected. The hunter rules by gaining strength and endurance, cunning and violence, but he must always return to his family if he is to find home, love, and tenderness.

The men's world, and the peripheral part women play in it, is established right away with the hunt. Wade is seen with his dogs, his men crouched in a swamp, aiming at ducks flying overhead. Just seconds before we hear the shot that hits Wade in the shoulder, Rafe notes that the attention of one dog has been distracted, and flings himself forward to knock Wade out of the line of fire. Rafe saves his father's life when the cuckolded husband of one of the many women Wade has slept with tries to kill him. Even wounded, Wade looks powerful. He sits on the table in the foreground, erect, bare-chested, wearing his Texan hat and drinking whiskey.

It's left to the doctor to convey the film's rather pessimistic message: "Wade, I'm going to tell you how we small-town Texans get our name for violence. It's grown men like you still playin' guns and cars. You never will grow up, will you? It's gettin' to where a man ain't a man around here anymore unless he uses a car, goes down a road at a hundred miles an hour, owns six or seven fancy shotguns, knows six or seven fancy ladies!" Which pretty much sums up Minnelli's personal critique of the macho code that prevailed in Hollywood and beyond.

Minnelli frames the characters so that each "event" illustrates a facet of their masculinity code. Masculinity is articulated in Mitchum's appearance, which is contrasted with that of his doctor, who's short, plump, balding, and bespectacled, perhaps even Jewish. Objecting to the hunt, the doctor sees it as adolescent ritual of masculinity, based on conquest and physical strength, much like the silly rituals of the boys in *Tea and Sympathy*.

Nonetheless, Hunnicutt is forced to pay for his macho lifestyle. He's fatally shot by a man who believes his daughter's child was fathered by Wade. The "right" to cross any man's fence when he is hunting signals Wade's basic deviance. Wade breaks the rules, which he believes exist only for the weak members of society—effeminate men like the doctor, women, and children, including his son Theron, with whom Minnelli identified completely.

For a month, the troupe filmed in Oxford, William Faulkner's hometown. At first, the shooting went smoothly, and Minnelli's work was inspired. The director and his star revealed surprising enthusiasm for their seemingly different styles. Mitchum favored the "just-do-it" approach, manifested in his anti-fussy acting style. Minnelli, in contrast, was an aesthete, a perfectionist, and a stylist who could spend a whole day positioning a leaf in a gutter before filming what would amount to a second on screen.

Nonetheless, Mitchum's acting was superb, far better than that of

Eleanor Parker or the film's younger males. It is one of the few performances for which he was acknowledged by critics, winning the 1960 Best Actor award from the National Board of Review. As the lecherous patriarch, Mitchum conveyed the character's masculine virtues, and a vague awareness of the heavy toll he had taken on his life and that of his family's. The philandering, violent captain was close to Mitchum's own personality as a young man. Mitchum told Minnelli that he would base his interpretation on his own past, as well on the many men he had met who were like Hunnicutt.

Over the years, Mitchum had developed a legendary reputation as the coolest actor in Hollywood. As a result, the two newcomers, the two Georges, were tiptoeing and trembling when around him. "They were impressed, because I was very impressive!" Mitchum later boasted.

"I don't know why Bob puts on his act," Minnelli later recalled. "Few actors I've worked with bring so much of themselves to a picture, and none do it with such total lack of affectation as Bob does." Minnelli admired Mitchum's powerful performance as the fierce Hunnicutt. He was distressed, however, when initially the press got more excited by the promising neophytes Peppard and Hamilton. To tabloid journalists, Mitchum was yesterday's news, Peppard was today's, and Hamilton tomorrow's.

It didn't help that Peppard arrived on the set with a lot of extra baggage—and a bloated ego for an actor of his youth and limited experience. A graduate of Lee Strasberg's prestigious Actors Studio—which was then at the height of its fame, having attracted students like James Dean and Marilyn Monroe—he was full of ideas on how to act and manage his career and, though he had not done much, he already showed contempt for Hollywood.

"Have you studied the Stanislavsky Method?" Peppard asked Mitchum during a break.

"No," said Mitchum scornfully, "but I've studied the Smirnoff Method." At which point, Peppard just walked away.

That Minnelli and Peppard did not get along is an understatement. Peppard refused to do his more challenging scenes until he could be, or feel, in the right mood to enact them persuasively. Minnelli told Peppard that his approach was fine for a small Greenwich Village theater, but not for a big-budget Hollywood movie. "You start to 'feel' the scene when you got off the bus at the location," Minnelli told him.

Stubborn and hot-tempered, Peppard decided not to compromise his principles, which meant giving his director a hard time. Peppard hoped that a rebellious actor like Mitchum would share his feelings and support him. To Peppard's surprise, Mitchum advised caution: "It's a very expensive hike. I'm sure the studio can sue you. I'm certain it will be your last job. Even though you think Minnelli is wrong, you have to do it his way." Privately, however, Mitchum had his own complaints, as he later recalled cynically: "Vincente mounted the film well. He got a lot of fan letters for the interior of the house!"

After three weeks in Mississippi, the company returned to the Metro lot in Culver City for a month, then went to Paris, Texas. "Minnelli shoots all his pictures in Paris," Mitchum cracked, alluding to the two vastly different Parises. The two weeks in Texas were spent shooting a wild boar hunt that was to be the film's big showpiece, a spectacle in its own right. Minnelli staged it with the flourishes and attention to detail he would lavish on an elaborate musical production number.

Minnelli began shooting in a wooded, sulfurous swamp filled with copperhead snakes and quicksand, though the final battle between the boar and the hunting dogs was shot on M-G-M's back lot. Unfortunately, the big boar, imported for the movie from Louisiana, died during the trip from unknown causes; Mitchum said it died of booze. Instead, they had to use a pig with tusks glued to its face. A large dosage of tranquilizers made sure that the pig would stagger and fall over at the precise moment Minnelli wanted it to.

In the end, *Home from the Hill* became a rugged experience for Minnelli. When the production manager informed him that they were shutting down the location and summoning the company back to Hollywood, Mitchum observed: "Vincente was in tears, very upset. He thought he was going to get a gold watch or medal or something for thirty years of diligent service to M-G-M. It was to get a pink slip instead."

The first cut, after the film's completion in August 1958, had the excessive running time of three hours. The picture was removed from Minnelli's control and the studio's editors trimmed it down to two and a half hours, still long for a 1950s melodrama. Among other things, such lengthy running time meant one less screening per day in theaters.

Dealing with pregnancy, illegitimacy, and other scandals, *Home from the Hill* is a melodrama where men are men, women are women, but it's the women who have the upper hand, which makes it a quintessential Minnelli movie. The theme is made clear in the very last scene, which, as in *Some Came Running,* takes place in the cemetery. Hannah, now a widow, reencounters Rafe, who's finally acknowledged as a legitimate son on his father's tombstone. A pleasant, small-chat between the two leads to something much more significant, the formation of a new kind of family, headed by Rafe, who meanwhile has married Theron's impregnated girlfriend and now raises Theron's son, with Hannah as the presiding matriarch-grandmother, establishing a "home" at Rafe's house. Moreover, Hannah's birth son, Theron, becomes the outsider; he leaves town to wander around until he finds himself, all the while grappling with a crucial, lingering question: Will he become like his patriarch father now that he himself is the father of an unacknowledged son?

Seen from a detached perspective, as Stephen Harvey has observed, *Home from the Hill* is a modern Texas melodrama that's a precursor to the popular television soap opera *Dallas*, with Mitchum as the proto-Jock, Eleanor Parker the suffering proto-Ellie, George Hamilton as proto-Bobby and George Peppard as a composite proto-J.R./proto-Ray. Which may explain why *Home from the Hill* is not just Minnelli's last good picture, but also a sampler of the end of classic melodrama as Hollywood's defining genre.

Twenty-one

The Party Is Over

AFTER ITS PEAK IN THE LATE 1950S, Minnelli's career began a sharp decline. His last six years at M-G-M, from 1960 through 1965, were characterized by inertia and mediocrity. Much valuable time was spent on film projects that for one reason or another didn't materialize.

For example, Minnelli asked Arthur Freed to acquire Lerner and Loewe's stage musical hit, *Camelot,* for him to direct, but the studio balked at the cost and the project fell apart. Several years later, Joshua Logan made the film, which was only moderately successful.

The status of M-G-M's musical films began to change in the mid-1950s. The biggest Broadway hits of 1956 were Alan Jay Lerner's *My Fair Lady* and Betty Comden and Adolph Green's *Bells Are Ringing.* These musicals represented not only their creators' divergent tastes, but also different approaches to the genre. Lerner and Loewe sought to elevate Broadway with classy Anglophilia, whereas Comden and Green wrote old-fashioned, simpler musical satires that were fun and aimed at a mainstream audience.

Minnelli didn't think *Bells Are Ringing* would be his last musical collaboration with Freed, but it was. Budgeted at three million dollars, *Bells Are Ringing* had a slender plot (less a plot than a premise, and a simple one at that) that served as an excuse for some musical numbers. At first glance, this didn't bother Minnelli since most of his good musicals lacked strong stories and stressed music, dance, and mise-en-scène over conventional narrative.

Judy Holliday, who had been friends with Comden and Green from the days of their old satirical nightclub act "The Revuers," was to star in the film. On Broadway, the whimsical musical comedy was directed by Jerome Robbins, co-choreographed by Robbins and Bob Fosse, and composed by Jule Styne. Some critics didn't like Holliday's vocal impersonations, but the public did. Holliday stayed with the show during its two-year run for a record of 924 performances. The film version of *Bells Are Ringing* was simply inconceivable without Holliday, who was eager to make it so that she could shake off her still best-known role in *Born Yesterday*, which she had played on stage and screen, winning the Oscar for it in a tough year when she was competing against Bette Davis and Gloria Swanson.

In *Bells Are Ringing,* Holliday plays Ella Peterson, a switchboard operator for an answering service who has no personal life of her own. Plugging into her clients' fantasies and frustrations, in due course, she engages to match Siamese cats with their owners, prescribe mustard plasters for a famous diva, and serve as agent to a Method actor.

A spinster working for Susan's Werphone, Ella literally lives by listening in—and sometimes horning in—on the lives of her company's clients. Ella's neediest case is a client known as Plaza 0 Double-4 Double 3, a playwright named Jeffrey Moss, who suffers from a writer's block. To help Jeffrey, Ella enters into his life as a mysterious fairy named Melisande Scott, and, predictably, he falls for her fabricated personality.

Minnelli committed to do the film in the summer of 1958, but the production was postponed twice. The movie finally began shooting on October 7, 1959. When Comden and Green took too long to deliver the final script, M-G-M-'s story department head Kenneth MacKenna complained of their lax behavior and busy schedule to their agent, Irving Lazar. After reading the first draft, which was 159 pages long without songs, Minnelli, too, was dissatisfied, and he requested a shorter, more streamlined scenario.

To dramatize the urgency of having a workable script, Minnelli left for New York in February 1959 to work with the writers. The second draft was more manageable, but new delays were now caused by Holliday's West Coast tour of *Bells Are Ringing*. Minnelli began rehearsals in

August 1959, on what appeared to be an easy job, since location shots were confined to a single brownstone, located on East 68th Street in Manhattan.

Minnelli summoned Holiday to Los Angeles for preproduction meetings in mid-August. They discussed her role and costumes in detail, and they seemed to be in agreement. Or so it seemed until shooting began. Holliday hated the script and Minnelli's approach to the film. She didn't understand why the story had to be opened up for the big screen, and instead demanded more close-ups than necessary.

The film reunited Minnelli with Dean Martin for the first time since *Some Came Running*. For Martin, it was just as agonizing an experience as it had been the first time around, except that on this film he did not get on with his director and costar. Sinatra had warned Martin, reminding him of the idle time and bad experience they both had on the set of *Some Came Running*, but the role of Jeffrey was good for Martin, who needed the job to maintain actively his onscreen exposure—and his cash flow.

At first, Holliday was baffled that a big star like Martin would play a supporting part. But once shooting began, and she observed the media blitz surrounding him, she resented the publicity Martin was getting, which was substantially bigger than hers. Moreover, Holliday resisted Minnelli's direction, and was only briefly appeased when he agreed to cast her lover, Gerry Mulligan, in a small part in the film. However, once that issue was settled, Holliday went back to being her usual difficult self.

Holliday's view of the script was not news to Minnelli, who had thought all along that it was pedestrian and severely flawed. Comden and Green cut a few scenes and added some others, but they couldn't correct the basic weaknesses. They had only prolonged the story without making it more entertaining or cinematic.

In the end, Minnelli failed to gain Holliday's confidence. A fan of hers since the days of her nightclub act, "The Revuers," Minnelli had expected no difficulties in working with her, but he was mistaken. Unable to communicate with her, Minnelli wondered why Holliday was so apprehensive about a role she knew inside out. Holliday claimed that she needed a stronger director. With no help from Minnelli, she felt she was at a complete loss. What made things worse is that she started to praise George Cukor while on the set, telling the crew how she wished Cukor was directing this movie, disregarding the fact that Cukor also had had problems with her on the set of *Born Yesterday*.

After the first week of shooting, Holliday became so distraught that she asked to be released from the picture. Out of desperation, she offered to return her salary so that production could start again with another actress; she even recommended Shirley MacLaine to take over her part. However, under pressure from Minnelli, Holliday resigned herself to finish the film. The cast and crew were extremely deferential to Holliday, but she remained convinced that the very concept was wrong. *Bells Are Ringing* became a nightmare for her, and sadly, it turned out to be her last movie; she died in 1965.

Another frustrating experience for Minnelli was *Say It with Music*, a cavalcade of Irving Berlin songs, both old and new. For three years, Minnelli and Freed struggled to get the project off the ground. Originally, the film had been planned as Freed's swan song, and Minnelli wanted it to be "the bang-up musical to end them all." Although Minnelli himself had serious doubts about the potential audience for a pricey Berlin musical, with a budget of $10 million, he continued to work on a new treatment with George Wells, who had penned *Designing Woman*.

The first draft, written by Arthur Laurents, had roles planned for Robert Goulet, Ann-Margret, and Sophia Loren. Subsequent scripts were done by Leonard Gershe (*Funny Face*), Betty Comden and Adolph Green, and others, with Julie Andrews in mind. But Minnelli was not to work his Oscar-winning magic on Julie Andrews. Internal politics at the studio meant that the whole project fizzled out, although the rapidly rising star followed her stage triumphs with an Oscar turn in *Mary Poppins*. The studio's new management deemed the Freed Unit's films nostalgic and old-fashioned and therefore non-commercial. M-G-M's new head, former CBS executive James Aubrey, canceled most of the projects he had inherited, including the Berlin musical.

Minnelli's next realized movie, *The Four Horsemen of the Apocalypse,* became a disaster that took four years of work and cost $8 million. It was a bad idea to begin with, which grew worse and worse during a lengthy production process. Uniformly panned by the critics, *Four Horsemen* was the first movie that really tarnished Minnelli's reputation; it also damaged his self-confidence. This movie signaled the beginning of Minnelli's decline as a major Hollywood filmmaker, and for the next decade he would make only mediocre movies.

Four Horsemen was meant to be an epic extravaganza in the *Quo Vadis?* tradition, with hopes of even outshining that popular 1950 picture. Rex Ingram had shot the original *Four Horsemen*, based on Vicente Blasco Ibáñez's bestselling book, in 1921. It was this film that had made a star of Rudolph Valentino. However, Minnelli neglected to take a more critical look at the original movie and reassess its merits for contemporary audiences.

Preproduction on *Four Horsemen* began before M-G-M put all of its energy and resources into *Ben-Hur,* a lavish remake of the 1926 Judeo-Christian Roman spectacular that had starred Ramón Novarro and Francis X. Bushman. However, released two years before *Four Horsemen,* in 1959, *Ben-Hur* was a smash box-office hit, sweeping all the Oscars, including Best Picture.

Everything about *Ben-Hur* was enormous, beginning with the three hundred sets that covered more than 340 acres. The arena that housed the chariot race took up about eighteen acres, the largest single set in film history. The studio's publicity machine, in one of its most successful campaigns, positioned *Ben-Hur* as an event movie before the term even existed. Budgeted at an unheard-of $12.5 million, *Ben-Hur* dwarfed everything in sight. Daily information about the epic production, formally released and sometimes informally leaked with gusto by *Ben-Hur*'s director, William Wyler, had a damaging moralizing effect on every movie in preproduction or production at M-G-M, including *Four Horsemen.*

For Minnelli, this was bad news in two ways. First, he knew that M-G-M would not rally behind his pet project with the same gusto and resources. And second, he cast envious eyes toward William Wyler, who shot the epic at Rome's famous Cinecittà studios, where Minnelli had always wanted to shoot a picture. Size mattered: When Wyler told Minnelli that Cinecittà was gutted of more than a million props, and the sculptors were hired to make more than two hundred giant statues specifically for his movie, Minnelli could only lament the lack of enthusiasm for his epic.

Even those who didn't like *Ben-Hur* had to acknowledge its pageantry, sweep, kitschy appeal, and the exciting climax of the chariot race. Despite the astounding budget, and predictions that it would bankrupt the studio, *Ben-Hur* grossed staggering amounts all over the world. In comparison, *Four Horsemen* was decidedly a mid-size project in budget and scope.

In June 1958, M-G-M announced its intent to remake *Four Horsemen* with Minnelli directing, but plans remained vague due to the failure of two WWI remakes: Selznick's production of *A Farewell to Arms,* with Rock Hudson and Jennifer Jones, and Kubrick's cynical war exposé *Paths of Glory,* starring Kirk Douglas, Minnelli's favorite actor. The two war films were radically different: Whereas the former was a nostalgic star-driven vehicle, the latter displayed a fresher, more cynical take on the war. Even so, Hollywood being Hollywood, when both movies failed to ignite the box office, the blame was quickly put on their underlining genre. In actuality, of course, the pictures failed for very different reasons, but they were lumped together into one syndrome that later included Minnelli's own contribution to the genre.

From the beginning, some of M-G-M's top administrators raised objections about the outdated nature of the story, a remote chapter from the past that seemed to have little relevance for modern viewers. A parable of an Argentinean playboy who finds redemption in the trenches of World War I might have been exotic and topical in 1921, since it captured the traumas of the postwar years. But in 1961, viewers couldn't relate to that war in either a romantic or tragic way.

At M-G-M, all involved agreed that the story needed a major update. When Graham Greene declined to write "a free treatment" of the novel, Robert Ardrey took over, spending six months trying to revitalize the script. At Minnelli's request, Ardrey changed the character of Julio into a dashing Argentinean living in occupied Paris, during the Second World War, poised between fascism and the Resistance. The new milieu was reflected in the way that the yarn's major characters were divided in their political philosophies and even personal behaviors.

Some years earlier, producer Julian Blaustein had supervised the costume drama *Desirée,* a smash hit with Marlon Brando and Jean Simmons, but he had not done a movie on the scale of *Four Horsemen,* not to mention one with such an unconventional narrative. The studio hoped that Minnelli's love of Paris would again inspire him—and overcome the picture's problems. They were encouraged that in his 1950s melodramas

Minnelli had generated sparks from generic and even routine material. Minnelli knew that the characters made no sense when taken out of their historical context, but he was flattered that his talent was considered indispensable to the project.

Minnelli began thinking about *Four Horsemen* after attending the Cannes Film Festival for the premiere of *Home from the Hill*. That picture was well received by the French, representing a high point for Minnelli, whose work began to be appreciated by international critics, not just the French but also the British in such magazines as *Sight and Sound*. He took advantage of being in Europe and went on a two-week vacation to Italy, sampling Rome, Milan, and Venice, to which he would return a year later to shoot his melodrama *Two Weeks in Another Town*.

The main allure in the silent version of *Four Horsemen* was the erotic appeal of its star, Valentino. Decades later, people still talked about Valentino's smoldering tango. Minnelli, too, wished to make the film a great showcase for a new international star, but he was clueless as to where such a star could be found. Minnelli first considered Dirk Bogarde, then Montgomery Clift, both a far cry from the script's macho-heroic conception of its protagonist. For a while, Minnelli considered *Home from the Hill*'s George Hamilton, because of his youth and dark good looks, but the studio ruled him out as a lightweight not able to carry such a movie, and hoped to find someone in the mold of *Ben-Hur*'s Charlton Heston.

Then, during his stay in Rome, Minnelli met and was immediately smitten with the stunning French actor Alain Delon, who recently had made an impression on the art-house circuit in René Clément's thriller *Purple Noon*. Luchino Visconti, who cast Delon in *Rocco and His Brothers* and had had, it was rumored, an affair with him, arranged for a meeting between Delon and Minnelli. Minnelli was impressed by Delon's dashing looks and good behavior. At their first meeting, he couldn't take his eyes off the young actor. Stories of Delon's suspected liaison with Visconti, while dating Romy Schneider, made him a desirable topic in the international press.

However, M-G-M undermined Minnelli's excitement, claiming that Delon's appeal was limited to the European market and that his command of English was limited and heavily accented. In vain, Minnelli reminded his superiors that Charles Boyer and Maurice Chevalier had never mastered English and still had become stars in Hollywood.

Minnelli's final recommendation, Horst Buchholz, the German matinee idol who had recently arrived in Hollywood, was also rejected. In the end, with trepidation, Minnelli consented to casting the role with the all-American Glenn Ford, who Minnelli thought was good-looking but whose acting was bland and stiff. Even so, Minnelli hoped to bring out Ford's erotic charm, from the times of *Gilda* and other noir melodramas, before he'd been turned into a conventional macho American hero in westerns and crime films.

As for the women, Swedish Ingrid Tulin (later Thulin), who had made a mark in Ingmar Bergman's movies, was cast as the female lead, Marguerite, and starlet Yvette Mimieux, who would soon become known in *Where the Boys Are* and other fluffy movies, was chosen to play a supporting role.

Neither Thulin nor Ford were helped by the overly explicit and banal dialogue, which was full of speeches and messages. To compensate for the lack of chemistry between the stars, Minnelli resorts to a sumptuous display of sound and light. When Julio and Marguerite meet at Versailles, the autumn radiance of the photography and the violin of André Previn's love theme were meant to distract the audience from paying attention to the inane dialogue.

Minnelli uses striking double-exposure montages, a blend of authentic wartime images with artfully faked shots in monochrome. Paying homage to Sergei Eisenstein, one of his most admired filmmakers, Minnelli staged the siege of Warsaw as a tribute to the Russian director's "Odessa Steps" sequence in *Battleship Potemkin*. There's even a close-up of a horror-struck, bespectacled woman colliding with the exploding bombs. But the visual vitality of these episodes emphasized even more how outdated the rest of the film was.

Minnelli's critics charged that he couldn't summon up the energy or passion for an epic film of the magnitude of *Four Horsemen*. It seemed that his apolitical nature as a director worked against him in a story that needed to ground its hero, Julio, in the story's particular political context.

On paper, Minnelli's next project, *Two Weeks in Another Town,* seemed to be a safer and better movie, a return to form, as M-G-M promised its exhibitors across the country. As a result, Minnelli plunged into the project with greater resolve and energy than on his last two pictures. Not only was he reunited with a familiar team, but he was also given an opportunity to explore a theme he understood well: the "New Hollywood," about a decade after *The Bad and the Beautiful* was made.

The movie offered Minnelli a chance to spend two months in Rome, his second-favorite city after Paris. However, the struggle to make the film and its eventual failure made the experience demoralizing and depressing. In the end, *Two Weeks* was mangled by the studio, reviled by the critics, and spurned by moviegoers.

Irwin Shaw's bestselling novel of the same title was about the neuroses that afflict the movie industry. Its "hero," Jack Andrus, is a middle-aged actor whose career was cut short by a wartime injury. Now a military adviser to NATO, he's summoned to Rome by his former mentor, a great director on the skids, to supervise the dubbing of his latest epic film. In the process, Andrus is thrown again into the process of Hollywood-style moviemaking, with all its allure, decadence, and corruption. At story's end, Andrus returns to Paris, to his French wife and diplomatic post.

In December 1959, Sol Siegel announced that *Two Weeks* would launch the new contract of producer John Houseman, who had proven his skills with Hollywood-driven stories. However, a six-month-long strike by the Writers' Guild delayed the production, which finally began shooting in mid-1960.

Siegel thought that the film was a perfect vehicle to reunite Clark Gable with Spencer Tracy, who had not acted together since *Boom Town,* in 1940. The veteran costars were meant to give the picture a more nostalgic and glamorous aura. Unfortunately, Gable died of sudden heart attack in 1960; without him, Tracy was uninterested in doing the film, even with Minnelli at the helm.

Charles Schnee, who wrote *The Bad and the Beautiful,* took a whole year to pen several drafts of a screenplay before Minnelli was satisfied. Part of the problem was Shaw's inert protagonist, a man suffering from a midlife crisis, or male menopause. In the book, Andrus had little to lose, since he could always go back to his secure job and wife. Minnelli asked Schnee to make Andrus more desperate and to imbue the film with angst, Hollywood-style.

To propel Andrus into both a physical and mental breakdown, Schnee added a hellish marriage for him and permeated the story in Hollywood corruption. In his version, instead of spending years at NATO, Andrus spent years in a psychiatric institution, and the new job is his last chance to regain his self-esteem.

The first draft prompted the wrath of the MPAA, still the bastion of old Hollywood morality. In a stern letter dated January 25, 1961, Geoffrey Shurlock reminded Joseph Vogel that, "The Code recognizes that men and women engage in premarital and extramarital relationships and agrees that stories dealing with these aspects of human behavior may be told if presented in a way which recognizes that these liaisons are immoral."

But for Shurlock, the script's current version "presents a panorama of affairs interlocked and overlapping in a way that would seem to indicate that the moral law was suspended, if not actually abolished." He went on to comment: "It's difficult to conceive that fornication could be any more casually portrayed than is done here. The portrayal of free and easy sexual intercourse is so graphically depicted that any pretense of presenting it in a moral light would appear to be almost ludicrous."

Under pressure, Schnee made some drastic changes to the sex scenes, and Vogel informed Minnelli and Houseman that the Production Code Administration's officers were now "highly enthusiastic over the ingenious way in which serious problems have been licked in the new script."

Minnelli was glad to offer the lead role of Andrus to Kirk Douglas after their great collaborations on *The Bad and the Beautiful* and *Lust for Life*. Times had changed, however, and whereas Douglas's fee was now $500,000, plus 10 percent of the grosses, Minnelli was to be paid only $200,000. M-G-M approved an eighty-one-day-shooting schedule and a budget of $4 million. However, due to Minnelli's slowness and other problems, the production was stretched to four and a half months, which made the picture much more expensive.

After changing the director's name from the Irish Delaney to the more Jewish Kruger, the role went to Edward G. Robinson. The female lead, the predatory Carlotta, Andrus's former wife, was handed to Cyd Charisse. Houseman and Douglas objected to Charisse, who had no dramatic experience or box-office clout, but Minnelli prevailed.

"Cyd ain't Lana," Douglas told Minnelli bluntly. Dissatisfied with his leading lady, Douglas insisted that Charisse's billing should be below the title.

For Robinson's wife, Minnelli settled on Claire Trevor, and M-G-M's boy-ingénu George Hamilton was cast as the decadent Davie Drew. An Italian starlet, Rosanna Schiaffino, played the star in the film-within-the-film, and the role of Douglas's wistful playmate went to Daliah Lavi, a young Israeli actress whose star was on the rise.

As rewritten, the brutal relationship between the philandering has-been director and his paranoid wife reflected Schnee's own domestic crisis. In the script, Clara Kruger attempts suicide to provoke remorse from her contemptuous hubby. Shockingly, Schnee's own wife, Mary, killed herself when the movie went into production, in October 1961. Minnelli was stunned by the real-life tragedy, which seemed to validate the film's scathing view of a typical Hollywood marriage. After all, was not Minnelli a victim of this syndrome himself?

The passion that had fueled Minnelli in the 1950s apparently was flagging, and he now failed to exert authority over what had become a sprawling project. The four years Minnelli had spent on *The Four Horsemen of the Apocalypse* had taken a severe toll on his energy and self-confidence. The combination of Minnelli's growing passivity (always a problem) and Houseman's lethargy resulted in an unsuccessful collaboration on any level.

In late August 1961, Minnelli flew to Rome for six weeks of preproduction and location scouting. In early October, he began shooting around the Piazza Navona, the Spanish Steps, Trastevere, and Via Veneto. Somewhat naïvely, Minnelli wished his version of Rome-by-night to be on a par with Fellini's scandalous hit, *La Dolce Vita*. Released in 1960 to great acclaim, winning the Best Foreign Language Film Oscar, it had made a big splash on the international scene with its portrait of the new, decadent international jet set. Indeed, one of the last scenes to be shot was truly Felliniesque. A wild party with Andrus as a depressed hero surrounded by the fashionable crowd, it was set against an erotic tableau that unfolded outside camera range. Minnelli was proud of this sequence, which combined his penchant for elegant surfaces with a more contemporary, edgy feel.

The film represents yet another example of a recurrent pattern in Minnelli's career. Whenever under strain, or hampered by a bad script, Minnelli would let loose his flair for flamboyant visual surfaces, as a camouflage for the lack of substantial narrative and sharp characterization.

With his own job on the line, Sol Siegel could not afford to indulge Minnelli. Siegel complained that Minnelli's footage lacked energy, urging him to speed up the pacing. In one alarming note, Siegel wrote: "It is a fresh story of today and requires that kind of treatment. You caught a wonderful spirit in *Some Came Running* and *Home from the Hill. Two Weeks in Another Town* needs the same care and attention. We have been criticized by the board of directors for our expensive productions. I am asking for your utmost cooperation, Vincente, to govern your schedule in Rome in order to cut it down to the number of days originally allotted to you."

Slower and more insecure than the usual, Minnelli stretched the nineteen-day location schedule to a month. Shooting in Venice, at the Lido's famous Excelsior Hotel, was more complicated than the shoot in Rome, due to the transporation costs. The company resumed work on the M-G-M back lot, on November 9. It took eleven additional weeks to get the picture done. Sets constructed for *Lady L.,* the recently canceled George Cukor–Gina Lollobrigida costume picture came in handy, as they were recycled for the film-within-the-film glimpsed in *Two Weeks in Another Town.*

Poor audience response to a spring 1962 sneak preview reaffirmed Siegel's decision to recut the film. Siegel assigned *Two Weeks in Another Town* to the studio's supervising editor, Margaret Booth, permitting her to do drastic cuts, without consulting Minnelli.

Minnelli's orgy-party scene was deleted, as well as Charisse's melancholy monologue. Like Nina Foch's excised final scene in *An American in Paris*, Charisse's speech was meant to humanize her character. Minnelli protested that without this explanation, Charisse's character would be perceived as just a predatory thrill-seeker. Alas, it was to no avail. Charisse's part was cut substantially, a move that satisfied Kirk Douglas and reaffirmed his verdict that she could not act much.

Booth's merciless, brutal cuts made the film's already neurotic characters even more sordid and unsympathetic than they had been in the script. Stripped of more nuanced psychological motivations, the characters now seemed just nasty, insecure, and paranoid. Held responsible for all the excesses, Minnelli was never consulted about any of the changes, which was a severe blow to his already shattered ego. No director could handle such bad treatment.

To avoid "unnecessary interference," as Siegel put it, the editing was done while producer Houseman was in Europe. As a result, when Houseman found out about the shenanigans, he sent an angry memo to the legal department that stated: "In 30 years of my accumulated reputation in the American theater, film, and television, I have taken full artistic responsibility for all the work which bore my name. *Two Weeks in Another Town* in its present form does not represent my work and I cannot permit my name to appear as its producer."

The studio disregarded Minnelli's and Houseman's protests and released its own version. In the process, *Two Weeks in Another Town* lost about fifteen minutes of crucial footage and was released with a running time of 107 minutes. The movie was then dumped without much publicity or fanfare, and M-G-M declared another flop.

In the 1960s, apart from one musical, *Bells Are Ringing*, Minnelli made four melodramas under the supervision of four different producers. Gone were the days of working with entrepreneurial producers such as Pandro Berman. Minnelli's latest Metro contract lapsed in early 1962, just as he was completing *Two Weeks in Another Town*. By that time, he had become one of few Hollywood directors of stature still working in the stable and protective environment of a studio like M-G-M.

The new Hollywood system benefited energetic filmmakers such as Hitchcock, John Huston, William Wyler, and Billy Wilder, who were also the producers and/or the writers of their films, which enabled them to take the initiative and develop their own properties. However, for someone like Minnelli or Cukor who had no production, business, or writing skills, and was not interested in cultivating them, it was a difficult adjustment to make. Both directors paid a heavy price when it came to making more personal and artistic films.

At sixty, Minnelli had spent two decades in the studio system. M-G-M, with its specialized departments, had always suited Minnelli's temperament as a director who had no producing ambitions. So long as there was no interference with his work, Minnelli was content to leave the less pleasant chores—pitching ideas, securing funds, managing budgets, scheduling locations—to the studio's other specialists. This passive approach had served him well, despite frequent regime changes. For two decades, Minnelli had gotten some of Metro's most lucrative and desirable projects, and he never had to fight for a movie he wished to helm. Not only was his talent recognized, his movies made money. Not a lot of money, but enough to recoup their expense and yield some profit.

However, M-G-M in the 1960s was a different studio. Sol Siegel, the last production head with any film knowledge, was ousted in 1961. Siegel admired directors like Minnelli, and during his tenure the studio still managed to make entertainment with strong artistic values. Siegel's successor was Robert Weitman, a bureaucrat, who established different priorities for the production department. For example, for several years, more pictures were produced at M-G-M's British studio than at its main home at Culver City.

It didn't help Minnelli's cause that certain big productions, such as a remake of *Mutiny on the Bounty,* with Marlon Brando, and the sprawling anthology, *How the West Was Won,* were high-budget box-office flops. The last vestiges of the studio's prestige projects were comedies with high-priced stars, or Broadway hits such as Richard Brooks's compromised version of Tennessee Williams's *Sweet Bird of Youth* and Stanley Kubrick's *Lolita,* based on Nabokov's novel. Metro's formerly reliable and steady production line began to suffer due to gradual attrition of its contract directors and craftsmen. Which came first? The decline of movie audiences or Hollywood's lagging behind the zeitgeist?

Unfortunately, Minnelli was caught in a major career dilemma. On the one hand, he couldn't conceive of a viable career way from Metro, and on the other, the studio didn't want to let him go but couldn't find suitable properties for his taste. In 1962, the relationship between M-G-M and Minnelli worsened thanks to the much-publicized conflict over *The Four Horsemen of the Apocalypse*, the most trouble-plagued film in Minnelli's career, and a big commercial failure. Minnelli then wrangled bitterly over the final cut of *Two Weeks in Another Town,* again losing the battle, and again experiencing failure. Minnelli continued to claim that his cut would have made the picture successful, but no one at the studio believed him.

In April 1962, yet another power shift occurred at Metro, this time one that strangely worked in Minnelli's favor. Under exclusive contract to make six pictures over the next four years, Minnelli was to head his own company, Venice Productions. The venture's name was a conflation of his first name with that of his third wife, Denise, whom he married in 1962. Though she assumed a more active role in his business affairs, Minnelli doesn't talk much about Denise in his memoirs, and neither does Liza. In interviews of the time, he talks about Denise as a nice, intelligent woman, a good companion who brought stability to his life. But it's hard to fathom what kind of marriage they had, despite the fact that it was the longest union he would have with any woman; they divorced in 1971.

According to the new arrangement, M-G-M would pay him $3,500 a week with small yearly increments, plus a $75,000 annual fee to Venice Productions. This amounted to a slightly higher sum than what he had received under his last contract, but money at that point was a secondary consideration. Minnelli also was guaranteed 25 percent of any net profits earned by the movies Venice produced and M-G-M distributed.

In addition to selecting his own properties and casting them, Minnelli was granted the final cut of each film through the second preview, and the ability to consult thereafter, in cases of disagreement between him and the studio. In theory, the Venice agreement confirmed Minnelli's high status in Hollywood, yet it also marked the beginning of his fade-out as a creative filmmaker in charge of his fate.

On a closer look, however, the new arrangement benefited no one. Only three of the six promised films would be made, and each represented a safe choice, a conventional project with major stars. Minnelli's hopes that the studio would come up with fresh ideas for him didn't materialize. In fact, the tired formulas chosen for him failed to draw on Minnelli's creativity on any level. And because he had vested interests in making commercial movies—he would, it was agreed, share in their profits—Minnelli was not particularly eager to press for more risky or innovative projects. Choosing a project for its potential commercial profit was never a motivation for Minnelli, and now his indifference backfired.

None of the three productions generated any profit, and none was really good artistically.

A retrospective of Minnelli's films at London's National Film Theatre, in May 1962, provided a most welcome respite. But it was also an all too useful reminder of how wonderful Minnelli's achievements of yesteryear had been, and how precarious and stale his career was becoming.

The Courtship of Eddie's Father, Minnelli's first film under the new Venice pact, was a modest comedy, based on Mark Toby's autobiographical novel about the readjustment problems of a recently widowed radio executive and his precocious son. Assembled by Toby and his friend Dorothy Wilson, the stories were later polished by another writer. The three women in the widower's new life actually represent different facets of Wilson, who owned the copyright to the text.

Hoping to grab the TV audience, Metro favored this kind of cute family portrait, but it didn't excite Minnelli. He found the story to be disappointing and feared that his efforts would result in "a very little picture," as he told his wife. It was produced by Joe Pasternak, a less demanding supervisor than either Freed or Berman, who specialized in broad, "corny" family fare. The film was written by John Gay, who was an odd choice since he had cowritten the disastrous *Four Horsemen of the Apocalypse.*

To everyone's surprise, even an innocuous film like *The Courtship of Eddie's Father* faced censorship problems. There were objections to Eddie's vague observations about female anatomy, which had to be modified to gain the Production Code's seal of approval.

Glenn Ford, then under contract at M-G-M, was cast in the lead, this time with Minnelli's approval. The three women were played by Shirley Jones, as the wholesome widow across the hall, Stella Stevens, as a sweet but dense Dollye, a role vaguely similar to Shirley MacLaine's Ginnie in *Some Came Running,* and Dina Merrill, as the girl he intends to marry.

Looking for a young boy to play the precocious kid, Minnelli cast Ronnie Howard, who had already scored big in the 1962 musical *The Music Man* and was a favorite tyke as Opie on TV's *The Andy Griffith Show.* (Howard later became the successful Hollywood director of *Apollo 13, Far and Away,* and *A Beautiful Mind,* among other films.)

Shooting began on August 1, 1962, and ended on time in early October. Minnelli was pressured to keep costs down, after the huge budgets spent on his last couple of pictures. As a result, the New York locations were re-created on the lot, and a wedding sequence was scaled down from a church ceremony to a reception in an apartment that was also used elsewhere in the picture. The studio allocated $1,800,000, the lowest budget for a Minnelli picture since 1950, of which his directorial fee, $195,000, was the biggest item, amounting to more than 10 percent of the figure.

When *The Courtship of Eddie's Father* opened, in June 1963, the critics found it sentimental and only mildly engaging. The public's response was mild too, and M-G-M declared a deficit. The story, however, enjoyed a future life on the small screen as a popular sitcom.

For Minnelli, *The Courtship of Eddie's Father* provided a kind of occupational therapy after the bickering and scandals on the set of *Four Horsemen* and *Two Weeks in Another Town*. But the film was modest to a fault. The cut-rate cast and studio look confirmed the film's status as a minor work, not more than a footnote in Minnelli's career. *The Courtship of Eddie's Father* does not even qualify as a stylish exercise; it's just a shallow and forgettable picture. To conform to the new production circumstances and movie market conditions, Minnelli lowered his standards, and, as a result, his customary signature is absent from the movie.

Moreover, the Panavision compositions clash with the film's intimate theme, a result of Milton Krasner's overlighting, further exposing the undernourished yarn. The movie's sound is even tackier than its visuals. Like many studio films, *The Courtship of Eddie's Father* lagged behind the taste and spirit of the times—too artificial to ring true as a family melodrama, too straight to qualify as a comedy.

Nonetheless, the film contains one vital element that had been missing from Minnelli's recent comedies, an emotional center. Like Frank Capra's 1959 *A Hole in the Head*—a better father-son film, with Frank Sinatra in the lead—Minnelli offers a melancholy portrait of a widowed father, then a relatively new type of screen hero in Hollywood movies. Set at the Corbett household just days after the death of Eddie's mom, the film observes the gradual adjustment of its two survivors, father and son, as they grow closer and and come to depend on each other.

As he showed in *Meet Me in St. Louis,* Minnelli views childhood not as a cheerful phase of life but as a painful period with a dark and brooding tone. Eddie exhibits a morbid sensibility similar to that of Margaret O'Brien's Tootie. Both Tootie and Eddie are forced to come to terms with such mature issues as death, and both have to endure growing pains with intense sorrow.

The year 1963 was frustrating for Minnelli. For the first time in decades, he couldn't put a single movie into production. Moreover, his wife Denise botched the negotiations for Minnelli to direct the screen version of *My Fair Lady,* the only project he really desired. Minnelli's last contract with M-G-M, signed in 1962, stipulated that the studio would obtain for him the rights to *My Fair Lady.* The studio had tried to acquire this hot Broadway property, a sure-fire movie if there ever was one, for Minnelli, but withdrew when the bidding reached the unheard-of sum of $5 million—a bigger sum than *Gigi*'s entire budget. In the end, Warner Bros. bought the rights.

Nevertheless, Minnelli's hopes revived when Lerner and Loewe urged Jack Warner to assign the film to their favorite director. From day one, the main obstacle was money. Minnelli's greedy wife and agents demanded half a million dollars plus points for his services. Minnelli later claimed that Denise's demands were made without his full consent. But after spending so much money on the film rights to the musical, Warner could not afford to indulge an artist like Minnelli, known as much for his perfectionism as for his slowness. He offered Minnelli a flat fee of $400,000, which Minnelli's wife deemed insulting to his stature.

Minnelli became a victim of the Hollywood maxim: You're as good as your last picture. Jack Warner offered the musical to Minnelli's rival, George Cukor, who had made *A Star Is Born* in 1954 with Judy Garland. Minnelli regretted his wife's ill-advised act of brinkmanship for the rest of his life. After seeing Cukor's 1964 movie, Minnelli felt that had he directed *My Fair Lady,* it would have been more stylish and more entertaining. It was the first time he criticized openly Cukor's approach to a film, which was more of a literal-minded Broadway/Edwardian series of tableaux, and not always tableaux vivant.

Throughout their simultaneous tenure as M-G-M's best directors,

Minnelli and Cukor were considered rivals, of the polite rather than the aggressive kind. Older than Minnelli by four years, Cukor had been the reigning director of Metro in the 1930s and 1940s, with four Oscar nominations to his credit. By the time Minnelli had made his first film, Cukor had already reached not one but two peaks in his career. Indeed, it was disturbing to many that, due to luck and circumstances rather than talent, Minnelli won a directing Oscar before Cukor, who finally was honored by the Academy in 1964, for *My Fair Lady*, at his fifth nomination.

Meanwhile, Minnelli remained idle, unable to find a worthwhile project to direct. Metro encouraged him to accept offers from other studios, which further offended him. Out of desperation, Minnelli accepted Twentieth Century–Fox's offer to direct *Goodbye, Charlie*, George Axelrod's stage farce about reincarnation, set in a Malibu beach house. For some reason, Minnelli took an unnecessarily long time, a full five months, from January to June of 1964, to prepare and shoot *Goodbye, Charlie*.

The Broadway play ran for only three months due to the then poor marquee value of Lauren Bacall, who was making her stage debut. Fox snared the play, hoping to shape it to the talents of Marilyn Monroe, who had triumphed in Axelrod's other famous comedy, *The Seven Year Itch*, directed by Billy Wilder. Initially, Minnelli was excited to work with Monroe, Hollywood's hottest star at the time, but by the time *Goodbye, Charlie* went into production, Monroe had been dead for a year, and her last film, *Something's Gotta Give*, under Cukor's helm, was never completed.

Reluctantly, Fox next turned to Debbie Reynolds, who enjoyed sudden popularity after *The Unsinkable Molly Brown* became the sleeper hit of 1964. Reynolds earned her first and only Oscar nomination for her performance in the title role, but Minnelli had serious doubts about his leading lady. Onstage, Bacall had brought a certain androgynous quality to her part, that of a Hollywood Don Juan type who's killed by an outraged hubby (before the play opens), and rematerializes in the incongruous form of the very kind of cute woman he's spent his life seducing. Minnelli could not see Reynolds in a bizarre story that was ahead of its times in terms of sexual politics.

It was ironic that Minnelli's first movie away from Metro found him directing Reynolds, with whom he had refused to work at Metro, where both were under contract for decades. In Minnelli's opinion, Reynolds was too crass and uneducated, lacking finesse. Fox, however, stood firm. Too eager to work to quibble, Minnelli acquiesced and bore his grudges against Reynolds quietly.

Unbeknownst to Minnelli, Reynolds also regretted her commitment to the film. She perceived the script as a one-joke story, describing it as "a tale of a dead man who comes back with the heart and mind of a reincarnated woman." However, Reynolds wanted to work with Minnelli, failing to realize the troubles she would have with her fussy director.

The part of Charlie's randy crony went to Tony Curtis, who had worked successfully with Debbie Reynolds on *The Rat Race.* Fortunately, Minnelli liked Curtis, and the two men enjoyed a cordial relationship on the set.

The contrived farce did not inspire Minnelli on any level. He tried to re-create the distinctive Metro ambience on the Fox lot by surrounding himself with longtime colleagues: cameraman Milton Krasner, composer André Previn, costumer Helen Rose, and set decorator Keogh Gleason. He relied most of all on art director Jack Martin Smith, who had designed most of Minnelli's Metro films.

Apart from a few location shots in Malibu, the film was made on the back lot, which underscored the tale's claustrophobic staginess. In fact, no less than half of the yarn takes place on a single set, Charlie's glitzy bachelor lair.

In the past, Minnelli was able to insert some wit into the simplest of his comedies, but *Goodbye, Charlie* suffers from a stiff script (with only a few acerbic lines) and the kind of morality that was cynical without being poignant. Nonetheless, Axelrod's point, that Charlie's fate represents a punishment for his sexual exploits, was a transgressive enough theme to appeal to Minnelli's sensibility. The hero says at one point, "It's as though I'd been a gourmet all my life, and suddenly I'm a lamb chop." The wit never rose above that level. The notions of bisexuality, effeminate men, and masculine women had always intrigued Minnelli as an artist and a man, since he himself combined those attributes in equal measure.

As he showed in *The Seven Year Itch* and *Will Success Spoil Rock Hunter?,* his anatomy of the all-American male was Axelrod's favorite theme. But in this work, there was only a thin line between his take on the opposite sex and that of the saps he satirized. Due to Axelrod's cartoonish idea of femininity, symbolized by tears and beauty parlors, Reynolds's gradual transformation into a woman is not as charming as it should have been. Worse, as his new self, Charlie is even duller than the male he was.

While screenwriter Harry Kurnitz preserved the play's spirit, he added some new wisecracks. "I don't have to go see Brigitte Bardot movies anymore," muses Charlie, "I can just stay home and pull down the shades." Kurnitz tried to open up the play by introducing two characters enamored of the new Charlie: A naïve, rich mama's boy (played by the singer Pat Boone), and the unseen trigger-happy producer (Walter Matthau), who had dispatched the hero before the story begins.

Fortunately, the Beverly Hills setting brings the movie closer to Minnelli's familiar sensibility. Like *The Bad and the Beautiful,* the movie contains allusions to Hollywood lore, but this time out they are played for broad laughs, not intensely emotional melodrama. The scene of Charlie being shot in the pants while on a yacht recalls the historical incident of the Thomas Ince scandal of the 1920s (which Peter Bogdanovich filmed in 2001 as *The Cat's Meow.*) The deadpan agent Crafty (Martin Gabel) is a clone of dealmaker Irving "Swifty" Lazar, and the movie's Hungarian mogul, Sir Leopold Sartori, resembles Sir Alexander Korda, the noted Hungarian-British producer-director, who helmed *That Hamilton Woman* and produced *The Tales of Hoffman* and Olivier's *Richard III*, among many credits.

In this picture again, Minnelli critiques the lifestyles of the rich and famous. Joanna Barnes and Ellen McRae (later known as Ellen Burstyn) play poisonous Hollywood wives with hilarious wardrobes to match. Whenever the secondary characters are onscreen, *Goodbye, Charlie* shows some of Minnelli's brio; the rest is just crass or second-rate.

Two sequences were meant to elevate the film above the routine. The opening orgy is sumptuous, a kind of Via Veneto–American style scene like that Minnelli had staged in *Two Weeks in Another Town,* but it was excised from the final cut. In the second, Minnelli moves the camera past a starlet toward the stateroom where Charlie disrobes a redhead.

Minnelli shows his taste for kitsch when Charlie visits Rodeo Drive, a West Coast variation of the all-female Park Avenue retreat that was seen in the opening sequence of Cukor's *The Women.* Delighted to be on an expansive set, Minnelli uses his camera with a droll flourish to record a place dominated by blue frescoes, with languid women dangling their toes in the fountains while gossiping about this and that.

The movie's vulgar touches, however, upstage Minnelli's parodic efforts. In the cheapest gag, the still male-at-heart heroine gets into the spirit of her new surroundings by goosing the nearest available fanny. With her notorious tomboy playfulness and aggressiveness, Reynolds's pat is more like a slug.

In *The Reluctant Debutante*, Minnelli showed some verve despite the slim text and restrictive set. But in *Goodbye, Charlie*, he doesn't care much. Curtis and Reynolds spend a good deal of time on-screen trading jokes in front of a back-projected seascape. For long stretches, it feels as if Minnelli retreats behind the camera, letting his stars do what comes naturally to them, without any interference or guidance.

As the expatriate novelist, Curtis belts out his repartee in a pale imitation of Cary Grant, though his performance is not as proficient and dead-on as his impersonation of Grant in Billy Wilder's *Some Like It Hot*. For such a crude man, the late Charlie still has too good a taste in paintings, which reflected Minnelli's aesthetics rather than that of his character's.

Except for Stanley Kubrick, who had directed Curtis in *Spartacus*, Minnelli was the most demanding director the actor had worked with. Curtis later recalled: "Minnelli was obsessed with tiny little details—everything had to match. He was always fidgeting with the set. He always wanted everything to look opulent and rich." Curtis also recalled, that "Minnelli and Ellen Burstyn (billed in the film as Ellen McRae) kicked the shit out of each other. They hated each other."

Compared to the indefatigably energetic Reynolds, Curtis is relatively subdued. Dressed in oversized pajamas, Reynolds comes across as an aggressive femme, and Minnelli saw his main task as restraining Reynolds's excessive physicality. He was always nudging Debbie to do things differently, a little more delicately. One day, Debbie came on the set and said quietly, "Good morning, everybody." Then she looked over and said to her director, "How was that for you, Vincente, or should I try again?" It was very much in the spirit of the joke that Judy had told on the set of *Meet Me in St. Louis* about Minnelli and his one-line actor.

Goodbye, Charlie became one of Minnelli's least impressive efforts, solely driven by his determination to keep working and getting paid without being able to adapt to the changing times. Most reviewers dismissed the film as just another verbose and stillborn farce.

The movie opened in New York in November 1964, playing only three blocks away from the theater where *My Fair Lady* had started its long triumphant engagement. While visiting New York City, Minnelli would walk around the block to avoid seeing the lines of people waiting to get into a screening of *My Fair Lady*. It was too painful to observe. Under different circumstances, if it were not for his damn wife, it could have been his picture—and a much better one.

Twenty-two

Being Idle

ALMOST EVERY FILMMAKER HAS at least one movie he's embarrassed about, a movie he'd like to erase from his filmography. In Minnelli's case, it's *The Sandpiper,* a silly soap opera intended to exploit the scandalous affair and then famous marriage between Elizabeth Taylor and Richard Burton. Indeed, M-G-M packaged the film hastily as a showcase for Taylor's and Burton's respective screen images.

Producer Martin Ransohoff concocted the premise of the story, an ill-starred alliance between a voluptuous free spirit and a married clergyman—and hired formerly blacklisted writers Dalton Trumbo and Michael Wilson to write the script. The hiring of these screenwriters was the first and last courageous act in this film, and, sadly, neither writer did a decent job.

Taylor was to play a flamboyant single mother who lives in a Big Sur beach house amid a close-knit community of bohemian artists. Burton was cast as an Episcopalian minister—the third clergyman he had portrayed—after *The Night of the Iguana* and *Becket*—since his romance with Taylor had begun. The minister and his devoted wife operate a private boys' school, and when the wife finds out about the tumultuous affair, the reverend leaves her for an uncertain future.

Burton and Taylor, who had director approval, first turned to William

Wyler, but the notoriously cantankerous director told them bluntly that the project was inane—"a piece of crap," in his words. As a replacement, the Burtons settled on Minnelli, who had successfully directed Taylor twice before, in *Father of the Bride* and *Father's Little Dividend*. Idle and readily available, Minnelli was more than happy to accept the offer.

After his loanout to Fox for *Goodbye, Charlie,* Minnelli had no projects to justify the money M-G-M was spending on Venice Productions. Like Wyler, Minnelli recognized immediately the script's limitations, but he also realized that, after *The Courtship of Eddie's Father* and *Goodbye, Charlie,* two stagy, mediocre comedies, principal photography on *The Sandpiper* would at least take him on location, and off the lot.

More important, Minnelli had not had a commercial hit in years, and *The Sandpiper* seemed to be a sure thing. At that point in their careers, the Burtons, as the most celebrated couple in the world, could ensure the commercial success of any venture, good or bad, they undertook. The film didn't do anything to maintain Minnelli's stature in the industry, except to serve as a reminder that he was still alive and kicking.

Eager to meet their director, Burton and Taylor invited Minnelli to come to New York at their expense, where Burton was appearing in *Hamlet* on stage. Vulnerable, Minnelli needed the flattery involved in their treatment. He reciprocated with a typically gentlemanly approach, never telling Taylor that she was actually the second choice for the lead; *The Sandpiper* had been designed for Kim Novak before she had a falling-out with producer Ransohoff.

With two mega-stars, Minnelli insisted on a respectable supporting cast, which included Eva Marie Saint as the pastor's steadfast wife. For the role of Taylor's neglected suitor, a sullen sculptor who made nude statues of her, Taylor proposed Rat Packer Sammy Davis Jr., who was then popular. She had befriended Davis in New York and thought it might be fun to work with him. Taylor disregarded Davis's dubious erotic appeal and the possibility that a black member of the cast would throw the picture off balance, turning the romance into an interracial affair, an idea that was not in the original script.

Like Minnelli, Ransohoff thought that casting Davis was a radical and even ridiculous idea. He told Liz candidly, "I'm a liberal—I had hired Dalton Trumbo, one of the Hollywood Ten, as coscreenwriter, but Sammy Davis Jr. as your love interest, in a 1964 movie, would have caused all kinds of grief." Taylor had to swallow her pride and forget about the Rat Packer.

Minnelli, too, objected to Davis, and instead cast Charles Bronson, before he became a big star in the 1970s vigilante action film *Death Wish.* Always loyal to actors he liked, Minnelli cast *Meet Me in St. Louis*'s Tom Drake for the small part of Burton's colleague and James Mason's son, Morgan as Taylor's love child.

Minnelli had hoped to shoot *The Sandpiper* soon and quickly, but it was not to happen. First, Taylor wanted to be in Mexico while Burton was making John Huston's *The Night of the Iguana,* fearing that his co-star, Ava Gardner, might have an affair with him, so the film was delayed to accommodate her private worries. Then, to protect the Burtons from the Internal Revenue Service, it was decided to shoot some of the story's California settings on a French sound stage, at the Boulogne-Billancourt studios. Minnelli was all too happy to return to the locale he had used in *The Reluctant Debutante,* six years earlier. Bad as the script was, how could Minnelli resist going to Paris at the producers' expense?

To obtain the requisite gloss for such a fluffy movie, Minnelli relied on a top-notch crew of longtime colleagues. This film represented his eighth collaboration with cinematographer Milton Krasner. George W. Davis and Urie McCleary, who had designed most of Minnelli's pictures after *Gigi,* drew Taylor's beachfront house. Minnelli asked his favorite costumer, Irene Sharaff (who had also designed *Cleopatra* and was thus trusted by Taylor), to try prodigiously to transform the then chubby star into a glamorous beatnik.

The trip to Paris was preceded by a month of location work. Minnelli spent all of September 1964 filming on the rocky coastline of Carmel and Big Sur. The golden seascapes were meant to convey Taylor's Thoreau-like communion with nature. Then, in early October, the company flew to Paris for a two-month shoot.

From day one, the set became a sideshow, a media circus. The world's most famous couple was besieged by paparazzi day and night. Minnelli's happy memories of working with Taylor on *Father of the Bride* and its sequel faded quickly. Hapless to begin with, Minnelli found himself in the midst of a chaotic shoot, unable to assert his authority. He did, however, finish principal photography on time, in December. A sneak preview in January led to reshoots of the Taylor-Burton love scenes at an Encino motel, using doubles.

Regardless of its quality, movie exhibitors across the country were eager to book *The Sandpiper* in their theaters. M-G-M scheduled the film as a big summer release with a steamy ad campaign: "She gave men a taste of life that made them hunger for more!" The film opened at Radio City Music Hall, the first Minnelli film to be shown there since *Bells Are Ringing* in 1960, and broke box-office records.

The reviews were derisive, and some downright nasty. *Time* declared: "How wanly art imitates life." The *New York Herald Tribune*'s Judith Crist wrote: "This is the most perfectly awful movie of the past several seasons. Miss Taylor and Mr. Burton were paid $1,750,000 for performing. If I were you, I wouldn't settle for less for watching them." Most critics showed contempt for the script's fatuities and giggled over the overripe curves that Taylor displayed in her seminude scenes.

The Village Voice's influential critic, Andrew Sarris, lamented Minnelli's diminished status in the new Hollywood: "Metro's most flamboyant stylist has been reduced to accepting assignments at the whim of an alleged actress he virtually started on the road to stardom." He correctly pointed out that "the studio's honchos will credit the Burtons for the good business and blame Minnelli for the bad reviews." "Ironically," Sarris wrote, "Minnelli was the only person connected with the production who has ever shown any genuine feeling and flair for the medium."

Predictably, *The Sandpiper* was critic-proof and made a lot of money. For an artist of Minnelli's pride, the success was a further humiliation, because it was the picture's appalling reputation that accounted for its mass appeal. Viewers went to see the movie to find out whether it was as risible and unwatchable as the critics had said.

Worse, Minnelli had inadvertently turned his star vehicle into a black comedy. *The Sandpiper* could be interpreted as a self-parody of Minnelli's other films about artists and nonconformity. Taylor's opulently scruffy home and the free spirits at Big Sur were preposterous, and the film is just as bad as the artworks painted by Taylor's protagonist, oils of seagulls and little boys.

Minnelli could not prevent his actors from showing contempt for their ridiculous lines. Consider Taylor's metaphoric bubble: "The only way you can tame a bird is to let him fly free." Once Taylor proves irresistible, Burton trumps her, begging the deity to "grant me some small remembrance of honor." Then Taylor delivers a fake feminist monologue about married women's barren lot, while the Big Sur surf is pounding the sands of her own cove.

In another scene, parading about in lurid lavender, Taylor smooches with Burton while a wounded fowl nests in her raven tresses. She then sports a violet-blue bra while she fends off a randy ex-lover by brandishing a dainty hatchet. Rather insensibly, Taylor was outfitted in caftans, some of the worst ever designed by Sharaff, which only emphasized her physical shortcomings. Taylor's long hair, flowing gowns, and soft lighting could not conceal her weight, which became a subject ridiculed with nasty jokes in Hollywood.

Worse yet, the erotic heat that allegedly prevailed between the stars offscreen remains invisible. Onscreen, their affair is carried on in an almost businesslike manner, with no sexual charge. Burton and Taylor seemed to be sleepwalking through their paces, including their pseudo-romantic scenes.

The shoot was turbulent, to say the least, from the start. When Minnelli placed a large pillow behind Burton's back to improve the camera angle, an angry Burton retorted, "Don't give me this rubbish that it looks all right. I know perfectly well that it doesn't look all right." As always, Minnelli insisted on doing the scene his way, and Burton eventually complied, but not before telling the director cynically, "For the money, we will dance."

Minnelli knew that *The Sandpiper* was not good for a smart actor like Burton, who was totally bored by it. For diversion, Burton ad-libbed, acting his life through the lines, which gave the performance a resonant subtext for those who cared to look. Unlike Burton, Taylor enjoyed the experience, realizing that, despite the media hype that surrounded her, she could not have otherwise gotten a job, due to her poor health. Deeply in love, Taylor was just happy to be on the same set with Burton, and even happier that she was being paid a lot of money for that.

Minnelli found the story's premise ludicrous and outdated. The dialogue was so awful that he was embarrassed to rehearse it. The script was turgid and rife with cliché—"I never knew it could be like this. Being with you is like having the whole world in my arms." When Burton missed a cue or blew a line, Taylor just giggled. "Oh, I'm so henpecked,"

Burton said, tossing her a wounded look. "I don't know why I bother to act."

"You don't!" Taylor retorted with sarcasm.

Burton then shut up, and Minnelli was dumbfounded by the exchange between the putative lovebirds.

"The film was so bad that it nearly broke up our marriage," Burton said later. "But the truth is, people didn't know we couldn't get any work, anywhere, not even in Europe."

The director and his leading man had one thing in common, though. Like Minnelli, Burton was of poor origins and obsessed with money. When asked what *The Sandpiper* was about, Burton said it was about $1.75 million and writing off some old debts. Burton's misgivings about the production were short-lived—money was the greatest balm for his fears. Burton was overpaid and he knew it. "It's quite indecent," he said in a moment of truth. Despite some vocal arguments with Minnelli, for the most part Burton did as he was told. Being obedient meant the cash continued to flow faster and more smoothly.

As cruel as the reviews for *Cleopatra* were, with critics describing Taylor as "overweight, overpaid, and under-talented," they were mild compared to those of *The Sandpiper*. The movie became the couple's most misconceived teaming. When Taylor read one decent review of the film, she laughed hysterically, threatening to sue for libel. Taylor knew she was no good, and that the whole movie was awful. The Burtons shrugged off the criticism. "Every once in a while you have to make a potboiler," Burton said. "We never thought it would be an artistic masterpiece," added Taylor, "We did it for the money."

Minnelli experienced other problems with his stars, who were always late on the set. Asked by the press whether lateness was not common among superstars, Minnelli squirmed and replied, "Not to the extent that we had in this situation." Nonetheless, when he talked to his crew, it was easier for him to rationalize the Burtons' bad habits, claiming "without them, there is no picture!"

Though a critical flop, *The Sandpiper* made more than $10 million at the box office, benefiting the Burtons as well as Metro. Audiences flocked to see the couple in their first pairing on screen after their respective divorces. After *Doctor Zhivago, The Sandpiper* was M-G-M's top-grosser of 1965, yielding $6 million in domestic and $4 million in foreign and TV revenue. Because of the studio's bizarre accounting system, however, M-G-M declared a loss and Minnelli never saw a penny beyond his base fee.

The vagaries and vicissitudes of the film industry are such that after making quick cash, Burton and Taylor managed to redeem the damage to their reputations caused by *The Sandpiper*. Their next joint project, *Who's Afraid of Virginia Woolf?*, based on Edward Albee's acclaimed play, was to be directed by Hollywood's brightest talent, Mike Nichols. Both stars would be nominated for Academy Awards and Taylor would win her second one, this time deservedly (her first had been for *Butterfield 8*).

It was no secret that Minnelli wished to direct the screen adaptation, and with that in mind, he even contacted Henry Fonda and Anne Bancroft. But he was not even considered. At sixty-two, with his career in severe decline, Minnelli felt that he had overstayed his welcome at Metro. The time was right to part ways, before being asked to do so.

In the past, work always compensated for personal frustrations, but now his priorities changed, and family life became more important. Suddenly, Minnelli began to feel guilty about neglecting his other, younger daughter, Tina Nina, having given most of his attention to Liza.

Minnelli always knew that Liza favored his company over Judy's. He also knew how difficult it was for Liza to be fair to both of her parents, and not to show favoritism. Liza could relax only in her father's company, since he made no demands on her. In contrast, Judy was always hyper, emotionally fragile, and needy. When Liza visited Los Angeles, she stayed with Minnelli, but she didn't want her mother to know, fearing her jealousy, so she lied to her that she was staying with friends or at a hotel.

Minnelli did not approve of Mickey, Garland's third husband and Liza's third stepfather, when Liza was living with them in London. In his own way, Minnelli would try to find out from Liza what kind of life she had in London, the nightclubs she frequented, the movies she saw, above all, who were her friends. He was always overly concerned that Liza would socialize with the "wrong" elements in Judy's life, specifically drug-driven, alcoholic artists and bohemian gay men.

In the 1960s, with Minnelli's Francophile encouragement, Liza enrolled at the Sorbonne, as the prestigious Université de Paris is informally known. The only advantage of going there was to acquire some rudimentary command of French, on which she would improve in the future, to the slight envy and great admiration of Minnelli, who could never really master the language. However, disliking academic life and Parisian snobbery, she stayed there for several months only.

Petrified of her father's reaction, Liza flew back to L.A. to tell him about dropping out of school and about her showbiz aspirations. But to her surprise, Minnelli just said, "I think it's about time. You have so much energy, you might as well start using it." Liza then confided in him that she was afraid of Judy's reaction. "Well," a calm Minnelli said, "tell your mom I'm all for it, if that helps."

For obvious reasons, at this phase of her life, Judy was more interested in finding Liza a companion than encouraging her showbiz plans. It was she, in fact, who chose Liza's first husband, Peter Allen, a twenty-year-old Australian singer-dancer, whom she saw performing during her stay in Hong Kong. Judy needed a new opening act, and she invited Allen and his partner, Chris Bell, to London.

Clearly, matchmaking was on Judy's mind from the get-go. She was certain that Allen, with his charming smile and infectious exuberance, would be the ideal mate for her daughter. Seated at a piano when Liza first met him, Allen greeted her with the appropriate Gershwin tune, "Isn't It a Pity (We Never Met Before)." Liza responded spontaneously, joining Allen at the keyboard. Before long, they were singing together. Judy was pleased—as a mother, for a change.

Initially, Minnelli was strongly against Liza's marriage to Allen. For one thing, he believed she was too young to get married. As he noted: "She was just twenty years old. They were both quite young and I thought she should wait. They were both also on the brink of professional careers and I knew the survival rate of such marriages was small."

Denise, Minnelli's wife at the time and Liza's stepmother, expressed even stronger disapproval, saying she wouldn't attend Liza's wedding. Yet, despite his concerns, Minnelli knew that marriage to Peter Allen was something Liza really wanted. As he later put it, "My eventual consent was one more request of Liza's I could not refuse."

There are indications that even Judy was beginning to change her mind about Allen when she learned about his wild gay lifestyle. Minnelli, too, was worried about the gossip about Allen as a flamboyant homosexual, trying to pass in straight society as bisexual to promote his career—this was, after all, 1967. Who better than Minnelli to understand Allen's urge to do that? Minnelli had always been discreet and cautious about his sexual orientation. But Allen belonged to a different generation, and he and his boyfriend, Chris, were known to have all-night orgies and to frequent the gay bathhouses in every city they performed in.

Allen did something smart and mature when Liza told him of her father's objections to the marriage. He sent a "respectful" letter in which he tried to dispel Minnelli's reservations about his marrying Liza. Minnelli later said, "I was impressed he was so tradition-bound he felt he had to ask for Liza's hand."

On March 3, 1967, Liza and Peter Allen were married in New York. At twenty-two, Liza was exactly her mother's age when she married Minnelli. Prophetically, Liza's marriage would last the same length of time as Judy's, about five years, though for half of this time, she was by herself.

Though Minnelli enjoyed women's company and liked being married, he was never completely fulfilled in his marriages. In his mannerisms, Peter Allen reminded Judy of Minnelli as a younger man. From the moment she met Allen in Hong Kong, Judy knew that Liza would be charmed by him. Though Allen was gay, Judy believed, or wanted to believe, that he was the right man for Liza.

Apart from her father, Peter Allen was the first man Liza really loved. It's hard to tell if it was a profound or an immature love. Minnelli always suspected that the relationship was Liza's subconscious attempt to launch a new life, independent of him and her mother.

Allen would become the first in a succession of gay brother figures who would define Liza's life. Like Judy, Liza was insecure about her looks and her desirability as a woman. Not surprisingly, she was drawn to the same type of mentor/companion figure that her mother was. In their obsessive quest for validation, both mother and daughter were attracted to either gay or older famous men, preferably both.

Judy and Liza similarly needed the same type of man. Having a bisexual father, whom she admired and with whom she also sympathized because she hated her mother, Judy gravitated toward soft, sensitive men. Liza would do the same. The parallels between Liza's life and her mother's were all too apparent. Just as Judy had surprised Minnelli when she found him with another man in bed, so now, only weeks into her marriage, Liza caught Allen in a compromising position. Judy's friends testified that, barely a year into her daughter's marriage, she cried over Liza's suffering from "Mama's repetition."

In fact, three generations—grandmother, mother, and daughter—found themselves in similar predicaments, with marriages blighted by their husbands' sexual orientation. All three women were doomed to make the same mistake: Ethel Gumm with Frank Gumm, Judy with Vincente, and Liza with Peter.

Once the wedding was over, and Liza had male protection, Judy was determined to help Liza launch her showbiz career. However, she was determined not to do it like her own domineering mother, who was a stereotypical stage mother. A close friend of Michael Medwin, the producer of *Charlie Bubbles,* Judy suggested Liza for a supporting role in the film that was to star Albert Finney and Billie Whitelaw.

Minnelli was nervous when Liza was cast in the role of Finney's adoring secretary and mistress, which required her to strip down to panties and bra. But, as usual and as expected, he offered most encouraging words of support: "I am delighted you are doing the picture, and I think it's a marvelous break for you. I feel absolutely sure you'll be fresh and great and appealing and something completely new."

For her first movie as an adult, Liza relied more on advice from Minnelli than from Judy. She followed to the letter his suggestion that she restrain her natural intensity. Time and again, father told his daughter: "Remember, such intensity is proper for the stage, where you need to project big, but not for the screen, which is much more subtle." "Don't press," Minnelli wrote to Liza on another occasion. "Remember you register so strongly and so easily you can project any emotion from ecstasy to anger and still be in control."

Liza immersed herself in a career that would serve her marriage to Peter Allen best, as he was a performer too. Nonetheless, the couple were soon living separate lives, while Peter and Chris were performing at gay clubs and hanging out with Allen's crowd. Liza either was left alone, or left to socialize with her own friends.

In the meantime, Minnelli's own marriage was collapsing. To his chagrin, Denise had fallen in love with the tycoon Prentice Hale. "Vincente was happy with Denise, and I think his heart was broken when she went off with Hale," wrote columnist Doris Lilly, who was also Minnelli's friend. The divorce was amicable, and Denise subsequently played a part in Minnelli's romantic involvement with British publicist Lee Anderson, whom he would marry in the 1980s. Anderson was a pretty blonde, twice-divorced, from the prominent French millionaire Eugene Suter and from cattle rancher Marion Getz.

When Judy died in June 1969, Liza's first call was to her father in Hollywood, where he was shooting the Barbra Streisand musical, *On a Clear Day You Can See Forever*. It was the biggest-budgeted musical he had ever been assigned to helm, and he was apprehensive. His anxiety was exacerbated by the fact that his marriage to Denise had collapsed, and a settlement had to be worked out quickly.

On Sunday, June 22, 1969, while organizing the shoot for the upcoming week, the telephone rang at Minnelli's house. It was Liza, calling from New York.

"Daddy."

"Darling!"

There was a pause on the other end of the line, before Liza could bring herself to say, "Mama died today."

"Oh, darling. I'm so sorry."

Though shaking, Liza seemed to be in total control, already dealing with the arrangements that needed to be made.

"I have to make sure she didn't kill herself," Liza said. "Mama couldn't have done that. She was in such a great mood during the last few days."

Minnelli comforted Liza as best he could. There was a long silence, until Liza said, "I'd better go, Daddy."

"Keep me informed, darling."

"Okay."

All by himself, Minnelli burst into tears. He had always feared that Judy would take her life or die of a drug overdose, but he hadn't expected it to happen quite so soon. After wiping away his tears, he fixed himself a martini that was twice as strong as his usual. He then sat down and sighed with relief. While his old fear about Judy had been realized and sort of dealt with, a new one had now emerged: What would happen to his darling Liza who, despite efforts at separation, was still too attached to her mom?

Twenty-three

Life Is a Cabaret

IN THE LATE 1960S, THE COUNTRY WAS in the midst of the Vietnam war and the antiwar movement. Hollywood, however, ignored the changing times, deluding itself that the public was nostalgic for old-fashioned studio fare. It was easy for an old-timer and inflexible filmmaker like Minnelli to embrace this mentality.

In 1964, *My Fair Lady,* the last classic musical, swept most of the Oscars. The following year, *The Sound of Music* grabbed all the important Academy Awards and the global box office. Instead of viewing these films as exceptions, Hollywood viewed them as the rule. These two films spawned a cycle of anachronistic musicals that tried to revive the declining genre with adaptations of Broadway hits, most of which had a distinct British flavor.

The studios acquired any show that had had a Broadway success, such as *Camelot, Funny Girl,* and *Oliver!* Other Broadway highlights, such as *Man of La Mancha, Mame,* and *Sweet Charity,* were all made into big-screen entertainment. Joshua Logan directed *Camelot* and *Paint Your Wagon,* whose greatest "distinction" was casting Clint Eastwood in a singing role! Rather dull and archaic, most of these pictures failed at the box office. *Doctor Dolittle,* with Rex Harrison, almost bankrupted Twentieth Century–Fox. The new cycle was retro not only in terms of material but in marketing. To make these movies seem like special events, the films opened on a reserved-seat basis, with full orchestras playing the overtures in the pit against lush curtains before the actual movies were screened.

Gene Kelly was selected to direct one of the most mediocre musicals of the cycle, *Hello, Dolly!,* starring Streisand, but for some reason, he kept the news to himself. Minnelli was upset that, while socializing with Kelly, the actor never bothered to mention the upcoming project, let alone ask for his advice.

Alan Jay Lerner's *On a Clear Day You Can See Forever,* which premiered on Broadway in 1965, served as a star vehicle for Barbara Harris. Like *Goodbye, Charlie,* it's a tale of reincarnation, shifting back and forth between Restoration-era England and present-day New York. The story concerns a love affair between a psychiatrist and a chain-smoker named Daisy Gamble, who discovers in therapy sessions that she is the reincarnation of a woman named Melinda Wells.

Like *Gigi* and *My Fair Lady, On a Clear Day* revolves around a cynical, middle-aged professor awakened to the possibilities of love by his protégée. However, *On a Clear Day* lacks the pedigree of those musicals, which drew on prestigious source material, such as Colette's witty novella and George Bernard Shaw's *Pygmalion.*

The stage production of *On a Clear Day* was criticized for its clumsy story. The lead role called for a singing personality who could play a period role as well as her modern-day alter ego. While the hypnosis sessions called for an actress who was a cookie, the period tale called for an irresistible seductress. Streisand seemed ideal for the dual role, but despite a meteoric rise to stage stardom, her big-screen appeal was not entirely proven yet. Nonetheless, holding that Streisand was indispensable, Paramount delayed its plans for producing *On a Clear Day* until 1968, when Streisand became available after the London run of *Funny Girl. On a Clear Day* would not be released until 1970, by which time Streisand had won a Best Actress Oscar for *Funny Girl.*

After the disappointment of not getting his favorite director to helm *My Fair Lady,* which George Cukor finally made, Lerner campaigned stronger than ever to get Minnelli for *On a Clear Day.* Lerner was cruelly reminded by studio executives that Minnelli had not directed a movie in five years, and had not done a musical in a decade, when *Bells Are Ring-*

ing had been a disappointment. Even so, Minnelli got the assignment. Although Streisand was signed before him, Minnelli was excited at the prospect of working with such a mega-talent, having seen her on stage a number of times.

In their first conference, Minnelli suggested that Lerner move up the period story's setting by a century, to the Napoleonic era, which he found to be more visually exciting. With Minnelli's encouragement, Lerner also embellished the story's melodramatic elements, such as the erotic dalliances of Melinda Wells and her trial for treason and murder.

To Minnelli's delight, Cecil Beaton agreed to design the costumes. After their successful teaming on *Gigi,* Minnelli was looking forward to another happy collaboration with Lerner and Beaton. Shooting began with grand publicity and fanfare on January 6, 1969, on what was scheduled to be an eighty-two-day shoot.

There were problems in casting the "romantic" shrink, Dr. Chabot, a sophisticated man who becomes distracted by Daisy's somewhat schizoid behavior. When Richard Harris, Frank Sinatra, and Gregory Peck all declined the role, Minnelli, ever the Francophile, turned to Yves Montand. Montand's track record with American movies had not been successful: Cukor's *Let's Make Love,* opposite Marilyn Monroe, *Sanctuary,* with Lee Remick, and *My Geisha,* with Shirley MacLaine, were all flops. But Montand possessed the requisite debonair manner for the role and an undeniably strong screen charisma. Minnelli hoped that his Gallic charm would spark a kind of "opposites attract" chemistry with Streisand's more pragmatic, Jewish-Brooklynese personality.

Minnelli had kept in touch with Montand and his wife, the actress Simone Signoret, whenever he was in Paris or they visited L.A. They all spent a memorable evening in 1960, when Signoret was up for Best Actress in the British drama, *Room at the Top.* It was the first time that the French couple attended the ceremonies together. They told Minnelli that they were shocked by how "Hollywood ecstatically abandons itself to its traditional narcissistic orgy, and all eyes were riveted on the procession of limousines, the black and white tuxedos, the bare shoulders and the long-considered gowns."

Simone Signoret had stage fright, as did Montand—he was to be one of the evening's performers; Minnelli had asked him to perform two songs, which meant two cases of stage fright, and then stage fright for

each other. When Montand's turn came, Bob Hope, the master of ceremonies, called on Fred Astaire, who then announced, "I have the great
honor, the great pleasure to present to you a French singer called Yves
Montand . . ." Whereupon Montand launched into *"Un garçon dansait,"*
his imitation of none other than Fred Astaire, and after that the staple
song, *"À Paris."*

Montand bowed and then rejoined Minnelli backstage. Minnelli suggested he return to his seat in the auditorium. "No, no," said Montand,
"the next Oscar is for Best Actress, and my wife is going to get it." Minnelli kept quiet, knowing that Signoret's chances were not very good, not
because of her performance, which was superb, but because of her
left-of-center politics. As this short exchange took place, Rock Hudson
was unsealing the envelope. A *Life* photographer caught Signoret at the
precise moment her name was read out. She had clapped her hands to
her chest and was exhaling with such energy that her breasts thrust forward as she rose. Joy struck her, and Signoret's entire body reflected that
feeling.

Afterward, Minnelli joined Montand and Signoret for the unbridled
jubilation. Along with the team of *Ben-Hur,* which swept ten Oscars,
Simone presided over a banquet at the Beverly Wilshire Hotel. Though
never political, Minnelli felt that Signoret's personal victory also represented a victory of Hollywood over itself. By voting for Signoret, the industry had finally exorcised its witches. Many of the evening's most
wildly applauded winners had been victims of the blacklist.

Unfortunately, a great deal had happened in American culture between 1968 and 1970, when *On a Clear Day* was released. Lerner made
brief allusions to the prevailing climate of student unrest, but overall, his
script was archaic and stiff. The only concession to the countercultural
times was the addition of a new character, Daisy's stepbrother, Tad Prin-
gle, a semi-hippie with sideburns and a guitar, played by Jack Nicholson.

On this picture, Minnelli worked with a new art director, John De-
Cuir, and with veteran cinematographer Harry Stradling, with whom
he had last collaborated on *The Pirate.* A park in Los Angeles served
as the rose garden for Streisand's solo, "Hurry! It's Lovely Up Here," and
the title song that opened and closed the film. The interiors for both the
flashbacks and the contemporary scenes were constructed on the Paramount lot.

The studio expected fireworks between Minnelli and Streisand, who already had developed a reputation as a temperamental and difficult actress—a diva. Instead, harmony prevailed from day one. Unlike William Wyler, a tyrannical director who didn't tolerate any artistic input from Streisand on *Funny Girl,* Minnelli encouraged his star to talk and was totally open to her ideas. Enraptured by Streisand, Minnelli made a special effort to make her shine in her solo songs, in the way he had served Lena Horne and Judy Garland at Metro.

Indeed, in his *New York Times* review, Vincent Canby wrote: "The high point of the film, and one of the most graceful Streisand moments ever put on film, is a royal dinner at which Minnelli's camera explores Miss Streisand in loving circling close-up while her voice is heard. Nothing is allowed to get in the way of Miss Streisand, but Minnelli has not been completely inhibited by her. He handles her with an appreciation of her beauty and of the largely unrealized possibilities of her talent." However, Minnelli's passive, laissez-faire attitude stranded the other performers. Montand struggled with his role from beginning to end, and Jack Nicholson really hated his director.

At this time, Jack Nicholson was known for his drive-in movies, such as Roger Corman's *The Terror* and *The Raven.* Nicholson's presence in the musical was weird, to say the least, though, at the time, the actor was desperate to get out of the Corman factory. *Easy Rider,* the cult movie that gave him his breakthrough role and made him an icon of the counterculture, which was beginning to influence the "New Hollywood," had not yet been released.

Easy Rider was still in the editing room when Paramount production head Robert Evans urged Minnelli to watch Nicholson in *Psych-Out,* a film about a rock band in San Francisco's Haight-Ashbury district. Evans said it would be useful for Minnelli to view the lighting effects, which could help in the reincarnation sequences in *On a Clear Day*, but he also gambled that Minnelli would take note of Nicholson's performance and unique screen appeal. Indeed, after seeing the film, Minnelli asked Nicholson to audition for the part of Tad. Nicholson was to play the sitar and sing a song with Streisand, "Who Is There Among Us Who Knows," written by Lerner and composer Burton Lane.

Nicholson initially declined the role, but Minnelli persisted, and the actor finally agreed to sing "Don't Blame Me," a standard song featured in M-G-M musicals. Evans recalled, "Jack wanted $12,500 and I would only pay him $10,000. He needed the extra money for alimony."

Though Nicholson eventually got the contract he wanted, shortly after committing to *On a Clear Day,* he realized he had made a mistake. Not only was he asked to cut his long hair, which was emblematic of his persona, he was dressed in button-down shirts and sweaters. For an actor known for his restless and dynamic image, there was little movement in Nicholson's scenes in the musical, in most of which Minnelli just leaned him against windowsills, or posed him in front of plants, motionless.

Bruce Dern, a friend of Nicholson's, observed: "Jack did that pitiful thing, and it was a total toilet job for him. You could see he was uncomfortable and awkward. Minnelli intimidated the shit out of him." Evans concurred: "Jack didn't get along with Minnelli. He's God-awful in it, and I think he'd offer me a percentage of the picture if I'd cut him out of it. The part was lousy, and the picture wasn't good. It wasn't Jack's fault, nobody else could have played it any better."

Minnelli insisted that he chose Nicholson not because of his countercultural reputation, but because he liked his awkward singing. For his part, Nicholson said that he was "fascinated by the idea of someone who doesn't sing doing a song." Ironically, Nicholson's solo ended on the cutting room floor.

In March 1970, Nicholson spoke with Rex Reed for a *New York Times* piece about the as-yet-unreleased film: "I am very frightened about it. I wanted to see what it would be like to be in a Vincente Minnelli musical. It's a radical departure for me, you know? I didn't take a step in the whole thing after I walked on carrying my suitcase. Once he let me get up to light someone's cigarette and I think my back went *crraccuhcchh*. You can probably hear it on screen. There was so little—uh—movement."

Nicholson yearned for direction from Minnelli, but he got none. "You have to sort of guess what he wants," Nicholson said. "One day I said, 'Look, Vincente, I really don't mind being directed, you know what I mean?' It was the clearest-cut job of acting for the money I've ever done."

"They had the good sense to leave me on the cutting room floor," Nicholson later said. Though he was set to play a hippie who would make this old-fashioned film attractive to younger viewers, Nicholson was told that his hair was too long and needed to be cut. The producers wanted to have it both ways: to make a film that would be hip and contemporary, yet would not be offensive to older demographics. But in 1970, the generation gap was too wide to permit a film to cautiously straddle the chasm, and ultimately, the movie appealed to no one.

Taking place in two different centuries, the film suffers from a severe identity crisis. Minnelli's preference for the 1812 era is obvious, as Joe Morgenstern pointed out in *Newsweek*: "Minnelli and his photographer Harry Stradling whip up some lovely old fluff in the regression sequences. The décor is sumptuous, the extravagance justifiable, the tone slightly self-mocking. But Minnelli and Stradling, custodians of a defunct tradition, bring a negligible sense of style or pacing or humor to those modern sequences which constitute, alas, most of the movie's running time. They, far more than poor Daisy Gamble, are haplessly trapped in the present."

The whole film suffered from clichés. *On a Clear Day* grafted its songs onto a sitcom plot of how Dr. Chabot hypnotizes Daisy to awaken her former self. The film's whimsy is based on the notion that Daisy and the doctor are karmic lovers whose incarnations clash: He yearns for the Melinda that was, and she pines for the shrink that is.

Minnelli alternates close-ups of the stars in their shared scenes, but he seldom shows them in the same frame together. The lack of chemistry between the two stars did not help, either. Streisand was already a self-contained star, lacking rapport with most of her leading men. For his part, removed from his French locale, Montand is unable to display onscreen the debonair quality he'd been hired for, and his concern with delivering his lines in an acceptable English accent came at the expense of acting. Miscast as a coolheaded intellectual with a skeptical mind and romantic soul, Montand seems too square and prematurely middle-aged.

Throughout the picture, Minnelli concentrates on Streisand, who was the kind of consummate performer with the aplomb he had always admired. The film was a good showcase for Streisand. As the contemporary schlemiel of a girl, Daisy, she does her Brooklyn-inflected shtick; as Melinda, she shows elegance and sophistication.

Minnelli's well-known fascination with spoofing plays is also evident in this movie. There is a send-up of a song from the recent hit musical

Oliver!, a cartoonish Dickensian account of Melinda's orphanage up-bringing, and a parody that's sumptuously lit and designed. In contrast, the contemporary episodes are done in a fluorescent flair against fake sets. But Minnelli had a hard time showing what passes as chic, and his escapist glamour doesn't gel with the movie's subtext.

Dr. Chabot's study is an office of marble steps and woodsy book-shelves. The expansive aerial shots of New York City and the frantic jump cuts are meant to show that Minnelli was au courant. In one of the few outdoor scenes, the final fadeout, Streisand sings her farewell against an expanse of pink and gray clouds.

Critics thought that her lyrics, "I'm out of date and outclassed by my past," could be applied to the film itself. Streisand's exuberance notwith-standing, *On a Clear Day* showed that Minnelli was out of touch with the times, both cinematically and socially. The harsher critics labeled the film "On a Clear Day You Shouldn't See This Ever." Minnelli's clout with the Hollywood establishment was rapidly slipping. Minnelli re-called that the film "made respectable money at the box office, but not enough to excite the bean counters."

To be fair, the film did receive some decent reviews. *Saturday Review's* Arthur Knight praised the direction: "What Minnelli does so well is to search out the essential qualities of his star performers, to frame them in ways that heighten the intimacy between them and the audiences and to surround them with an aura of glamour that makes them at once larger than life and very real."

Despite the lukewarm reception of *On a Clear Day*, Minnelli refused to concede that his career was over. In the next few years, he tried hard to develop new projects at Paramount: a chronicle of Billie Holiday intended for Tina Turner (the movie was later made as *Lady Sings the Blues,* starring Diana Ross). Minnelli also entertained the idea of a biopic about Zelda Fitzgerald, adapted from Nancy Milford's book, with Liza in the lead.

Father and daughter had been long nurturing mutual hopes of work-ing together. After the collapse of the *Zelda* project, Minnelli sought other possible projects for Liza. Various financial backers approached the two for a possible film about Judy Garland, an idea that both perceived—quite rightly—as grossly insensitive.

Sadly, around that time, Minnelli and Liza further bonded over another matter. Both had gone through their respective divorces within months of each other. First, Liza announced to the press that her marriage to Peter Allen was over, and soon a similar announcement was made about her father's divorce from Denise. It took Liza years to tell her dad that she had caught Peter in a compromising position with another man. Minnelli understood, though he couldn't share with his daughter his own scandal of getting caught by Judy in a similar position.

While he was directing *On a Clear Day,* Minnelli heard rumors that his wife Denise was dating other men. In an uncharacteristic move, the troubled Minnelli confronted Denise about the gossip. At first, she dismissed the rumors, saying, "Don't worry about it. It's nothing."

However, when Minnelli returned to California, Denise confided in him that she was no longer sure she wanted to stay married to him. It was "a great shock," he later recalled. Denise complained that they had drifted apart, that Minnelli was so self-absorbed and preoccupied with work that he wasn't even aware of her frustrations. One major issue was their sex life, which had never been active in the first place, and had declined dramatically over the past few years. They were spending most of their evenings in separate rooms, going to bed at different times, getting up at different hours. Reluctantly, Denise had become a live-in companion, and a frustrated one.

Even so, up until then, Minnelli felt that Denise had been a marvelous wife who'd made a happy life for him. He determined that, if this was what she desired, he wouldn't stand in her way. It took Denise a few months to make up her mind, but eventually she opted for divorce, which was granted in August 1971. A self-described "three-time loser," Minnelli vowed never to marry again. However, ten years later, he would again violate his vow and marry for the fourth time.

According to gossiper Doris Lilly, the divorce from Denise was on amiable terms. In fact, it was Denise who later played a part in Minnelli's romantic involvement with British publicist Lee Anderson. Anderson was an attractive divorcée, whose previous husbands were the socially prominent French millionaire Eugene Suter and the cattle rancher Marion Getz.

With Denise's blessing, Lee moved into Minnelli's house in the late 1970s. Denise knew that Minnelli couldn't live by himself, that he needed somebody to tend to his needs. Cordial and sensitive, Lee would be good at that.

All of his friends were rooting for him to marry Lee right away. But Minnelli took his time. He and Lee were together for a very long time before they officially married in 1983, just three years before Minnelli's death. Lee's warmth and companionship meant a great deal to Minnelli, as it also did to Liza, who would say, "You're the only woman who's really doing what a mother should do, be kind and supportive of me."

Meanwhile, rumors in town were spreading that Minnelli had lost his stamina, and that the studios were reluctant to entrust him with another major movie. Indeed, there was a sharp decline in Minnelli's health. A lifelong chain-smoker who never did any physical exercise, Minnelli suffered a series of minor strokes, which exacerbated his chronic stutter and clouded his already vague memory. Then, a near-fatal chest ailment necessitated an operation to remove part of one lung, which increased his frailty. Minnelli's lifelong habit of concealing his true age—claiming to have been born in 1910 instead of 1903—now backfired. All of a sudden, he looked very old for a man who was only sixty-nine in 1972.

The happiest distraction from an increasingly frustrating career came through Liza's growing success as an actress and concert performer. Always the doting father, Minnelli took an active role in guiding Liza's career. He had always encouraged her talent and flair for fantasy, and she came to rely on his loving counsel. Liza later claimed that Sally Bowles, her Oscar-winning part in *Cabaret,* was influenced more by her father's insights than by her director Bob Fosse's ideas.

Designed as a star vehicle for Liza, the movie musical *Cabaret* opened to rave reviews. As expected, it gathered numerous Oscar nominations, including Best Picture, Director, Actress, and Supporting Actor. In 1972, the competition for Best Actress was quite intense. There were so many excellent performances that narrowing them down to five became an impossibly difficult job for the Academy. Liza was facing Oscar anxiety for the second time. She had been nominated in 1969, for her first starring role, in Alan Pakula's *The Sterile Cuckoo*, but hadn't expected to win. Three years later, with her second nomination for *Cabaret,* the expectations were higher.

Liza's first nomination was not a happy occasion for her or her father. A week before the Academy Awards show, she fell off a motor scooter, and the doctors had to patch her up so that she could attend the ceremonies. As Liza recalled, "Part of my front tooth was missing, and the doctor gave me a shot because I had a busted shoulder. I had my arm in a sling." Hanging on her ailing father, Liza joked about how they qualified, each for his own reasons, as Hollywood's "hottest" and "coolest" couple that night. When Maggie Smith was announced the winner (for *The Prime of Miss Jean Brodie*), Liza applauded spontaneously. Minnelli was nervous, but Liza claimed that she didn't even know that it was her category. "I'd been in such pain," Liza recalled. "Whatever the doctor had given me had made me woozy."

While Liza was rehearsing *Cabaret*, Minnelli helped her conduct extensive research about her role, stressing Sally's physical and psychological transformation as the story unfolds. Liza was trying to visualize Sally's look because the author of the literary source, Christopher Isherwood, had provided only a sketchy description of her in his *Berlin Stories*.

When Minnelli first asked Liza, "What are you going to look like as Sally?" she went blank.

"I don't know," she said. "What should I look like?"

"I don't know yet," Minnelli said, "but don't you worry, we'll find out."

Three days later, Liza walked into her father's study and found on his desk stacks of books and photos about the era for her to study. Over the years, when Minnelli had been talking about the necessary research that goes into preproduction for each movie, it had sounded vague to Liza. But now that it applied directly to her work, Liza immediately grasped the practical meaning of extensive research.

Minnelli told Liza, "You should look special, but like your real self." But what exactly did he mean by that? To Liza, it sounded like a contradiction in terms.

Based on her own research, Liza initially chose a Marlene Dietrich look, but Minnelli convinced her to create instead a more pixieish appearance with hat, halter top, bow tie, garters, and black net stockings, elements that would later become Liza's unique *Cabaret* trademark, a signature style that would mark her future one-woman shows.

A meticulous director, known for his rigorous attention to detail, Minnelli advised Liza to listen carefully to Bob Fosse's direction and to watch her dailies in his presence. Liza obeyed, and she reported to her father about the good rapport that prevailed between her and Fosse, on screen and off.

During the shoot of *Cabaret,* Minnelli began to experience a strange feeling that something extraordinary was happening to his daughter. Excited about getting the part, Liza immediately immersed herself in studying Sally Bowles's multifaceted personality. It was a great part for any actress, but particularly for Liza at this early but crucial juncture of her career.

While shooting in Germany, Minnelli would get periodic telephone calls from her, some of them in the middle of the night, due to her neglect to take into account the time difference between the continents. But he didn't care.

"I don't know if I'm doing it right, Daddy," Liza said.

"Listen to Bob Fosse," Minnelli advised, "he knows if it's fine. What are you uncomfortable about anyway?"

"Nothing in particular," Liza said, "except that it seems terribly hard."

"How does Fosse feel about it?" Minnelli asked.

"Well, he's pleased."

"Then, I'm sure it's okay," Minnelli said. "More to the point, how does your hair look?"

"It is cut in a point at the forehead."

Minnelli persisted, "In the rushes, darling, do you see yourself or do you see somebody else?"

"I think I see somebody else."

"Then you're on the right track," Minnelli reassured his daughter.

Several months later, Minnelli was extremely apprehensive when Liza took him to see a rough cut of *Cabaret.* Though Liza knew that the movie was good, she was uncertain about her own performance and was eager to find out her father's reaction. When the lights came up, Minnelli turned to Liza and said quietly but firmly, "It's truly one of a kind, and so are you, for that matter."

"Do you really think so, Daddy?"

"Absolutely," Minnelli said, "just trust me, just wait and see the reviews."

Minnelli was right. He liked the visual style of *Cabaret*, which he found to be more vivid than the stage play upon which the movie was loosely based. Assisted by Geoffrey Unsworth's evocative cinematography, Fosse captured the cynical and decadent mood of Berlin at the dawn of the Nazi era in a manner that would have been impossible in the Hollywood of Minnelli's era. Brilliant and innovative, *Cabaret* was the kind of movie musical that Minnelli would have liked to direct, particularly after the stale *On a Clear Day*. Made only two years apart, the two musicals were like day and night.

Minnelli praised Fosse's ingenious direction, which made the film a uniquely visual and visceral experience. *Cabaret* represented significant progress in the evolution of the Hollywood musical, after the stagnant 1960s, his own work included. It dazzled and thrilled, filled audiences with despair, and gave pause for sober thought. Boasting sophisticated if decadent wit and a singular vision, here was a real musical about a real issue, Nazism, not the escapist fluff that M-G-M was known for.

Minnelli was proud that Liza came through brilliantly. Her vitality was evident in every frame. Liza caught her character's defiance, her desperation, her sexual anxieties, her identity crisis. She was also impressive in her quiet moments, "like an animal in repose," Minnelli said. He had suggested that Liza play Sally Bowles as a girl who improvises her whole life, a woman whose fantasies distract her from the harsher reality. Minnelli saw immediately the personal dimensions of a role that, for better or worse, fitted Liza's own life like a glove.

At Oscar time, the pressures on the five nominated actresses, including Liza, were enormous. Minnelli escorted Liza to several industry functions before the March 27 Academy Awards presentation. "Are they doing to you what they're doing to me?" Liza asked fellow nominee Diana Ross. "Am I supposed to be your enemy?" Listening to these conversations made Minnelli more nervous about Liza's nomination than he had been about his own, years before. Times had obviously changed. Though there had always been tension surrounding the competition, in Minnelli's day there had been no nasty Oscar campaigns, no media blitz, no bad-mouthing, all of which began in the 1970s (and was to become even more pronounced in the future).

Minnelli grew increasingly disturbed by the inaccurate reports from the sob-sister stories in the press that Liza was penniless, still burdened with paying Judy's debts. With great dismay, he observed how Liza's annoyance changed into anger, and then from anger to impatience. Being a real trouper ran in the family, however, and she got through the agonizing weeks of Oscar campaigning just fine.

Meanwhile, Minnelli himself kept busy putting the final touches on a presentation he had written for a meeting with the principal backers of the picture he was eager to make with Liza. He suspected that the meeting had been scheduled for the day after the Oscars to distract Liza, in case she lost.

Oscar night was a very special occasion. Minnelli and Lee Anderson were ready at five o'clock sharp, when Liza and her date, Desi Arnaz Jr., came to pick them up in a studio limousine. Liza was dressed in yellow—as always, her father's favorite color. Sensing her dad's nervousness, Liza treated the event as if it were just another premiere. They chatted about this and that in the car, and jokes were exchanged; laughing the subject away was the only way to get through the ordeal.

Twenty-four

The Swan Song

THE SUCCESS OF *CABARET* AND LIZA'S ACADEMY AWARD enabled her to become more selective in choosing screen roles—at least in the short run. She now wanted to materialize a dream she had nurtured for decades. Ever since she first rode the camera boom at M-G-M watching her father direct, Liza had been dreaming of making a movie with him. Now, because of Minnelli's age, heart problems, and other ailments, time was running out. It was now or never, literally.

For several years now, Minnelli and Liza had been looking for the right property. It became a major challenge because *On a Clear Day* hadn't done well, even with La Streisand as its star. Minnelli had been interested in Maurice Druon's 1954 novel, *La volupté d'être,* translated as *The Film of Memory,* and inspired by the fabled adventures of the Marchesa Luisa Casati, circa 1910. The book chronicles the last days of a countess who had once subdued financiers, warriors, and other luminaries, but who now resides in a cheap hotel, where all she can do is relive her former triumphs. She's encouraged to do so by an awestruck chambermaid who, inspired by the countess, embarks on her own adventure.

Paul Osborn's stage version of the novel, *La Contessa,* which starred Vivien Leigh, was a failure. But Minnelli remained confident about the story's bittersweet tone, hoping that with a shift of emphasis in the script, the waiflike maid, Carmela, would be a good role for his Liza, under his helm.

Without a producer like Arthur Freed at his side, Minnelli struggled to adapt to the much harsher and more pragmatic Hollywood of the 1970s. He knew that the film would have to be an independent production. After acquiring the screen rights, Minnelli commissioned a script and began looking for financial backing. Writer John Gay, who had collaborated with Minnelli before, shifted Carmela from a bystander to the center of the countess's time-travel reveries. However, even with Liza's elevated post-Oscar clout, every major studio in town rejected the film.

As a last resort, Minnelli approached American International Pictures (AIP), best known for its cheap bikini, biker, and horror flicks of the 1950s and 1960s. Seeing an opportunity to upgrade AIP's image, its president, Samuel Z. Arkoff, allocated a budget of $5 million, which was way above the company's norm. Minnelli, anxious to terminate his creative drought, threw himself completely into the project, unwisely signing a contract that denied him final cut.

Minnelli flew to Europe to scout locations and assemble a skillful cast and crew for a film to be shot in Rome and Venice. The big challenge was to find a leading actress who could embody the countess's charisma and mystique. Minnelli wanted to cast Italian actress Valentina Cortese, but Arkoff wanted a bigger name and went after Ingrid Bergman, who had just won a third Academy Award for her supporting role in *Murder on the Orient Express*.

Well cast, Bergman played the senile, white-haired countess, once a gorgeous courtesan, but now lost in reverie, living in a seedy hotel. Bergman had her twin daughters in the picture as well: Ingrid and Isabella, in her first small part, as a nurse-nun named Sister Pia (the real-life name of Bergman's eldest daughter). Once Bergman was aboard, Minnelli coaxed Charles Boyer out of retirement to play her long-estranged husband; Boyer was initially happy, as he had costarred with Bergman in Cukor's 1944 thriller *Gaslight*.

The rest of the international ensemble evoked decades of movie history. Minnelli cast Amedeo Nazzari, the romantic Italian star of the postwar era, and for the part of the countess's lover, the veteran Spanish actor Fernando Rey. Tina Aumont, the daughter of Jean-Pierre Aumont and Maria Montez, played the chambermaid's cousin.

Enthusiastically, Minnelli hired cinematographer Geoffrey Unsworth, who had shot Liza's previous films, *Cabaret* and *Lucky Lady.* Though *Carmela,* as the film was first titled (after the name of the chambermaid), was not a musical, John Kander and Fred Ebb were asked to write two songs, one of them the title song.

Minnelli and Arkoff fought over Gay's scenario, which followed the book's parallels between the countess's past and her protégée's present. Arkoff demanded a bigger, more dramatic climax. Reluctantly, Minnelli agreed to shoot a few scenes with Carmela, now renamed Nina, as a screen legend in her own right. Rather naïvely, Minnelli believed that he could excise those additional scenes in the editing room, disregarding the fact that he had no final cut.

After six years of forced hiatus, Minnelli was now back at work. Shooting began in late 1975, as soon as Liza finished her commitments on *Lucky Lady.* He enjoyed directing Liza and Bergman in the same film. And he got a kick out of the locations, including the Venetian Palazzo Ca' Rezzonico, where he staged Nina's opulent imaginary incarnation. Working in the winter, however, was grueling for Minnelli, forcing him to move slower than usual. As a result, the budget began to escalate, and to the dismay of AIP, the scheduled fourteen-week shoot expanded to twenty weeks.

The stages were heated with portable gas burners that sucked much of the oxygen from the air, which left some of the cast with constant headaches. Working conditions in Italy and later problems at the film laboratories caused further delays, all of which were unfairly attributed to Minnelli's waning powers. The shoot, jinxed from the start, was aggravated by labor strikes and the shorter working hours that were customary in Italy.

In the past, Minnelli could always rely on M-G-M's expert technicians, who knew exactly what he wanted. However, he now found himself working with an unfamiliar crew and inadequate resources. On top of that, there was a language barrier: Minnelli's understanding of the Italian language was rudimentary. And his neurological problems, inarticulate speech, and lack of smooth communication with the cast only made things worse on the set.

People believed that the only reason Minnelli had gotten to direct the movie, which smelled of disaster from the start, was because of Liza. Understandably, Liza was overly anxious, knowing that this would be the only film she would make with her ailing father. She wanted the movie to be perfect. "I always wanted to work with Daddy," she recalled. "He's a genius, a perfectionist. From watching Daddy on the set, I learned not only about film but about life." During the shoot there were several kidnap threats against Liza, but she didn't tell her father about them and just arranged for tighter security.

Throughout the shoot the mood on the set was gloomy. Boyer was still depressed by the 1965 suicide of his only child and the terminal illness of his wife. (Two years later, in 1978, after his wife's death, he would take his own life.) Bergman tried to leaven the atmosphere of a doomed production, but she had a limited part, which basically called on her to encourage Liza's maid to become a kind of Italian Gigi.

In most of Bergman's movies it took only several takes to get her scenes right, but she had particular difficulties on the set of *A Matter of Time*. One morning, after blowing yet another long scene several times, she had lunch with the scholar Joel E. Siegel. "It's really not my business," he said, "but I think there's a typo in the text. There's a word missing, that's why it doesn't make sense." Leaning over, Ingrid whispered maliciously into Siegel's ear: "It's all rubbish." Siegel was stunned. No one had noticed—or cared.

Minnelli, nevertheless, was determined to make an "impressive yet personal" movie, one for which he and Liza would be remembered. While on the set, a blissfully happy Minnelli said, "It was only a matter of time. I've wanted to do a film with Liza much sooner than this. It's really the perfect part for her." Asked how it was to work with a legend like Ingrid, he replied, "They both are legends, Ingrid and Liza. Just look at Liza. She is as big a star today as Judy was, and yet she can go much further, if that's possible. I don't think the surface of Liza's talent has been scratched. There's much more to come out." As for similarities between Judy and Liza, Minnelli noted, "It's so hard to compare them. Liza is great, just like her mother, but she is great in different ways."

During the shoot Minnelli and Liza stayed at the Ambasciatori Palace Hotel in Rome. They both loved the Piazza Navona and the Roman

Forum, where Liza played a scene overlooking the site of Julius Caesar's assassination. Could life be better than that?

Journalist John Gideon Bachmann, who observed the production, wrote in *The Guardian*: "There is no doubt that this is a couple in love, and there's no doubt that they are not afraid of Judy's shadow. I have watched them shoot and rehearse and eat lunch and wait for Geoffrey Unsworth's lighting setups, and I have watched them watch the result of their labors in a screening room and with well-placed radio microphones, have listened in upon their intimate exchanges, and have found no chink in their oedophile armor."

Liza believed that in several scenes her father unintentionally made her look like Judy. Bachmann reported: "No wonder they both tell me, independently in conversation, that they have waited to work together until 'the perfect story came along.' Inasmuch as this one tells the tale of a young woman taking the place of an old one in the affections of a father figure . . . this is the perfect story."

The crew cracked up when, after every single scene, Liza eagerly asked, "Was I all right, Daddy, or should I do the scene again?" Minnelli adored every minute of directing Liza. "When I directed her," he later said, "I treated her just like I treated her mother, as a fine actress, marvelous comedian, and great tragedian."

During the shoot, while Bergman was doing a scene with Liza, Minnelli overheard the veteran actress, who was known for her pragmatically healthy attitude, sharing secrets of her trade, including how to survive tough films, how to maneuver in Hollywood, and even how to cry on screen. "Just use glycerin, darling," Bergman told Liza. "Don't be bashful. It works, trust me."

When edited, the film's first assemblage clocked in at three hours. Fearful that the whole project would collapse, Arkoff took the movie out of its director's hands. Minnelli's vision clashed with that of Arkoff, who threw out many of the flashbacks and eliminated one character entirely. Arkoff also tossed in some travelogue footage of Rome that Minnelli hadn't even shot. He disfigured the structure by enclosing the story within that of Nina-as-diva, which turned it into yet another vulgar version of *A Star Is Born*.

Arkoff's butchered editing resulted in a violent reaction, practically a crusade, by many of Hollywood's most powerful celebs. Director Martin Scorsese solicited every possible director to sign a protest petition, but to no avail. Appalled at the final cut, Minnelli disavowed association with the picture.

Sadly, Bergman took out her anger on Minnelli. Deeply upset, she realized that even if she took her name off the credits, everyone would still see her in the movie. Liza was the most miserable, for this was the movie she had long wanted to make with her father. The picture had been conceived as a showcase for Liza, but it turned out to be her second flop in a row, following *Lucky Lady,* which had opened on Christmas Day 1975, to poor reviews.

Even Vincent Canby, the usually generous *New York Times* critic, didn't like *A Matter of Time,* which opened October 7, 1976, at Radio City Music Hall. He wrote: "The film is full of glittery costumes and spectacular props. Liza Minnelli, whose appearance recalls her father and whose voice and mannerisms recall her mother, has talent of her own but it comes to us through the presence of others. Liza's eyes seem to have been widened surgically to play this part. *A Matter of Time* has moments of real visual beauty, but because what the characters say to each other is mostly dumb, it may be a film to attend while wearing your earplugs."

The New Yorker's Pauline Kael, outraged by Arkoff's mangling of the film, protested: "From what is being shown, it is almost impossible to judge what the tone of the film was, or whether it would have worked at any level. But even if his own version was less than a triumph, that was the film I wanted to see, not this chopped-up shambles."

Not surprisingly, with such a production history and negative reception, the film became a financial disaster. The consensus was that Minnelli's style of direction was dated, and that he had "lost his touch." To add insult to injury, the film was never released in Britain, France, and other European countries where Minnelli's work was popular.

Ultimately, *A Matter of Time* had less to do with moviemaking than with a father-daughter relationship. "Despite so many blunders and miscalculations," the critic Stephen Harvey said, "for those who care about Minnelli's movie legacy, *A Matter of Time* is a touching last farewell to the obsessions of three decades." For some, it was Minnelli's own memory film, in which he surveys his most treasured motifs, based on his knowledge that there would be no other chance to express them.

Minnelli's former wife, Georgette, held that *A Matter of Time* was Liza's gift to her father. Tina Nina, too, knew how much the project meant to her father. She recalled, "Daddy had so many ideas about the movie. He had me read the book, and we talked about it. He didn't have anything else on his mind."

Despite Scorsese's petition the film was an unmitigated disaster for both Minnelli and Liza. Rex Reed commented, "Liza should call it 'What I Did for Love.' How else can you explain this brainless gumbo of incompetence? Liza obviously did it to help out Daddy, who hasn't been getting too many jobs lately as a director."

While the failure of *A Matter of Time* was a blow to Liza, it was a real tragedy for her father. Minnelli's long-held fantasy of making a film with Liza was now being ridiculed. Minnelli knew that, with or without Liza, he would never be given the opportunity to make another film. Their only collaboration, *A Matter of Time* became the last hurrah for Minnelli, once one of Hollywood's most revered directors.

In the hot summer of 1976, several months before *A Matter of Time* opened, Liza was already involved in a new movie musical, *New York, New York,* a tribute to Hollywood's classic musicals, including Minnelli's own. The film costarred Robert De Niro and was directed by Martin Scorsese, who had become a hot director in the wake of *Taxi Driver,* which won the Cannes Festival's Palme d'Or. For the first time in her career, Liza was working at M-G-M, home studio of both her parents. Liza was assigned to Judy's old dressing room, and her hairdresser was none other than the veteran Sydney Guilaroff, the legendary stylist who had done Judy's hair.

Links to Liza's childhood pervaded the production. Scorsese extended an open invitation to visit the set, and Minnelli spent a number of days there. Scorsese had always admired Minnelli, and the two formed an instant rapport that would last until Minnelli's death.

During the shooting of the ballroom scene, when Liza, De Niro, and numerous extras celebrated VJ Day, Minnelli, seeing Liza with her 1940s hairdo, was overcome with emotion. In a shaky voice and trembling hands, he told Scorsese, "You know, Marty, Liza looks so much like Judy." Scorsese remained speechless.

Minnelli's visits to the set were emotional for other reasons. *New York, New York* was shot at the same studio where he had filmed his legendary musicals, *Meet Me in St. Louis* and *Gigi*. And some individual scenes were shot on Stage 29, where *An American in Paris* was filmed.

During the 1970s and '80s, the only real solace in Minnelli's life was his marriage to Lee Anderson. Despite his conviction that he was not suited for marriage, his fourth one was the happiest. Minnelli's life was enriched by Lee, and the new marriage became the most serene he had had. His close friends held that Lee's loving care and selfless devotion extended Minnelli's life by at least five years. Frustrated and unhealthy, he now suffered from cancer and was also developing Alzheimer's.

The failure of *A Matter of Time* brought Minnelli closer to Liza than he had been in years. However, he was unaware of the conflict between his two daughters and remained oblivious to the ongoing jealousy between them.

Occasionally, Liza visited Tina Nina in Mexico, on one occasion bringing her then husband, Jack Haley Jr. Tina Nina remembered, "We talked about Daddy a great deal, and Liza told me that he had a lot of financial problems because he couldn't work. Liza explained to me that it was hard for Daddy to understand that they weren't making films anymore like in the old days. He was used to working with choreographers, writers, and costumers, but not to working with the money men, which is how they made movies now."

Because of distance and other reasons, Minnelli didn't feel particularly close to his two grandchildren, Vincent Miro Minnelli, born in 1977, and Karla Ximena Miro Minnelli, born two years later. For years he had been sending Tina Nina a small monthly allowance. But now Liza pleaded with her half sister to ask their father not to send money anymore, promising to provide an allowance out of her own pocket. It was hard for Tina Nina to accept the new arrangement, because she needed the money to support her family. She also knew that Liza would not send her money—and Liza never did.

In her effort to terminate her half sister's allowance, Liza also appealed separately to Tina Nina's mother. Georgette recalled: "When Liza was in Mexico, she told me that I should write and tell Vincente not to send any money to Tina Nina. The law didn't dictate that he still contribute financially to Tina Nina, but as he still sent her money, I told Liza I thought it must make him happy. The money was a great help to Tina Nina, so I didn't write to him."

Liza then talked to her father about it. Weeks later, Minnelli called Tina Nina to say: "You know, I'm not doing very well, I'm not going to be able to send you the same amount of money, I'm going to send you a little less." A few months later, Minnelli just stopped sending money completely. Tina Nina said she never complained about it.

Georgette believed that Liza was instrumental in depriving Tina Nina of her father's allowance. But, as Georgette admitted, "We could all see that people were after Liza for money. We invited her to stay, to be in a family, so we could give her our love. When you are with Liza, she makes you feel you are important to her, and you believe it. Then, the very next day, there is nothing."

As many had predicted, Liza's marriage to Haley did not endure, but she didn't remain single for too long. Friends introduced her to Mark Gero, whom she later married. After the wedding ceremony, Halston hosted a black-tie reception for the newlyweds, attended by Hollywood's glitterati. Liza later said, "I only married Mark because my father told me to. I was proud of my mother, but I was really a daddy's girl." Asked how she had ever found a man to match her father, Liza noted, "Well, it took three tries." When Liza met Gero, he was a stage manager from a show business family. His decision to give up his work in the theater in order to concentrate on his art was viewed favorably by Minnelli the artist. But, alas, this marriage didn't work either.

Liza's devotion to her father grew even deeper as he got older and was fitted with a pacemaker. A frequent visitor to his home, Liza spent at least one day a month with her father, jazzing up his life with the latest showbiz gossip. She introduced him to some of her hip friends, like Michael Jackson, who were in awe of him and amazed by his unusual modesty.

Tina Nina continued to live in Mexico with her children, Vincent and Ximena. They were Minnelli's only grandchildren, but he never felt close to them. Tina Nina visited Minnelli from time to time, but she and Liza were never close because Liza was jealous. After all those years Liza still refused to acknowledge that her father had another child. Tina Nina recalled, "Liza was much more at ease and much closer to Daddy than I was. Daddy was her stability, and Liza was practically in love with him."

On Friday, November 23, 1980, Don Bachardy, the artist and Christopher Isherwood's longtime companion, was invited to draw Minnelli in his house. He worked in Minnelli's office, which was also the room where he and Lee were watching television. When Bachardy arrived at the side entrance off the driveway, the door was opened by a male servant dressed in a white jacket. Minnelli soon appeared and led him through the first floor of the house.

Bachardy's first impression of the house was that of a vast restaurant from the forties, one that had been sealed up for years but meticulously maintained. In the large living room, Minnelli pointed proudly to a self-portrait in oil by "the only painter allowed to work in the Vatican." "Liza loves it," Minnelli said. But Bachardy found the portrait characterless and ineptly done.

Lee had asked Bachardy to come at two thirty, and he began work around three, too late to use natural light at this season of the year. Minnelli and Bachardy were both nervous, but neither cared to admit it, each relying on his professionalism to fortify his attitude. Minnelli mustered concentration and showed no resistance. He sat motionless for two hours, during which he asked for only one brief coffee break. Occasionally, Minnelli looked Bachardy in the eye, though the artist felt that direct confrontation didn't come easily to him.

Bachardy proceeded to record what he perceived as Minnelli's wide-eyed, almost crazed stare. Dreading disapproval, Bachardy was relieved when the Minnellis professed enthusiasm for the drawing. However, Lee made a strange comment: "I've never before seen Vincente with his mouth open." She left the room to get Bachardy a drink and didn't return for nearly twenty minutes, which made him nervous.

During Lee's absence, Minnelli watched TV. Enervated by the ordeal of being drawn, he had no strength to do anything else. Bachardy noticed a book about his movies on a cocktail table, along with magazines with essays about him and a book of photographs of American directors, which included one of Minnelli. Through the television's distracting drone, Minnelli spoke occasionally, though he had trouble finding the words he wanted. Bachardy got the impression that the words existed in the back of Minnelli's head, but that he was struggling to search for the right word and then say it.

Lee finally returned with the drinks, and they all watched the TV news together. The Minnellis' behavior with each other was mutually affectionate, though Bachardy became suspicious of their extraordinary patience and sweetness toward each other. For him, it was tainted with the fear of death.

On December 4, Lee called Bachardy and told him that they didn't like his drawing. She cited the "staring eyes" and "open mouth," describing both gestures as "untrue" of her husband's expression. Bachardy sensed that their belated reaction must have been brewing. Since they hadn't asked for a photograph of the drawing, he hadn't sent them one. Lee's call must have been prompted by Bachardy's letter, in which he sincerely thanked Minnelli for his patient cooperation. Bachardy also confided that he was still uncertain about his feelings about the drawing, though he was intrigued by its "unusual intensity."

Bachardy promised Lee not to exhibit the drawing in public. But then he realized that she expected more of him, perhaps to do another drawing of Minnelli. She didn't want to suggest it herself, fearing it might sound like a paid commission. "I'd be delighted to try again," Bachardy said, "if Mr. Minnelli would be willing to sit a second time."

Bachardy did a second drawing of Minnelli, on December 12. Minnelli's concentration and stillness were as flawless as at the first sitting, though he was careful to keep his mouth shut. This time around, the Minnellis were delighted with the result. As for Bachardy, he was as pleased with the second drawing as he was with the first. Forced to choose, however, he favored the first, partly because of Minnelli's stare and open mouth, which revealed a delicate sensitivity that he thought essential to Minnelli's character. At the very least, the earlier drawing had a "real aliveness."

On February 19, 1983, for her father's eightieth birthday (on the 28th), Liza orchestrated a reception for him at the Palm Springs Desert Museum. Several weeks after the Palm Springs tribute, Liza included a tribute to her father's movies in her new concert tour.

In March, Liza paid another tribute to her father at New York's Museum of Modern Art. Minnelli was too ill to make the cross-country trip, but he sent his daughter a telegram that, unsurprisingly, began with stage instructions: "My darling Liza, first of all, as your father, let me remind you to stand up straight and speak slowly."

The evening's most exciting moment was a speech delivered by Lillian Gish, who had starred in *The Cobweb*. Making a toast, Gish said: "Liza, you're Vincente's greatest production!" Liza was always troubled by the fact that the world adored her mother but ignored her father. She had always thought that her equally talented dad had never been given the accolades he deserved.

Minnelli's health deteriorated rapidly in the mid-1980s, and he very seldom left his house. In addition to his heart ailment and cancer, Minnelli was now suffering from a severe case of Alzheimer's. He would begin a sentence quite coherently, but after uttering a few words, he would get stuck and end up stuttering.

When Liza received word that her father was seriously ill, she canceled the rest of her tour and rushed to his side in Los Angeles. Minnelli took great comfort in Liza's company. Being near his wife and daughter had a soothing effect on him. Liza spent two days with her father, reassuring him he was going to get better, and that she and Mark were still hoping to have a baby.

Comedian-director Carl Reiner recalled that he once arrived at Minnelli's house to find Liza sobbing. Liza explained that she had been crying because, for the first time in years, she and her father had watched *Meet Me in St. Louis*, together the first film in which Minnelli had directed her mother.

Sadness descended on the Minnelli household. Suffering from various terminal illnesses, Minnelli found it hard to talk and he couldn't write. He could understand what was going on, but he couldn't really express himself. Once, when Liza took him to see a show, he suddenly clutched her arm. Looking at her helplessly, he said, "You know, I live inside myself."

Liza spent July 23 and 24 of 1986 with her father at his house. They talked about her plans to have a baby, and she asked for his advice on songs and clothes for her concert tours. Then, on the 25th, feeling that her father was holding his own, she took a plane to Nice for her next concert date.

That night, Lee cooked her husband one of his favorite suppers, scallops and snow peas. After dinner, Minnelli quietly slipped away and went to bed. It was that night, while Liza was flying to France, that Minnelli died in his sleep. The cause of death was a fatal combination of pneumonia and emphysema, after years of heavy smoking.

Liza was still on the plane over the Atlantic when Frank Sinatra learned through the Hollywood grapevine of Minnelli's death. Fearing that the media would surround Liza before she even learned of her father's death, and before she was prepared to cope, he arranged for a phone call to the Nice airport to reach Liza before she would be confronted by the newshounds.

As soon as she landed and heard her name paged, Liza knew that something very bad must have happened. Sinatra tried to convey the sad news to her as gently as he could. Stunned that her father had died only a few hours after she had seen him, Liza immediately flew back to Los Angeles.

Tina Nina learned of her father's death from her stepfather, who had just heard it on the radio. He had guessed correctly that no one else had called to inform Tina Nina.

When Minnelli was in the hospital, Lee kept telling Tina Nina that everything was all right and that she didn't need to come up from Mexico. Tina Nina had become friendly with Minnelli's nurse, Brenda Moore. When Tina Nina arrived for the funeral, Moore told her, "I'm so glad you came. They weren't going to tell you anything until everything was organized."

Tina Nina was not sure whether Moore meant that it had just slipped their mind, or whether they had decided to wait until the details were worked out to make it less painful for her.

Having gone through agony with her mother's funeral, Liza was faced with another emotionally charged event, exacerbated by conflicting expectations of the family members. Minnelli had requested that his ashes be disposed of by the survivors as they saw fit. However, as it had been when Judy Garland died, everyone was against cremation. Wishing to preserve Minnelli's reputation as a great artist, Liza and Lee were determined to give Minnelli a Hollywood funeral that would befit his status. On the other hand, respectful of her father, Tina Nina wanted to follow his wishes. She reminded Liza that their father hadn't wanted a funeral, but Liza went ahead and arranged for one anyway, a big show-biz affair with buffet and drinks at the house afterward.

Minnelli couldn't be buried in Beverly Hills because the city has no cemeteries. An elegant funeral service was therefore held at Forest Lawn Memorial Park five days after his death. Landscaped with sculptures and murals, Forest Lawn has been the resting place for many of Hollywood's famous stars. The service took place in the "Wee Kirk of the Heather" chapel with a priest, George O'Brien, presiding. More than a hundred friends, family, and three generations of Hollywood stars gathered at what became a grand ceremony, in a place that resembled one of M-G-M's lavish sets.

Among the mourners were Bob Hope, Kenny Rogers, Jimmy Stewart, Henry Mancini. As the mourners left the chapel, the organist played "Embraceable You," the song that several years earlier Minnelli had sung to his daughter, upon her request. Actors Kirk Douglas and Gregory Peck, both of whom had worked with Minnelli, spoke most eloquently about him. Peck referred to Liza's recent performance in New York at the Statue of Liberty celebration on July 4. "I've been thinking of how much of Vincente there was in Liza's performance, that sensibility that is beyond professionalism, to the point that transcends reality." Of Minnelli the person, Peck said, "He was a man who literally gave his life to reach for the distant star, to create works that a hundred years later will glow with life and power."

Douglas called Minnelli a wonderful man with mysterious ways, noting that despite their years of collaboration and friendship, the core of

Minnelli's nature remained private, and the actor could never quite pen-
etrate it. Douglas speculated that perhaps that secret place was where his
art came from. Minnelli himself would have been the last person capable
of explaining its mystery. For Douglas, Minnelli's movies endure as both
his own composite self-portrait and a glass that reflects the time and
place that nurtured him. But, as Minnelli always insisted, "the mirrors
must be beautiful."

Douglas then concluded his remarks with a poignant observation
about Minnelli, the artist and the man: "I loved Vincente, but I found he
was a difficult man to know. Enigmatic Vincente with that boyish laugh.
He was a man of mystery. The mystery unfolds in his work and the
vivid memories he has given the world for generations to come."

But perhaps it was Liza who said it best, when she compared the impact that her parents had on her life: "My mother gave me my drive,
which is the basic way I am, but my father gave me my dream. My father
taught me nothing was impossible, nothing was out of the question.
There's always a way to accomplish something."

Indeed, accomplishment is a key word to describe Minnelli's existence. As noted, he was never entirely pleased with his work, or with his
life. Early in his childhood, he stood in front of a mirror and observed,
"You're nothing. Really nothing. What have you done?" It's an image
that continued to preoccupy him for the duration of his life, despite numerous artistic achievements, box-office hits, Academy Awards, and
various other tributes.

Minnelli was always gratified that the French and British critics understood and appreciated his work better than their American counterparts, a partial result of his "specialized" genres, the cheerful musical
and the somber melodrama, two relatively debased types of films in the
eyes of American critics. The principal adornment on Minnelli's mantel-
piece was the French parchment naming him Commander of the Legion of Honor.

He treasured a personal call that he received from Gene Kelly before
they worked together. It came after the premiere of *Meet Me in St. Louis,*
and the star both enthused and complained: "I'm angry. God damn it.
They don't appreciate what a fine thing you did. They don't realize what
went into it." Kelly thought that Minnelli deserved at least an Oscar
nomination for that picture, and so did producer Mike Todd after seeing

another underestimated picture, *Lust for Life*. Using the same words as Kelly, Todd wrote: "God damn it. They don't appreciate it."

The relatively low esteem in which Minnelli was held by most American critics of his era was also evident in his obituaries, in July 1986. In Paris, in the pages of the prestigious *Le Monde,* Minnelli's death was front-page news, prompting lengthy essays on his unique stature and distinguished contribution as Hollywood's "preeminent magician of color and camera movement." By contrast, in his own country, the *New York Times* obituary devoted more space to Minnelli's marriage to Judy Garland (and her suicide attempt with him as hapless witness) than to his Broadway and Hollywood work.

As Stephen Harvey wrote in his eloquent essay in *Film Comment*: "This was the predictable finale to Minnelli's slow fade over the last two decades, during which he was the least honored of Hollywood's great directors emeriti. Ford, Wyler, and Capra got their medallions from the AFI, while Lincoln Center paid homage to Cukor and Huston; Wilder and Hitchcock were respectfully roasted on both coasts."

Some of this neglect stemmed from Minnelli's personality as a shy, modest, and insecure artist, who never understood the prerequisites for canonization, unlike Capra and, especially, Hitchcock, who manipulated the press and orchestrated campaigns to elevate his stature.

Cut to seven or so years ago, when I committed to do a full-length biography of Minnelli and told friends and colleagues that it was going to be the first one in English. "No way," they said. "Are you sure?" I was, and with the exception of two academic books, there's still not a single account of Minnelli the artist and the man, placed against the social and cultural context of the times in which he lived and worked.

It is with the hope that I have made some contribution to the understanding of Minnelli the man, the artist, and his work that I'd like to conclude this book.

Conclusion

Minnelli's Legacy

BETWEEN 1942 AND 1962, MINNELLI DIRECTED twenty-nine films at
M-G-M, eventually becoming the studio's longest-tenured, highest-paid,
and most prestigious director. Minnelli's career at the studio was by no
means restricted to musicals; he also directed many successful comedies
and elegant melodramas.

Minnelli's career was the single driving force of his life. His wives,
companions, and friends always complained that he was married to his
work. In their arguments and eventual divorce, his first wife, Judy Garland, accused him of favoring the interests of M-G-M over her personal
and professional ones.

Like some other Hollywood directors, Minnelli first received serious
critical recognition from foreign film critics. French critics writing in
Cahiers du Cinéma and British critics in *Movie* championed him in the
late 1950s and early 1960s as one of Hollywood's consummate filmmakers, an artist and craftsman of the first order.

Now, in the first decade of a new century, it is time to ask, what is
Vincente Minnelli's film legacy? What did he accomplish as a film artist
and under what conditions?

The Artist in a Factory

Several notions about Minnelli have persisted over the years, such as the idea that he was an artist trapped in Hollywood's factory, a victim of the studio system who suffered under the tight control of M-G-M's top executives. However, my research shows that nothing is further from the truth. Unlike some directors who floundered and often crashed in the studio system, Minnelli blossomed, reaching artistic heights that he could not have accomplished without the steady support of M-G-M and its specialized departments. Yes, there were strains and conflicts, but there was also tremendous help, based on the division of labor along more or less defined lines, that prevailed at M-G-M.

As a member of the Freed Unit, he benefited from the opportunity to work with the biggest stars, greatest musical talents, and finest craftsmen. This roster of varied and gifted personnel helped Minnelli form his uniquely cinematic vision, which encompassed all aspects of production. Although a perfectionist, Minnelli knew his limitations. He was not a producer or a writer, which worked against him in the 1960s, when the studio system declined. Moreover, he was endowed with a passive-aggressive personality, on the set and off, and while he always knew intuitively what he wanted, he often found it hard to articulate it and communicate it to his actors.

In good times and bad, Minnelli never lost his passion for work and for the creative process. As he once observed: "There's nothing as exhilarating and challenging as getting a film project off the ground: The tantrums, the feuds, the emergencies, the race against time, the sudden salvation of high humor, which comes on and has you pounding the floor."

High Art and Mass Culture

For many moviegoers, Minnelli exemplified the best of Hollywood's mass entertainment, a positive concept in his world. Admired for his wild sense of color and dynamic camera movement, Minnelli was blessed with an aesthete's temperament that recalled a long tradition of painters. Even while in Hollywood, he continued dreaming about being a painter in Paris, and toward the end of his life, he spent more and more time on his drawings and paintings.

It's crucial to remember that Minnelli was a modernist artist whose sensibilities were shaped in the 1920s and 1930s by the same forces that gave birth to modernist literature, painting, architecture, and dance. As such, his work bridged the gap between high art and popular culture, showing that the latter could have genuine artistic dimensions and that high art could have a popular base and wide commercial appeal.

James Naremore has correctly observed that Minnelli served as an emissary between the cultural margins and the center, feeding mainstream entertainment with its needs for novelty, innovation, and change—up to a point. Minnelli's historical importance at M-G-M rests on his ability to modernize entertainment, drawing on various, mostly nonfilmic sources.

From a very early age, Minnelli spent the little extra money he had collecting art books. First, they served as escape routes from solitude and shyness and later as sources of inspiration for his Broadway and Hollywood work. He consciously borrowed ideas from French art movements, such as the decorative art nouveau and the impressionist styles of the late nineteenth century and the post-impressionism of the twentieth.

He was particularly influenced by the romantic visions of the surrealists, exposing in Freudian ways the sexual and political unconscious. Minnelli directed the first surrealist ballet presented on Broadway, choreographed by the Russian immigrant George Balanchine, who later founded the New York City Ballet. Like his mentor and friend George Gershwin, he blended a European aesthetic with a uniquely American idiom, drawing on jazz, folklore, and other sources that combined the Old World with the New, a similarity of taste that explains his attraction to Gershwin's *An American in Paris*. Minnelli popularized ballet, which suffered from the American public's view of it as an elitist art form. In his correspondence, he often chose the word "dance," rather than ballet, to avoid the European (and feminine) connotations of the term.

In both his look and his outlook, Minnelli wedded the notions of the dandy aesthete with that of the commercial entertainer. In 1937, *Esquire* described him as "the incarnation of our preconceived notion of a 'Village type,' with the flat black hat with a wide brim, loose collar and no tie around his thin neck." In publicity releases, the Shubert Organization and Radio City Music Hall emphasized his vanguard taste: "A modernist, Minnelli revels in torch songs, music from the heart of Harlem, and picturesque angular furniture."

Never an intellectual, Minnelli considered himself to be something of a cultural sponge who absorbed all kinds of ideas from books, paintings, movies, and the zeitgeist. "I'm just as apt to throw myself into a thing that's very low class as the next guy," he used to say. Nonetheless, he made very few films that were crass or beneath his refined taste. Films such as *The Courtship of Eddie's Father, Goodbye, Charlie,* and *The Sandpiper* are exceptions to his usual high standards. But these pictures were directed in the last decade of his career, and not so much by choice. The first two were concessions to Hollywood's competition with television; the third was made when he was in his sixties and lacked the clout to demand more challenging projects.

Minnelli was an intuitive artist, more a flamboyant fabulist than a conventional storyteller. The critic Richard Schickel noted that Minnelli did not have an analytical mind, that he "seems to feel his way toward the solution of creative problems, clued more by visual ideas and, of course, musical ones than by any of the signs one might term 'literary.' "

Like some other major filmmakers—Hitchcock, Ford, and Sirk, among them—Minnelli firmly believed that genre pictures could serve as personal expressions of their directors' idiosyncratic sensibilities. Nonetheless, and for better or worse, Minnelli is mostly associated with one signature genre, musicals, even if, of his thirty-four features, only a third were musicals. As the "master of musicals," Minnelli is seldom given credit for his contribution to comedy, in the same way that Hitchcock is always described as the "master of suspense," Ford the "master of westerns," and Sirk the "master of melodrama," though all three had worked well in a wide variety of genres.

Genuine Auteur or Just Stylist?

As noted elsewhere, I consider Andrew Sarris to be the most influential film critic in American history. Yet one of the few disagreements I have had with his assessments of directors concerns Minnelli. For most of his career, Minnelli suffered from the notion that he was more of a decorative artist than an auteur, a perception that took hold after the 1968 publication of Sarris's *The American Cinema,* still considered the bible of auteurism.

Minnelli was often attacked for his stylistic flourishes, for believing in beauty rather than in art. He was charged with distracting audiences from narrative and dialogue with fancy camera angles. For Sarris, Minnelli was a director who believed that style could transcend substance, that the camera was powerful enough to transform trash into art. Hence, he deemed Minnelli's art as more visual than personal, more decorative than meaningful.

But even Sarris acknowledged that Minnelli "had an unusually somber outlook for musical comedy," a point of view that lent most of his films unexpected levels of depth and gravity. What provides justification for the subtitle of my book is the dark sensibility that prevails in all of Minnelli's films, not only his melodramas, a form expected to be somber and grave, but also his seemingly bright musicals and sunny comedies. He was the first to admit, "I love comedy that's played as tragedy, and vice versa." Of the comedies he saw later in his life, Minnelli particularly liked Elaine May's *The Heartbreak Kid* (1972) because "it was played for blood and was sophisticated, dealing with real feelings."

In a rare instance of self-aggrandizement, Minnelli once observed: "Some erudite types point to *An American in Paris* as the perfect example of the studio as auteur theory. I disagree. Though I don't minimize anyone's contributions, one man was responsible for bringing it all together. That man was me."

Nonetheless, his stylistic accomplishments worked against his being taken seriously as an auteur. By the late 1950s, he was dubbed by the critic Albert Johnson as "the master of the decorative image." No doubt, his films are impeccably crafted, filled with lush and stylized sets, exuberant long takes, subtly executed dissolves, and a fluidly mobile camera—all devices particularly suitable for presenting song-and-dance sequences in exciting spatial arrangements. Yet as Ed Lowry noted, this sensibility also informs the nonmusical sequences of Minnelli's films, which are marked by a liberal, nonjudgmental approach that allows both his screen characters and their audience greater freedom of movement and interpretation within time and space.

Thus, it's possible to demonstrate that Minnelli was an auteur in thematic, stylistic, and ideological terms. His films demonstrate vividly that concepts of art and artificiality run throughout his work. Stylization and artifice are addressed by musicals naturally, as in the baroque otherworldliness in *Yolanda and the Thief* or the interplay of character and actor in Fred Astaire's interpretation in *The Band Wagon,* but they also prevail in his melodramas.

Though style may occasionally overwhelm theme, it ultimately confirms Minnelli's contribution to the refinement of the strategies by which Hollywood films translate visual style into meaningful entertainment. A painful sense of self, and the impossibility of meaningful relationships, inform melodramas like *Some Came Running* and *Home from the Hill,* and it's no coincidence that principal characters in both films—Shirley MacLaine in the former, Robert Mitchum in the latter—end in death.

The dichotomy between appearance and reality is a theme that Minnelli explored repeatedly. He acknowledges the need for individualized existence, defined by innermost fantasies that strive for fulfillment. The tensions in his screen narrative (and his own life off screen) derive from the necessity to accommodate an ideal (and idealistic) world within the bounds of a more mundane reality.

The gap between dreaming and the waking life could be narrow or wide, but it's a recurrent motif throughout his oeuvre, often realized in his expressive use of light, color, décor, and composition. In *Cabin in the Sky,* waking up is more than a metaphor; it's a narrative device. The movie ends when Little Joe awakens in his bed and learns that his odyssey was a delirious and haunting nightmare adventure.

The artist's struggle to control or appropriate his external reality often fails, but it's a worthwhile pursuit, for without such battle there is no chance for freedom. Throughout Minnelli's work, he is concerned with different levels of reality and unreality, as in the self-reflexive meditation on the Hollywood industry, *The Bad and the Beautiful*. Contrast, however, the cynical and bitter view of Billy Wilder in *Sunset Boulevard* with Minnelli's more complex, ambiguous, and ultimately positive view of industry types in *The Bad and the Beautiful*.

This exploration of levels of fantasy/reality reaches its limitation in his last film, *A Matter of Time,* where the story of an aspiring actress (played by Liza Minnelli) becomes an examination of his own daughter's talents and persona, haunted by the ghost of her mother (and Minnelli's first wife, Judy Garland), not to mention the casting of the iconic Hollywood star Ingrid Bergman as the woman who feeds the young girl's fantasies.

Fantasies are almost always present in Minnelli's films, even when they address more "ordinary" themes in "realistic" settings. In these fantasies the narratives recede in order to allow free play of ideas on both symbolic and formal levels. In the musicals, they take the shape of an extended "ballet," most memorably the seventeen-minute dance that concludes *An American in Paris.* But equally powerful is Garland's erotic fantasy of Gene Kelly as "Mack the Black" in *The Pirate.*

In *Meet Me in St. Louis,* the strongest expression of style occurs in the nonmusical sequences, including the romantic interludes between Judy Garland and the boy next door played by Tom Drake, and of course in the horrific Halloween sequence, dominated by Margaret O'Brien, a child star who at the time was known for her upbeat personality. O'Brien's obsession with death (including the killing of the snow figures) and the overt morbidity in the movie as a whole may account for audiences' ongoing interest in the film.

In the comedy *Father of the Bride,* it's the sequence in which Spencer Tracy's fatherly anxieties come to the fore during the wedding, upon the realization that he is about to "lose" his daughter. The hallucinatory chase through a carnival in *Some Came Running* and the fast, hysterical car drives in *The Bad and Beautiful* and it quasi-sequel, *Two Weeks in Another Town,* are more about intense emotions and visual stylization than plot elements per se, offering escapes from the banalities of the real world, which Minnelli depicts as frustrating, limiting, and suffocating.

All of Minnelli's comedies explore rather serious themes. Some are critiques of America's new consumer culture of the 1950s. Notice the unnecessarily huge amounts of money spent on weddings and the lengthy, overblown, and exhausting preparations for them in *Father of the Bride.* Or the use of an outsize mechanical trailer as a metaphor for the shaky marriage of newlyweds Lucille Ball and Desi Arnaz in *The Long, Long Trailer. Father of the Bride* and its sequel, *Father's Little Dividend,* deal with the inevitable loss of a daughter, while *The Courtship of Eddie's Father,* a serio-comedy about a one-parent family headed by a male (Glenn Ford), was one of Hollywood's first films about the changing structure of American families. In this picture, the images that linger are those of the young boy (Ron Howard), forced to adjust to his mother's death, who is horrified to discover his deceased goldfish, his first real encounter with death.

The tentative or unstable nature of love, and the inability to reconcile domestic and professional demands, are evident in all of Minnelli's melodramas. But they may be at their most explicit in *The Cobweb,* where an argument over drapes for the recreation room in a mental institution ultimately reveals dark secrets, neuroses, and disorders among the staff members and their families, which are not much different from those of the patients they're supposed to "cure."

The Four Horsemen of the Apocalypse is considered to be one of Minnelli's weakest films, and yet in terms of visual style and color scheme it had a far-reaching impact on French, Italian, and American directors. Jean-Luc Godard's *Contempt,* considered to be one of his masterpieces, Luchino Visconti's *The Damned,* which costarred Ingrid Thulin (who had appeared in *Four Horsemen*), Bernardo Bertolucci's *The Conformist,* and Vittorio De Sica's elegiac period piece, *The Garden of the Finzi-Continis* all owe a debt and/or pay tribute to Minnelli. You can't understand Martin Scorsese's musical *New York, New York* without acknowledging Minnelli's influence, and not only because Liza Minnelli is the star and is made up to look like her mother in the 1940s.

Kinetic Art and Stylized Spectacles

Kinetic art defines Minnelli's work through deliberate camera movements and judicious use of color. Even his lesser musicals, such as *Yolanda and the Thief* or *Brigadoon,* rise above the polished if mediocre films produced by Arthur Freed in the 1940s and 1950s. Minnelli's talent was in blending a large number of seemingly random details into a visually harmonious and integrated format. But there were always exceptions, dizzying images and dazzling elements, which almost gave M-G-M art director Cedric Gibbons heart attacks.

To the best of my knowledge, scholars have not applied the concept of cinematic excess to Minnelli's work. By drawing on the work of Kristin Thompson, Linda Williams, and others, it's possible to show that Minnelli's films exemplify the struggle of two opposing forces, one that strives to unify a work and hold it together, and the other that defies inclusion in the structure and inevitably calls attention to itself.

As Stephen Heath noted, excess is useful in understanding films that do not or cannot exhaust the full range of visual imagery. This is particularly the case of Minnelli's richest and most complex narratives, which either defy or simply cannot contain the whole filmic system. The dense materiality of Minnelli's imagery creates spectacles that go beyond the nominal stories. In his elaborate mise-en-scène, there are elements not integral to the smooth and coherent operation of the narrative.

But excess doesn't necessarily weaken a film's emotional meaning or aesthetic impact, and in Minnelli's case, it may be more fruitful to focus on those excesses and tensions. Unlike most Hollywood directors of his time, Minnelli didn't hold that imagery must always serve the plot; he deviated from the classical Hollywood model that typically strives to minimize excess in favor of a seamless and invisible style.

Excess and spectacle are probably the reasons Minnelli admired Orson Welles for his good and coherent films (*Citizen Kane*) as well as the good and less coherent (*Touch of Evil*), which contain scenes that have no direct causal function for the plot and in fact divert attention from the action.

In Minnelli's work the most emotional moments are often excessive in terms of narrative needs, such as Margaret O'Brien's Halloween outburst in *Meet Me in St. Louis,* Lana Turner's hysterical drive in *The Bad and the Beautiful* (arguably the most powerful image in the picture), the Girl Hunt sequence in *The Band Wagon,* and of course the lengthy ballet in *An American in Paris,* which is virtually a film-within-a-film. Minnelli cultivated and cherished dissident thematic and stylistic moments that disrupt a movie's overtly intentional design, reflected in unmotivated events, rhythmic montages, parallel constructions, images flashed in ultra-light, and other self-conscious and playful sequences.

Queer Sensibility: Channeling Sexual Anxieties into Art

Over the past decade there's been a growing literature of queer sensibility, a rather vague but useful concept. As I discussed in my book *Cinema of Outsiders,* there are directors who imbue their work with a gay/queer sensibility regardless of the particular genre or narrative they work in; among them are Gus Van Sant, Todd Haynes, and Gregg Araki. This sensibility goes as far back as the studio system, reflected in the work of openly gay directors, such as James Whale and George Cukor, and bisexual ones, such as Minnelli.

Not surprisingly, Minnelli's most personal films, the good (*Lust for Life* and *Home from the Hill*) and the mediocre (*Tea and Sympathy* and *Designing Woman*), deal explicitly with sexual politics, gender roles as imposed by society, the meanings of masculinity, and stigmas and punishments that result from deviations from cultural definitions of manhood. I have devoted a lengthy analysis to these issues in the chapters discussing those films.

Which leads directly to the prevalence of creative types—artists, writers, journalists, dancers—in Minnelli's musicals, melodramas, and comedies. In his world, artists are gifted individuals doomed to existential isolation and emotional loneliness. Minnelli's humanistic perspective doesn't romanticize artists as "special" people—they're just more sensitive, and he devotes as much attention to their neuroses, petty jealousies, and moral and professional fears as to their unique talents and singular accomplishments.

Two Weeks in Another Town is a highly personal movie in more ways than one: It concerns the loss of control experienced by a once-powerful director (Edward G. Robinson) who now operates in an unfamiliar social and commercial environment. One of the harshest sequences in any Minnelli picture is the argument between Robinson and Claire Trevor, who plays his drug-addicted, suicide-prone wife, when he tells her not to take another overdose of sleeping pills, because they would just have to pump her stomach out again—and she knows how sick that makes her. You wonder how many times Minnelli had said something like this to Judy Garland.

Consider the artists and the sponsors in *An American in Paris*. Who's Milo Roberts, the woman enamored of Jerry who wants to help him financially and professionally? An American expatriate and nouveau riche, she bears a male name, is older than Jerry, and is not particularly attractive; we also get a feeling that Milo has done it before and will do it again. Is she a stand-in, as one of my students suggested, for a sugar daddy, an older rich man, perhaps gay, who's attracted to younger, attractive, potentially gifted males? Kelly's Jerry expresses his fear of being owned and patronized by Milo, and some questions remain. What would have happened if he had stayed with Milo and not Lise? Would he have developed into his own artist? Would she have continued to support (and to love) him if he didn't show results as a painter?

Laura in *Tea and Sympathy* is also more complex than she seems to be. Though married to a macho man, she is not the typical housewife; it's also her second marriage. She's seldom seen in the kitchen or indoors, which is traditionally women's domain, and the most crucial scenes are played out in exteriors, in her garden, on the beach, in the park.

In Minnelli's criticism of the gender roles as prescribed and proscribed by society, he dresses Tom in a blue suit before he goes to the town's whore, Elly. At one point, Tom himself states explicitly, "Put me in a blue suit and I look like a kid." Similarly, Laura is repeatedly told that she needs more blue, a color associated with maleness.

An Actors' Director

There is a misconception that Minnelli did not place emphasis on acting and didn't care about maintaining M-G-M's prestige as the studio of the stars, expressed in its popular catchphrase, "More Stars Than There Are in Heaven." A closer look, however, reveals that he worked mostly with stars, or with actors on the verge of stardom, and that he did care about acting, even if he despised the pretentiousness that often accompanied Method acting. For starters, Minnelli is single-handedly responsible for turning Judy Garland from a popular adolescent and Mickey Rooney's costar into a mature and beautiful dramatic actress, by directing two of her best performances in *Meet Me in St. Louis* and *The Clock,* her first nonmusical role.

While always reliable, Spencer Tracy also distinguished himself in a Minnelli film, *Father of the Bride,* giving a resonant performance for which he received his fourth Best Actor nomination, and which surpasses his back-to-back Oscar-winning turns in *Captains Courageous* and *Boys Town*.

Kirk Douglas, Minnelli's favorite actor, collaborated with him on three films in which the actor did his most iconic work as egotistical producer Jonathan Shields in *The Bad and the Beautiful,* the troubled artist Van Gogh in *Lust for Life,* and in *Two Weeks in Another Town*. The Rat Packers Frank Sinatra and Dean Martin complained about Minnelli's slowness and meticulous attention to the smallest detail, but they were assigned good roles in his pictures and delivered mightily.

Minnelli brought Fred Astaire out of semiretirement and displayed a new facet of him in *The Band Wagon*. He also encouraged Gene Kelly to polish his comedic and athletic skills in *The Pirate* and *An American in Paris*.

Although Minnelli didn't have a good professional rapport with Katharine Hepburn, due to a bad choice of vehicle in *Undercurrent,* he did develop a friendship with her off-screen. He often said that he regretted that Garbo was already retired from the screen by the time he arrived in Hollywood. He didn't care for the studio's other two queens,

Joan Crawford and Norma Shearer, who retired from acting in 1942, and he never worked with Greer Garson, Louis B. Mayer's favorite star in the 1940s, because he found her too stately. He also disliked another dominant M-G-M figure, Debbie Reynolds, because she was, as he put it, "unrefined," though he directed her in the 1960s at a movie made at Fox. On the other hand, he coaxed a haunting performance from Jennifer Jones in *Madame Bovary* that was far more impressive than her more celebrated Oscar-winning or Oscar-nominated roles.

Sheer Pleasure

Finally, a note about the sheer pleasure we derive from watching Minnelli's musicals, comedies, and melodramas, and why we keep revisiting such films as *Meet Me in St. Louis,* a staple on television every holiday season, which occupies a mythical status similar to that of Capra's *It's a Wonderful Life* or even *Casablanca.*

More than anything else, *An American in Paris* is a musical about visual pleasure, in which the protagonist creates through song and dance his own live and lively audience of children on the street, patrons of fancy cafés, and his own pals. It's also a movie about rhythm, as the American ex-G.I. makes clear when he sings "I Got Rhythm," and it's a stylized spectacle of and about Paris, a city whose long history and varied cityscapes offer Jerry (and Minnelli) the subject and inspiration for his paintings.

Hollywood's pleasure principle was a structure that governed a film's narrative, emotional, and psychological energy, leading to intense audience involvement and engagement, and sometimes even to complete identification. It's not necessary to be a film critic or a scholar to recognize the exuberance and charm that Minnelli's films and his stars continue to exude. What Vincente Minnelli, the dark dreamer, did better than other directors—and what Hollywood achieved better than other national cinemas—was to bind its audiences on deep psychological and emotional levels to movies, which went way beyond plot and character.

Notes

This book is based on four principal sources. First, the Special Minnelli Collection of letters, production files, photographs, drawings, and other materials at the Academy of Motion Picture Arts and Sciences Center for Motion Picture Study (AMPAS). Second, letters and documents that Minnelli's widow, Lee Anderson Minnelli, shared with me. Third, Minnelli's memoir, *I Remember It Well,* along with earlier versions of the manuscript, which are longer and more detailed, in the Special Collection. Last, the AMPAS Library has wonderfully detailed production files for each movie Minnelli directed. Unless otherwise specified, quoted passages come from the above sources. Complete bibliographical information on other sources mentioned below may be found in the section that follows.

1: Childhood
Sketches and notes for *The Show Is On* were provided by Lee Anderson Minnelli.
For a discussion of family influences on *Meet Me in St. Louis* and *The Long, Long Trailer,* see chapters 7 and 16, respectively.
For background information: Richard Schickel, *The Men Who Made the Movies*.

2: Chicago
For a discussion of Chicago as a cultural and architectural center, see William Howland Kenny, *Chicago Jazz: A Cultural History 1904–1930*.

The section on Whistler is based on E. R. and J. Pennell, *The Life of James McNeill Whistler*; and David Gerstner, "Queer Modernism: The Cinematic Aesthetic of Vincente Minnelli."

For details on the Balaban and Katz theaters, see David Balaban, *The Chicago Movie Palaces of Balaban and Katz*.

The history of Radio City Music Hall draws on various books, including Brooks Atkinson, *Broadway,* and Atkinson and Al Hirschfeld, *The Lively Years*.

3: Radio City Music Hall

For a detailed discussion of the New York theater scene in the 1930s, see Atkinson, *Broadway* and Atkinson and Hirschfeld, *The Lively Years*.

The section on *Vanities* is based on files at the New York Public Library for the Performing Arts at Lincoln Center.

Reviews of Minnelli's stage work are taken from *The New York Times* and the *Boston Herald*.

The discussion of Minnelli's social clique, which included the Gershwins, Dorothy Parker, and Oscar Levant, draws on books by and about these people: Levant, *The Memoirs of Amnesia* and *The Unimportance of Being Oscar;* Sam Kashner and Nancy Schroeder, *A Talent for Genius: The Life and Times of Oscar Levant;* John Keats, *You Might As Well Live: The Life and Times of Dorothy Parker;* Leslie Ferwin, *The Late Miss Dorothy Parker;* Steven Bach, *Dazzler: The Life and Times of Moss Hart;* Edward Jablonski, *Gershwin;* and Howard Pollack, *George Gershwin: His Life and Work*.

The anecdotes about Moss Hart are taken from the Special Minnelli Collection and Bach, *Dazzler: The Life and Times of Moss Hart*.

For Minnelli's work with Fanny Brice and Bert Lahr, see Herbert Goldman, *Fanny Brice: The Original Funny Girl;* Barbara Grossman, *Funny Lady: The Life and Times of Fanny Brice;* and John Lahr, *Notes on a Cowardly Lion: The Biography of Bert Lahr*.

Minnelli's work with Grace Moore is discussed in her memoir, *You're Only Human Once*.

4: New York, New York

Sketches and notes for Minnelli's shows *At Home Abroad, Hooray for What?* and *Very Warm for May* are in the collections of the Museum of the City of New York and the Metropolitan Museum of Art.

Brooks Atkinson's reviews of *At Home Abroad* and *Very Warm for May* appeared in *The New York Times*, September 20, 1935, and November 18, 1939, respectively.

"Prodigy," a profile of Minnelli, was published in *The New Yorker*.

The section on Josephine Baker is based on Jean-Claude Baker and Chris Chase, *Josephine Baker: The Hungry Heart;* Lynn Haney, *Naked at the Feast: A Biography of Josephine Baker;* and on Minnelli's letters.

Elliot Norton's articles about *The Ziegfeld Follies* appeared in *The Boston Post,* December 30 and 31, 1935.

Brooks Atkinson's review of *The Ziegfeld Follies* appeared in *The New York Times,* January 30, 1936.

Description of Minnelli's friendship with and admiration for Ira and Lee Gershwin is drawn from the Special Minnelli Collection and Edward Jablonski, *Gershwin;* William Hyland, *George Gershwin: A New Biography;* and Howard Pollock, *George Gershwin: His Life and Work.*

Born in 1904 and recently arrived from Russia, George Balanchine was not only the same age as Minnelli, but, like Minnelli, was an outsider in New York, albeit for different reasons. Minnelli's interaction with Balanchine and the influence the choreographer had on Minnelli's sensibility is drawn from Bernard Taper, *George Balanchine,* and Robert Gottlieb, *George Balanchine: The Ballet Maker.*

The Royal Family by Edna Ferber and George S. Kaufman opened on Broadway, December 28, 1927.

Minnelli hired the young Gordon Jenkins, who began his career doing arrangements for radio, to conduct *The Show Is On* after hearing the artist's arrangements for André Kostelanetz, which Minnelli admired.

John Mason Brown's review of *The Show Is On* appeared in *The New York Evening Post.*

On the friendship and the collaboration between Minnelli and Eleanor Lambert, see her notes on Minnelli in the Shubert Theatre

press releases at the Library for the Performing Arts at Lincoln
Center.

5: Broadway

For more on the Broadway theater scene in the late 1930s, see Atkinson, *Broadway*.

For a discussion of Jacques Feyder's *Carnival in Flanders,* see Roy
Armes, *French Cinema*. Paramount's *The Big Broadcast* movies and
Bing Crosby's "Road" Musicals.

S. J. Perelman's interaction with Minnelli draws on correspondence in
the Special Minnelli Collection.

For a detailed discussion of *Serena Blandish* by S. N. Behrman, see
Harvey, *Directed by Vincente Minnelli*.

On Minnelli's relationship and work with New York artists, see Vernon Duke, *Passport to Paris*.

On Minnelli's meeting with Samuel Goldwyn, see A. Scott Berg,
Goldwyn.

6: Hollywood: Early Years

For Busby Berkeley's approach to musicals, see Rubin Martin, *Show-
stoppers: Busby Berkeley and the Tradition of Spectacle;* and David
Thompson's 1988 documentary *Busby Berkeley: Going Through the
Roof*.

Minnelli had little respect for Busby Berkeley as a director. They were
barely on speaking terms after their interaction on *Cabin in the Sky*.
In fact, Berkeley's career as a director terminated just as Minnelli's
took off, though Berkeley continued to work in Hollywood as a
choreographer.

My description of Minnelli's association with producer Pandro Berman is drawn from Stephen Harvey, *Directed by Vincente Minnelli*
and correspondence belonging to Lee Anderson Minnelli.

My account of the making of *Panama Hattie* is drawn from AMPAS
production files. My discussion of Minnelli's musicals produced by
the Freed Unit is drawn heavily from detailed accounts in Hugh
Fordin, *M-G-M's Greatest Musicals: The Arthur Freed Unit*. Minnelli
never worked with Mickey Rooney, though he was one of M-G-M's
major stars of the 1940s.

Minnelli's work with Ethel Waters in *Cabin in the Sky* is described in her memoirs, *His Eye Is on the Sparrow* and *To Me It's Wonderful*.

Minnelli's work with Louis Armstrong is discussed in James Lincoln Collier, *Louis Armstrong: An American Genius*; Laurence Bergreen, *Louis Armstrong*, and Max Jones and John Chilton, *Louis: The Louis Armstrong Story, 1900–1971*.

The discussion of Lena Horne in *Cabin in the Sky* is drawn from an interview with her, as well as her book *Lena,* cowritten by Richard Schickel, and from James Haskins, *Lena*.

The notion of *Cabin in the Sky* as a version of the Faust legend is explored in Thomas Cooksey, "*The Devil and Daniel Webster, Cabin in the Sky,* and *Damn Yankees*: American Contributions to the Faust Legend."

Discussion of the censorship issues concerning *Cabin in the Sky* is drawn from files of the Production Code Administration at the AMPAS Library.

The reviews of *Cabin in the Sky* are from *The New York Times*, May 28, 1943; *Daily Variety* and *The Hollywood Reporter* January 1, 1943.

Minnelli's work on *I Dood It* is discussed in the film's AMPAS production files.

Bosley Crowther's review of *I Dood It* appeared in *The New York Times*, November 11, 1943.

7: The First Peak: *Meet Me in St. Louis*

My account of the making of *Meet Me in St. Louis* draws on many sources, including Fordin, *M-G-M's Greatest Musicals* and biographies of Judy Garland, among them Joe Morella and Edward Epstein, *Judy: The Films and Career of Judy Garland;* David Shipman, *Judy Garland: The Secret Life of an American Legend;* Gerold Frank, *Judy;* Gerald Clarke, *Get Happy: The Life of Judy Garland;* and Christopher Finch, *Rainbow: The Stormy Life of Judy Garland*. The analysis also draws on Scott Higgins, "Minnelli's Technicolor Style in *Meet Me in St. Louis*."

Mary Astor's role is discussed in her memoir, *A Life on Film*.

Bosley Crowther's review of *Meet Me in St. Louis* appeared in *The New York Times,* November 29, 1944.

Judy Garland's affair with Joseph Mankiewicz is discussed in Kenneth Geist's biography, *Pictures Will Talk: The Life and Films of J. L. Mankiewicz,* and Clarke, *Get Happy.*

Judy Garland's relationship with Yul Brynner is referred to in Rock Brynner's memoir of his father, *Yul: The Man Who Would Be King.*

8: A Fresh Look at Old Genres: *Ziegfeld Follies* and *The Clock*

For details on the making of *Ziegfeld Follies,* see Fordin, *M-G-M's Greatest Musicals;* and Harvey, *Directed by Vincente Minnelli.*

Bosley Crowther's review of *Ziegfeld Follies* appeared in *The New York Times,* March 23, 1946.

Judy's correspondence with Minnelli regarding *The Clock* and the personal letters are in the Special Minnelli Collection.

For Robert Walker's problems during the shoot of *The Clock*, I've drawn on correspondence in the Special Minnelli Collection and on Frank, *Judy.*

James Agee's review of *The Clock* appeared in *The Nation,* June 9, 1945.

A. H. Weiler's review of *The Clock* appeared in *The New York Times*, May 4, 1945.

9: Falling in Love

Lena Horne's description of Minnelli's role as a Svengali comes from an interview with her, as well as material from her 1981 one-woman show, *Lena Horne: The Lady and Her Music.* Judy's affair with Orson Welles is described in several biographies, among them Barbara Learning, *Orson Welles.*

Accounts of Judy's marriage as they appeared in the press are drawn from the syndicated columns of Hedda Hopper and Louella Parsons.

Lester Gaba had a successful career staging elaborate fashion shows in the 1940s and '50s. He also wrote a weekly column for *Women's Wear Daily*, but he was best known for the life-size mannequins that he carved from soap for store window displays. Gaba died in 1987.

Bosley Crowther's review of *Yolanda and the Thief* appeared in *The New York Times,* November 23, 1945.

The Minnellis' wedding took place on June 15, 1945, followed by their honeymoon in New York later that month.

Laurette Taylor's impression of Judy appears in the Special Minnelli Collection.

10: Husband and Father

For Minnelli's work on *Till the Clouds Roll By,* I've drawn on Fordin, *M-G-M's Greatest Musicals* and the Special Minnelli Collection.

Bosley Crowther's review of *Till the Clouds Roll By* appeared in *The New York Times,* December 6, 1946.

Discussion of Oscar Hammerstein's lyrics draws on Fordin, *M-G-M's Greatest Musicals* and his *Getting to Know You: A Biography of Oscar Hammerstein II.*

Minnelli's and Judy's work conditions and compensation at M-G-M are taken from their contracts in the Special Minnelli Collection.

Oscar Levant described the Minnellis' social life in great detail in *The Memoirs of Amnesia* and *The Unimportance of Being Oscar;* see also Kashner and Schoenberger, *A Talent for Genius.*

The section on *Undercurrent* is based on the film's AMPAS production files as well as an interview with Katharine Hepburn.

Bosley Crowther's review of *Undercurrent* appeared in *The New York Times*, November 29, 1944.

11: The Great Debacle: *The Pirate*

S. N. Behrman's *The Pirate* opened on Broadway on November 23, 1942, and starred Alfred Lunt and Lynn Fontanne.

Cole Porter's music for *The Pirate* is discussed in William McBrien, *Cole Porter: The Definitive Biography.*

Gene Kelly's observations on the making of *The Pirate* derive from Kelly's published interviews; Clive Hirshhorn, *Gene Kelly;* and the 2005 PBS *American Masters* documentary "Gene Kelly: Anatomy of a Dancer."

Hedda Hopper's visit to the set is documented in the Special Minnelli Collection and in Clarke, *Get Happy.*

The *New York Times* review of *The Pirate* appeared May 21, 1945. Charles Walters replaced Minnelli as director on *Easter Parade* and was later nominated for an Academy Award for *Lili,* which was offered first to Minnelli.

12: Scandalous Melodrama: *Madame Bovary*

Correspondence regarding censorship issues about *Madame Bovary* is
found in the MPAA and AMPAS production files of the film.

The casting of Jennifer Jones is discussed in Rudy Behlmer, *Memo
from David O. Selznick,* and Edward Epstein, *Portrait of Jennifer*.

My description of Minnelli's work with James Mason is drawn from
Mason's memoir, *Before I Forget*.

The comparison of *Madame Bovary* to Minnelli's musicals is drawn
from Harvey, *Directed by Vincente Minnelli*. My discussion of the
film also derives from Robert Lang, *American Melodrama: Griffith,
Vidor, Minnelli*.

Bosley Crowther's review of *Madame Bovary* appeared in *The New
York Times,* August 26, 1948.

13: Problems with Judy

Judy's stay at Casa de las Campanas and Austen Riggs clinics is documented in various books and documentaries about her, but the account here is drawn primarily from Clarke, *Get Happy*. Minnelli's
views of Judy's mental problems are described in his letters in the
Special Minnelli Collection.

The account of the Minnellis' separation and divorce is taken from
contemporary newspaper reports, Minnelli's memoir, and various
Garland biographies, including Clarke, *Get Happy;* Morella and
Epstein, *Judy: The Films and Career of Judy Garland;* Shipman, *Judy
Garland: The Secret Life of an American Legend;* Frank, *Judy;* and
Finch, *Rainbow: The Stormy Life of Judy Garland*.

14: *An American in Paris*

Minnelli's relationship with Dore Schary, head of M-G-M, is described in the latter's autobiography, *Heyday*.

The account of the casting of Spencer Tracy in *Father of the Bride* is
drawn from an interview with Katharine Hepburn and biographies of Spencer Tracy by Bill Davidson and Larry Swindell.

The previews of *Father of the Bride* and its sequel are documented in
the films' press files at AMPAS.

Bosley Crowther's review of *Father of the Bride* appeared in *The New
York Times*, May 19, 1950.

Bosley Crowther's review of *Father's Little Dividend* appeared in *The New York Times*, April 13, 1951.

My account of the making of *An American in Paris* draws on numerous sources, primarily Fordin, *M-G-M's Greatest Musicals;* Rick Altman, *The American Film Musical;* and Gerald Mast, *Can't Help Singin': The American Musical on Stage and Screen*.

Interpretation of the musical draws on Donald Knox, *The Magic Factory: How MGM Made An American in Paris;* and Lindsay Anderson, "Minnelli, Kelly, and *An American in Paris*."

Alan Jay Lerner discusses his work on the picture in Paris in his memoir, *The Street Where I Live;* see also Edward Jablonski's biography, *Alan Jay Lerner*.

For the casting of Leslie Caron, I've drawn on interviews given by her at the Los Angeles County Museum of Art tribute to *An American in Paris* and *Gigi,* interviews given by Gene Kelly, and Hirschhorn, *Gene Kelly*.

The analysis of the lengthy ballet in *An American in Paris* is based on Minnelli's letters and drawings in the Special Minnelli Collection.

The influence of French painting on the ballet is discussed in Angela Dalle Vacche, *Cinema and Painting: How Art Is Used in Film*.

The analysis of the symbolic meaning of French and American culture is drawn from Mast, *Can't Help Singin': The American Musical on Stage and Screen*.

My account of the critical and public response to *An American in Paris* was drawn from the AMPAS production files.

The Oscar campaign for *An American in Paris* and the account of the Academy Award ceremony draws on my book *All About Oscar* and the film's Academy Awards files at AMPAS.

Bosley Crowther's review of *An American in Paris* appeared in *The New York Times,* October 5, 1951.

Observations of Liza Minnelli's childhood are drawn from letters in the Special Minnelli Collection.

15: Minnelli's Masterpieces: *The Bad and the Beautiful* and *The Band Wagon*

The comparison between *The Bad and the Beautiful* and *Citizen Kane* is drawn from James Naremore, *The Films of Vincente Minnelli*.

The cycle of pictures on show business that began in 1950 with *All About Eve* and *Sunset Boulevard* continued for several years, and included *The Barefoot Contessa, In a Lonely Place,* and *The Big Knife*.

For Kirk Douglas's work in *The Bad and the Beautiful* (and later, in *Lust for Life*), I've drawn on an interview with him, letters exchanged between him and Minnelli in the Special Minnelli Collection, and Michael Munn, *Kirk Douglas*.

Descriptions of Lana Turner's work in *The Bad and the Beautiful* draw on her autobiography, *Lana: The Lady, the Legend, the Truth;* Morella and Epstein, *Lana Turner;* and the film's AMPAS production files.

Discussion of design elements, color, and editorial cuts on *The Bad and the Beautiful* draws on correspondence between Dore Schary and producer John Houseman in the film's AMPAS production files.

My account of Minnelli's work with John Houseman, here and throughout, on *The Bad and the Beautiful, The Cobweb,* and *Lust for Life* draws on various volumes written by Houseman, including *Run-Through, Final Dress, Front and Center*, and *Unfinished Business: A Memoir*. Information about the previews and public response to *The Bad and the Beautiful* are taken from the film's AMPAS production files.

Bosley Crowther's review of *The Bad and the Beautiful* appeared in *The New York Times,* January 16, 1953.

The *Los Angeles Times* review of *The Bad and the Beautiful* appeared December 28, 1952.

Naremore, in *The Films of Vincente Minnelli,* makes an interesting comparison between Minnelli and Orson Welles, who was an inspirational model for Minnelli.

For Minnelli's failed effort to make *Huckleberry Finn,* I've drawn on this film's AMPAS production file.

For *The Story of Three Loves* and Minnelli's work with Ethel Barrymore, I've drawn on her memoir, *Memories: An Autobiography,* as well as materials in the Special Minnelli Collection.

For a detailed comparison between "Mademoiselle" and Minnelli's last film, *A Matter of Time,* see Harvey, *Directed by Vincente Minnelli*.

Bosley Crowther's review of *The Story of Three Loves* appeared in *The New York Times,* March 6, 1953.

The discussion of the screenplay for *The Band Wagon* is based on an interview with Betty Comden.

The selection of songs for *The Band Wagon* is discussed in Fordin, *M-G-M's Greatest Musicals.*

The images of Hollywood and American society in *The Band Wagon* are analyzed in Dennis Barone, "A 'Natural' Environment: Hollywood."

The discussion of the musical's structure draws on Mast, *Can't Help Singin': The American Musical on Stage and Screen.*

My analysis of the "Dancing in the Dark" sequence draws on Eric de Kuyper, "Step by Step."

For Minnelli's work with Fred Astaire and Cyd Charisse, I've drawn on the Special Minnelli Collection; Harvey, *Fred Astaire;* and Tony Martin and Cyd Charisse, *The Two of Us.*

Bosley Crowther's review of *The Band Wagon* appeared in *The New York Times,* July 10, 1953.

16: Minnelli Loves Lucy

Minnelli's work with Lucille Ball is discussed in the AMPAS production files on *The Long, Long Trailer* and in Kathleen Brady, *Lucille: The Life of Lucille Ball;* and Charles Higham, *The Life of Lucille Ball.*

Bosley Crowther's review of *The Long, Long Trailer* appeared in *The New York Times,* February 19, 1954.

For a discussion of consumerism in American culture, see Harvey, *Directed by Vincente Minnelli.*

The section on *Brigadoon* is based on Fordin, *M-G-M's Greatest Musicals.*

Bosley Crowther's review of *Brigadoon* appeared in *The New York Times,* September 17, 1954.

Alan Jay Lerner describes his disappointment with *Brigadoon* in *The Street Where I Live.*

Liza Minnelli's recollection of her childhood is based on her essay in Minnelli's memoir, *I Remember It Well.*

Christiane Nina Minnelli's relationship with her sister, Liza Minnelli, draws on George Mair, *Under the Rainbow: The Real Liza Minnelli* and other sources.

17: Up and Down: Contract Director

My account of the making of *The Cobweb* draws on files in the Special Minnelli Collection as well as the film's AMPAS production files.

The correspondence between Dore Schary, John Houseman, and Minnelli is taken from the Special Minnelli Collection.

The *New York Times* review of *The Cobweb* appeared August 5, 1955.

For a discussion of Minnelli's melodramas, see Thomas Schatz's *Film Genres*.

Jack Cole's work on *Kismet* draws on the film's AMPAS production files, as well as Glenn Loney, *Unsung Genius: The Passion of Dancer-Choreographer Jack Cole* and Stephen M. Silverman, *Dancing on the Ceiling: Stanley Donen and His Movies*.

Stanley Donen's contribution to *Kismet* is analyzed in Joseph Andrew Casper, *Stanley Donen*.

Bosley Crowther's review of *Kismet* appeared in *The New York Times,* December 9, 1955.

18: Personal Films: *Lust for Life* and *Tea and Sympathy*

The discussion of the production of *Lust for Life* is based on material in the Special Minnelli Collection.

For analysis of *Lust for Life*'s color and design scheme, see Naremore, *The Films of Vincente Minnelli*.

Anthony Quinn's account derives from his memoir, *The Original Sin: A Self Portrait*.

Bosley Crowther's review of *Lust for Life* appeared in *The New York Times,* September 18, 1956.

The standing of the film at the Oscars is based on the film's Academy Awards files at AMPAS.

The discussion of Deborah Kerr's role in *Tea and Sympathy* is taken from an interview with her and from Eric Braun's *Deborah Kerr*.

The correspondence between *Tea and Sympathy* playwright Robert Anderson, producer Pandro Berman, and Minnelli is based on the PCA and production files at AMPAS, as well as on Jerold Simmons's article, "The Production Code Under New Management: Geoffrey Shurlock, *The Bad Seed,* and *Tea and Sympathy*" and John

Lewis, *Hollywood v. Hard Core: How the Struggle over Censorship Saved the Modern Film Industry.*

For more on Elia Kazan's Broadway production of *Tea and Sympathy,* see Richard Schickel's biography, *Elia Kazan,* and Kazan's memoir, *A Life.*

For an anaylsis of the symbolic meaning of *Tea and Sympathy*'s color scheme, see David Gerstner, "The Production and Display of the Closet: Making Minnelli's *Tea and Sympathy.*" Some of my ideas regarding *Tea and Sympathy* came out of a stimulating panel on the film at the 2003 Provincetown Film Festival with my colleague, Thomas Doherty.

For a discussion of Minnelli's preoccupation with masculinity, see Harvey, *Directed by Vincente Minnelli.*

The discussion of *Tea and Sympathy* draws on David Zinman, *50 from the 50's: Vintage Films from America's Mid-Century.*

Bosley Crowther's piece on *Tea and Sympathy* appeared in *The New York Times,* October 7, 1956. His review ran on September 28, 1956.

For Minnelli's work with Gregory Peck and Lauren Bacall on *Designing Woman,* I've drawn on interviews with the actors, the film's AMPAS production files, Bacall's memoir, *By Myself,* and Michael Freedland's biography, *Gregory Peck.*

Bosley Crowther's review of *Designing Woman* appeared in *The New York Times,* May 17, 1957.

19: The Height of His Career: *Gigi*

The analysis of the making of *Gigi* draws on the Special Minnelli Collection and Digby Diehl's article, "Vincente Minnelli and *Gigi.*"

The correspondence between Arthur Freed, Cecil Beaton, and Minnelli draws heavily on Fordin, *M-G-M's Greatest Musicals.*

Cecil Beaton's correspondence draws on his article, "Beaton's Guide to Hollywood," and his book, *The Restless Years: Diaries 1953–63.*

The account of Minnelli's work with Maurice Chevalier is taken from Michael Freedland's biography, *Maurice Chevalier.*

Discussion of *Gigi*'s previews and commercial performance, and the response of critics is drawn from the film's AMPAS production files.

Minnelli's correspondence with Colette's husband, Maurice Goudeket, is documented in the Special Minnelli Collection.

Bosley Crowther's review of *Gigi* appeared in *The New York Times,*
May 18, 1958.

The analysis of *The Reluctant Debutante* is based on an interview with
Rex Harrison as well as on his memoir, *Rex: An Autobiography*.

Minnelli's admiration for Kay Kendall was expressed in a series of letters and interviews about her given after her death in 1958.

My account of Minnelli's work with Sandra Dee and John Saxon is
taken from Darin Dodd and Maxine Paetro, *Dream Lovers: The
Magnificent Shattered Lives of Sandra Dee and Bobby Darin*.

A. H. Weiler's review of *The Reluctant Debutante* appeared in *The
New York Times* on August 15, 1958.

20: Master of Melodramas: *Some Came Running* and *Home from the Hill*

The discussion of Minnelli's work with Frank Sinatra and Dean Martin in *Some Came Running* derives from the film's AMPAS production files as well as Alan Frank, *Sinatra*, and William Schoell,
Martini Man: The Life of Dean Martin.

The casting of Shirley MacLaine is discussed in correspondence between Minnelli and Frank Sinatra in the Special Minnelli Collection.

Minnelli's expressed complaints about the misconduct of the Rat Pack
actors in his letters are held in the Special Minnelli Collection.

Some Came Running was part of Hollywood's late-1950s cycle of
small-town melodramas, which included, among others, *The Long
Hot Summer* and *Cat on a Hot Tin Roof*. For a discussion of this
cycle, see Harvey, *Directed by Vincente Minnelli* and my *Small-Town
America in Film*.

Location shooting problems on *Some Came Running* are discussed
in producer Sol Spiegel's letters in the film's AMPAS production
file.

Bosley Crowther's review of *Some Came Running* appeared in *The
New York Times,* January 23, 1959.

My account of Minnelli's work with Robert Mitchum and George
Peppard on *Home from the Hill* comes from my interviews with
Mitchum and the film's AMPAS production files, as well as Jerry

Roberts, *Mitchum: In His Own Words;* and George Eels, *The Robert Mitchum Story.*

Bosley Crowther's review of *Home from the Hill* appeared in *The New York Times,* March 4, 1960.

The analysis of melodrama as a genre draws on the writings of Andrew Sarris in a series of articles published in *The Village Voice,* as well as Frank Rahill, *The World of Melodrama.*

The issues of melodrama as a genre that deals with moral and legal concerns derives from Robert Lang, *American Film Melodrama: Griffith, Vidor, Minnelli.*

21: The Party Is Over

My account of the making of *Bells Are Ringing* draws on an interview with Betty Comden.

Minnelli's communication with Judy Holliday and Dean Martin derives from the film's AMPAS production files; Gary Carey, *Judy Holliday: An Intimate Life Story;* and Schoell, *Martini Man: The Life of Dean Martin.*

Bosley Crowther's review of *Bells Are Ringing* appeared in *The New York Times,* June 24, 1960.

For background information on *The Four Horsemen of the Apocalypse,* see Harvey, *Directed by Vincente Minnelli.*

The casting of Glenn Ford and Ingrid Thulin is discussed in correspondence between Minnelli and producer Pandro S. Berman in the Special Minnelli Collection.

Charles Boyer's reluctance to appear in the film is discussed in Larry Swindell, *Charles Boyer: The Reluctant Lover.*

Bosley Crowther's review of *The Four Horsemen of the Apocalypse* appeared in *The New York Times,* March 10, 1962.

My account of the making of *Two Weeks in Another Town* draws on an interview with Kirk Douglas, Minnelli's interview about the film in *Wide Angle,* the film's AMPAS production file, and Peter Bogdanovich, *Pieces of Time.*

My discussion of melodrama draws on Lang, *American Film Melodrama: Griffith, Vidor, Minnelli.*

The casting of the film, specifically Edward G. Robinson and Cyd Charisse, is discussed in the film's AMPAS production files.

The influence of Fellini's *La Dolce Vita* is mentioned in Harvey, *Directed by Vincente Minnelli*.

The location shoot of *Two Weeks in Another Town* in Rome and Venice is discussed in articles in *Photoplay* and *Films and Filmmakers*.

Bosley Crowther's review of *Two Weeks in Another Town* appeared in *The New York Times,* August 18, 1962.

Most of the information on *The Courtship of Eddie's Father* comes from the Special Minnelli Collection and the film's AMPAS production files.

Bosley Crowther's review of *The Courtship of Eddie's Father* appeared in *The New York Times,* March 28, 1963.

My comparison between the careers of Minnelli and George Cukor draws on my *George Cukor: Master of Elegance*.

Minnelli's negotiations for, and his failure to be assigned to, the film version of *My Fair Lady* draws on my interview with agent Irving Lazar, as well as Richard Stirling, *Julie Andrews: An Intimate Biography*.

The description of the making of *Goodbye, Charlie* is based on the film's AMPAS production files.

Minnelli's interaction with Tony Curtis and Debbie Reynolds derives from Curtis and Barry Doris, *Tony Curtis: The Autobiography*.

22: Being Idle

My account of the making of *The Sandpiper* draws on the Special Minnelli Collection.

The casting of Elizabeth Taylor and Richard Burton is discussed in Donald Spoto, *A Passion for Life: The Biography of Elizabeth Taylor* and is drawn from biographies of Richard Burton, including Hollis Alpert, *Burton*; John Cottrell and Fergus Cashin, *Richard Burton: Very Close up*; and Paul Ferris, *Richard Burton*.

Minnelli's problems on the set of *The Sandpiper* were detailed in a 1964 interview with Richard Burton in *Newsweek*.

Andrew Sarris's evaluation of *The Sandpiper* and the stars appeared in *The Village Voice* on July 21, 1965.

Bosley Crowther's review of *The Sandpiper* appeared in *The New York Times,* July 16, 1965.

Judith Crist's review of *The Sandpiper* appeared in the *New York Herald Tribune*, July 16, 1965.

Despite negative reviews, *The Sandpiper* was one of Minnelli's most commercially successful films.

Minnelli's wish to work with Henry Fonda and direct *Who's Afraid of Virginia Woolf?* are mentioned in the film's AMPAS production file.

Liza Minnelli's relationship with her stepmother Denise is described in an early version of her father's memoir held in the Special Minnelli Collection, as well as in books about Liza Minnelli.

Liza Minnelli's courtship and marriage to Peter Allen is discussed in Minnelli's memoirs as well as in biographies of Judy Garland, including Clarke, *Get Happy;* and Frank, *Judy*.

23: Life Is a Cabaret

For a detailed account of the making of *On a Clear Day You Can See Forever,* see the Special Minnelli Connection.

Alan Jay Lerner's screenplay for the picture is discussed in his book *The Street Where I Live,* and in Jablonski, *Alan Jay Lerner*.

Minnelli expressed admiration for Barbra Streisand in letters held in the Special Minnelli Collection as well as in published interviews at the time the film was made.

Streisand's, work on the picture is described in Donald Zee and Anthony Fowle, *Barbra*.

The casting of Yves Montand draws on correspondence in the Special Minnelli Collection, as well as on Yves Montand with Hervé Hamon and Patrick Rotman, *You See, I Haven't Forgotten*.

My account of Jack Nicholson's casting is based on the film's AMPAS production files and David Robert Crane and Christopher Fryer, *Jack Nicholson: Face to Face*.

Vincent Canby's review of *On a Clear Day You Can See Forever* appeared in *The New York Times,* June 18, 1970.

Nicholson's description of Minnelli's work appeared in an interview he gave to Rex Reed, which appeared in *The New York Times,* March 21, 1970.

Joe Morgenstern's review of *On a Clear Day* appeared in *Newsweek*, June 25, 1970.

Arthur Knight's assessment of *On a Clear Day* appeared in *The Saturday Review,* November 6, 1965.

Minnelli's failed effort to make a picture with Liza about Zelda
Fitzgerald draws on Unrealized Film Projects files in the Special
Minnelli Collection.

Minnelli's contribution to Liza's look and his advice about her performance in *Cabaret* is drawn from letters exchanged between them
held in the Special Minnelli Collection.

My account of the Academy Awards presentation at which Liza won
for Best Actress draws on my *All About Oscar*.

24: The Swan Song

My account of the making of *A Matter of Time* is drawn from Harvey,
Directed by Vincent Minnelli.

The casting of Ingrid Bergman and Charles Boyer is described in
Donald Spoto, *Notorious: The Life of Ingrid Bergman*.

The description of location shooting draws on Gideon Bachmann's
reporting in *The Guardian,* and *Film Comment*.

Ingrid Bergman's view of the production is taken from an interview
conducted by Joel Siegel.

Vincent Canby's review of *A Matter of Time* appeared in *The New
York Times,* October 8, 1976.

Pauline Kael's protest against the cutting of the film appeared in *The
New Yorker* on November 1, 1976.

Minnelli's visit to the set of *New York, New York* is based on interviews given by Martin Scorsese, as well as on my interview with
Lee Anderson Minnelli.

The account of Don Bachardy's visits to the Minnellis' home is taken
from his book, *Stars in My Eyes*.

The 1983 tribute to Minnelli at New York's Museum of Modern Art
is described in a booklet published by MoMA to benefit the Annual
Fund, March 2, 1983.

Minnelli's last months were described to me by Mrs. Lee Anderson
Minnelli.

Minnelli's funeral, including the eulogies delivered by Gregory Peck
and Kirk Douglas, were described to me by Douglas and were
quoted in the obituary in *Variety*, July 30, 1986.

Stephen Harvey's eulogy appeared in *Film Comment*.

Conclusion: Minnelli's Legacy

Thomas Elsaesser, a professor at the University of Amsterdam, discusses Hollywood's pleasure principle as a governing structure for movie studio films in two essays on Minnelli published in the *Brighton Film Review*, 1969 and 1972.

Index

VM stands for Vincente Minnelli.

Academy Awards, 1, 367–68, 377–78
Actors Studio, 328
Adams, Stanley, 52
Adrian (costume designer), 46, 196, 221
adultery, as movie theme, 173, 281, 289
Adventures of Huckleberry Finn (1939),
    230
affairs, as movie theme, 259
Agee, James, 128
Albee, Edward, 360
All About Eve, 225
Allen, Peter, 361–63
Allen, Richard, 39
Allenberg, Bert, 280
Allenby, Frank, 180
Alsop, Carleton, 182–83, 187, 189–90
Alton, John, 200, 208, 213, 291
Alton, Robert, 72, 147, 162
An American in Paris, 1–2, 28, 166, 175,
    195, 198, 240, 386, 397, 399, 404,
    405, 406

Best Picture Oscar, 214–17
reviews of, 217
seventeen-minute dance in, 214, 401,
    403
American International Pictures (AIP),
    380
American middle class, 321
Ames, Leon, 97, 114, 203
Ames, Preston, 95, 208, 209, 212, 213,
    237, 257, 266, 279, 291, 299
Anderson, Eddie "Rochester," 86, 89
Anderson, Iain F., 248
Anderson, John Murray, 46–47
Anderson, Lee (VM's fourth wife), 7,
    364, 373–74, 378, 386, 388–89, 392
Anderson, Lindsay, 324
Anderson, Robert, 280, 289
Anderson, Sherwood, 22
Andrews, Edward, 284
Andrews, Julie, 334
Angeli, Pier, 258

Annie Get Your Gun, 181, 184, 188–91, 206

Ansco Color (Metrocolor), 244, 273

Anski, S., 60

Araki, Gregg, 403

Arden, Eve, 47

Ardrey, Robert, 173, 175, 271, 336

Arkoff, Samuel Z., 380–81, 383–84

Arlen, Annie, 52

Arlen, Harold, 29, 38, 52–53, 56, 62, 63, 71, 91, 145

Armstrong, Louis, 62, 86, 89

Arnaz, Desi, 10, 241, 243, 401

Arnaz, Desi, Jr., 378

Arnold, Edward, 119

Aronson, Boris, 39

Around the World in 80 Days, 279

Art Institute of Chicago, 17, 22

artists, tormented, as protagonists, 317, 404

Artists & Models, 61, 62

Asher, Betty, 123, 132, 139

Astaire, Adele, 238

Astaire, Fred, 60, 72, 115–16, 118, 119, 120, 136, 138–39, 171, 186–87, 221, 235, 238, 368, 405
   top hat and cane, 235–36

Astor, Mary, 104

At Home Abroad, 41–43, 47, 55, 119, 235

Atkinson, Brooks, 44, 51, 54, 68

Aubrey, James, 334

Aumont, Tina, 381

auteur theory, 239, 399

Axelrod, George, 349, 350–51

Ayres, Lemuel, 99

Baba (black poodle), 68, 95

Bacall, Lauren, 260, 261, 290, 349

Bachardy, Don, 388

Bachmann, John Gideon, 383

The Bad and the Beautiful, 74, 178, 198, 223–30, 234, 241, 279, 400, 401, 403, 405
   reviews of, 228–30

Baker, Josephine, 48–49, 132

Bakst, Leon, 29, 197

Balaban, A. J., 23

Balaban and Katz chain, 22–24

Balanchine, George, 39, 47, 48, 72, 397, 409

Ball, Lucille, 10, 33, 118, 120, 241, 242, 243, 313, 401

Ballard, Dr. Francis, 190

Ballbusch, Peter, 209–10

ballet in film, 72, 214, 397

Ballets Russes, 29

Balmain, Pierre, 313

Bancroft, Anne, 360

The Band Wagon, 27, 68, 138, 175, 178, 198, 221, 224, 230–40, 293, 310, 399, 403, 405
   reviews of, 240
   title for, 236

The Barefoot Contessa, 225

The Barkleys of Broadway, 182, 186–87, 206

Barnes, Howard, 139

Barnes, Joanna, 351

Barrett, Rona, 218

Barrie, Grace, 52

Barrymore, Ethel, 232–33

Barrymore, John, 226

Beardsley, Aubrey, 22

Beaton, Cecil, 297, 299–300, 302, 303–4, 307–8, 367

Behrman, S. N., 65, 145, 160

Beiderbecke, Bix, 22

Bell, Chris, 361–62, 363

Bell, Marion, 120

Bells Are Ringing, 310, 331–34

Bemelmans, Ludwig, 136–37

Benchley, Robert, 29

Ben-Hur, 335–36, 368

Bennett, Joan, 199–200, 205

Benny, Jack, 123, 198–99, 202

Benny, Mary, 123

Benson, Sally, 96, 230

Bergerac, Jacques, 300
Bergman, Ingrid, 158, 234, 288–89, 380, 382, 383, 384, 400
Berkeley, Busby, 76, 80, 104, 147, 188
  VM's dislike of work of, 72–73
Berkson, Seymour, 27–28, 410
Berlin, Irving, 56, 167, 184, 186, 206, 334
Berman, Pandro, 75–76, 156–57, 172–73, 175, 180, 198–99, 242, 243, 282, 310–11
  biography, 198
Berry Brothers, 77–78
Bertolucci, Bernardo, 402
The Big Knife, 225
biopictures, 148, 150, 270, 271, 372
Birinski, Leo, 57, 58
bisexuality movie theme, 350
bisexuals, as Judy's and Liza's mates, 361–63
black and white films, 229
Blackboard Jungle, 264
black press, 85
blacks, childlike stereotypes of, in musicals, 85
Blair, Betsy, 167
Blake, Madge, 251
Blane, Hugh, 230
Blane, Ralph, 99
Blasco Ibáñez, Vicente, 335
Blaustein, Julian, 336
blue, VM's use of, 286–87
Blyth, Ann, 266
Bogarde, Dirk, 297, 337
Bogart, Humphrey, 291
Bolger, Ray, 38
Bonwit Teller, 16
Boone, Pat, 351
Booth, Margaret, 342–43
Borodin, Aleksandr, 265
Boudin, Eugène, 299, 307
Bowles, Paul, 39
Box Office Blue Ribbon Award, 250

Boyer, Charles, 260, 337, 380, 382
Bradley, Josephine, 311
Bradshaw, George, 224
Brady, Ruth, 108
Brecher, Irving, 97, 99, 105, 137
Brecht, Bertolt, 44
Breen, Joseph, 90, 248
Breen office, 161, 173, 280
Bremer, Lucille, 101, 105, 115–16, 120, 136, 138, 148
Brentano's bookstore, 21
Brice, Fanny, 38, 47, 48, 50, 118, 119
Brigadoon, 246–50, 297, 402
The Broadway Melody, 70
Broadway theater, 27, 32–33, 62–69
  big-screen adaptations of, 73
Bromfield, Louis, 65–66
Bronson, Charles, 356
Brooks, Richard, 70, 324
Broun, Heywood, 21, 34
Brown, Clarence, 33
Brown, John Mason, 54
Bruce, Virginia, 57
Bryna production company, 271
Brynner, Yul, 112
Buchanan, Jack, 236–37, 238
Buchholz, Horst, 338
Buñuel, Luis, 22, 57
Burke, Billie, 46, 202
Burstyn, Ellen, 351, 352
Burton, Richard, 354–60

Cabaret, 374–78
Cabin in the Sky, 29, 67, 76, 83–93, 132, 137, 175, 400, 410
Cabot, Sebastian, 266
Cagney, Jimmy, 62
Cahiers du Cinéma, 217, 224, 309, 395
calendar art, 276
Cambria, Frank, 23, 25, 26
Camelot, 331, 365
camera, movement of the, 82–83, 227
camp sensibility, 161

Canby, Vincent, 369, 384
Cannes Film Festival, 337
Canova, Judy, 48
Carlisle, Kitty, 145
Carmichael, Hoagy, 52
Caron, Leslie, 1, 208, 211–12, 217, 223,
    232–33, 297, 298, 303, 304, 307
Carousel (show), 144
Carroll, Earl, 29–30
Carroll, Leo G., 202
Carter, Desmond, 30
Cartier, Jacques, 27
Casanova's Memoirs, 22
Catholic Legion of Decency, 282, 284
Cat on a Hot Tin Roof, 323
censorship, 90, 173, 175, 280, 288, 340,
    346
  self-, 305
  of sex scenes, 340
Cézanne, Paul, 22
Champion, Marge and Gower, 197
Chaplin, Charlie, 14, 64, 235
Chaplin, Saul, 209, 212
Charisse, Cyd, 115, 120, 228, 238,
    248–50, 291, 340–41, 342
Charisse, Nico, 221
Chesterton, G. K., 26
Chevalier, Maurice, 208, 297–98, 300,
    302, 308, 309, 337
Chicago, 15–26
  art scene, 22
  French Colony, 15
Chicago Theatre, 22–24
child abuse
  in filmmaking, 102–3
  as hidden movie theme, 296
Chodorov, Edward, 156–57
Chumley's, 27
Cinecittà studios, 335
CinemaScope, 242, 272
cinematographers, 208
Citizen Kane, 224–25, 403
Claire, Ina, 19, 252, 298

Cleopatra, 359
Clift, Montgomery, 337
The Clock, 121–27, 134, 203, 233, 405
  reviews, 128
Coast to Coast, 37–38
The Cobweb, 28, 238, 243, 258–65,
    401–2
  critics on, 264–65
Cocteau, Jean, 22, 57
Cole, Jack, 46, 266–67, 291
Colette, 207, 254, 296, 305, 307, 309, 366
Colman, Benita, 183
Colman, Ronald, 183, 265
color
  in the European theater, 29
  in films, 116
  VM's use of, 20, 50–51, 197, 274,
    286–87
color films, 229, 272–73
Columbus, Ohio, 12, 13–14
Comden, Betty, 207, 235, 240, 331–33,
    334
comedies, 243, 313, 399
  noir, 202
composers for films, 79
Condon, Eddie, 22
The Conformist, 402
Connelly, Marc, 41
Constantin Guys, 299
consumer culture, 401
Contempt, 402
Coppock, Al, 56
Corman, Roger, 369
Cortese, Valentina, 380
Corwin, Norman, 271–72, 279
The Courtship of Eddie's Father, 243,
    346–48, 398, 401
  critics on, 347
Craig, Gordon, 21
Crane, Norma, 288
Crawford, Joan, 79, 406
creative types as protagonists, 404
Crist, Judith, 357

Crouse, Russell, 63

Crowther, Bosley, 95, 139, 216, 240, 250, 289, 322–23

Cukor, George, 79, 83, 96, 133–34, 177, 232, 294, 313, 333–34, 345, 348–49, 403

Cummings, Jack, 75, 95, 195–96, 197

Curtis, Tony, 350, 352

Curtiz, Michael, 1

Dailey, Dan, 77

The Daily Variety, review, 92

Dalí, Salvador, 16, 22

The Damned, 402

Damone, Vic, 266

Dana, Leora, 322

Dancing in the Dark, 235

Dancing Sambo toy, 8

Davis, George W., 356

Davis, Lutor, 265

Davis, Sammy, Jr., 355–56

Dean, James, 260, 287

Deans, Mickey (Garland's third husband), 360

Decision Before Dawn, 215

de Cordova, Freddie, 50, 53, 111

DeCuir, John, 368

Dee, Sandra, 311

Degas, Edgar, 274

Delaware, Ohio, 9–10, 13

Minnelli family move to, 7

Delon, Alain, 337

Del Ruth, Roy, 77, 93, 119

de Mille, Agnes, 249

DeMille, Cecil B., 59

De Niro, Robert, 385

Derain, André, 263

Dern, Bruce, 370

De Sica, Vittorio, 402

Designing Woman, 241, 243, 290–95, 403

Deutsch, Adolph, 203

Deutsch, Helen, 223

diegetic sound, 203

Dietrich, Marlene, 265

Dietz, Howard, 41–42, 234–35, 237, 240, 300, 303

directors, gay, 403

Directors Guild of America, 206, 309

Disney animated musicals, 239

dissolves, 83

Donen, Stanley, 2, 70, 216, 237–39, 267, 308

Douglas, Kirk, 223–24, 226, 228, 230, 236, 264, 271, 277, 278–79, 340, 342, 392–93, 405

Douglas-Home, William, 310–11

Dowling, Eddie, 50

Drake, Alfred, 265

Drake, Tom, 111, 356, 401

Dreiser, Theodore, 22

Dreyer, Carl Theodor, 57

Druon, Maurice, 379

The Dubarry, 30

Duchamp, Marcel, 22

Dufy, Raoul, 22, 210–11

Duke, Vernon, 39, 47, 49, 52, 65

Dunham, Katherine, 86

Dunne, Irene, 298

Duquette, Tony, 266

Durante, Jimmy, 118

Eakins, Thomas, 99

Earl Carroll's Vanities, 27, 29

Easter Parade, 169–71, 172, 184, 186, 206

East Lynne, 4–5

Eastman Color, 272–73

Ebb, Fred, 381

Eddy, Nelson, 54, 70

Edens, Roger, 72, 77, 110, 117, 186

effeminacy, condemned in the 1950s, 294

Eisenstein, Sergei, 57, 338

Ellington, Duke, 37, 86

Epstein, Julius, 311

Erickson, Leif, 282
Ernst, Max, 22
Erté, 29
Evans, Robert, 369–70

Fabray, Nanette, 208, 236
fade-outs, 83
family life, as movie theme, 200–203, 263
A Farewell to Arms, 336
Farmer, Frances, 190
Father of the Bride, 76, 195, 198–204, 241, 401, 405
Father's Little Dividend, 76, 195, 203–6, 210, 212, 401
Faulkner, William, 56, 327
Fazan, Adrienne, 208, 299, 304, 308
Federal Theatre, 63
Fellini, Federico, 341
Ferber, Edna, 53
Ferrer, José, 236
Fetter, Ted, 52
Feyder, Jacques, 57
Fields, Dorothy, 56, 66
Fields, Joe, 296
filming
   on back lots, 209–10
   camaraderie of, 79
   on location, 209–10, 270, 273, 301–2
film noir, 156, 176
   comedic, 202
Finklehoffe, Fred, 97, 99, 101
Firbank, Ronald, 22
Fitzgerald, F. Scott, 13, 56
Flaubert, Gustave, 172, 175, 178
Fleming, Victor, 83
Foch, Nina, 208
Folies Bergère, 29
Folsey, George, 106, 126, 237, 261
Fonda, Henry, 360
Fontanne, Lynn, 133
Ford, Glenn, 338, 346, 401

Ford, John, 73, 398
Forest Lawn Memorial Park, 392
For Me and My Gal, 160
Forrest, George, 265
Fosse, Bob, 376–77
Four Horsemen of the Apocalypse, 209, 334–38, 344, 402
   VM's reputation tarnished by, 335
Four Saints in Three Acts, 65
Fox, Henry, 81
France, 253, 269
France Soir, review, 309
Frank, Harriet Jr., 325
Franklin, Sidney, 231
Frazier, Mr. (Chicago), 16–17
Freed, Arthur, 75–77, 92, 103–4, 113, 120, 121, 136, 139, 146–48, 160, 167, 206, 209, 211, 234, 246–47, 249, 258, 265, 296–300, 304, 331, 402
   advice to VM, 79
   biography, 70–72
   impressed by VM, 80–81
   independent production company of, on M-G-M lot, 295
   Irving Thalberg Memorial Award, 216
   last big hit (*Gigi*), 310
   and Lucille Bremer, 101
   as singer, 114
   sponsorship of VM to direct films, 83–85, 96–98
   takes VM off a film, 169–70
Freed Unit, 70–72, 98, 115, 117, 206, 238, 247, 334, 396
Freedman, David, 47, 50, 53, 68
French art movements, influence on VM, 397
Freud, Sigmund, 22, 173
Froeschel, George, 232

Gaba, Lester, 32–33, 142, 412
Gabel, Martin, 351

Gable, Clark, 224, 325, 339

Gabor, Zsa Zsa, 220, 232

Gabriel, Gilbert W., 28

Gaby, 303

Gallico, Paul, 121

Garbo, Greta, 78–79, 405

The Garden of the Finzi-Continis, 402

Gardiner, Reginald, 53

Gardner, Ava, 356

Garland, Judy
  British tour (1951), 193
  cast by VM as a woman, not a child
    star, 101, 107, 405
  caught VM in compromising
    positions, 282
  comic impersonation of Greer
    Garson in *Ziegfeld Follies,* 79
  concern for Liza Minnelli, 360–64
  death of, 364
  directed by VM, 103–7, 120–21,
    123–27
  as dramatic actress, 128
  early movie appearances, 76, 80–81
  finances, 184, 187
  gay friends, 152
  a Gemini, 140
  health, 187–88
  and Hepburn, 158–59
  housewife phase, 153–55
  image as a child star, 142
  marriage to Sid Luft, 251, 255
  marriage to VM, 7, 14, 46, 139–40
  in *Meet Me in St. Louis,* 97–101
  M-G-M contract, 151, 182–84,
    189–91
  observations about VM, 275, 305,
    395
  penalty deductions from salary,
    182–83
  pill use, 64, 110, 131, 141, 155,
    163–64, 184–86
  pregnancy, 146, 155–56
  proposed marriage to VM, 134–36
  and psychiatrists, 164, 169, 186
  public's affection for, 142
  at rehab centers, 184–86, 414
  sharp humor, 144
  sex life and lovers, 112, 132–33, 320
  sex need, 142, 152
  shaky emotional state, 158
  similarity of Liza to, 385–86, 400,
    402
  singing voice, 136
  songs of, 99, 222
  in *A Star Is Born,* 3
  suicide attempt, 190
  suspended (fired) from M-G-M,
    189–91
  in *Till the Clouds Roll By,* 147–50
  turns against VM as director, 169–73
  VM's courting of, 107–13, 128–36
  VM's first meeting with, 81, 97–101
  VM's transformation of, 234
  in *Ziegfeld Follies,* 118–19

Garson, Greer, 79, 117, 174, 175, 406

Gauguin, Paul, 276
  ghost of, 277–79

Gay, John, 346, 380–81

gay directors, 403

gender roles as movie theme, 403–4

generation gap, 371

George White's Scandals, 27, 29

Gero, Mark, 387

Gershe, Leonard, 334

Gershwin, George, 1, 34, 35, 59–62,
  209, 213, 397
  Concerto in F, 211
  musical (*An American in Paris*) based
    on songs by, 206

Gershwin, Ira, 34, 35, 38, 39, 47, 48, 49,
  51, 59–62, 139–40, 155, 206, 209

Gershwin, Leonore (Lee), 34, 36, 38,
  39, 51, 59–62, 152, 165, 219

Gershwin brothers, 34, 52, 56, 118,
  164–65, 207
  social salon of, 28, 34–35

Gibbons, Cedric, 74–75, 100, 161, 197, 232, 279, 402
Gibbons, Irene, 139
Gibson, George, 212
Gibson, William, 258–59
Gielgud, John, 53
Giersdorf singing sisters, 33
Gigi, 210, 234, 243, 247, 253, 295–310, 312, 366, 386
  critics on, 304, 306
Gilks, Alfred, 208
Gilmore, Ethel Gumm, 130–31, 134, 139, 146, 190, 363
Gingold, Hermione, 298, 302
Gish, Lillian, 252, 260, 261, 390
The Glass Menagerie, 144
Gleason, F. Keogh, 212, 279, 350
Gobo (dog), 143
Godard, Jean-Luc, 402
Goddard, Paulette, 60
Goldwyn, Samuel, 55–56, 247
The Goldwyn Follies (project), 61, 72
Gone with the Wind, 78, 280
Goodbye, Charlie, 243, 349–53, 398
Goodman, Benny, 22
Goodman, Lillian Rosedale, 24
Goodrich, Frances, 161, 198, 241, 310
Goudeket, Maurice, 309
Goulet, Robert, 144
Graham, Martha, 46
Grahame, Gloria, 260, 261
Granger, Farley, 232–33
Grant, Cary, 352
Gray, Dolores, 266, 267, 291
Grayson, Kathryn, 21, 120, 148, 197, 248
The Great Ziegfeld, 70
Green, Adolph, 207, 235, 240, 331–33, 334
Green, Johnny, 152, 208, 212, 266
Green, Morris, 30
green, VM's use of, 287
Greene, Graham, 336
Green Mansions (project), 257–58, 297

The Green Pastures, 85
Greenwich Village, 26, 27, 34, 141
Greer, Howard, 46
Greutert, Henry, 213
Grimm Brothers' fairy tales, 96
Grofé, Ferde, *Tabloid Suite,* 36
Guétary, Georges, 208, 209, 211, 212
Guilaroff, Sydney, 385
Gumm, Frank, 363
Guys and Dolls, 247

Haakon, Paul, 41–42
Hackett, Albert, 161, 198, 241, 310
Haggin, Ben Ali, 30
Hale, Prentice, 363–64
Haley, Jack, Jr., 386
Halston, 221
Hamilton, George, 325, 328, 337, 341
Hammerstein, Dorothy, 145
Hammerstein, Oscar, 67, 92, 145, 149
Hammett, Dashiell, 34
"Happiness Is Just a Thing Called Joe" (song), 29
Hara (valet), 36–37, 42, 63
Harburg, E. Y. (Yip), 28–29, 34, 37–38, 39, 52, 56, 60, 70, 71, 230
Harding, Warren G., 9
Harlan, Russell, 274
Harlem, 46
Harris, Jed, 224–25
Harris, Richard, 367
Harris, Winonie, 93
Harrison, Rex, 310–11, 313–14
Hart, Lorenz, 52, 68
Hart, Moss, 34–35, 53, 63, 145
The Harvey Girls, 123
Hayes, Rutherford B., 9
Haynes, Todd, 403
Hayton, Lennie, 92, 93
Hayworth, Rita, 133
The Heartbreak Kid, 399
Heflin, Van, 175, 180
Hellman, Lillian, 34, 55, 79

Hello, Dolly! 366
Henrici's (bakery-restaurant), 17
Henry, O., 11
Hepburn, Audrey, 296, 297, 298
Hepburn, Katharine, 156–59, 184, 199,
    205, 290, 405
Herrmann, Bernard, 203
Herwood, Marian, 33–34, 39, 45, 56
Herzig, Sig, 93
Hessler, James, 148
Heston, Charlton, 337
heterosexuality, proof of, 294
High Society, 247
Hitchcock, Alfred, 203, 261, 343, 398
Hoctor, Harriet, 47
Hodiak, John, 93
Holliday, Judy, 332
Hollywood
    actresses ruined by, 190
    audience involvement with films
        and stars from, 406
    ignored the changing times,
        in 1960s, 365
    new system starting in the 1950s, 343
    New York people not happy in, 60
    studio system, 79, 81, 84, 212, 247,
        282, 344, 396
    Sunday pool parties, 81
    VM's early years in, 70–95
    writers in, 56, 80
Hollywood Reporter, articles in, 92, 216
Hollywood themes, 339, 351
    self-reflexive, 225, 400
Home from the Hill, 201, 261, 263, 294,
    321, 323–30, 400, 403
homosexuality
    in Broadway theater, 32–33
    Hollywood's belief that it was
        self-chosen and could be
        overcome, 134
    as movie theme, 259–60, 281–83
    need for concealment of, in the
        1950s, 294

Hooray for What! 63–65
Hope, Bob, 47, 50, 243, 368, 392
Hopper, Hedda, 167, 229
Horne, Lena, 77–78, 86, 87–88, 92–93,
    94, 118, 148, 234
Houseman, John, 224–25, 229, 258–65,
    267, 270, 271, 339–40, 343
House Un-American Activities
    Committee, 194, 230
Howard, Ron, 346, 401
Huckleberry Finn (project), 195,
    230–31
Hudson, Rock, 368
Hudson, W. H., 257
Humphrey, Doris, 46
Humphrey, William, 324
Huston, John, 343
Hutton, Betty, 190
Hyer, Martha, 321, 322

I Dood It, 93–95, 139
"Illustrated Literary Classic" movie
    genre, 174
I Love Lucy (TV show), 241
Ince, Thomas, scandal of, 351
Ingram, Rex, 86, 89, 335
In the Good Old Summertime, 180,
    188
Isherwood, Christopher, 375, 388
Ivanhoe, 240

Jackson, Harry, 237
Jackson, Michael, 387
James, Henry, 173
Japan, surrender of, 146
Jeanette (nanny), 254
Jeanmaire, Zizi, 236
Jenkins, Gordon, 54, 409
Jennings, Al, 108, 163
Jennings, Juanita, 109
Jews, 15
Johnson, Albert, 399
Johnson, Hall, 86–87

Johnson, Van, 152, 246, 250
Jolson, Al, 193
Jones, Barry, 250
Jones, James, 316–17
Jones, Jennifer, 122–23, 175, 177, 179–80, 406
Jones, Robert Edmond, 18, 21, 28, 31
Jones, Shirley, 346
Jourdan, Louis, 175, 180, 297, 301, 303, 304, 308
June, Ray, 304

Kael, Pauline, 228–29, 384
Kalmus, Natalie, 100
Kander, John, 381
Kaufman, George S., 53, 63, 236
Kaufman, Harry, 38
Kaye, Danny, 202, 216, 230–31
Kazan, Elia, 2, 281
Keaton, Buster, 14, 93–94
Keel, Howard, 197, 266
Keim, Betty Lou, 322
Kelly, Gene, 115–16, 160, 162–63, 170–71, 206, 219, 230–31, 238, 246, 248–50, 401
  in An American in Paris, 1, 207, 209, 210, 212
  appreciation of VM, 393
  comes to Hollywood, 72
  compared to Astaire, 235
  as director, 366
  honorary Oscar to, 2, 216–17
  in The Pirate, 166–68
  as singer, 186
  VM's directing of, 405
Kelly, Grace, 259, 260, 290
Kendall, Kay, 310–11, 313–14
Kennedy, Arthur, 321, 322
Kent, Christopher, 180
Kern, Eva, 148
Kern, Jerome, 51, 52–53, 56, 67, 146, 147, 195–96
  memorial for, 151

Kerr, Deborah, 175, 280–82, 285, 287–88
Kerr, John, 258, 260, 261, 282, 285–86, 288
Keyes, Marian Herwood, 111–12
Kidd, Michael, 237–38, 240
Kipling, Rudyard, 11
Kismet (stage and film), 265
Knight, Arthur, 372
Knight, Raymond, 41
Knights of the Round Table, 243
Knoblock, Edward, 265
Korda, Sir Alexander, 351
Koster, Henry, 147
Krasner, Milton, 350, 356
Kress, Harold F., 262
Kupper, Dr., 169–70
Kurnitz, Harry, 351

La Contessa, 379
La Dolce Vita, 341
Lady Be Good, 76
Lady in the Dark, 59, 76
Lady Sings the Blues, 372
Lahr, Bert, 38, 53, 54
Laing, Hugh, 250
Lambert, Eleanor, 27–28, 45, 57–58, 66, 145, 153
Lamour, Dorothy, 57
Lane, Burton, 230, 369
Lansbury, Angela, 148, 311
Lasky, Jesse, 2, 216
Laurents, Arthur, 334
Lavi, Daliah, 341
Lazar, Irving "Swifty," 351
LeBaron, William, 57, 58
LeBeau, Amy (aunt), 6, 15–16
LeBeau, May (grandmother), 6, 15
LeBeau, Mina Mary LaLouche (mother), 3–9, 132, 135
LeBeau, uncle, 6
Lederer, Charles, 265
Lee, Gypsy Rose, 130

Lee, Spike, 202
Le Figaro, review, 309
Leigh, Rowland, 30
Leisen, Mitchell, 59
Le Maire, Charles, 46
Le Monde, 394
Leonidoff, Leon, 37
Lerner, Alan Jay, 72, 206–7, 210–11,
        215, 217, 231, 246, 248–49, 296–98,
        299–300, 301, 303–4, 331, 348,
        366–67, 368, 369
    biography, 207
LeRoy, Mervyn, 71, 195–96
Les Girls, 313
Levant, Amanda, 221
Levant, June, 152
Levant, Oscar, 28, 34, 39, 152, 182, 207,
        209, 211, 236, 238, 260
Lewis, Albert, 84
Life magazine, 11
The Light Fantastic, 65, 67
lighting, 19
    in film, 73–74
Lili, 223, 303
Lillie, Beatrice, 41, 42–43, 53, 54, 65,
        66, 145
Lilly, Doris, 364, 373
Lindsay, Howard, 63
Locher, Robert, 22, 23
Loew, Arthur, 272
Loewe, Frederick, 248, 297, 299–300,
        303, 331, 348
Loew's theater chain, 194, 281
Logan, Ella, 92
Logan, Joshua, 290
Lombard, Carole, 314
Long, Avon, 118
The Long, Long Trailer, 10, 33, 76,
        241–46, 247, 401
The Long Hot Summer, 323
Look Back in Anger, 324
Loos, Anita, 296
Loper, Don, 107–8, 111

Los Angeles, social life in, compared to
        New York, 82, 142
Los Angeles Times, review, 230
Lovely to Look At, 195–98
Lowry, Ed, 399
Lubitsch, Ernst, 42, 59, 307
Luft, Joey, 255
Luft, Lorna, 254
Luft, Sid, 251
Lunt, Alfred, 133, 160
Lust for Life, 253, 266, 269–80, 283,
        394, 403, 405
    Oscars for, 279
Lustig, Jan, 232
Lynes, George Platt, 45

MacDonald, Jeanette, 70
MacKenna, Kenneth, 310
MacLaine, Shirley, 309, 318–19, 334,
        400
Madame Bovary, 76, 172–81, 194, 198,
        204, 306, 406
    waltz sequence, 176
"Mademoiselle" (episode in *The Story
        of Three Loves*), 231–34
Magnani, Georgette (VM's third wife),
        250–55, 302, 385, 387
    files for divorce, 312
Main, Marjorie, 10, 245
Maine, Grandmother, 8
Maine (farmer), 8
male weepie, 263
Mamita, 298
Mamoulian, Rouben, 56–57
Mancini, Henry, 392
Mankiewicz, Joseph, 109, 111–12, 132,
        225
Mannix, Eddie, 74–75
Marion, Ohio, 9
Markert, Russell, 31, 33, 37
marriages, open, European style, 134
Marshall, George, 61
Marshall Field, Chicago, 16–18

Martel, Christiane, 250

Martin, Dean, 318–20, 333, 405

Martin, Gayle, 221

Martin, Hugh, 99

Martin, Ralph, 230

Martin, Tony, 148

Marton, Andrew, 84

Marx, Harpo, 34

Marx Brothers, 75

masculinity, as movie theme, 284–85,
　　290, 293, 324, 326–27, 403

Mason, James, 175, 178

Mason, Morgan, 356

Matisse, Henri, 22

A Matter of Time, 218, 234, 379–85, 400
　　critics on, 384
　　disastrous history of, 382

Matthau, Walter, 351

Maugham, Somerset, 173, 295

Mayer, Louis B., 70, 81, 98, 108, 119,
　　121, 131, 133–34, 135, 140, 141,
　　146, 184, 187, 189, 191, 194,
　　216–17, 281

Mayfair, Mitzi, 52

McCambridge, Mercedes, 208

McCarthy era, 281

McCleary, Urie, 356

McKay, William R., 192

McLeod, Norman Z., 77

McPartland, Jimmy, 22

McQueen, Butterfly, 95

McRae, Ellen, 351

Medwin, Michael, 363

Meerson, Lazare, 57

Meet Me in St. Louis, 1, 9, 10, 22,
　　96–114, 134, 162, 163, 200–201,
　　312, 348, 386, 390, 393, 401, 403,
　　405, 406
　　Halloween sequence in, 113
　　premiere, 129
　　reviews, 114

melodramas, 177–78, 243, 275, 323–24,
　　330, 336, 393

Melton, James, 120

Merman, Ethel, 76, 184

Merrill, Dina, 346

Messenger, Lillie, 98

Method acting, 405

Mexican divorces, 130

M-G-M (Metro)
　　accounting system, 360
　　actors "imprisoned" by, 151
　　art department, 90, 99, 232
　　biopics, 148
　　color film, 272
　　crisis and change in, in 1950s, 194–95
　　film credit "Made entirely in
　　　Hollywood, U.S.A," 214
　　legal department, 230
　　middlebrow sensibility, 119
　　musicals, 2, 44, 70–71, 72, 136, 310
　　1960s changes and demise of the
　　　studio system, 344
　　silver anniversary, 183–84
　　stars brought up by, 405
　　technical advances, 242

middle-class anxieties, theme of, 201,
　　241

Miller, Ann, 197

Miller, Gilbert, 296

Mimieux, Yvette, 338

Minnelli, Anna (aunt), 10

Minnelli, Christiana Nina (Tina
　　Nina), 251–56, 360, 385, 386–88,
　　391–92
　　stepfather of, 391

Minnelli, Edna (aunt), 8

Minnelli, Elsie (aunt), 10

Minnelli, Francine (cousin), 8

Minnelli, Frank (uncle), 3, 8

Minnelli, Karla Ximena Miro
　　(grandchild), 386

Minnelli, Liza
　　birth of, 156
　　bounced between parents, 185–86,
　　　192–93

career, 374–78

competition for VM's love, 251

custody agreement with Judy
    Garland, 218

learning French, 360–61

making a movie with VM (*A Matter
    of Time*), 234, 379–85, 400

marriages, 363, 373, 386, 387

memories of VM, 218

Oscar for, 377–78

rivalry with step-mother Georgette
    and half-sister Tina Nina, 250–56

similarity to Judy Garland, 385–86,
    400, 402

success as actor, 374–78

and Tina Nina, 386

tribute to VM, 390

visits VM on set at early age, 217–20

VM looking for projects for, 372–73

at VM's funeral, 392–93

VM's parenting of, 14

young adulthood and early
    marriage, 360–64

Minnelli, Professor (grandfather), 7–8

died while pruning a tree, 8, 52

Minnelli, Stella (aunt), 8

Minnelli, Vincent Charles (father), 3,
    7–9, 10, 12, 135

move to Florida, 37

Minnelli, Vincente

absentmindedness, 7

as actor, 13, 18

Alzheimer's developing in, 390

apolitical nature of, 64

applied makeup to leading ladies,
    318–19

apprentice status at M-G-M, 74

art book collection, 153

artistic interests as a child, 11, 20,
    21–22, 153, 307

artistic talents, 12, 13, 17, 18, 23–24,
    28, 29, 31–32, 36, 74, 76, 343, 380,
    396, 398–99

artists admired by, 307

astrology belief, 140

attitude toward drugs and
    physicians, 64

attitude toward psychiatrists, 222

as auteur, 399

awards, 2, 206, 309, 393

beliefs, 5, 15, 64, 140

Best Director Oscar, 2, 309

bisexuality, 17, 111, 112, 129, 133–34,
    156, 362

black poodles, 143

as book illustrator, 29

"born in the trunk," 3

bringing Liza up (spoiling her),
    218–22, 254

brothers died young, 4, 8

career, 3, 55, 68, 71, 83, 172, 188, 191,
    269, 323, 331, 343, 344, 345, 366,
    372

career decline in 1960s, 331, 366

career peak in 1959, 323

Catholicism, 5, 15

celebrity and cult status, 45, 169

Chicago apartment, 18

as child actor, 5

childhood, 3–14, 21, 32, 76

comfortable in the company of
    women, 10, 35–36

Commander of the Legion of
    Honor, 393

as costume designer, 23–24

could spend hours arranging flowers
    the way he wanted them, 301

courting Judy Garland, 107–13,
    128–36

as dance director, 74

dark sensibility, 399

a decorative artist more than an
    auteur, per Sarris, 398–99

did not care for glitzy parties, 152

died in his sleep, 391

as director, 18, 103, 333, 352

Minnelli, Vincente *(continued)*
   Directors Guild of America award,
     206
   dreaming about being a painter, 396
   driving skills, lack of, 58
   early jobs, 12–13, 16–18, 19, 74
   effeminate behavior, 10, 16–17, 156
   energy and self-confidence, 341
   escorting older women to dinner
     and nightclubs, 33
   facial tics, 20
   as father, 14, 218–22, 254, 375
   favorite colors, yellow and red, 20
   filmmaking, 11, 18, 80–81, 103–4,
     174, 195, 197, 199, 210, 217, 274,
     302, 318–19, 327, 333, 342, 352,
     381, 395, 398, 399, 400
   final illnesses, 390–92
   financial problems, 31, 253
   first big flop, 68
   forgetfulness, 66
   forgoing screen credit, 195
   fought to get right cast for his
     pictures, 199
   frugal existence, 12
   funeral, 392
   gay lifestyle, 24, 33
   gentleman of the old school, 121
   going to the theater, 17
   in gossip columns, 45
   health, 64, 312, 374, 386, 390
   high school, 13
   Hollywood career, 55
   homosexual liaisons not given up
     upon marriage, 193
   idle with no assignments, 172, 188
   imagination nurtured by books as
     child, 11
   as independent producer, 380
   interior decoration of residences, 20
   an intuitive artist, 398
   job in window display, 16–18
   jobs as youth, 12–13

   lack of formal higher education,
     14, 21
   lonely, shy boy, 5, 11
   Los Angeles, house at 10000 Sunset
     Boulevard, 187
   loved dressing women, 132
   love of literature and avant-garde,
     21–22
   marijuana anecdote, 46–47
   marriages, 7, 14, 45–46, 107–13,
     128–36, 141, 152–53, 164–66, 184,
     191–92, 193, 250–55, 302, 312, 345,
     373–74
   marriage to Denise Radosavljev
     (q.v.), 345, 373
   marriage to Georgette Magnani
     (q.v.), 250–55, 302, 312
   marriage to Judy Garland (q.v.), 14,
     141, 152–53, 164–66, 184, 191–93
   marriage to Lee Anderson (q.v.),
     373–74
   married to his work, 177, 395
   "master of musicals," 398
   mentoring of Liza, 375
   M-G-M contract lapsed in early
     1962, 343
   M-G-M's longest-tenured, highest-
     paid, and most prestigious
     director, 191, 344, 395
   mixing with the upper class, 14
   mother wished he would get
     married, 45–46
   multiple marriages, and
     appreciation of stability, 7, 373
   name change to Vincente, 3, 21, 32
   name originally Lester Anthony, 3
   natural charm and generosity, 98
   neurosis and hysteria of, 98, 275
   never received a writing credit, 76
   never satisfied with his work, 12
   New York, East 52nd Street
     apartment, 34, 36
   New York, studio on 53rd Street, 39

no production, business, or writing skills, 343

obituaries, 394

one-year apprenticeship with M-G-M, 83

only one movie initiated by, 269

paintings as child, 12

part Svengali and part Pygmalion, 132

passive-aggressive nature, 320, 396

pay and compensation, 71, 345

perfectionism, 49, 327

personal traits, 5–6, 7, 9, 12, 13–14, 20–21, 30, 49, 58, 64, 66, 98, 121, 132, 136, 152, 177, 210, 234, 242, 275, 285, 294, 305, 320, 327, 341, 396

philosophy of entertainment, 217

as photographer's apprentice, 19

poor communication with cast, 381

poor memory for names, 30, 66

pragmatic approach to film making, 80–81

reality and unreality in working, 400

refused to concede that his career was over, 372

rehearsals, 103–4

reinvention of himself, 21–22

relied on fantasy as an escape from harsh reality, 234

residences, 18, 20, 34, 36, 39, 187

rumors about his sexuality, 46, 111, 129

said children "might look like me," 136

sat for portrait, 388–90

as scenery designer, 36

as a scout for new Broadway shows, 76

sense of failure, 5–6

sensitivity to women, 178

as set designer, 28

sex life, 51–52, 152, 373

sexual orientation, 17, 24–26, 32–33, 46, 112, 362

shyness, 13–14

sketching of shows, 17

slow schedules of, 302, 342

a smoker, 64, 374

soundstages, magic and mystery of, 210

spoke falteringly and vaguely, 210

strong inner tensions, 305

studio as an escape from home, 177

as style designer, 31–32

sympathy with the underdog, 294

too shy to court girls as youth, 13

tribute to, at New York Museum of Modern Art, 390

unattractive appearance, 20–21, 136

upbringing, 6

volunteered for the Army but rejected, 96

warm and generous yet extremely demanding, 242

wearing light makeup, 285

and women, 10, 13, 33, 35–36, 132, 178

work habits, 12, 177, 395, 400

Minnelli, Vincente, work of

American critics on, 217, 393–94

appreciated by international critics, 217, 337, 393, 395

butchered editing of a film, 383–84

camera movement, 227

color symbolism in, 197, 274, 286–87

commercial appeal of his films abroad, 217

failure of pictures, 169

fantasy/reality in, 400

feminist streak in movies, 305–6

flashback structure, 241

grosses, 2, 118

high art and mass culture in work of, 396–98

Minnelli, Vincente, work of *(continued)*
  legacy of, 395
  lowered standards in comedies, 347
  male protagonists in, 178
  melodramas hold up a dark mirror
    to his musicals, 177–78
  mises-en-scène, 83, 119, 402
  pleasure we derive from, 406
  previews, 229, 303
  recycling of routines, 245
  retrospective of (London 1962), 346
  reviews, 49, 54, 139
  running times, 262, 329
  stylism of, 275, 327, 398–99, 400–403
  visual excess, 274, 402–3
Minnelli, Vincent Miro (grandchild),
  386
Minnelli Brothers Tent Theater, 3, 6–7
Minnelli on Minnelli, 221
"The Minnellium" (VM's studio in
  New York), 40
mirrors in VM's films, 91
Mitchum, Robert, 157–58, 325, 327–30,
  400
modern-dance movement, 46
modernism, 396–97
Monroe, Marilyn, 349
montage school of cutting and
  splicing, 73
Montand, Yves, 367–68, 369, 371
Moore, Brenda, 391
Moore, Florence, 30
Moore, Grace, 30
Moore, Victor, 119
"More Stars Than There Are in
  Heaven" (song), 405
Morgan, Frank, 137
Morgenstern, Joe, 371
Moscow Museum of Modern Art, 273
Motion Picture Association of America
  (MPAA), 175, 296, 340
Moulin Rouge, 270
Movie film magazine, 395

Mrs. Miniver, 174
Mulligan, Gerry, 333
Museum of Modern Art (New York),
  273
musical biopictures, 150
musical films, 44, 50, 51, 56, 72–73, 214,
  306, 331, 365, 377, 398, 399
  all-black, 85
  dance-oriented, 206
  decline of, in 1950's, 247
  last classic (*My Fair Lady*), 365
  movie type of, redefined, 211
musical revues, 27, 52, 63, 117, 119
music in film, 203
My Fair Lady, 296, 304–5, 331, 366
  last classic musical, 365
  VM's desire to direct, disappointed,
    348–49, 353

Nash, Ogden, 56
Nathan, Robert, 121, 137
National Film Theatre, 346
Natwick, Mildred, 137
Nazism
  as movie theme, 377
  ridiculed in theater pieces, 64
Nazzari, Amedeo, 380
NBC-TV, 189
Neame, Ronald, 295
Negulesco, Jean, 271
Nelson, Ricky, 232
Newcombe, Warren, 232
New Deal, 63
New York, New York, 385, 402
New York City
  most exciting era of, 145–46
  scenes in movies, 122
  VM and Judy's honeymoon in,
    141–46
  VM's early adulthood in, 26–27,
    34–39
The New Yorker, profile of VM (1935),
  45

The New York Times
  obituary of VM, 394
  reviews in, 78, 91
New York World, review in, 21
Nichols, Mike, 360
Nicholson, Jack, 368–71
  felt he got no direction from VM,
    370
Niesen, Gertrude, 48
The Night of the Iguana, 356
the 1950s, 294
the 1960s, 365, 368
noir films, 156, 176, 202
nonconformity, fear of, in the 1950s, 284
Norton, Elliot, 49, 50
Novak, Kim, 355
Now I'm a Grandfather (working title),
  203

O'Brien, George (priest), 392
O'Brien, Margaret, 101–3, 113, 203,
    401, 403
O'Day, Nell, 33
Odets, Clifford, 63
O'Hara, John, 34
O'Keeffe, Georgia, 39–40
Oklahoma! (Broadway musical), 129, 144
Oklahoma! (movie), 113
Olsen, Moroni, 202, 245
omnibus films, 231
On a Clear Day You Can See Forever,
    73, 364, 366–72
  critics on, 369, 371–72
One Flew Over the Cuckoo's Nest, 264
O'Neill, Eugene, 18
On the Town, 206
Ophuls, Max, 82
Osborn, Paul, 379
"Over the Rainbow" (song), 71

Pagan Love Song, 206
Pal Joey, 76
Palmer, Mrs. Potter, 18

Palm Springs Desert Museum, 390
Panama Hattie, 76–78, 87–88
Paramount Pictures, 56–59, 71
Paramount-Publix chain, 26, 28, 30
Paramount Theater, New York City, 26
Paris, France, 209–10, 215, 273–74, 295,
    299–302, 307–8, 329, 406
Paris, Tex., 329
Parker, Dorothy, 32–33, 34, 39, 56, 79
Parker, Eleanor, 325, 328
Parsons, Louella, 135, 151, 184, 192
Pasternak, Joe (Joseph), 71, 239, 346
Pat and Mike, 292
Paths of Glory, 336
Patricia, Sister, 13
Patrick, Dorothy, 148
Patrick, John, 316, 323
Paxton, John, 258
Peck, Gregory, 290–91, 367, 392
pedophilia, as hidden movie theme,
    296
Pène Du Bois, Raoul, 63
Peppard, George, 325, 328–29
Pepper, Buddy, 193
Perelman, S. J., 44, 56, 57–58, 65, 80
Peter Bent Brigham Hospital, 185–86
Peters, Hans, 279
Peyton Place, 316, 323
Pins and Needles, 63, 65
The Pirate, 160–69, 175, 182, 195, 204,
    266, 306, 405
  failed to yield a profit, 168
  "Mack the Black" in, 401
A Place in the Sun, 2, 215
Platt, Ernie, 231
Ponedel, Dorothy (Dottie), 101, 106,
    123, 125, 133, 136
Porter, Cole, 56, 63, 65, 77, 78, 161, 164,
    168, 219, 313
Powell, Eddie, 74, 79, 167
Powell, Eleanor, 41–42, 93–94
Powell, William, 120
Presenting Lily Mars, 97

Previn, André, 299, 300, 303, 312, 350
prima donnas, 30
producers, independent, 295, 380
Production Code, 173, 175, 248, 264,
    281, 283, 289, 296, 346
Production Code Administration
    (PCA), 90, 281–82, 289
psychiatrists, VM's attitude toward,
    222
Psych-Out, 369
Purdom, Edmund, 258
Pye, Merrill, 120

queer sensibility, 403–5
Quinn, Anthony, 276–78, 279
Quo Vadis? 215

Radio City Music Hall, 23, 31–34,
    36–39, 266, 397
Radosavljev, Denise (Minnelli's third
    wife), 345, 348, 361, 363–64
    dating other men, 373
Ragland, Rags, 92
rain forest, filming in, 257
Rainier, Prince, 290
Ransohoff, Martin, 354–55
Rat Pack, 320
Ravetch, Irving, 325
Ray, Man, 39
Raye, Martha, 62
The Red Shoes, 206
Reed, Rex, 370, 385
Reiner, Carl, 390
Reinhardt, Gottfried, 231
The Reluctant Debutante, 303–4,
    310–15
Remisoff, Nicholas, 29
Renoir, Jean, 174
Renoir, Pierre-Auguste, 22
Rewald, John, 273
Rey, Fernando, 381
Reynolds, Debbie, 349–50, 352, 406
Reynolds, James, 21, 28, 46

Rhapsody in Blue, 207
Rice, Elmer, 85
Richardson, Tony, 324
Ringling Brothers Circus, 6
Rio Rita, 76
RKO musicals, 72
Roberta, 195
Roberts, James, 23
Roberts, Rev. William E., 140
Robinson, Clark, 31
Robinson, Edward G., 273, 340, 404
Rockettes, 33
rock 'n' roll, 247
Rodgers, Dorothy, 129
Rodgers, Richard, 52, 68, 129
Rogers, Ginger, 59, 60, 72, 187
Rogers, Kenny, 392
Rogge, Florence, 37
Roland, Gilbert, 230
Rome, Italy, 341
Room at the Top, 324
Rooney, Mickey, 21, 76, 80–81, 108,
    118, 187, 410
Rose, Billy, 47
Rose, David, 81, 97, 110, 130, 139, 146,
    152, 182
Rose, Helen, 290, 291, 350
Rosenman, Leonard, 261
Ross, Diana, 377
Rosson, Hal, 213
Rothafel, S. L. (Roxy), 31–32
Rozsa, Miklos, 176, 232, 275
Ruttenberg, Joseph, 273, 299, 300–301,
    304

Saidy, Fred, 93
Saint, Eva Marie, 355
St. John, Adela Rogers, 134
Salinger, Conrad, 212, 303
Sandburg, Carl, 22
The Sandpiper, 354–60, 398, 423
    reviews, 357
Sandrich, Mark, 60, 115

Sargeant, Anne, 207

Saroyan, William, 21, 68–69

   The Human Comedy, 21

Sarris, Andrew, 228, 357, 398–99

Saturday Night and Sunday Morning, 324

Saxon, John, 311

Say It with Music (project), 334

Schary, Dore, 191, 194–95, 198, 206, 217, 229, 262, 265–66, 281, 290, 316

Schary, Mrs. Dore, 269

Scheherazade (Rimsky-Korsakov), 31

Schenck, Nicholas, 184, 191

Schiaffino, Rosanna, 341

Schickel, Richard, 398

Schnee, Charles, 225, 339–40, 341

Schnee, Mary, 341

Schramm, Charles, 220

Schrank, Joseph, 121, 137

Schwartz, Arthur, 41, 234–35, 237

Scorsese, Martin, 384, 385–86, 402

Scott, Hazel, 93, 94

Sears, Jerry, 37

seduction fantasies, movie theme of, 174–75

Selznick, David O., 78, 123, 175, 177, 225

Selznick, Irene, 123

Sem, 299, 307

sequels, 206

Serena Blandish, 65, 87

sets, unprofessional behavior on, 319

Seurat, Georges, 307

Seven Brides for Seven Brothers, 247

The Seventh Sin, 295

sex scenes, censorship of, 340

sexual politics, as movie theme, 403

Shafter, Robert, 52

Shall We Dance? 60

Sharaff, Irene, 72, 99, 101, 105, 111, 128, 161, 212, 221, 231, 356, 358

Shaughnessy, Mickey, 292

Shaw, Artie, 182

Shaw, George Bernard, 366

Shaw, Irwin, 339

Shearer, Moira, 248

Shearer, Norma, 78–79, 174, 406

Sheekman, Arthur, 316, 323

Sheldon, Sidney, 170

Sheriff, Paul, 270

Sherman, Hiram, 67–68

She's Gotta Have It, 202

"Shine On, Harvest Moon" (song), 10

Shore, Dinah, 148

Show Boat, 240

The Show Is On, 10, 52–54, 63, 118, 119

Shubert, Jake, 53

Shubert, Lee, 38–39, 46, 53, 54, 62, 65

Shubert Organization, 38–39, 41–42, 63, 65, 397

   revues, 52

Shurlock, Geoffrey, 281, 283, 340

Sidney, George, 117, 118, 147, 190

Sidney, Sylvia, 154, 183, 185

Siegel, Joel E., 382

Siegel, Sol C., 316, 320, 339, 342–43, 344

Sight and Sound, 357

Signoret, Simone, 367–68

silent movies, 9, 82, 228

Simonson, Lee, 23

Sinatra, Frank, 112, 147, 185, 206, 317–20, 333, 367, 391, 405

Singin' in the Rain, 2, 229, 238–39, 240

Sirk, Douglas, 324, 398

sitcoms, 200

Skelton, Edna, 94

Skelton, Red, 93–95, 118, 196–97

The Skipper Surprised His Wife, 198

Skolsky, Sidney, 216

Slezak, Walter, 161

Smith, Jack Martin, 161, 176, 212, 350

Smith, Oliver, 72, 237, 239–40

Smith, Pete, 91

Snappy Stories magazine, 11

soap operas, 323, 330
social deviance in film, 281
social order, rightness of, as movie theme, 324
Society of Painters and Paper Hangers, 28
Some Came Running, 11, 22, 201, 215, 243, 263, 293, 309, 312, 316–23, 400, 401
songwriters, in Hollywood, 56
Sothern, Ann, 77
Soudeikine, Serge, 29
The Sound and the Fury, 323
The Sound of Music, 365
sound pictures, 82
Spear, Bill, 152
The Stage, review, 65
stage mothers, 130, 363
Stahr, Leo, 25
A Star Is Born, 3, 153, 225, 229
stars
    importance of, 261
    Judy's parody sketch about, 117
    not allowed to appear on television, 242
    VM's work with, 405–6
The Sterile Cuckoo, 374
Stevens, George, 2, 115, 290
Stevens, Stella, 346
Stewart, Donald Ogden, 230
Stewart, Jimmy, 290, 392
Stieglitz, Alfred, 39–40
Stockwell, Dean, 230
Stone, Irving, 270
Stone, Paul, 18–19
The Story of Three Loves, 220, 231–34
Strabel, Thelma, 156
Stradling, Harry, 73, 162, 368, 371
Strasberg, Lee, 328
A Streetcar Named Desire, 2, 215, 216
Streeter, Edward, 198
Streisand, Barbra, 366–67, 368–72
Strickling, Howard, 140, 229, 240

Strike Up the Band (film), 75, 76, 80–81
studio system
    abundant work under, 282
    advantages of working in, 81, 212
    coordination of talent, 212
    decline and fall of, 79, 84, 247
    at M-G-M, 344
    VM not hindered by, 396
style as a way of life (in *Gigi*), 306–7
Sullivan, Barry, 230
Summer Stock, 200
Sunset Boulevard, 225, 400
surrealism, 22, 65, 397
surrogate family, as movie theme, 263
Swift, Kay, 37, 40

Take Me Out to the Ball Game, 206
A Tale of Two Cities, 11
Taradash, Daniel, 271
Taurog, Norman, 120
Taylor, Elizabeth, 199, 354–60
Taylor, Laurette, 144–45
Taylor, Robert, 157, 259
Tchelitchev, Pavel, 39
Tea and Sympathy (film), 263, 280–90, 306, 403, 404
    reviews of, 284, 289–90
    a severely flawed picture, 287–88
Tea and Sympathy (French production of stage play), 288–89
Tea and Sympathy (play), 280
Technicolor, 50–51, 100, 208, 244, 272
television
    competition with, 194, 242–43, 262
    sitcoms, 200
The Ten Commandments, 280
tent-show business, 9
"That's Entertainment" (song and title), 237
Thau, Benny, 199, 299, 302
theater chains, 194
theater life, on the road, 6–7, 10

Theatre Guild, 63

Théry, Jacques, 136

Thompson, Jimmy, 250

Thompson, Kay, 72, 95, 117, 152

Thompson, Woodman, 28

Thorson, Marjorie, 310

3-D, 244

Till the Clouds Roll By, 146, 147–50, 317

Time, reviews in, 65, 114, 126, 357

Times Square, VM's appreciation of, 26

Times Square (project), 58, 61

Titheradge, Dion, 41

titles of films, 229

Tivoli Theater, 24

Toby, Mark, 346

Todd, Mike, 393–94

Torrington, Mr. D., 217

Touch of Evil, 403

Toulouse-Lautrec, Henri de, 210–11

Tracy, Spencer, 159, 199–200, 202, 204, 270, 290, 313, 339, 401, 405

Trevor, Claire, 341, 404

Tribute to a Bad Man (working title), 198, 223

Trinidad, 51

Trumbo, Dalton, 354, 355

Tulin, Ingrid, 338

Tully, Myrtle, 189–90

Turner, Lana, 108, 175, 224, 227, 259, 403

Twentieth Century-Fox, 247, 349

Twiss, Clinton, 241

Two Weeks in Another Town, 228, 236, 243, 263, 338–43, 344, 401, 404, 405

Undercurrent, 155, 156–58, 306, 405

Unsworth, Geoffrey, 377, 381, 383

Uptown Theater, 24

Vakhtangov, Yevgeny, 60

Valentino, Rudolph, 335, 337

Van Gogh, Theo, 272

Van Gogh, Vincent, 22, 265, 269, 270, 276

Van Sant, Gus, 403

Van Schmus, W. G., 32, 37

Variety, reports in, 56, 264

variety shows, 44

vaudeville

  circuit, 13

  routines, 119

Venice Productions, 345, 355

Verdi, Giuseppe, *La Traviata,* 120

Vertes, Marcel, 270

Very Warm for May, 67–68

Vidor, King, 82

Villa-Lobos, Heitor, 257

Visconti, Luchino, 337, 402

Vizzard, Jack, 281

Vogel, Joseph, 303, 340

Walker, Judy, 122

Walker, Robert, 121, 122–23, 125–26, 148

Wallis, Hal, 318

Walters, Charles, 72, 111, 170, 186, 189, 190, 223, 231, 302, 304, 413

Wand, Betty, 303

war films, 336

Warner, Jack, 348

Warner Brothers, 72, 348

  musicals, 50, 51

Warren, Harry, 120, 136

Waters, Ethel, 41, 76, 86, 88–89

Webb, Clifton, 236

Weill, Kurt, 59

Weingarten, Lawrence, 206

Weitman, Robert, 344

Welles, Orson, 63, 74, 112, 132–33, 224, 236, 403

Wells, George, 137, 290, 291, 334

Whale, James, 294, 403

Wheeling, W. Va., 8

Whistler, James McNeill, 19–21

White, George, 29

Whorf, Richard, 147

Who's Afraid of Virginia Woolf? 360
widescreen format, 272
Widmark, Richard, 260, 261
Wilder, Billy, 343
Williams, Esther, 115, 120, 206
Williams, Herb, 41
Willis, Edwin B., 279
Wilson, Dooley, 86
Wilson, Dorothy, 346
Wilson, Michael, 354
Winchell, Walter, 45
Winter Garden Theater (New York), 43, 51
The Wizard of Oz, 71, 78
Woman of the Year, 290
women viewers, pictures aimed at, 174
Wood, Mrs. Henry, 4
Wood, Sam, 83
Woollcott, Alexander, 21
Woolley, Monty, 63
Words and Music, 183, 187
"Words Without Music" (ballet), 120
Worsley, Wallace, 163
Wright, Robert, 265

writers for films, 56, 80
Writer's Guild, 339
Written on the Wind, 323
Wyler, William, 335, 343, 355, 369
Wynn, Ed, 65
Wynn, Keenan, 245

Yankee Doodle Dandy, 1
yellow, VM's use of, 273, 286–87
Yolanda and the Thief, 116, 136–39, 175, 399, 402
Young, Frederick, 274
Young, Victor, 25

Zelda (project), 372
Ziegfeld, Florenz, 50
Ziegfeld Follies (1946 film), 21, 47, 79, 111, 115, 136
Ziegfeld Follies of 1931, 27, 30
Ziegfeld Follies of 1936, 46–51, 52, 63
Ziegfeld revues (stage), 118
Zinnemann, Fred, 121, 316
Zorina, Vera, 72
Zukor, Adolph, 58